SUBSTANCE ABUSE ON CAMPUS

A HANDBOOK FOR COLLEGE AND UNIVERSITY PERSONNEL

Edited by
P. Clayton Rivers and Elsie R. Shore

Copy 1

The Greenwood Educators' Reference Collection

GREENWOOD PRESS
Westport, Connecticut • London

Library of Congress Cataloging-in-Publication Data

Substance abuse on campus : a handbook for college and university
    personnel / edited by P. Clayton Rivers, Elsie R. Shore.
            p.   cm. — (The Greenwood educators' reference collection, ISSN
    1056–2192)
    Includes bibliographical references and index.
    ISBN 0–313–29310–4 (alk. paper)
    1. College students—Substance use—United States.   2. College
students—Alcohol use—United States.   3. Substance abuse—United
States—Prevention.   4. Alcoholism—United States—Prevention.
5. Universities and colleges—Health promotion services—United
States.   I. Rivers, P. Clayton.   II. Shore, Elsie R.   III. Series.
HV4999.Y68S82   1997
362.29'088'375—dc21   97–18722

British Library Cataloguing in Publication Data is available.

Library of Congress Catalog Card Number: 97–18722
ISBN: 0–313–29310–4
ISSN: 1056–2192

First published in 1997

Greenwood Press, 88 Post Road West, Westport, CT 06881
An imprint of Greenwood Publishing Group, Inc.

Printed in the United States of America

The paper used in this book complies with the
Permanent Paper Standard issued by the National
Information Standards Organization (Z39.48–1984).

10   9   8   7   6   5   4   3   2   1

To Dick and Linda, our partners
with heartfelt thanks for all their love and support
over the years and during the editing of this volume

Contents

Preface

Alcohol and drug abuse on college campuses are serious problems for the academic community. For example, a recent edition of the *Chronicle of Higher Education* had the following to say about alcohol abuse:

Alcohol abuse is a common, not marginal activity at most colleges and we only fool ourselves if we expect marginal efforts to reduce it. If we really want to deal with the problem, administrators, faculty members, students and parents must first gain a better understanding of how excessive drinking is affecting the academic and social climate of their institutions. Second, they must believe there are promising practical strategies they can adopt to improve the situation. Finally, they must be prepared to contend with the skepticism and resistance bound to be aroused by actions designed to curb the abuse. (April 14, 1994, p. B1)

This volume is written for the many academic personnel who are faced with dealing with a student who has an alcohol or drug problem. Most academic personnel, ranging from university president, to faculty member, to librarian and academic support staff, are often ill prepared to cope with substance abuse problems in the students they serve. This handbook is designed to give them a broader understanding of how substance abuse is viewed by theoreticians, researchers, and clinicians who deal with the problem, and also some practical suggestions of how to intervene with a student. While several abused substances are discussed in this volume, alcohol, the number-one drug of abuse on college campuses, is emphasized.

To accomplish the task of introducing the reader to the complex issues involved in substance abuse, the book is divided into three parts: (1) Basic

Issues and Models, (2) Policies, Programming, and Prevention, and (3) Assessment, Intervention, and Treatment.

The first part, Basic Issues and Models, has chapters that deal with the concepts, theories, and models used in the alcohol and drug field. Zucker, Reider, Ellis, and Fitzgerald's developmental theory of alcohol use and abuse compares this theoretical position with the disease concept and with the American Psychiatric Association's Diagnostic and Statistical Manual categories. Zucker and colleagues use the developmental perspective to help us understand the processes underlying the development or failure to develop alcohol problems. They make the point that what we know about treatment is based on clinical samples. These clinical samples have far fewer resources than are found in the selected, stable, and psychologically supported people that are in the majority on college campuses. Zucker and colleagues feel strongly that any attempt to deal with alcohol problems on campus (and elsewhere) must take into account the multiple factors which arise out of historical and developmental contexts.

The physiological and neuropsychological effects of substance abuse are systematically covered in a chapter by Woltersdorf. This author defines important substance abuse concepts such as dependence, tolerance, and withdrawal from drugs. He covers addiction problems ranging from alcohol and cocaine to coffee. His focus is on the physiological–behavioral impact of these substances and their neurological effects. He is also specific about the signs and symptoms of substance abuse and the recovery of function following abstinence from the substance. He informs the reader of the risk for chronic, nonrecoverable effects of a given drug and contrasts those with the substance's acute effects. Finally, he reviews fetal alcohol syndrome and other substances which are capable of crossing the blood–placenta barrier.

Dennis Thombs reviews the disease or "twelve-step" model. He notes that the majority of Americans see alcoholism as a disease and this medical model is the basis for most treatment programs in the United States. He traces the history of this model of alcohol abuse and points out its impact on reducing stigma and encouraging treatment of alcohol and substance abuse. The tie between the medical model and Alcoholics Anonymous (AA) is highlighted. He takes the reader through the process of treatment from intake to treatment planning to discharge and followup using this model. Thombs notes that almost all current recovery programs incorporate the disease model and the twelve-step approach advocated by AA. The strengths and weaknesses of the disease model are compared and the contributions of this model, historically and presently, are detailed.

Calamari and Cox's major aim is to contrast alternative models to the classic disease model presented by Thombs. Using a case example, they follow a freshman student who gets into difficulty related to abusive drinking. They then use the case to demonstrate how traditional disease theory and alternative theories would conceptualize the problem. The difference that seems most central is the use of a broader, more flexible continuum of severity in the alternative theories and a narrower, more rigid approach by disease theory. For example, "harm reduction," or changing aspects of the student's drinking pattern (not having the student quit drinking entirely), would be considered by alternative theorists as a proper approach, while total abstinence would be the only option in disease theory. These two authors, like Zucker and colleagues, also conceptually define substance abuse problems from the perspective of the Diagnostic and Statistical Manual of the American Psychiatric Association, carefully distinguishing between alcohol abuse and alcohol dependency as specified by this diagnostic manual.

The second part of the book deals with policies, programming, and prevention. The chapter on policy by Schuh and Shore points out some of the legal, educational, and social factors which must be taken into account when developing a campus policy on substance abuse. In particular, the fact that alcohol use is legal for students over twenty-one years of age and not legal for those under that age causes problems with both education and social actions on campuses. One important guideline for developing an alcohol and drug policy is making sure that it is consistent with the educational institution's mission and philosophy statements. If these statements are coherent and clear and the substance abuse policy is consistent with the mission and philosophy statements, then the policy is likely to be more understandable and effective. These authors provide guidelines that need to be considered when developing a campus alcohol and drug policy.

Berkowitz deals with prevention and programming on college campuses. He distinguishes between reactive and proactive prevention; his chapter is based on the latter approach. Berkowitz notes that most alcohol and drug programs have focused on the abusers on campus, and outlines the growing evidence that focusing on campus substance abusers may, paradoxically, perpetuate problem alcohol and drug use. Following his approach to prevention of alcohol and drug abuse, campus communities must be provided with accurate information about the norms for drinking that actually exist on campus. Students, through surveys, are provided accurate information about their alcohol and drug abuse. This information is used for "norming" the campus. Typically, these surveys indicate that students overestimate the number of people on campus who abuse alcohol and the general level of abusive drinking. Students discover, to their surprise, that the majority of campus drinkers are moderate to low users of alcohol and drugs. Becoming more aware of the actual substance-using norms and making these norms public has the effect of reducing substance abuse, even in those who abuse alcohol and drugs.

The final chapter in this part is Rubington's chapter on university housing. His writing is based on an empirical study at a major city university. While the findings are based on housing policies at one university, many of the concerns raised by the research are generalizable to other institutions. In particular, alcohol policy and its level of enforcement by resident directors and resident assistants have a powerful impact on the potential for alcohol problems in dormitories. This research suggests both directly and indirectly that policy decisions and their enforcement (or lack thereof) can affect alcohol use and abuse in resident halls.

The final part of the book covers assessment, intervention, and treatment. When working with substance abusers, intervention and assessment often overlap in terms of which comes first and which comes second. The assessment chapter is presented first with the rationale that the problem and its severity must be known before intervening. The chapter by Patrick D. Smith, Dedra B. Wells, and Katurah Abdul-Salaam covers assessment in terms of (1) when assessment is appropriate, (2) how a potential abuser gets to assessment, and (3) how assessment information is used. The question to be asked is simply, "Is the alcohol or drug abuse affecting the student's life in a negative fashion?" If the answer is yes, then assessment is needed to establish the severity of the problem. Smith's chapter suggests some of the steps which might be necessary to get an alcohol or drug assessment completed. He also recommends some possible sources for this service. The chapter ends with some thumbnail sketches of alcohol and drug assessment instruments appropriate for use with college-level substance users and abusers.

Deisinger, in his intervention chapter, notes that early intervention with a student's substance abuse problem means that the problem is easier and more cost effective to treat. He defines intervention as a process that does not allow individuals to avoid the awareness of the natural outcome and consequence of their substance abuse. Deisinger asserts that if the intervener takes action, there are two positive results. Action gives the intervener hope and it helps the abusing student to take charge of his or her problem. The intervener needs to be carefully trained so that he or she develops confidence and feels empowered to intercede. The author reviews formal versus informal interventions and group versus individual interventions. Whatever the mode, intervention is considered an integral part of successful substance abuse programs on college campuses.

The next to last chapter, written by Kenneth Gregoire, focuses on treatment of college-age substance abusers. One of the complicating factors in treating college-age students is that they are often going through a transition in life; that is, moving from adolescence to adulthood. Gregoire points out that just being a college student has aspects that can support substance abuse. He discusses the Minnesota Model, the primary model for substance abuse treatment in this country and thus the treatment model most likely to be available to college students. In contrast to Calamari and Cox (see Chapter 4), Gregoire views the Minnesota Model programs as becoming increasingly flexible. He discusses assessing motivation for change, treatment settings, and levels of care. The multifaceted nature of substance abuse means that many different people must work together to provide treatment for the student. Treatment success with college students, as well as with other populations, is heavily dependent on close collaboration between all sources of support and care.

The final chapter, written by Gary and Ann Lawson, focuses on the important role of self-help groups in treatment and aftercare. While they spend considerable time on the self-help groups based on the twelve-step model of Alcoholics Anonymous (and there are many), they also discuss Rational Recovery, Self-Management and Recovery Training, and Women for Sobriety groups. They show how self-help groups can be utilized by the recovering student and suggest that on-campus groups are frequently available and a better fit for college students. They take the reader into twelve-step groups so they can understand what to expect at a typical self-help group meeting. They also point out how twelve-step groups can interface with ongoing formal treatment and how these groups can be used in aftercare.

This work allows the reader to focus on a single chapter or to read the entire volume. The book is comprehensive and the reader will find many practical and useful suggestions from the contributors. We hope that the information will inform college personnel and, ultimately, lead to more effective prevention, intervention, and treatment of college substance abuse.

Acknowledgments

An edited book of this size is put together with the aid of many people. At the risk of leaving out some very important individuals who helped us in getting the book to press, we would like to recognize as many as we can. First, we thank the contributors, whose names are listed at the end of the book. Without their scholarship, wisdom, and openness to our editorial suggestions it would have been much more difficult to see the task to fruition. We also thank the secretarial staffs in the psychology departments at Wichita State University and the University of Nebraska–Lincoln (UNL).

Prior to the submission of the outline for consideration to publish, several people read and commented on the prospectus for the book. At Wichita State University, Dr. Gregory Buell, Associate Director and Director of Clinical Services of that university's Counseling and Testing Center, made helpful comments and assured us that the outlined topics were relevant. Given his close contact with students on campus and their problems, this was very reassuring to us.

At the University of Nebraska–Lincoln, three people reviewed the outline and gave us comments. Dr. Douglas Zatechka, Director of Housing, was kind enough to look over our preliminary plans and to say that the outline suggested a book that was needed and long overdue. Dr. Vernon Williams, Coordinator of Career Counseling at UNL, had similar comments after his review. These were much needed words of encouragement from two people who are keenly aware of the substance abuse problems that face students on campus.

The late Brian Sarata, a faculty member in the psychology department, was the third UNL reviewer. Knowing the high standards that he set for himself and the students with whom he worked, it was gratifying to hear from him that the volume seemed to be well thought out and to cover many of the important issues faced by university and college personnel. Brian was a friend, colleague, and mentor to both of us; an important person from whom we wanted feedback early in the process; and one who could readily see the blindspots we might overlook. While he will be missed for his insight and intelligence, he will be missed most for his care, concern, kindness, friendship, and love of "community." We hope this volume will be helpful to those working in the campus community. If it is, we know that Brian would be pleased.

PART I

BASIC ISSUES AND MODELS

1

Alcohol Involvement over the Life Span: A Developmental Perspective on Etiology and Course

Robert A. Zucker, Eve E. Reider,
Deborah A. Ellis, and Hiram E. Fitzgerald

A DEVELOPMENTAL PERSPECTIVE

The developmental perspective is concerned with understanding the growth, maturation, and decline of the individual organism, from conception, through birth, and through all stages of the life cycle. Whether used in biology (Waddington, 1968) or in the behavioral sciences (Baltes, 1987; Gottlieb, 1991; Lerner, 1991), it is concerned with mapping the many processes that affect development. Researchers using this perspective seek to document the relationship of maturation to environmental trigger events, to establish the extent to which the basic structure of developmental processes can be modified by environmental experiences, and to describe the organism–environment interchanges that are necessary either to bring about such change or to resist it.

In this chapter we describe the developmental perspective and compare it to other current typologies, specifically the disease concept and the American system of diagnosis of addictive disorders. This perspective is especially useful because it allows us to account for the vagaries of alcohol involvement and alcohol problems over the life course better than is currently possible with paradigms that ignore the time-based and context-embedded nature of such phenomena. The perspective may be especially useful when trying to understand and respond to alcohol-related issues and problems in college populations (both traditional and nontraditional).

The notion of time flow is basic to the developmental approach. What is loosely and typically referred to by the shorthand title of "age" is, in reality, a way of referring to the fact that all of what we need to understand is taking place in a time that is multidetermined and differently measured. We may refer to the different ways of measuring time as "clocks."

A *biological clock* starts running at the moment of conception and continues to tick thereafter. The clock regulates structural and functional sequencing, and genetic codes provide a game plan for differentiation. The developmental perspective, however, requires that we attend to two other clocks that are running from the time of conception and that interact with the biological clock throughout the life span.

The *sociohistorical clock* marks the unfolding of epochs. Such time is of relevance to the issues being considered in this volume because it directs our attention to differences in the availability of alcohol and differences in attitudes about temperate and intemperate use; such differences in "drinking cultures" form the context in which learning about alcohol takes place, and in which environments work to suppress or enhance drinking and its many sequelae. Living in the passionately abstinent Mormon Salt Lake City of the 1880s or the bacchanalian Gin Lanes of eighteenth-century London (Coffey, 1966), the rural and temperate Kansas of the mid-1950s or the regularly-drinking middle class suburbs of the sixties (Cahalan, Cisin, & Crossley, 1969), provide different contexts in which alcohol-related processes are gauged and unfold. So also, current attitudes about temperate use and moderation are very different than the "turn-on, tune-in, drop-out" attitudes of the 1960s.

There is also the *psychosocial clock*, linking organismic time to the sequencing of age grades within each society (Erickson, 1959). This is the social clock that has received the bulk of attention in the developmental literature on the onset of drinking in urban Western European and North American societies. It is this clock that leads us to regard the availability of alcoholic beverages for a three year old, and the encouragement of the three year old's use by others in the child's environment, as a clear sign of abuse on the part of the caretakers. The same clock informs us that parallel phenomena occurring in the environment of a sixteen year old are part of the process of normal growth and social development (Jessor and Jessor, 1977). Thus, contextual differences lead to grossly different ramifications of two ostensibly similar sets of events. These examples underscore the need for awareness of interactive relationships, and for sensitivity to the time-linked nature of etiology, whether it be in the evolution of normal drinking patterns or in the evolution of what later will become alcoholism.

Because of its recognition of the presence and influence of different "clocks" and their effect on each other, the developmental approach often is also termed *biopsychosocial*. As with other theoretical systems, it is concerned with constancy and change, recognizing that both are always present in the life of the organism. The perspective is different from some others, however, in its emphasis on contextualism and its desire to define and map the multiple interacting factors that produce behavior.

SOME TYPOLOGIES OF ALCOHOL INVOLVEMENT

Alcohol is a substance that is used for pleasure, celebration, relief, and even sometimes for escape. A truly developmental approach to understanding these patterns of use would require us to make inferences about the discovery and early consumption of this ubiquitous substance, far back in prehistoric time. Somewhere in that prehistory, humankind decided to put energy into figuring out how to manufacture ethanol, and we have been doing so ever since. Out of consideration of space, however, we will skip what we know of earlier epochs and move instead to more recent history, first to the seventeenth century and then to the nineteenth and twentieth, paying particular attention to the disease theory of alcoholism (see also Chapter 3). Finally, we will move to 1994 for a look at the most recent formal statement/definition we have concerning the phenomenon of problematic alcohol involvement by individuals. This brief trip through history will provide the reader with an understanding of current definitions of alcohol dependence and alcoholism and will set the stage for looking at developmental factors affecting alcohol involvement.

Levine (1978), in his definitive historical review of the concept of addiction, informs us that the idea that alcoholism is a progressive disease, the chief symptom of which is loss of control over drinking behavior and whose only remedy is abstinence from all alcoholic beverages, is now about 175 or 200 years old, but no older. He states that this concept "constituted a radical break with traditional ideas about the problems involved in drinking alcohol" (p. 143).

During the seventeenth and most of the eighteenth centuries, it was assumed that people drank because they wanted to rather than because they had to. Alcohol was not thought to disable the will nor was it considered to be addicting. By the end of the eighteenth century, however, Americans began to report having irresistible desires for alcohol. People affiliated with temperance groups asserted that intemperance was a disease which arose from the moderate use of alcohol (Levine, 1978). In his analysis, Levine demonstrates that there is a basic continuity between the ideology of the Temperance Movement and the post–Prohibition (and present day) paradigm of alcoholism as a progressive disorder or disease, one marked by loss of control.

It is relevant to note, however, that although the temperance position was the dominant one, there was an anti-temperance thread to be identified during this period. This was the moral position asserting that drunkenness was a vice, not a disease (Todd, 1882), and that it involved both personal choice and the lack of willpower. We note this "minority position" because it is a clear precursor to the notion of psychopathology as "moral insanity" (Cleckley, 1950), which itself is the intellectual forbearer of the position that some forms of alcoholism are associated with antisocial character (Cloninger, Bohman, & Sigvardsson, 1981; Cadoret, O'Gorman, Troughton, & Haywood, 1985; Zucker, 1987).

Although E. M. Jellinek is usually considered to be the father of the disease concept of alcoholism, an examination of earlier writing indicates that the disease concept is an old one. Within the work of Benjamin Rush, the father of American psychiatry, one can find the four elements necessary to characterize the addictive disease paradigm: (1) There is loss of control; (2) there is a causal agent; (3) there is the identification of the involvement as a disease (i.e., inability to abstain by will alone); and (4) there is a cure—abstinence (Levine, 1978). It was Jellinek's powerful work, however, that most clearly articulated the disease concept for modern time.

Jellinek described several species of alcoholism, named alpha, beta, gamma, delta, and epsilon. Although he was willing to embrace a broad definition of alcoholism, involving "any use of alcoholic beverages that causes any damage to the individual or society or both" (1960, p. 35), Jellinek reserved the notion of a disease entity for only two of the alcoholic subspecies, gamma and delta alcoholism. Both of these species are seen as having (1) acquired tissue tolerance, (2) adaptive cell metabolism, (3) withdrawal symptoms and craving (i.e., physical dependence), and (4) for gamma alcoholism, loss of control. Excluded from the disease classification are those forms of alcoholism that are seen as purely psychologically motivated, that do not involve progression (e.g., periodic but not progressive dipsomania), or that may be the residue of an underlying psychopathological rather than a physiological etiology.

In other words, for Jellinek, it was possible to be considered to be alcoholic without being addicted and having a disease in the classical sense. This distinction may also be important when considering the drinking behaviors of college-age people, who may exhibit problems (such as frequent drunkenness, drunk driving, vandalism, school failure) without experiencing loss of control, withdrawal (other than hangovers), or other signs of addiction to alcohol. The presence of an alcohol abuse problem different from classical alcoholism also has ramifications for the choice of intervention and treatment adopted. Thus, if we see the individual as "having a set of problems," then perhaps the most efficacious treatment is to deal with these problems, one by one. When they are successfully addressed, then the abuse no longer exists (see Baer, 1993).

Given the developmental perspective we are following here, it is also important to note that the two syndromes Jellinek viewed as disease entities are the only ones that involve a clear progression and the presumption of underlying physiological processes at work (see Jellinek, 1960, pp. 37–38). Progression has been viewed by some as irreversible and unavoidable. That is, once a person shows early signs of problems with alcohol it is assumed that, unless the person completely abstains, additional and more severe symptoms will emerge, leading inevitably to the complete loss of health, family, and livelihood, and, finally, to death.

There have been major changes in the level of our understanding of the vagaries of display, unfolding, and natural history of alcohol problems since

Jellinek's time, but his basic definitional paradigm remains. This can be seen in the *Diagnostic and Statistical Manual of Mental Disorders (DSM IV)* (American Psychiatric Association, 1994). This manual is used in virtually every clinic, hospital, and treatment facility in the United States and its definitions of mental illness are accepted as the basis for insurance and other reimbursement for treatment. In it there is heavy emphasis on characteristics of physical dependence (Edwards & Gross, 1976) to establish a diagnosis of substance dependence, which is the more severe of two possible DSM-IV diagnoses (the less severe being labeled substance abuse). There is also relative downplay of criteria concerned with impaired social and occupational functioning, nonphysical signs of problems related to alcohol use (Institute of Medicine, 1987). The DSM-IV markers for alcohol dependence include tolerance, withdrawal, drinking to relieve withdrawal, greater use than the person intends, a persistent desire to control use, inability to cut down or control, much time spent in activities related to obtaining alcohol or recovering from use, continuing use despite problems connected to use, and reduction of role involvements because of use. A minimum of three of these symptoms must be present at any time during the same twelve-month period in order to make the diagnosis (see Chapter 4).

ISSUES AND PROBLEMS

From the perspective of a developmentalist there are a number of problems with this clinical picture. These problems may be subsumed under three main points, concerning context, underlying processes, and the type of people studied.

A clinically based alcohol dependence definition fails to adequately represent the context within which alcohol problems evolve. The simplest way to summarize this deficit is to note that the contribution of psychosocial factors to the onset, maintenance, and possible exacerbation of alcohol-related difficulties is downplayed in clinical accounts and in formal, medically based definitions. This is so despite the by now overwhelming evidence that alcohol problems vary with culture, social class, and sex, factors that are powerful determinants of the rule structures which govern roles and regulate social behavior (Ojesjo, Hagnell, & Lanke, 1983; Cahalan & Room, 1974; Heath, 1988). Recent evidence even indicates that influences at this level of social structure can interact with differences in level of genetic susceptibility to produce different rates of alcoholic incidence in a culture (Reich, Cloninger, Van Eerdewegh, Rice, & Mullaney, 1988). Thus, to either minimize (as in the case of DSM IV) or exclude (as with Jellinek) contextual influences as largely irrelevant to the disease process simply because they are necessary for onset but do not in an obvious way drive the addictive time sequence is to leave out major contributions to variation in susceptibility. By way of historical comment, changes in the DSM-IV criteria from those found in DSM III-R indicate that this situation is slowly shifting. A close reading of the new text shows that there is some awareness of cultural influences and variations in course as a function of environmental factors.

Another problem with the current disease typologies is that, with the exception of attention paid to etiological factors at the biological level, they fail to specify other underlying or core processes involved in the production of the disorder(s). A disease is a system whose structure and operation is more than the sum of its subsidiary parts (von Bertalanffy, 1968). Although the evidence at this point in time clearly indicates that alcohol-related problems result from a multifactorial, biopsychosocial process (or set of processes, if we conceive of more than one alcohol involvement pathway) (Kissen & Begleiter, 1983; Zucker, Fitzgerald, & Moses, 1995) that eventually coalesces into a structure which is larger than its immediate addictive determinants, the current typologies do not take this into account. A developmental perspective would help researchers generate an adequate model of the processes involved in the development, or avoidance, of alcoholism and alcohol-related problems.

The alcoholism categorization is drawn almost entirely from observations of clinical phenomena, made either by clinicians or by researchers who recruit subjects from hospitals or other treatment facilities. Such observations are heavily biased in the direction of showing continuity of time flow and an accumulation of ever-worsening signs and symptoms. Starting with patients in treatment for alcohol problems and working backward to construct a history virtually guarantees the appearance of an identifiable progression toward a recognizable disease entity. People whose drinking does not proceed in this manner may not enter treatment programs, and thus are lost to the clinical researcher. A close reading of Jellinek, as well as the DSM IV, reveals that the authors were in an intuitive way aware of this anomaly; one notes observations here and there which indicate that progress does not always take place at the same rate, does not always unfold, and that reversibility and remission may occur. These observations, however, are not well articulated, leaving the impression that such variations are rare and anomalous events and that progression to a disease state is the most usual consequence.

The almost exclusive utilization of clinical samples and the failure to consider context have serious ramifications for work with college students. Making assumptions from such samples about the likely course, intervention, and treatment needs of younger healthier men and women of diverse ethnicity, with shorter histories of alcohol-related problems and intact and usually rich and elaborate support systems, is certainly risky. Fortunately, more recent findings (including those from research by developmentalists) have begun to affect theory and practice, providing alternatives that are more appropriate for college students.

VARIATION IN DRINKING OVER THE LIFE COURSE

The evidence for a substantial degree of instability/epiphenomenality of alcohol problems over the life course is now significant. Heavily based upon population rather than clinical samples, it ranges from studies of youth (Andersson & Magnusson, 1988; Donovan, Jessor, & Jessor, 1983; Temple & Fillmore, 1986), to studies of adults (Cahalan, 1970; Clark & Cahalan, 1976; Knupfer, 1972; Roizen, Cahalan, & Shanks, 1978; Skog & Duckert, 1993), to studies of the elderly (Gomberg, 1982, 1989). All of this work reports significant shifts into and out of problem drinking classifications over intervals even as short as one year, suggesting that consumption level and related problems are very unstable over longer intervals of time.

By the same token, evidence for stability of drinking patterns and for the operation of a cumulative process is likewise present (Grant, Harford, & Grigson, 1988; Penick, Powell, Liskow, Jackson, & Nickel, 1988). To add to the apparent contradiction, some of these studies are the same ones that provide evidence for instability and shift (Windle, 1988; Andersson & Magnusson, 1988). In part, the issue of change versus stability may have to do with how data are analyzed and with what attributes of the problem are being studied. Another interpretation, however, is important when considering college age drinkers: Fillmore, in two papers, has suggested that the paradox of stability and change is age connected (Fillmore & Midanik, 1984; Fillmore, 1987). She provides evidence that instability in drinking behaviors and consequences is the rule among younger people and in old age, while chronicity is more common in the middle years.

Nicki Erlenmeyer-Kimling and her colleagues, noted researchers studying the antecedents of schizophrenia, have found that individuals follow widely differing courses (Erlenmeyer-Kimling, Corblatt, Bassett, Moldin, Adamo, & Roberts, 1990). Although most subjects who showed poor adjustment in childhood also were dysfunctional in early adulthood and most who were nondysfunctional as children continued to show good adjustment, there were numerous exceptions in both cases. The variability in functioning over time that is shown in such data provide another piece of evidence indicating the need for a revision in our notions that early risk unalterably leads to a preset trajectory. What is needed is a developmental paradigm that can more adequately reflect what our data indicate is actually taking place.

A PROBABILISTIC DEVELOPMENTAL
FRAMEWORK FOR COURSE

As has been discussed, the evidence for the operation of multiple processes in the development of alcohol problems is such that the notion of a single progressive and irreversible pathway of outcome is no longer workable. A more appropriate way to take into account multiple processes is to move to a probabilistic conceptual framework of both risk and clinical disorder (Zucker, 1987, 1989). In such a framework, risk is viewed as a fluid characteristic that increases or decreases depending on the momentum of earlier risk experience, as well as the influence of new external and internal agents of liability. Risk is construed as the end result of a set of dynamic processes, anchored within both developmental and sociohistorical time, that operates in varying degrees throughout the life span of the individual. Risk ebbs and flows.

Within this framework, the onset of "caseness" (i.e., the discovery that a clinical case has developed) is best understood as a threshold phenomenon. It may be that a pattern of continuity develops or becomes evident or that previous manifestations of problems display with greater intensity, frequency, or regularity. Once the clinical level is reached, one no longer speaks about risk, but instead about disease or disorder. In the college setting, "going critical" may lead to identification of a clinical entity (alcoholism), a preclinical problem (drinking behavior with high risk for future negative consequences), or a school-specific disorder (school failure, rules violations).

This reformulation is offered as a more accurate representation of the probabilistic nature of alcohol use over time. It allows for specification of interactional processes, and acknowledges that these processes sometimes result in the development of "disease" and sometimes lead to a "resilient outcome" (cf. Rutter, 1987). The model is prospective; one must specify what alternative paths are possible before they occur, as well as what interaction of contextual and intrinsic factors will lead to which path. Such models will be more helpful for those interested in prevention, especially as compared with retrospectively derived models that present one fixed and invariant developmental path.

Alcohol and drug use in young adulthood is one example of how age-stage influences can affect later behaviors. Age of onset for alcohol and harder drug use has in recent years been regarded as a proxy indicator of a gateway phenomenon. Thus, if the onset of drug use can be prevented until the early twenties, then risk for later drug use becomes negligible (Kandel & Yamaguchi, 1985; Robins, 1984). Differences between adolescent-stage pressures and those of early adulthood are important here. One of the dominant themes of adolescence in our society is increasing development of independence, along with increasing rebelliousness, heightened peer socialization for deviant behavior, and heightened alcohol and other drug involvement (Jessor & Jessor, 1977). In contrast, the role demands of early adulthood are for achievement, conventionality, and marriage, all of which are conducive to lessened alcohol and other drug use (Donovan et al., 1983). Thus, if one makes it through adolescence without drug involvement, one misses the window of exposure, availability, and peer pressure which drives onset of the phenomenon. Thereafter, without earlier use, even if the biopsychological structure is appropriate for a pattern of abuse (alcoholism in the family, for example), the environmental triggers and the significant substance availability are absent.

Traditionally, going to college is thought to prolong adolescence. Thus, for college-bound youth the window of exposure may be extended past high school. In some cases, college may even constitute the first significant exposure to increased availability, peer pressure, and freedom from adult control. One question is whether drinking behavior in college is significantly predictive of future drinking. For some, behaviors freely engaged in during the college years are abandoned upon graduation and the assumption of the adult role. For others, however, such behaviors are continued despite the fact that they are less appropriate, and more dangerous, than they were in the college environment.

Nontraditional college students, as well as an increasing number of traditional-aged students, are less likely to experience college attendance as an extension of high school and adolescence. Like noncollege young adults, nontraditional students are likely to have families, jobs, and other responsibilities and, thus, are less likely to frequent college hangouts, feel the need for rebellion, or face peer pressure to drink. Nontraditional students with alcohol abuse problems may, therefore, be on another path, requiring different types of intervention.

These variations are additional examples of pathways to be understood, and further illustrate the limitations of typologies that assume that abusive behavior at one point in time is always predictive of future problems. It is of course true that problems in college must be addressed regardless of the likelihood that they will continue in the future. The question is one of assessment of appropriate intervention and/or treatment. For example, should college students who are drinking abusively be referred to programs that prepare them for lifelong abstinence?

ELABORATING THE MODEL

Figure 1.1 is a graphic representation of a probabilistic model. The grid illustrates the developmental flow of risk factors over the lifetime of the individual (X axis), and highlights the potential for both continuity and discontinuity. The power of the developmental paradigm comes from its emphasis on contextualism, both cross-sectionally and maturationally (Harris, 1957). Studies which ignore the complexity of the influencing network are ultimately invitations to dead ends, for the simple reason that the data sets so produced will not allow for tests of competing hypotheses about major sources of variation.

The Y axis of Figure 1.1 lists what we regard as the major domains of the biopsychosocial influencing structure. They were selected on the grounds that substantial evidence currently exists demonstrating the significant role they play in etiologic processes. Thus, factors within each of these domains need to be regarded as potentially available influencing systems for risk, and for insulation against risk, at each age stage.

The domains listed, ranging from the biological to the socio-cultural, are an attempt to cover the biopsychosocial continuum. This and similar catalog attempts have proven to be necessary whenever one wishes to describe process relationships among complex multilevel systems (cf. Anderson, 1972; Salthe, 1985), or where the primary question is understanding stability and change over time (cf. Lerner, 1984). In order to adequately represent the forces

Figure 1.1
A Probabilistic Developmental Model of the Flow of Risk across the Biopsychosocial Domain Structure, and over the Life Course

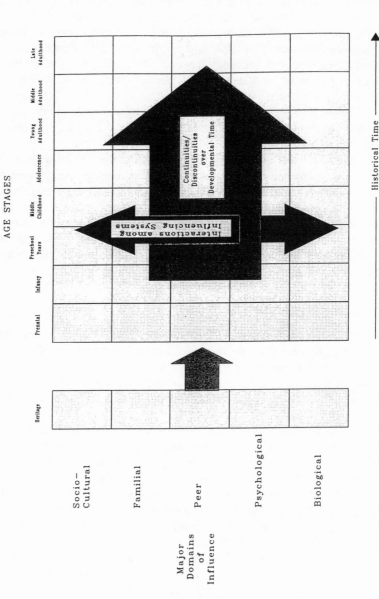

Source: Adapted from Zucker (1987).
Note: Relative risk at any age involves additive and subtractive elements in the grid that may, at a particular age stage, go over threshold to display as a clinical case.

at work, the domains must include both alcohol-specific and nonalcohol-specific influences. Recent studies that have included both sets of factors have been able to represent (and model) the chain of interplay between the specific and the nonspecific in ways which offer considerable promise for understanding how the building blocks cumulate to produce risky (and in some instances damaged) outcomes (Brook, Whiteman, Gordon, & Cohen, 1989; McCord, 1988; Sher, Walitzer, Wood, & Brent, 1991).

The high-risk-for-alcoholism Michigan State University–University of Michigan Longitudinal Study being conducted by Zucker, Fitzgerald, and colleagues (Zucker, Ellis, Bingham, & Fitzgerald, 1996; Zucker, 1987) shows how models are built and provides some illustrations of the potentially thick network of causal structures necessary to adequately account for alcoholic etiologic processes. The project utilizes a population-based sample of alcoholic men, their spouses, and their male children. Data collected from the families at three-year intervals explicitly attempt to sample across the multiple domains depicted in Figure 1.1.

One of the study's overarching hypotheses is that both factors nonspecific to alcohol—in particular, pertaining to the development of aggression and negative mood—and factors specific to alcohol are necessary to turn risk into the actuality of symptomatic outcome (Zucker, 1987). In her doctoral dissertation research, Reider (1991) attempted to model the way that early factors are linked to the development of child behavior problems. (Because these children are too young for evaluation of any obvious alcohol-specific outcomes, only nonspecific factors are examined here.[1]) Figure 1.2 presents the result of path analyses indicating how factors are linked with child behavior problems. Figure 1.3 translates the path analysis map into the domain structure depicted in Figure 1.1. The figures indicate that the mother's lifetime trouble and family conflict contribute to the mother's depression, which in turn affects the child's behavior. Although the father's depression is linked to similar variables, it is not significantly related to the child's behavior.

As is clear from the figures, this is currently an incomplete representation because it contains no evaluation of either sociocultural or biological variation. Other analyses of this data set (Fitzgerald & Zucker, 1995; Jansen, Fitzgerald, Ham, & Zucker, 1995) in fact suggest that socioeconomic status (a sociocultural variable) and child temperament (at least partially a constitutional variable) may also play some role in child outcome.

Wynblatt's (1990) research, also using the longitudinal data set, investigated the pathways for two types of alcoholism: early onset, antisocial and later onset, nonantisocial alcoholism (Cloninger, Bohman, & Sigvardsson, 1981; Cloninger, 1987). She found two paths to the former type; one in which delinquent or conduct-disorder behavior in childhood was predictive of antisociality in adulthood, which in turn drove adult alcohol-related difficulty, and the other in which childhood antisociality and family risk also contributed. In contrast,

Figure 1.2
Final Trimmed Path Model Linking Parental and Familial Influences to Child Aggression (Mother CBCL Ratings)

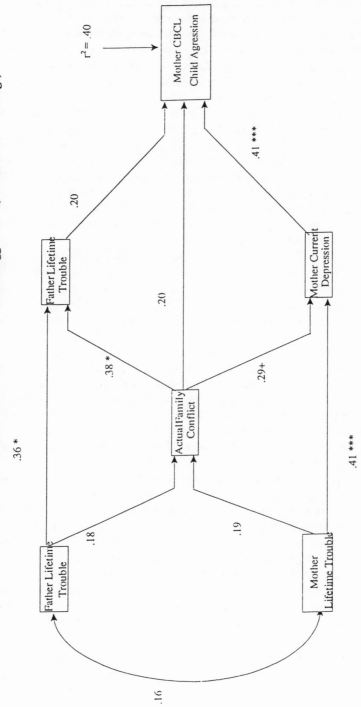

Source: Adapted from Reider (1991).

Figure 1.3
**Trimmed Path Model of Parental and Familial Influences Leading to Child
Aggression Mapped onto the Domain Structure of the Probabilistic
Developmental Grid**

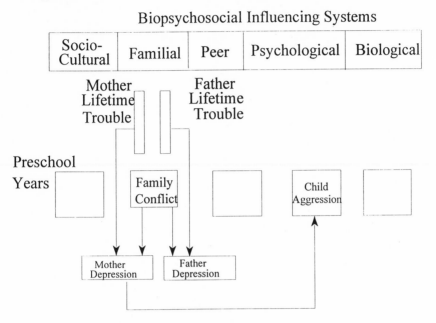

only exposure to an alcoholic rearing environment was predictive of later
alcoholic difficulty (see also Zucker, Ellis, & Fitzgerald, 1994).

Wynblatt's and Reider's maps can be combined (with some assumptions
made explicit) to reveal a complex web (Figure 1.4) that begins in parental
history and makes its way, via family processes, to impact the behavioral
adaptation, or lack thereof, of the child during the preschool years. The presence, at this juncture, of ongoing behavioral difficulty in turn creates a window of opportunity for the initiation of a pathway involving a pattern of
antisocial behavior. Should such a pattern be sustained over the years of middle
childhood and adolescence, it then, in conjunction with genetic factors, produces both more severe adult alcoholism and a pattern of adult antisociality.
Such is the thick causal structure of developmental processes; it involves
multiple domains, some constancy of life trajectory, and the potential for different causal mechanisms operating at different life stages.

DRINKING PATTERNS AMONG YOUNG PEOPLE:
A DEVELOPMENTAL VIEW

So what are the concrete implications of such a probabilistic model in understanding the drinking behavior of the college years? From a developmen-

Figure 1.4
Composite Life Span Path Model for the Developmental Course of Risk from Childhood to Adulthood for Type II Alcoholics

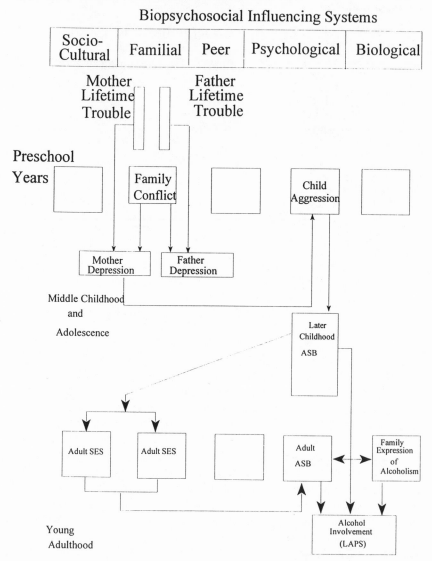

tal perspective, problem drinking among college students needs to be viewed as a multiple process phenomenon, encompassing a number of different pathways into (and out of) problem alcohol use. For some, it is a continuation of the normative deviance of adolescence. As we have already noted, this is a process that the Jessors (1977) and their coworkers (Jessor, Donovan, & Costa,

1991; Donovan, Jessor, & Jessor, 1983) have described, involving increasing valuation of independence over achievement, increasing dependence on peer influences over those of parents, and participation in a variety of more socially deviant and externalizing activities, including heavier drinking, earlier and more sexual involvement, and participation in minor delinquent activity. For this subset of young people, the problematic alcohol involvement of the college years, and related trouble, can be expected to moderate with the onset of adulthood and its expectancies of commitment to career and marriage.

For others, an apparently similar pattern of deviance and problem alcohol involvement during college will not moderate, but continues thereafter (Zucker, 1987; Zucker, Fitzgerald, & Moses, 1995). What distinguishes these two different pathways? For one, this second group has had a pattern of social misbehavior substantially prior to college. So the deviance is of earlier onset, and, if one looks closely, minor delinquency is detectable even prior to the high school years. In addition, there is more commonly a family history that is positive for alcoholism. Thus, for a variety of reasons the problem shown during college is actually one involving a trajectory of misbehavior that is driven by more elements of risk, is therefore more likely to be of greater severity, and is also more likely to persist once college is over.

Both of these groups may meet formal diagnostic criteria of alcohol dependence, and both are deserving of intervention that addresses the immediate drinking difficulty. For the first subset of problem drinkers, this strategy is more likely to be sufficient; for the second subset it is not, and a substantially broader armamentarium of clinical skills, applied for a significantly longer period of time, is likely to be called for.

What has been described here are two of the more common patterns of alcohol involvement during this life stage. There are more, some that reflect simple differences in symptomatic variability during the years of late adolescence to early adulthood, and others that reflect early manifestations of subtype variation among the alcoholisms that can be expected to play out in different ways as adulthood progresses.

More generally, the college years need to be regarded as a narrow time window through which a variety of longer-term trajectories of normal and problematic alcohol involvement pass. If the counselor is to make sense out of the developmentally small amount of observational data available, he or she needs to (1) be aware of the variety of longer-term drinking trajectories that have been identified, (2) be sensitive to markers of earlier life-course variations that may help establish which of the trajectories is showing itself, and (3) be aware as well that different treatment strategies may be called for, even though the observed symptomatology appears to be the same. A detailed description of these trajectories is beyond the scope of this chapter, but the interested reader is referred to the chapter by Zucker, Fitzgerald, and Moses (1995), and the article by Schulenberg, O'Malley, Bachman, Wadsworth, and Johnston (1996) for more information.

SOME LARGER IMPLICATIONS OF A PROBABILISTIC DEVELOPMENTAL FRAMEWORK

There are several quite practical implications of such elaborate developmental models of causes. At the most general level, they require both the policy maker and the change agent to recognize that a change in level of alcohol problems may impact more than simple alcoholic symptomatology. These changes are likely to impact social relationships and the legal system, and may have economic implications as well. For the same reason, the policy maker and change agent must also recognize that, to sustain change, other systems of action will have to be impacted.

At the level of policy, the developmental framework implies that a push for social change involving changing the drinking age or changing availability through price increases is a push to modify a structure that is both behaviorally interwoven with other structural systems (from the biological to the social), and also is embedded in a particular historical era. Thus, to attempt to influence the one element (alcohol) without dealing with other neighboring domains may lead, in the long run, to failure of the change attempt. Conversely, programming that focuses on multiple domains, and that is more closely tied to both developmental and historical contexts, is more likely to become integrated and form the basis for a structure which can successfully sustain itself.

NOTES

The research reported in this article was supported in part by grants to Robert A. Zucker, Hiram E. Fitzgerald, and Robert B. Noll from the National Institute on Alcohol Abuse and Alcoholism (AA 07065) and from the Michigan Department of Mental Health, Prevention Services Unit.

1. In fact, the theory guiding this study suggests that some alcohol-specific factors should be present, even at this early an age, but that such factors are not what would typically be regarded as markers of symptomatic alcohol use. We refer to early individual differences in the availability of cognitions about drugs and the precocious development of cognitive schemas about drugs (see Noll, Zucker, & Greenberg, 1990; Zucker, Fitzgerald, & Noll, 1991; Zucker, Kincaid, Fitzgerald, & Bingham, 1995). However, the present set of analyses was not designed to explore these issues.

REFERENCES

American Psychiatric Association. (1994). *Diagnostic and statistical manual of mental disorders* (4th ed.). Washington, DC: Author.

Anderson, P. W. (1972). More is different. *Science, 177,* 393–396.

Andersson, T., & Magnusson, D. (1988). Drinking habits and alcohol abuse among young men: A prospective longitudinal study. *Journal of Studies on Alcohol, 49,* 245–252.

Baer, J. S. (1993). Etiology and secondary prevention of alcohol problems with young adults. In J. S. Baer, G. A. Marlatt, & R. J. McMahon (Eds.), *Addictive behaviors across the life span: Prevention, treatment, and policy* (pp. 111–137). Newbury Park, CA: Sage.

Baltes, P. B. (1987). Theoretical propositions of life-span developmental psychology: On the dynamics between growth and decline. *Developmental Psychology, 23,* 611–626.

Brook, J. S., Whiteman, M., Gordon, A. S., & Cohen, P. (1989). Changes in drug involvement: A longitudinal study of childhood and adolescent determinants. *Psychological Reports, 65,* 707–726.

Cadoret, R. J., O'Gorman, T., Troughton, E., & Haywood, E. (1985). Alcoholism and antisocial personality: Interrelationships, genetic and environmental factors. *Archives of General Psychiatry, 42,* 161–167.

Cahalan, D. (1970). *Problem drinkers.* San Francisco: Jossey-Bass.

Cahalan, D., Cisin, I., & Crossley, H. (1969). *American drinking practices: A national study of drinking behavior and attitudes.* New Brunswick, NJ: Publications Division, Rutgers Center of Alcohol Studies.

Cahalan, D., & Room, R. (1974). *Problem drinking among American men* (Monograph No. 7). New Brunswick, NJ: Publications Division, Rutgers Center of Alcohol Studies.

Clark, W., & Cahalan, D. (1976). Changes in problem drinking over a four-year span. *Addictive Behaviors, 1,* 251–259.

Cleckley, H. (1950). *The mask of sanity.* St. Louis: C. V. Mosby.

Cloninger, R. (1987). Neurogenetic adaptive mechanisms in alcoholism. *Science, 236,* 410–416.

Cloninger, R., Bohman, M., & Sigvardsson, S. (1981). Inheritance of substance abuse: Cross-fostering analysis of adopted men. *Archives of General Psychiatry, 38,* 861–867.

Coffey, T. G. (1966). Beer Street: Gin Lane—Some views of 18th century drinking. *Quarterly Journal of Studies on Alcohol, 27,* 669–692.

Donovan, J. E., Jessor, R., & Jessor, S. L. (1983). Problem drinking in adolescence and early adulthood: A follow-up study. *Journal of Studies on Alcohol, 44,* 109–137.

Edwards, G., & Gross, M. M. (1976). Alcohol dependence: Provisional description of a clinical syndrome. *British Medical Journal, 1,* 1058–1061.

Erickson, E. H. (1959). *Identity and the life cycle.* New York: International Universities Press.

Erlenmayer-Kimling, L., Corblatt, B. A., Bassett, A. S., Moldin, S. O., Adamo, U. H., & Roberts, S. (1990). High risk children in adolescence and young adulthood: Course of global adjustment. In L. N. Robins & M. E. Rutter (Eds.), *Pathways to mental illness.* London: Cambridge University Press.

Fillmore, K. M. (1987). Prevalence, incidence and chronicity of drinking patterns and problems among men as a function of age: A longitudinal and cohort analysis. *British Journal of Addictions, 82,* 77–83.

Fillmore, K. M., & Midanik, L. (1984). Chronicity of drinking problems among men: A longitudinal study. *Journal of Studies on Alcohol, 45,* 228–236.

Fitzgerald, H. E., & Zucker, R. A. (1995). Socioeconomic status and alcoholism: Structuring developmental pathways to addiction. In H. E. Fitzgerald, B. M. Lester, & B. Zuckerman (Eds.), *Children of poverty* (pp. 125–147). New York: Garland Press.

Gomberg, E. S. L. (1982). Alcohol use and alcohol problems among the elderly. In N.I.A.A.A. (Ed.), *Alcohol and Health Monographs, No. 4. Special Populations*. Rockville, MD: National Institute on Alcohol Abuse and Alcoholism.

Gomberg, E. S. L. (1989). Drugs, alcohol, and aging. *Research Advances in Alcohol and Drug Problems* (Vol. 10). New York: Plenum Press.

Gottlieb, G. (1991). Experimental canalization of behavioral development: Theory. *Developmental Psychology, 27,* 4–13.

Grant, B. F., Harford, T. C., & Grigson, M. B. (1988). Stability of alcohol consumption among youth: A national longitudinal survey. *Journal of Studies on Alcohol, 49,* 253–260.

Harris, D. B. (1957). *The concept of development*. Minneapolis: University of Minnesota Press.

Heath, D. B. (1988). Emerging anthropological theory and models of alcohol use and alcoholism. In C. D. Chaudron & D. A. Wilkinson (Eds.), *Theories on alcoholism*. Toronto: Alcoholism and Drug Addiction Research Foundation.

Institute of Medicine. (1987). *Causes and consequences of alcohol problems: An agenda for research*. Washington, DC: National Academy Press.

Jansen, R. L., Fitzgerald, H. E., Ham, H. P., & Zucker, R. A. (1995). Difficult temperament and problem behavior in three-to-five-year-old sons of alcoholics. *Alcoholism: Clinical and Experimental Research, 19,* 501–509.

Jellinek, E. M. (1960). *The disease concept of alcoholism*. New Haven, CT: Hillhouse Press.

Jessor, R., Donovan, J. E., & Costa, F. M. (1991). *Beyond adolescence: Problem behavior and young adult development*. New York: Cambridge University Press.

Jessor, R., & Jessor, S. L. (1977). *Problem behavior and psychosocial development: A longitudinal study of youth*. New York: Academic Press.

Kandel, D. B., & Yamaguchi, K. (1985). Developmental patterns of the use of legal, illegal, and medically prescribed psychotropic drugs from adolescence to young adulthood. In C. L. Jones & R. J. Battjes (Eds.), *Etiology of drug abuse: Implications for prevention* (NIDA Monograph No. 56). Rockville, MD: National Institute on Drug Abuse.

Kissin, B., & Begleiter, H. (1983). Preface. In B. Kissin & H. Begleiter (Eds.), *The pathogenesis of alcoholism: Psychosocial factors. The biology of alcoholism* (Vol. 6, pp. vii–x). New York: Plenum Press.

Knupfer, G. (1972). Ex-problem drinker. In M. Roff, L. Robins, & M. Pollick (Eds.), *Life history research in psychopathology* (Vol. 2). Minneapolis: University of Minnesota Press.

Lerner, R. M. (1984). *On the nature of human plasticity*. Cambridge: Cambridge University Press.

Lerner, R. M. (1991). Changing organism-context relations as the basic process of development: A developmental contextual perspective. *Developmental Psychology, 27,* 27–32.

Levine, H. G. (1978). The discovery of addiction: Changing conceptions of habitual drunkenness in America. *Journal of Studies on Alcohol, 39*(1), 143–174.

McCord, J. (1988). Identifying developmental paradigms leading to alcoholism. *Journal of Studies on Alcohol, 49,* 357–362.

Noll, R. B., Zucker, R. A., & Greenberg, G. S. (1990). Identification of alcohol by smell among preschoolers: Evidence for early socialization about drugs occurring in the home. *Child Development, 61,* 1520–1527.

Ojesjo, L., Hagnell, O., & Lanke, J. (1983). Class variations in the incidence of alcoholism in the Lundby Study, Sweden. *Social Psychiatry, 18,* 123–128.

Penick, E. C., Powell, B. J., Liskow, B. I., Jackson, J. O., & Nickel, E. J. (1988). The stability of coexisting psychiatric syndromes in alcoholic men after one year. *Journal of Studies on Alcohol, 49,* 395–405.

Reich, T. R., Cloninger, C. R., Van Eerdewegh, P., Rice, J. P., & Mullaney, J. (1988). Secular trends in the familial transmission of alcoholism. *Alcoholism: Clinical and Experimental Research, 12,* 458–464.

Reider, E. E. (1991). *Relationships between parental psychopathology, family conflict, and child behavior problems in young alcoholic families.* Unpublished doctoral dissertation, Michigan State University, East Lansing, MI.

Robins, L. N. (1984). The natural history of adolescent drug use. *American Journal of Public Health, 74,* 656–657.

Roizen, R., Cahalan, D., & Shanks, P. (1978). "Spontaneous remission" among untreated problem drinkers. In D. B. Kandel (Ed.), *Longitudinal Research on Drug Use* (pp. 197–221). Washington, DC: John Wiley & Sons.

Rutter, M. (1987). Psychological resilience and protective mechanisms. *American Journal of Orthopsychiatry, 57,* 316–331.

Salthe, S. N. (1985). *Evolving hierarchical systems: Their structure and representation.* New York: Columbia University Press.

Schulenberg, J., O'Malley, P. M., Bachman, J. G., Wadsworth, K. N., & Johnston, L. D. (1996). Getting drunk and growing up: Trajectories of frequent binge drinking during the transition to young adulthood. *Journal of Studies on Alcohol, 57,* 289–304.

Sher, K. J., Walitzer, K. S., Wood, P., & Brent, E. E. (1991). Characteristics of children of alcoholics: Putative risk factors, substance use and abuse, and psychopathology. *Journal of Abnormal Psychology, 100,* 427–448.

Skog, O. J., & Duckert, F. (1993). The stability of alcoholics' and heavy drinkers' consumption: A longitudinal study. *Journal of Studies on Alcohol, 53,* 178–188.

Temple, M., & Fillmore, K. M. (1986). The variability of drinking patterns and problems among young men, age 16–31: A longitudinal study. *International Journal of the Addictions, 20,* 1595–1620, 1985–1986.

Todd, J. E. (1882). *Drunkenness: A vice, not a disease.* Hartford, CT: Case, Lockwood, & Brainard. Cited in Jellinek, E. M. (1960). *The disease concept of alcoholism.* New Haven, CT: Hillhouse Press.

von Bertalanffy, L. (Ed.). (1968). *General system theory.* New York: Braziller.

Waddington, C. H. (1968). The basic ideas of biology. In C. H. Waddington (Ed.), *Towards a theoretical biology: Vol. 1. Prolegomena.* Chicago: Adline.

Windle, M. (1988). Are those adolescent to early adulthood drinking patterns so discontinuous? A response to Temple & Fillmore. *International Journal of the Addictions, 23,* 907–912.

Wynblatt, D. A. (1990). *Genetic loading for alcoholism: New evidence for subtypes.* Unpublished master's thesis, Michigan State University, East Lansing, MI.

Zucker, R. A. (1987) The four alcoholisms: A developmental account of the etiologic process. In P. C. Rivers (Ed.), *Nebraska symposium on motivation: Vol. 34. Alcohol and addictive behaviors* (pp. 27–83). Lincoln: University of Nebraska Press.

Zucker, R. A. (1989). Is risk for alcoholism predictable? A probabilistic approach to a developmental problem. *Drugs and Society, 4,* 69–93.

Zucker, R. A., Ellis, D. A., Bingham, C. R., & Fitzgerald, H. E. (1996). The development of alcoholic subtypes: Risk variation among alcoholic families during
early childhood. *Alcohol Health and Research World, 20,* 46–54.

Zucker, R. A., Ellis, D. A., & Fitzgerald, H. E. (1994). Developmental evidence for at
least two alcoholisms: I. Biopsychosocial variation among pathways into symptomatic difficulty. *Annals of the New York Academy of Sciences, 708,* 134–146.

Zucker, R. A., Fitzgerald, H. E., & Moses, H. D. (1995). Emergence of alcohol problems and the several alcoholisms: A developmental perspective on etiologic
theory and life course trajectory. In D. Cicchetti & D. J. Cohen (Eds.), *Manual
of developmental psychopathology* (pp. 667–711). New York: Wiley.

Zucker, R. A., Fitzgerald, H. E., & Noll, R. B. (1991, April). *The development of
cognitive schemas about drugs among preschoolers.* Paper presented at the
meeting of the Society for Research in Child Development, Seattle, WA.

Zucker, R. A., Kincaid, S. B., Fitzgerald, H. E., & Bingham, C. R. (1995). Alcohol
schema acquisition in preschoolers: Differences between children of alcoholics and children of nonalcoholics. *Alcoholism: Clinical and Experimental Research, 19,* 1011–1017.

2

Neuropsychological Effects of Substance Abuse

Mitchel A. Woltersdorf

NEUROPSYCHOLOGY

Neuropsychology is the study of brain–behavior relationships. It seeks to understand and predict the consequences of various central nervous system factors on the behavior of the individual (Lezak, 1995). Behavior, for a neuropsychologist, is more than readily observed gross motor behavior, which is often the lay understanding of behavior; for example, "Don't behave (running in the halls) that way!" Behavior is any response produced by the brain, whether it can be observed (e.g., running) or not. Thinking is a behavior; retrieving a memory is too. Feeling strong emotions is also a behavior, even though it can be elusive to the observer as well as the owner.

In the area of substance abuse behavior neuropsychologists are interested in the antecedents of abuse (why do they drink so much?), the patterns of abuse (how much do they consume over how much time?), the cognitive consequences of abuse (what cognitive components have been affected?), the emotional consequences of abuse (are they developing psychological problems related to abuse?), the permanency of behavioral consequences (is the memory permanently damaged?), and intervention strategies for both the abusive behavior and the potential consequences (how can we change their behavior and work around the deficits created by their abuse?). Because of space limitations, this chapter is dedicated to the question of the cognitive consequences of substance use and abuse. The reader will leave with an overview of the typical substances abused and the footprints of their presence in a person's life.

SUBSTANCE USE AND ABUSE

Substances are nonnutritive agents used for recreational or repressional purposes (Lawson, Peterson, & Lawson, 1983). They have no food value, are not necessary for survival (except in the mind of the abuser), and do not produce greater individual adjustment or personal growth (again, except in the mind of the abuser).

Recreational is actually an unfortunate misnomer, since it is popularly used to mean not productive, a poor application of the term. Recreation in its truest form is highly productive when seen for its restorative and creative role, a well-planned and lengthy vacation being the best example. Substance use and abuse is not productive time or activity.

Repressional means the abuser is not trying to uncover new facts about him or herself, but is trying to hide or ignore facts about themselves, life, or others around them (Alcoholics Anonymous World Services, 1986). Abusers think they have an excuse for inappropriate behavior since they were "not in control of their faculties," even though this was a self-induced dyscontrol. What they fail to ask is why they felt they had to perform an act that needed such an excuse. This failure results in the repression of personal revelations and the inhibition of potential growth as the human being remains in a fog of substance use and abuse.

Abuse can be a slippery term. When does use become abnormal use? This slipperiness becomes more obvious when one considers the most abused drug of all, caffeine. If I have a cup of coffee with each meal, is that use or abuse? Two cups with each meal? When is the line crossed? To combat this ambiguity abuse is defined by the American Psychiatric Association's *Diagnostic and Statistical Manual*, Fourth Edition (DSMIV), as a "maladaptive pattern of substance use manifested by recurrent and significant adverse consequences related to the repeated use of substances" (1994, p. 182). So caffeine abuse occurs when its use in my life results in frequent adverse consequences, such as high blood pressure.

The issue of abuse is further complicated when use of the drug is illegal. Some say, "Even one joint of marijuana is abuse because it is illegal." However, bringing in legal considerations does not help clarify the matter of the neuropsychological effects, including psychological effects, brain damage, behavior changes, driving while intoxicated, and dependence. For this reason, the legal status of the substance will not be a criterion dealt with in this chapter. With this caveat in mind, trying one joint of marijuana, even if one inhales, is not defined as abuse, because the issues of recurrence, significant adverse consequences, and repeated use are not applicable. Thus, by scientific rather than legal or social criteria, this one encounter with marijuana would be considered use, not abuse.

The DSM IV states that abuse is a maladaptive pattern of substance use leading to clinically significant impairment or distress as manifested by one or more of the following occurring within a twelve-month period:

1. Recurrent substance use resulting in a failure to fulfill major role obligations at work, school, or home. For example, a student misses classes repeatedly, fails to submit work assignments, fails exams, forgets to go to his or her part-time job or visit the folks at the holidays.
2. Recurrent substance use in situations in which it is physically hazardous to do so. For example, driving a car or operating dangerous machinery, such as a power saw.
3. Recurrent substance-related legal problems. This is typically seen with frequent DUIs (driving under the influence) or DWIs (driving while intoxicated).
4. Continued substance use despite having persistent or recurrent social or interpersonal problems caused or exacerbated by the effects of the substance. For example, a person continues to drink even though it leads to arguments, fighting, or loss of privileges at home, school, or work.

This definition of abuse will be used with all eight agents mentioned in this chapter. Going back to my caffeine example, one can see that the twelve-cup-a-day drinker may not perceive him or herself as fitting criterion 1, but the employer may because of the frequent trips to the coffee machine. Excessive caffeine can affect blood pressure, a silent killer, so criterion 2 is fulfilled. However, caffeine is not likely to cause criterion 3. The husband with the elevated blood pressure who comes home intolerant of the normal noise of children has fulfilled criterion 4. What this illustrates is that the abuser is seldom the best determiner of whether abuse occurs. This tenet will hold true throughout this chapter.

INTOXICATION AND DEPENDENCE

The essential feature of dependence is a cluster of cognitive, behavioral, and physiological symptoms indicating that the individual continues use of the substance despite significant substance-related problems. The older term used for dependence was addiction. According to studies, of all the substances covered in this chapter the only one a person cannot become dependent on is caffeine.

According to DSM IV, in order for a person to be diagnosed as dependent three or more of the following criteria must occur within a twelve-month period. As with abuse, this definition of dependence applies to all the drugs mentioned in this chapter, except caffeine.

1. Tolerance, which can be defined either as a need for increased amounts of the substance in question or as diminished effect with the same amount of the substance in question. For example, the new beer drinker will notice the effects of alcohol within one or two cans, but the experienced beer drinker will not be affected until near the end of a six pack.
2. Withdrawal, which can be manifested either by a physical response to cessation of the substance or by the use of a closely related substance to avoid a physical response. The caffeine abuser will get a tremendous headache within twenty-four to forty-eight hours of abstinence and will get better relief from Excedrin, which contains caffeine, than from standard aspirin, which contains no caffeine.

3. The substance is taken in larger amounts or over a longer period than planned (as may be the case for over-the-counter medications [OTCs] or prescription pain relievers). This is also seen in "social drinkers" who go for a drink after class but find themselves still drinking in the wee hours of the morning.

4. A persistent desire or unsuccessful efforts to stop substance use. The subtle key here is that the final word in the previous sentence is "use," not "abuse." Dependence is present because the alcohol abuser, for example, wants badly to stop all use of alcohol but has been unable to stop any contact with the substance of alcohol. The same applies to all substance abusers. Some abusers try to say they have no dependence because they have not had a "drunk" or "high" for a long time; the issue, however, is not "persistent abuse" but "persistent use."

5. Much time spent in activities necessary to obtain the substance. This is often seen in the "hard" drug users and abusers, such as heroin and cocaine addicts. However, many alcohol-dependent individuals cannot wait for the next weekend party and go to any lengths to find where one may be or to adjust their work and school schedule to fit the party schedule.

6. Social, occupational, and recreational activities are curtailed. Hobbies and pastimes may be abandoned, work or school missed, and old friends avoided as drug use becomes a more dominant factor in the person's life.

7. Continued use in the face of growing physical and psychological problems related to its use. This is best exemplified by alcohol abusers who continue to drink even though they are experiencing frequent blackouts or have more and more people refusing to spend time with them.

Intoxication is defined as the loss of motor and/or cognitive control brought about by the ingestion of an external agent. From this, one can see a spectrum emerge. Drinking one can of beer is using alcohol, six cans of beer is being intoxicated by alcohol; a period of use can lead to abuse, which can lead to dependence on alcohol. How quickly this process develops is unique to the person, since genetics, body size, metabolism, and other intrinsic factors are involved.

In addition, before abuse or dependence can be assigned to a person's behavior with substances, the DSM IV states that one of two things need be present in addition to the items already mentioned: (1) significant distress reported by the abusing person, or (2) significant impairment in social, occupational, or academic functions. Obviously, intoxication will temporarily produce the latter; abuse and dependence will likely produce both, depending on the level of awareness of the person who is using, abusing, or depending on drugs. Also note that the first is reported by the person who is using drugs while the second is often only noted by observers of the person using drugs.

SUBSTANCES

Substances for abuse include but are not limited to the following:

Alcohol	Cocaine
Amphetamines	Hallucinogens

Caffeine   Inhalants

Cannabis   Opioids

The list is not exhaustive, but these are the most frequent agents of abuse and will be the focus of this chapter. It is worthy of note that some list entrants are illicit, some medicinal, and some readily and legally available. Each will be addressed in its own section.

Alcohol

Along with nicotine and caffeine, alcohol is one of the most common legal substances abused. Alcoholism is America's third largest health problem, behind heart disease and cancer, with more than 10 million people at some stage in the illness (Clinebell, 1990). There are twice as many males as females afflicted (Hilton, 1989). Alcohol is the drug most frequently indicted by college and university administrators as having disastrous effects on students' lives. Some indications of the role alcohol can play in student lives include these:

- Almost 4 percent of the college population drinks daily.
- 26 to 48 percent of college students get intoxicated at least once a month.
- Over one-half of college students participate in drinking games which involve the consumption of dangerously high quantities of alcohol (six to ten drinks in a short period of time).
- A survey of college administrators indicates that alcohol is a factor in 34 percent of all academic problems and 25 percent of dropout cases.
- In 1987, American hospitals discharged approximately 96 thousand patients in the eighteen- to twenty-five-year-old age group with at least one alcohol-related illness. These figures do not include alcohol-related injuries from falls, automobile crashes, and other accidents.
- Between 2 and 3 percent of present university students will eventually die from alcohol-related causes, about the same percentage as will eventually be awarded master's and doctoral degrees. (U.S. Department of Health and Human Services, 1991)

Acute impairment is determined by blood alcohol level (BAL), which is computed with the following formula (Segal & Sisson, 1985):

$$BAL = \frac{80 \times grams}{f \times w} = mg/100ml$$

Grams is the amount of alcohol consumed, f is the estimate of the person's body water content (with 0.7 for lean, 0.6 for average, and 0.5 for fat individuals), and w is the person's weight in kilograms (1 kilogram = 2.2 pounds).

Acute Impairment Alcohol is an irregular depressant of the central nervous system (i.e., it affects parts of the brain differently at different dose levels). Being an irregular depressant means that alcohol affects the higher levels of the brain first (such as the cerebrum, which controls higher order judgment and decision making), and leaves the life sustaining functions of the medulla (which controls heartbeat, blood flow, and breathing) intact except at very high blood alcohol levels. Alcohol use can lead to acute and chronic impairment.

Acute impairment begins when the person's BAL exceeds 50 mg/ml (most commonly reported as 0.05) and manifests as slowed reaction time, blurred vision, and motor incoordination. As BAL increases up to 300 mg/ml (0.3), the person begins to experience visual acuity impairment, staggered gait, and slurred speech. As BAL approaches 500 mg/ml (0.5), marked motor incoordination and stupor presents. Over 500 mg/ml, the risk of coma and death looms (Klassen, Amdur, & Doull, 1986).

Scientific descriptions of levels of impairment often lead unwary people to believe that until their blood alcohol level reaches 0.05 there are no dangerous effects of alcohol on functioning. This is not the case. Even before the blood alcohol level reaches 0.05, a person's system has been affected by the toxin. This impairment at low BALs has been shown repeatedly in studies and used as support for groups trying to obtain even more stringent BALs for drivers who chose to drink irresponsibly.

Acute effects in college students are often tied to drinking challenges and/ or games. These games can result in threats to students' lives. For example, *chugalugging* (drinking a large amount of an alcoholic beverage rapidly without stopping) makes it possible for the student to defeat the body's natural tendency to regurgitate high levels of alcohol (i.e., to throw up). If a student chugalugs a pint of whiskey, his or her stomach, and later bloodstream, may contain enough alcohol to send him or her into a coma. While in this state, the BAL may continue to rise, depressing the functioning of the medulla area of the brain and resulting in breathing that is too shallow to support life. Asphyxiation is one of the dangers of rapid, heavy alcohol intake, and a student with a high BAL should be viewed as a potential medical emergency (i.e., suffering from a drug overdose).

Another threat to life can come about by a drunken student aspirating vomit while passed out. Such aspiration can block the trachea and lead to death, or fill the lungs with vomit and cause pneumonia. This is another reason that no student should be left alone when heavily intoxicated.

Chronic Impairment There are two types of students on university campuses these days. One group is comprised of the so-called "traditional" students. The second group is comprised of older "nontraditional" students. While chronic effects of alcohol may not occur as often in younger students, one can observe such effects as delirium tremens (DTs) in college populations. Delirium tremens are an extreme reaction of the central nervous system to the withdrawal of alcohol. Like a track athlete waiting for the starting gun, the person with DTs has an overresponsive sensory system. The person overreacts to common stimuli and is in a state of panic as he or she misreads sounds, sights, and touch as terrifying threats to his or her life. DTs-based terrors have been so great that people have hurled themselves from windows to their deaths. Medication, a quiet surrounding, and a watchful eye provided by soothing companions are necessary when DTs occur. Careful supervision of the afflicted person is of utmost urgency.

A second neurological problem is the alcoholic blackout. Although usually found in chronic heavy drinkers (after as little as two years of heavy drinking), blackouts also can occur to light and to first-time drinkers, and can be brought on by as few as two to four drinks. Victims of blackouts continue to behave as they normally would and exhibit no behavior changes that would be noticed by observers. After the blackout is over (the next morning or perhaps several days later) the person will be amnesic for the period of the blackout; that is, he or she will not remember anything that happened during that period. Many former heavy drinkers who developed this problem say that one of the nice things about being sober is that they wake up on Sunday morning and know where they left their car.

While these patterns and changes are most characteristic of the person who has a longer drinking career, they can also be found in the traditional student. In point of fact, most alcohol treatment centers are seeing younger and younger patients. The number of people in the age range between eighteen and twenty-five years who are in treatment for alcohol problems has increased dramatically in the past two decades. In addition, many students will have begun their drinking careers when they were twelve or thirteen years old, and some of them will have been drinking heavily for five or six years prior to entering college. Therefore, it should be said that chronic effects, while much rarer, can also be found among traditional students, particularly those with long drinking histories. In addition, the increased presence of nontraditional students on campuses increases the possibility that university personnel will confront chronic alcohol abuse and its consequences.

Chronic alcohol effects are not limited to DTs, blackouts, or brain-damage syndromes (as will be discussed). Chronic alcohol effects also occur in fetal alcohol syndrome (FAS), a developmental disorder in a newborn brought about by the presence of alcohol in a pregnant woman. FAS is precipitated by a pregnant woman who consumes at least one ounce of alcohol on a daily basis during the term of the pregnancy (Jacobson et al., 1994). This would amount to a mere glass of beer or wine with supper. The spectrum runs the gamut from full-fledged FAS, with facial deformities and mental retardation in the infant, to the newly discovered and scantily researched Fetal Alcohol Effects (FAE), with less spectacular but still educationally and socially crippling results (Streissguth, Barr, & Sampson, 1990). While new federal guidelines suggest that light drinking is safe for pregnant women, the reader must keep in mind that this addresses the more damaging FAS and not FAE, which is still a topic of much heated debate. A conservative approach would suggest abstinence during pregnancy until all the votes are in. Naturally, a person who becomes heated about this "enforced abstinence," as one recent client phrased it, should probably realize she is likely attempting to cover up a problem with dependence or abuse under the guise of "righteous indignation."

Wernicke-Korsakoff syndrome is a brain disorder brought about by chronic alcohol ingestion by a person with a thiamine-deficient diet, resulting in destruction of brain tissue around the third ventricle. As the path of intoxication through abuse into dependence continues, the person consumes more alcohol than nutritive foods, resulting in the thiamine deficiency. Though it sounds extreme and certainly rare, the syndrome is not. Investigators have found that 80 percent of individuals with Wernicke-Korsakoff syndrome were discovered at autopsy, not during life, suggesting it is often missed and confused with other illness states (Harper, 1983).

The condition is notable for two stages: Wernicke's encephalopathy and Korsakoff's syndrome. The former consists of gait disturbances, eye gaze imbalance, and memory disturbances. The latter by dense amnesia for new information, confabulation (the tendency to ramble when talking and make up information to fill in the void created by the amnesia), plus the continuation of the Wernicke factors (Brandt & Butters, 1986). Wernicke's encephalopathy is seen more frequently in members of lower socioeconomic groups, while Korsakoff's syndrome tends to be more prevalent among better educated groups (Hartman, 1995).

It must be remembered that alcohol is a solvent. It essentially dissolves brain cells. It also has indirect effects through cerebrovascular vasospasm, reduction of system available thiamine, and diminished recovery from injury and illness (Charness, 1994). Additional problems include liver dysfunction, which leads to loss of short-term memory, poor visual tracking, and reduced hand–eye coordination as the damaged liver metabolism wrecks its havoc upon delicate brain tissue (Tarter, Edwards, & Van Thiel, 1988).

Testing for Impairment Besides the obvious signs of intoxication and the subtle signs mentioned, there are typical deficiencies detectable by the type of standard testing often provided by campus counseling services.

Loss of nonverbal abstract reasoning is common among acute and chronic alcohol abusers. Their poorest performances occur on the Ravens Progressive Matrices, the Halstead Category Test, and the Wisconsin Card Sorting Test (Jones & Parsons, 1972; Braun & Richter, 1993). Problems with memory are easily discerned with the Wechsler Memory Scale–Revised (Lezak, 1995). Interestingly, few studies have been able to show the direct effects of alcohol on verbal intelligence, as expressed by the Wechsler Adult Intelligence Scale–Revised (WAIS–R) (Lezak, 1995; Brandt & Butters, 1986). Last, visual–spatial tests show marked impairment in most alcohol abusers, as expressed by the performance subtests of the WAIS–R (Lezak, 1995; Parsons & Farr, 1981).

Recovery of Function Studies of detoxified alcohol abusers with alcohol-related cognitive deficits show that they steadily improve over the first twenty-three weeks of abstinence and then plateau; that is, they do not reach premorbid (pre-drinking) levels even after another six months of abstinence (Goldman, 1986).

Numerous studies show that age and recovery are linked, since the older a person is the longer they had the chance to imbibe. Results are confounded by the normal aging process, which itself produces some cognitive decline.

There is no recent research showing the neuropsychological correlates of social drinking and "recovery" from it (Parsons, 1986). This last issue addresses the paucity of research aimed at what many consider to be a "non-problem." The myth that one drink destroys a million brain cells may have been started by parents or pastors worried about alcohol experimentation or social drinking in children. However, at this point, the neuropsychological effects of "low volume drinking" (i.e., social drinking) are without research support. One exception should be noted: The vast majority of traumatic brain injuries, such as may result from auto crashes, occur in eighteen- to thirty-five-year-old males with significant blood alcohol levels (Ruff et al., 1990).

The treatment of alcohol problems must be multimodal, with the use of outpatient individual therapy, community support groups, and family therapy (Lawson et al., 1983). The use of just one intervention has been found to be less effective than using multiple interventions. When students are found with significant drinking problems, a solution will not be found until the whole "village" is brought in on the problem. The power of family therapy and community support groups, like AA, take advantage of this village motif by making the problem drinker visible. Misapplication of the appeal to the "rights of the individual" and "confidentiality" only keeps the drinker a drinker.

Summary There is little doubt that alcohol is detrimental to brain function, even in low doses and that it does indeed appear to have lasting effects. As the dose increases, so does the response curve of behavioral and cognitive deficits. In other words, with steady and frequent consumption, the possibility for dependence and withdrawal looms large, as does the potential for irreversible damage, not only to cognitive processes but also to other organ systems (Hunt & Nixon, 1993). While complete abstinence is not likely to be a factor in the life of the average college student, the continued education of youth to the scientific findings of alcohol's danger remains paramount for educators and administrators.

Amphetamines

Also known as speed and ice (when smoked), these are powerful central nervous system stimulants with psychoactive and sympathomimetic effects (mirroring the effect of the sympathetic nervous system to maintain arousal and fight–flight qualities). These are frequently prescribed drugs and thus can be quite readily available. Physicians use them effectively against narcolepsy, Attention Deficit–Hyperactivity Disorder, and obesity. However, since drug abuse continues to be profitable, more potent varieties are becoming available on the street and do not require a prescription (Smith, Ehrlich, & Seymour, 1991).

Signs and Symptoms The presence of amphetamines in a person's system is marked by (in order of increasing seriousness) increased or decreased heart rate, dilated pupils, significantly elevated or lowered blood pressure, increased perspiration, nausea or vomiting, decreased appetite, motor agitation, muscle weakness, and confusion and/or coma. DSM IV states that only two of the above need be present for amphetamine abuse to be diagnosed. Withdrawal ("crashing") from amphetamines typically occurs after cessation of prolonged use or after a brief episode of intense, high-dose use ("speed run"). The signs include depressed mood, fatigue, unpleasant dreams, hypersomnia, increased appetite, and agitation when not asleep. Suicidal ideation (thoughts) is also common and needs to be monitored. (Keep in mind the definitions of abuse and dependence mentioned in earlier sections of this chapter. The behavioral patterns described in those sections are applicable to amphetamines.)

A student who is currently using amphetamines inappropriately (beyond prescribed limits) will be easy to recognize by the dilated pupils, hyperactivity, expansive mood, and giddiness. It is, however, very difficult to distinguish an amphetamine high from a psychiatric illness called mania. If caused by amphetamines, the elevated state will be short lived and followed by the opposite state of lethargy, sleepiness, and irritability if more amphetamines are not ingested. Typically, abused drugs have strong reinforcement potential, and amphetamines such as Ritalin, Cylert, and their derivatives are at the top of the list in this regard.

Neurological, developmental, and psychiatric consequences are common with this class of drugs. The primary psychiatric complication is amphetamine psychosis, which looks similar to paranoid schizophrenia and develops with chronic amphetamine use. Neurological complications include hypertension, stroke, kidney failure, and eye damage (Kane & Lieberman, 1992). Developmental complications for women using amphetamines during pregnancy are similar to the problems with cocaine in producing "cocaine babies" with marked lethargy and motor agitation. Strangely enough, there are few studies of the psychological complications following amphetamine abuse beyond those already addressing psychological dependence.

Recovery of Function Recovery from acute use often occurs after cessation of the drug plus the passage of sufficient time for a return to premorbid function levels, usually twenty-four to seventy-two hours. Chronic users experiencing withdrawal symptoms can often take several weeks to return to premorbid levels of functioning. The use of medical management for the chronic abuser, along with outpatient support groups, is highly recommended.

Caffeine

Caffeine is the most widely used psychoactive drug worldwide by most reports (see Usenet news group at alt.drugs.caffeine). I have had several cups of coffee typing this chapter, as you, the reader, may have had while perusing it.

The DSM IV only reports on caffeine intoxication, not abuse or dependence. Figuring 80 to 100 mg of caffeine per brewed cup of coffee or tea, intoxication begins at about 250 to 300 mg, obviously depending on rate of consumption. Other equivalent sources of caffeine include soft drinks (Mountain Dew® has the highest level of caffeine), chocolate, and some over-the-counter medications (such as Excedrin®).

Signs and Symptoms Five of the following cardinal signs need be present for intoxication: restlessness, nervousness, excitement, insomnia, flushed face, frequent urination, stomach disturbance, muscle twitching, rambling flow of thought and/or speech, heart palpitations, episodic inexhaustibility, and motor agitation. There are no adequate research studies on the neuropsychological correlates of caffeine consumption. However, the caffeine consumer knows all too well the "caffeine headache" that follows the cessation of a long period of overconsumption. Medical complications from overconsumption of caffeine include increased blood pressure, increased heart rate, and vasoconstriction of blood vessels; the import of these stimulant-derived symptoms depends on the health, age, and medical history of the consumer.

While university officials are unlikely to view caffeine abuse as an issue, residence hall personnel and others in close contact with students will see excessive use of caffeine, especially before exams, and may see students with caffeine headaches afterward. In the spirit of a well-rounded education, it might be valuable to educate students on the short- and long-term effects of caffeine consumption.

Recovery of Function Caffeine intoxication will last approximately twenty-four to forty-eight hours, depending on the level of consumption and the general health and age of the consumer. Some report caffeine headaches only after a period of intoxication, others report headaches after any degree of consumption. Some have said caffeine intoxication is pandemic on campuses and recovery only comes with graduation.

Cannabis

Also known as marijuana, pot, and grass, cannabis is derived from the cannabis plant when the leaves, stems, and tops are dried and the product is smoked. Hashish is the exudate from the underside of the cannabis leaf and top flora. The active ingredient in cannabis is tetrahydrocannabinol (THC). Its initial medical use was as a treatment for glaucoma, to relieve the nausea of chemotherapy patients, and to combat weight loss in AIDS patients (see National Clearinghouse for Alcohol and Drug Information web site at gopher.health.org).

The incidence of cannabis use is reportedly on the decline since the 1960s, with current U.S. estimates indicating that almost 30 million people use it episodically. There are reportedly more than 8 million daily users (DEA, 1990). Its continued popularity, however, is probably no more underscored than by the presence of numerous Internet and web sites extolling its virtues as well as the dangers of its use (e.g., Usenet news group at alt.drugs.pot.cultivation;

web site at http://www.paranoia.com/maryjane/; and Usenet news group at alt.drugs.pot). If these sites are not available at the time this volume is published, the reader interested in following the electronic debate on marijuana can find new sites by using simple key-term searches to browse the Internet.

Signs and Symptoms Cannabis intoxication displays with impaired motor coordination (Janowsky, Meacham, Blaine, Schoor, & Bozzetti, 1976), euphoria, memory problems (Miller & Branconnier, 1983), anxiety, slowed reaction times (Yesavage, Leirer, Denari, & Hollister, 1985), social withdrawal, bloodshot eyes, increased appetite (the "stoned munchies"), and dry mouth (American Psychiatric Association, 1994). The latter two signs easily distinguish the cannabis user from the alcohol user. Cannabis abuse and dependence are defined by the behavioral presentations mentioned in the introduction to this chapter.

The student who is using cannabis will appear intoxicated but not like the alcoholic, who is often staggering, aggressive, and boorish if not downright stuporous. Marijuana intoxication is more subtle, often leaving the user calm, amotivational, and giddy. While substances affect different people differently, the marijuana user can be pleasant to be around and less intrusive, while the alcohol intoxicant often is unpleasant and intrusive. The smell of marijuana smoke is not easily covered by colognes or perfumes, while the drinker often does not even care to attempt camouflage. Police are often suspicious of students who smell too good to be true; professors and administrators should be suspicious too.

The usual cannabis pattern on campuses tends to be intense brief exposure, often found during weekend binges of more than three joints (0.3 oz) within a one-hour period and repeated frequently throughout the weekend. The usual results of such a scenario will be students who display aberrant behavior during the weekend in the form of hallucinations (psychosis), agitation (anxiety), and severe disorientation (delirium). When the new week begins they will be fatigued, unusually disheveled, and likely still feeling some of the effects they experienced during the weekend, but of less intensity.

Acute and Chronic Effects Studies using electroencephalographs (EEG) on cannabis users showed marked changes in the amygdala regions of the brain (responsible for memory and emotional control) that persisted up to eight months after the cessation of smoking equivalent to three joints per day for three years (Jones, 1980). While EEG studies show minute electrical effects of cannabis, functional or neuropsychological effects are another way one can look for proof of neuropsychological deficits from chronic cannabis use. Some studies have shown there are no lasting behavioral and cognitive effects from long-term use (Satz, Fletcher, & Sutker, 1976), and others have shown only deficits in attention and cognitive efficiency (handling more than one task at a time), and then only when the use of cannabis was astronomical (equivalent to ten joints a day, every day, for seventeen years) (Page, Fletcher, & True, 1988).

Cannabis-derived psychiatric disorders, stemming from both intense brief exposure and from chronic exposure intermingled with brief intense episodes, include cannabis-induced psychosis, cannabis-induced anxiety disorder, and cannabis-induced delirium, all of which include loss of orientation, agitation, social impairment, and, for the delirium, hallucinations (American Psychiatric Association, 1994).

Perhaps the most telling studies relate to prenatal cannabis use by pregnant women. Cannabis use during pregnancy is correlated with low fetal birth weight, complications during labor and delivery, and potential for early delivery. Breast-fed babies whose mothers smoked cannabis postpartum also showed signs of cannabis toxicity, since THC bonds to a mother's milk with a greater tenacity than it does to blood (Astley & Little, 1990).

Studies comparing cigarette and cannabis smokers have found that carbon monoxide levels were far higher in cannabis smokers than in cigarette smokers, a finding that has profound implications for cardiovascular risk and health (Tashkin, Wu, & Djahed, 1988).

Recovery of Function Since the duration of effects of THC is brief, usually two to four hours, the ability to recover from brief, infrequent cannabis smoking is excellent. As the dose and frequency increases, recovery is protracted, with some studies indicating that effects may last up to several weeks, although the possibility of significant permanent impairment is unlikely (DEA, 1990). Depending on the dose and frequency, urinalysis can detect the presence of THC for up to thirty days, and some recent unpublished studies suggest that more appropriate reagent methodologies could detect THC for up to six months.

Summary Cannabis use is widespread and many feel there is no downside to moderate use. Results are benign when it comes to occasional use, defined as weekly rather than daily use. Antagonists claim that the most telling problems with cannabis use are the amotivational state of even the infrequent user, the financial drain on personal finances, the strain on the legal system, and accidents on the road and work site while under the influence of cannabis (see Usenet news group at clari.news.drugs). No studies can be currently found that look at the interaction of these variables.

Cocaine

Also known as coke, crack, flake, and snow, cocaine is a natural substance derived from the coca plant common in Central and South America. Cocaine is the active ingredient, much as THC is the active ingredient in cannabis. Cocaine hydrochloride powder is the most common form, revered in movies as the quintessential expression of drug sophistication. It is snorted by the user, often using a rolled dollar bill as the nasal siphon. Student snorters can often be detected at the lunch counter when they produce a bill that cannot lie flat.

Crack cocaine, on the other hand, is extracted from the hydrochloride form, mixed with sodium bicarbonate, and then allowed to dry into small rocks. It is easily vaporized and thus has an extremely rapid onset when compared to other forms of cocaine. Before crack was discovered, cocaine was separated from its hydrochloride base by heating it with ether, resulting in freebase cocaine, which is smoked. Freebasing was dangerous because of the volatility of the ether, which often exploded during the process (see Usenet news group on heroin and cocaine at alt.drugs.hard). Comedian Richard Pryor is a well-known victim of a freebasing explosion, which produced serious burns and almost killed him.

Cocaine use has reached epidemic levels, with 33 million users in the United States alone, an increase of approximately 10 million persons per decade since the 1960s (Nicholi, 1984). In fact, Kain, Kain, and Scarpelli (1992) claim that 14 percent of the entire U.S. population has tried cocaine in some form at least once.

It has been reported that 40 percent use the drug intranasally, 30 percent freebase, 20 percent inject, and 10 percent use some combination of the other three (Kain et al., 1992). When inhaled, the most common route, the typical dose is about 50 to 150 mg, with the maximum safe dose about 200 to 300 mg. Naturally, toxicity and fatality are dose and administration-route dependent, with 1,000 mg the absolute standard cutoff for safety when the product is smoked.

Signs and Symptoms Cocaine has an amphetamine-like intoxication and withdrawal picture, as well as the standard problems of abuse and dependence explicated. Intoxication, according to DSM IV, requires maladaptive behavioral changes evidenced by euphoria, hypervigilance (miniparanoia), impaired judgment, anxiety or anger, and impaired social and occupational (school) functions. In addition, two or more of the following symptoms (in order of increasing seriousness) must also be present: heart rate change, dilated pupils, change in blood pressure, perspiration, nausea or vomiting, weight loss, motor agitation, weakness, and confusion, seizures, or coma (depending on the dose). The careful reader will note that this spectrum of symptoms is parallel to those found with amphetamine intoxication. In fact, they are identical, because both cocaine and amphetamines are considered stimulants and thus have similar physiological effects upon organ systems.

Withdrawal, typically occurring after heavy and prolonged use, is characterized by depression, fatigue, unpleasant dreams, sleep disturbances, increased appetite, and agitation. Again, the same picture was present for amphetamine withdrawal, highlighting the impossibility of detecting drug of choice by outward symptom picture alone.

Cocaine has a host of associated psychiatric problems: cocaine-induced psychosis, cocaine-induced mood disorder, cocaine-induced anxiety disorder, cocaine-induced sexual dysfunction, and cocaine-induced sleep disorder (American Psychiatric Association, 1994). These look just like their nondrug cousins of psychosis, depression, anxiety, sexual dysfunction, and sleep problems. The only difference between the disorders is the etiology of the problem.

According to the DEA (1990), cocaine has high potential for physical and psychological dependence, as do the amphetamines. Tolerance is a major problem, as more and more cocaine is required by the user to achieve equivalent highs. Tolerance typically develops quickly, but cannot be measured as it is dependent on the route of administration, the amount of the dose, the user's body weight and metabolism, and associated health issues (Is he also a drinker or a user of other drugs in the past?). With its short effect duration (approximately three hours, again depending on the dose and frequency of use) and quick development of tolerance, cocaine use can easily lead to overdose.

Acute and Chronic Effects Cocaine is a mean master. The literature records neurochemical effects, neuropsychological effects, psychological effects, and prenatal effects.

The neurochemical effects are potent since cocaine is lipophilic (fat soluble), crosses the blood–brain barrier with ease, and can produce an intense experience in five minutes. It is quickly broken down by plasma, but this breakdown is slowed in individuals with reduced blood cholinesterases, such as infants, pregnant women, and the elderly (Dial, 1992). The neurochemical effects are not limited to the central nervous system, but also affect the peripheral nervous system by causing vasoconstriction (blood vessels constrict) and pupil dilation. Cocaine essentially produces its high through dopaminergic channels by increasing the production of dopamine, a neurotransmitter, and preventing its reabsorption (Daigle, Clark, & Landry, 1988). The pleasure dopamine's presence brings to organisms, such as rats and people, is obvious in the research studies where animals quit the self-administration of cocaine when they were also administered dopamine-blocking agents which prevented the increased dopamine production by the cocaine (Wise, 1984). Cessation of long-term use often results in a profound depression in the user because of the depletion of neurotransmitter sites producing not only dopamine but also another naturally occurring strong mood elevator, serotonin (Taylor & Ho, 1978).

The neuropsychological effects can be placed into three groups: damage due to excessive central nervous stimulation, EEG findings, and metabolic damage. Since cocaine is a strong stimulant it produces excessive adrenalin activity, the fight or flight response. If one imagines what a field mouse experiences when it knows a hawk is about to swoop down and snatch it from the earth, then one can know the effect excessive adrenalin has upon the body: panic, near heart attack, lung overexpansion, and blood leaving the core and flooding the limbs. Organism burnout and fatigue results with chronic use, causing enough vascular system deterioration to result in strokes. The EEG findings related to cocaine highlight the likelihood of "brain kindling," the slow spread of errant electrical impulses at a subseizure level, and the production of actual seizure activity (Spiers, Schomer, Blume, & Mesulam, 1985).

Metabolic studies have taken advantage of PET scans and SPECT scans, which register the glucose metabolism of the living brain. Cocaine ingestion lowered glucose metabolism significantly, which affects the brain's ability to handle the processing of input from the outside world (London et al., 1990).

Insofar as neuropsychological assessment studies are concerned, the principle findings are these: Deficits tend to be mild in the area of attention, speed of processing, handling of complex information, and memory; deficits worsen with the use of crack cocaine over cocaine hydrochloride, and worsen further with the addition of polydrug use, although no new areas of deficit arise other than those already mentioned (Hartman, 1995). Methodological problems are inherent in these studies because of the use of multiple substances, interactional effects, and the likelihood of "dirty" crack used by chronic users. Dirty crack is pure cocaine that has been thinned with cheaper agents that can be neutral, such as baking soda, or toxic, such as rat poison.

The psychological effects of cocaine cover a spectrum paralleling the route of administration and duration of use. The nasal route produces the most instantaneous results, while the oral route produces the slowest; other methods of ingestion fall somewhere between these extremes (DEA, 1990). Many people are familiar with the initial appearances of acute cocaine use: elevated mood, euphoria, alertness, reduced appetite and sleep. However, as the habit continues more serious psychological implications appear in the form of panic attacks, paranoia, anxiety, and amotivational states (Washton & Gold, 1984; Washton & Tatarsky, 1984). As use escalates to toxic levels, the advent of cocaine psychosis begins, with prominent hallucination behavior (American Psychiatric Association, 1994).

The prenatal effects occur because, like with the brain, cocaine can cross the placenta and wreck its havoc on the unborn. The principle factor in fetal developmental problems appears to be cocaine's vasoconstrictive capabilities, which effectively rob the fetus of appropriate oxygen and blood-born nutrients during the crucial nine-month growth process (Schneider & Chasnoff, 1992; Coles, Platzman, Smith, James, & Falek, 1992). These same authors also explicate the incremental damage wrought by the prenatal use of cocaine combined with other substances, such as alcohol. When the babies are born they typically exhibit motor disturbances; sleep problems; irritability; frequent, if not constant, crying; low birth weight; and apathy (Kain et al., 1992).

Recovery of Function There does not appear to be permanent loss of neurocognitive or neuroemotional functions after brief exposure to cocaine within organism-tolerant doses. As dose intensity (volume of each dose) or dose frequency (number of doses) increases, the multiple effects outlined begin to figure prominently in the health of the user. Once a medical crisis occurs, such as with stroke secondary to cocaine, the permanency of deficits secondary to cocaine become less arguable and more obvious. However, the lack of longitudinal neuropsychological studies leaves the proof of subtle functional problems an open question.

Summary Perhaps the best summary to this section is best expressed by two users of cocaine who are patients of the author. One said, "If I had to do it over again I wouldn't." The other was a bit more philosophical: "Everyone who uses cocaine either ends up wanting to quit or destroying themselves; there's no middle ground."

Hallucinogens

According to the DEA (1990), hallucinogens are lysergic acid diethylamide (LSD, acid), mescaline (peyote, cactus), phencyclidine (PCP, angel dust), and a cadre of "designer drugs," such as 3,4-methylenedioxymethamphetamine (MDMA, ecstasy) and 1-methyl-4-phenyl-4-proprionoxy-piperidine (MPPP, or MPTP if mixed wrong).

Due to lack of space and the editorial desire to provide coverage based on frequency of occurrence, I will not spend any time on the designer drugs other than to say they are horribly toxic with severe permanent deficits blessed upon those who choose to indulge. Campuses are often rampant with stories of someone who used MDMA without any problems: "So what's the problem?" It is my experience that few students or faculty are versed enough to know when they are given the real thing or a safer corollary. The majority of space will be dedicated to LSD and PCP, since they are most widespread hallucinogens, although their effects are different. Other than the distant veterinary use of PCP as an anesthetic, there are no medical uses known for the hallucinogenics or "psychedelics" as the Age of Aquarius termed them.

The duration of effect for both LSD and PCP is quite long, with the average range cited by the DEA (1990) being eight to twelve hours. Duration will, of course, depend upon dose, body weight, and user tolerance. Tolerance is relatively easily developed with both drugs. Nothing is known about the development of physical or psychological dependence on either LSD or PCP.

Route of administration for both is typically oral, although there are reports of PCP also being smoked and injected. Both the DEA (1990) and the World Wide Web (see Usenet news group at alt.drugs.psychedelics) indicate that LSD use is on the rise, and penetrating high schools (about 5 percent reported use). Confiscated caches are increasing in size.

Signs and Symptoms The DSM IV separates the LSD and other hallucinogenic disorders from the PCP disorders because the actual symptoms of intoxication are different. As before, the determination of abuse and dependence is not based on the substance itself but on the behavioral correlates manifested by the user. Withdrawal is not common with hallucinogenics, but users do report a craving.

LSD intoxication is evidenced by maladaptive behavioral and psychological changes such as paranoia, impaired judgment, impaired social skills, marked anxiety ("bad trips"), and/or occupational dysfunction. There are also perceptual changes, even though the person is awake and alert. These changes may take the form of hallucinations (perceiving without stimulation), intensification of perceptions, or illusions (misperceiving with stimulation). In addition, two or more of the following are often present: pupils dilated, sweating, blurred vision, tremors, incoordination, and racing heart rate. The types of perceptual changes often are geometric hallucinations, flashes of color, trails following moving objects, positive afterimages, halos around objects, or objects appearing very small or very large.

PCP intoxication is evidenced by the same maladaptive changes as noted for LSD, but there are no perceptual changes. Instead, the user manifests belligerence, assaultiveness, unpredictability, and impulsiveness. In addition, two or more of the following are often present: racing heart rate or elevated blood pressure, diminished responsiveness to pain, gait disturbances, slurred speech, increased muscle tone, vertical or horizontal nystagmus (minute, repetitive tremor of the eye in either a horizontal or vertical direction), hyperacusis (highly sensitive hearing), and possibly seizures or coma.

Both LSD and PCP have psychiatric disorders linked to heavy and/or chronic use. DSM IV lists them as hallucinogenic-induced (HI) psychotic disorder with hallucinations, HI psychotic disorder with delusions, HI mood disorder, and HI anxiety disorder. As before, these will appear similar to their nondrug cousins. However, LSD also has a unique addition in the name of LSD persisting perception disorder (flashbacks). The essential feature is a distressing reexperience, after cessation of drug use, of one or more of the perceptual symptoms that were experienced while under the influence of an hallucinogenic. Timothy Leary, well-known advocate of the use of LSD, denied any difficulty with flashbacks after cessation of use of LSD, even after his earlier extensive use.

Behaviorally, separating the LSD user from the PCP user can often be accomplished by the observer asking, "Is any aggressive behavior present?" The PCP user almost always displays aggressive behavior, even at low doses, while the LSD user seldom does at low doses.

Acute and Chronic Effects Of all the hallucinogens, only LSD has been neuropsychologically investigated, with mixed results. This is due to the fact that LSD is seldom used alone and controlled human studies would not be ethical. The few methodologically sound investigations offer little in the way of clinically valid results.

McGlothin, Arnold, and Freedman (1969) found that users with more than fifty LSD experiences had diminished capacity to do nonverbal complex problem solving but no overall functional or global impairments were found. Nonverbal complex problem solving was assessed by the Category Test. In the same year, Cohen and Edwards studied users with more than thirty "trips" and found they had impaired visuospatial abilities, as measured by Raven's Progressive Matrices and Trail Making Test. Unfortunately, the experimental group contained some polydrug users.

In 1975, a meta-analytic review was completed (Grant & Mohns, 1975) which concluded that there were no chronic neuropsychological impairments from LSD use. However, Abraham (1982) found that users who averaged more than eighty LSD experiences developed permanent color-vision impairment. Smith and Seymour (1994) also used highly experienced LSD users to determine that post-hallucinogenic perceptual disorder, an impairment of visuospatial orientation accompanied by depression or anxiety, is a possible, though infrequent, artifact of heavy use. My clinical experience tells me that, while longitudinal studies may be absent and methodologies may be poor, the user of hallucinogenics suffers more from the social destruction brought about by legal problems following arrest, financial loss through frequent purchases, interactional effects and potential polydrug use, being enmeshed in the drug culture, and traumatic accidents while under their influence than from their neuropsychological effects.

Summary Recovery of function cannot be adequately addressed, as few studies of sufficient duration exist for the hallucinogenics. What appears to be clear is that LSD has some remote neuropsychological ramifications with chronic use. However, the most damaging effects of LSD and other hallucinogenics may not take place within the body but within the social system in which the body resides.

Inhalants

There are literally hundreds of inhalable substances that produce psychoactive effects and neuropsychological impairments. College students do not appear to use inhalants to any great extent, but the products certainly are readily available should they choose to do so. Inhalant use may be more common at junior colleges and technical schools as a result of different student demographics and the availability of solvents and inhalants in labs and shops. Nevertheless, all college students eventually attempt to find work and often find themselves in jobs where these toxins occur in abundance and where work conditions are not optimal to protect them from the effects of these powerful agents. Some of the more common agents that can be abused or abuse the innocent are the following:

cleaning fluid	refrigerant	indelible ink
nail polish remover	typewriter correction fluid	plastic adhesive
gas engine primer	furniture spray	paint stripper
carburetor spray	kerosene	degreasers
diesel fuel	model paint	hair spray
jet fuel	model glue	disinfectants
room deodorizer	solvents	all aerosols
spot remover	lacquer paint	all polish

Because of the sheer number of abusable inhalants, this discussion is limited to the two most frequently abused classes of inhalants: aliphatic hydrocarbons and aromatic hydrocarbons. These are essentially solvents and cleaners. Because inhalants do not exist in pure form as they might at a factory which uses pure methyl ethyl ketone (MEK) for cleaning equipment, the psychoactive and neuropsychological effects from abuse are complex and, at times, difficult to distinguish from each other. For example, a person who chooses to sniff cleaning fluid from a bag is not just inhaling trichlorethylene but also naphtha, perchloroethylene, and carbon tetrachloride. This "toxic cocktail" has disastrous consequences for the nervous system, often from just one use. It is, however, almost impossible to determine which ingredient in the cocktail did the most damage.

The usual route of administration is inhaling or "sniffing," although different techniques are used. Some users soak a rag and drape it over the mouth and nose as they breathe normally; some inhale directly from the container the substance is in; some put the substance in a plastic or paper bag to inhale from; some heat the substances before inhaling to increase vaporization.

Hartman (1995) notes that the typical inhalant abuser is young, male, between the ages of seven and seventeen, and inhales out of boredom or to reduce the impact of a hostile environment. Giovacchini (1985) reports that solvent abuse involves approximately 50 percent of the adolescent population, with frequency of abuse and choice of substance differing by ethnic group. He found gasoline inhalation most common among Native Americans and solvent sniffers overrepresented in the Hispanic culture.

Signs and Symptoms   DSM IV notes that inhalant dependence, while technically the same as for other substances, has some unique differences worth noting. Inhalant dependence does not have a withdrawal syndrome nor is there evidence of the benefit of repeat inhalant use to relieve withdrawal symptoms. Also, because inhalants are cheap, legal, common, and readily available, time spent procuring will not be a sign of dependence as it is with other substances.

Inhalant intoxication includes the usual rubric of significant behavioral and psychological changes. Inhalants produce changes that are quite similar to PCP, with belligerence, assaultiveness, and impaired judgment at the top of the list. In addition, two or more of the following are often present: dizziness, nystagmus (moving of the eyes laterally with quick, short tremors), incoordination, slurred speech, unsteady gait, lethargy, slowed reflexes, motor slowing, tremor, muscle weakness, blurred vision, stupor, coma, or euphoria. As with other substances, the psychiatric disorders following inhalant abuse include Inhalant induced (Ii) dementia, Ii psychotic disorder with delusions, Ii psychotic disorder with hallucinations, Ii mood disorder, and Ii anxiety disorder.

Wyse (1973) adds a diagnostic taxonomy that posits a four-stage neurotoxic process with inhalants. Stage I is characterized by euphoria, dizziness, and hallucinations. Stage II includes confusion, disorientation, loss of self-control, and vision and hearing changes. Stage III introduces sleepiness, incoordination, nystagmus, and dyspraxias. Stage IV culminates in seizures and EEG changes. Inhalants users will go through each of these stages in succession but, depending on the inhalant and the strength of dose, can go through them quite rapidly as they move toward organ damage.

People using inhalants will appear "not present." Their eyes will be open but not seeing. They appear drunk and disoriented but will have a chemical smell about them.

Acute and Chronic Effects Solvent vapors are absorbed by the lungs and deposited into organs with a high lipid structure, such as the brain and liver. Peak blood levels occur between fifteen and thirty minutes after inhalation, with peak tissue levels occurring much later. Acute toxic reactions occur because of anoxia as the inhaled substance displaces oxygen consumption. Neurotoxicity from inhaled substances is related to structural damage rather than degradation of neurotransmitter function as with other abused substances. The aliphatic and aromatic hydrocarbons are the most neurotoxic, with permanent damage practically guaranteed (Hartman, 1995).

Chronic inhalers have a whole host of symptoms not necessarily related to acute intoxication as described by DSM IV. Hartman (1995) describes muscle weakness, anorexia, weight loss, fatigue, and paresthesias (sensory changes); he also mentions a stocking–glove pattern of sensory change that appears in the areas normally covered by stockings and gloves; that is, both feet up to mid-shin and both hands up to the wrist.

Recovery of Function Studies are not very promising for recovery from chronic abuse or acute use. It is clear that the effects of acute intoxication may be short lived, depending on the substance, but that does not mean the substance has not left its footprints behind. For example, MEK and toluene (both found plentifully in cements, glues, and thinners) are notorious for permanent cognitive deficits in the users, even after one brief exposure for the first-time user. Use of these types of substances can wreck havoc on the nervous system of the abuser for a lifetime (Grigsby, Rosenberg, Dreisbach, Busenbark, & Grisby, 1993). The real threat of inhalant use is this Russian roulette feature: "Can I use it once and get away with it?" Some do; many do not.

Opioids

The DEA (1990) includes opium (Dover's powder, paregoric), morphine (pectoral syrup), codeine (Robitussin A & C®, Empirin® Compound with codeine, Tylenol® with codeine), heroin (horse, smack), and methadone in the class of opioids. An additional catchall category includes other prescription medications, such as Darvon, Talwin, and Percocet. Almost all are orally ingested, injected, or snorted; morphine and heroin can also be smoked. All have high physical and psychological dependence potential. Tolerance comes quickly to the unwary user. Opioids are prescribed as analgesics, antidiarrheal agents, and cough suppressants. Heroin is the most abused drug in this category, although drugs available by prescription are a close second. The old terminology for this group was narcotics (DEA, 1990). There are no different criteria for opioid dependence and opioid abuse than for the generic abuse and dependence criteria mentioned. However, there is a specific pattern of opioid withdrawal.

The power of opioids is the attraction of the high, which allows the user to escape from the pressures of this world in what one user describes as "heaven with sex." Tolerance is quick, dependence in strong, and withdrawal is excruciating. All of this combines to seduce the light user into becoming a much heavier user. The negative legal, financial, and health consequences of use become blurred by the rapidity with which opiods take control of the user.

Signs and Symptoms Opioid withdrawal requires either the cessation of heavy opioid use or the administration of an opioid antagonist (such as Narcane, Naloxone, or Naltrexone, agents that block the effects of the original opioid). There must also be three or more of the following, which develop within minutes or days: dysphoric mood (depressed), nausea or vomiting, muscle ache, profuse tearing or runny nose, physiological overresponse (pupils dilated, sweating, erect hair on limbs), diarrhea, excessive yawning, fever, or insomnia. Antagonists are not to be confused with Methadone, which is used in the treatment of opiod dependency because it is an opiod substitute without the tendency to make the user tolerant or dependent to the degree that opiods do.

DSM IV states that opioid intoxication occurs when a known opioid has been ingested and there are maladaptive behavioral and/or psychological changes (initial euphoria followed by apathy, dysphoria, agitation, impaired judgment, and impaired social and/or occupational functioning) immediately following the ingestion. In addition, there will be pupil constriction or dilation (if an overdose) and one or more of the following signs: drowsiness or coma, slurred speech, or impairment in attention and memory. As with other substances, psychiatric disturbances also follow opioid abuse and can include opioid-induced (OI) psychotic disorder with delusions, OI psychotic disorder with hallucinations, OI mood disorder, OI sleep disorder, and OI sexual dysfunction.

Acute and Chronic Effects Surprisingly enough, there are no studies capable of showing cortical damage from acute or chronic opioid abuse. In fact, on some studies chronic abusers even outperformed control subjects on tests of psychomotor speed (Rousanville, Jones, Novelly, & Kleber, 1982). Mutti and colleagues (1992) suggest that the destructive qualities of opioids do not occur at the cortical level but at the neuroendocrine level, affecting plasma electrolytes and enzymatic agents. However, their study was the only one found that even approached the issue of neuroendocrine versus cortical etiology.

The clear acute and chronic effects of opioid use are attached to the avenue of administration rather than to direct drug effects. Newspapers and news broadcasts are replete with stories of secondary infections through the sharing of intravenous needles and poor hygiene at the time of injection. Hartman (1995) highlights AIDS, as well as neurotoxic bacterial, fungal, and viral infections. In addition, because the placenta is breached by opiod compounds, as it is by cocaine, developing fetuses can be affected by maternal use. Opioid infants display similar symptoms as cocaine-poisoned babies.

Recovery of Function There is little to discuss here, since the studies have yet to show direct neuropsychological or neurological consequences from even chronic opioid abuse. The greatest destruction comes from the secondary infections and perhaps the tertiary effects upon family, finances, and work.

While the individual abuser may physically recover, there may be no reclaiming of opportunities lost in these other domains of life (Lawson et al., 1983).

Summary It would be easy for the reader to assume that of all the substances available for abuse the opiods would be the safest. From a neuropsychological standpoint, that may be true since studies proving otherwise do not yet exist. However, one only needs to look at the devastation opioids have had upon communities, families, work sites, and the jail population to know that believing them safe is tantamount to denial of the obvious.

EPILOGUE

Given space limitations, only the most frequently abused substances have been covered. The careful reader needs to be mindful that the substance abuse picture is complex and multifacted. In addition, there is literature on drug interactions describing the multiplication of effects when any of these categories of drugs are combined with each other.

We have not covered nicotine, although it is now politically correct to do so. We have not covered the damage brought about by indiscriminate use of health additives, which is not yet politically correct but which can be serious. For example, as a resident at the University of Washington I was involved in studies, not yet published, of blood dyscrasias (abnormal cell development) caused by the use of L-tryptophan, a naturally occurring amino acid frequently purchased from health food stores for the treatment of insomnia. We have also not covered the prescription drug abuse scene, which runs the spectrum from overt abuse by the adolescent to the often hidden abuse brought about by the overmedication of the elderly by well-intentioned but poorly informed physicians.

The job of the campus professional is daunting, to say the least, when one considers the tremendous threat these substances pose to the individual organism. However, with material such as contained in this text, the work of educating America may be made somewhat easier.

REFERENCES

Abraham, H. (1982). Chronic impairment of color vision in users of LSD. *British Journal of Psychiatry, 140,* 518–521.

Alcoholics Anonymous. (1976). *Alcoholics Anonymous: The story of how many thousands of men and women recovered from alcoholism* (3rd ed.). New York: Alcoholics Anonymous World Services.

American Psychiatric Association. (1994). *Diagnostic and statistical manual of mental disorders* (4th ed.). Washington, DC: Author.

Astley, S., & Little, R. (1990). Maternal marijuana use during lactation and infant development at one year. *Neurotoxicology and Teratology, 12,* 161–168.

Brandt, J., & Butters, N. (1986). The alcoholic Wernicke-Korsakoff syndrome and its relationship to long-term alcohol abuse. In I. Grant & N. Butters (Eds.), *Neuropsychological assessment of neuropsychiatric disorders.* New York: Oxford University Press.

Braun, C., & Richter, M. (1993). A comparison of functional indices derived from screening tests of chronic alcoholic neurotoxicity in the cerebral cortex, retina, and peripheral nervous system. *Journal of Studies on Alcohol, 54*(1), 11–16.

Charness, M. (1994). Brain lesions in alcoholics. *Alcoholism: Clinical and Experimental Research, 17,* 2–11.

Clinebell, H. (1990). Alcohol abuse, addiction, and therapy. In R. Hunter (Ed.), *Dictionary of pastoral care and counseling.* Nashville, TN: Abingdon Press.

Cohen, S., & Edwards, A. (1969). LSD and organic brain impairment. *Drug Dependence, 2,* 3–12.

Coles, C., Platzman, K., Smith, L., James, M., & Falek, A. (1992). Effects of cocaine and alcohol use in pregnancy on neonatal growth and neurobehavioral status. *Neurotoxicology and Teratology, 14,* 23–33.

Daigle, R., Clark, H., & Landry, M. (1988). A primer on neurotransmitters and cocaine. *Journal of Psychoactive Drugs, 20,* 283–295.

Dial, J. (1992). The interaction of alcohol and cocaine: A review. *Psychobiology, 20,* 179–183.

Drug Enforcement Administration (DEA). (1990). *Drug enforcement: Fall 1990.* Washington, DC: U.S. Department of Justice.

Giovacchini, R. (1985). Abusing the volatile organic chemicals. *Regulatory Toxicology and Pharmacology, 5,* 18–37.

Goldman, M. (1986). Neuropsychological recovery in alcoholics: Endogenous and exogenous processes. *Alcoholism: Clinical and Experimental Research, 10,* 136–144.

Grant, I., & Mohns, L. (1975). Chronic cerebral effects of alcohol and drug abuse. *International Journal of the Addictions, 10*(5), 883–921.

Grigsby, J., Rosenberg, N., Dreisbach, J., Busenbark, D., & Grisby, P. (1993). Chronic toluene abuse produces neurological and neuropsychological deficits. *Archives of Clinical Neuropsychology, 8,* 229–230.

Harper, C. (1983). The incidence of Wernicke-Korsakoff syndrome in Australia: A neuropathological study of 131 cases. *Journal of Neurology, Neurosurgery and Psychiatry, 46,* 593–598.

Hartman, D. (1995). *Neuropsychological toxicology: Identification and assessment of human neurotoxic syndromes* (2nd ed.). New York: Plenum Press.

Hilton, M. (1989). How many alcoholics are there in the United States? *British Journal of Addiction, 84,* 459–460.

Hunt, W., & Nixon, S. (1993). *Alcohol-induced brain damage* (Research Monograph No. 22). Washington, DC: U.S. Department of Health and Human Services, National Institute on Alcohol Abuse and Alcoholism.

Jacobson, L., Jacobson, S., Sokol, R., Martier, R., Martier, S., Ager, J., & Kaplan-Estrin, M. (1994). Teratogenic effects of alcohol on infant development. *Alcoholism: Clinical and Experimental Research, 17,* 174–183.

Janowsky, D., Meacham, M., Blaine, J., Schoor, M., & Bozzetti, L. (1976). Marijuana effects on simulated flying ability. *American Journal of Psychiatry, 133,* 384–388.

Jones, B., & Parsons, O. (1972). Specific vs. generalized deficits of subtracting ability in chronic alcoholics. *Archives of General Psychiatry, 26,* 380–384.

Jones, R. (1980). Human effects: An overview. In R. Peterson (Ed.), *Marijuana research findings 1980.* (NIDA Research Monograph No. 31, pp. 54–80). Washington, DC: Department of Health and Human Services.

Kain, Z., Kain, T., & Scarpelli, E. (1992). Cocaine exposure in utero: Perinatal development and neonatal manifestations. *Clinical Toxicology, 30*(4), 607–636.

Kane, J., & Lieberman J. (1992). *Adverse effects of psychotropic drugs.* New York: Guilford Press.

Klassen, C., Amdur, M., & Doull, J. (Eds.). (1986). *Casarett and Doull's toxicology.* New York: Macmillan.

Lawson, G., Peterson, J., & Lawson, A. (1983). *Alcoholism and the family.* Rockville, MD: Aspen.

Lezak, M. (1995). *Neuropsychological assessment* (3rd ed.). New York: Oxford University Press.

London, E., Cascella, N., Wong, D., Phillips, R., Danais, F., Links, J., Herning, R., Grayson R., Jaffe, J., & Wagner, H. (1990). Cocaine-induced reduction in glucose utilization in the human brain. *Archives of General Psychiatry, 47,* 567–575.

McGlothin, W., Arnold, D., & Freedman, D. (1969). Organicity measures following repeated LSD use. *Archives of General Psychiatry, 21,* 704–710.

Miller, L., & Branconnier, R. (1983). Cannabis: Effects on memory and the cholinergic limbic system. *Psychological Bulletin, 93,* 441–456.

Mutti, A., Folli, D., Der Venne, V., Berlin, A., Gerra, G., Caccavari, R., Vescovi, P., & Franchini, I. (1992). Long-lasting impairment of neuroendocrine response to psychological stress in heroin addicts. *Neurotoxicology, 13,* 255–260.

Nicholi, A. (1984). Cocaine use among the college age group: Biological and psychological effects: Clinical and laboratory research findings. *Journal of American College Health, 32,* 258–261.

Page, J., Fletcher, J., & True, W. (1988). Psychosociocultural perspectives on chronic cannabis use: The Costa Rican follow-up. *Journal of Psychoactive Drugs, 20,* 57–64.

Parsons, O. (1986). Overview of the Halstead-Reitan battery. In T. Incagnoli, G. Goldstein, & C. Goldstein (Eds.), *Clinical applications of neuropsychological test batteries.* New York: Plenum Press.

Parsons, O., & Farr, S. (1981). The neuropsychology of drug and alcohol abuse. In S. Filskov & T. Boll (Eds.), *Handbook of clinical neuropsychology.* New York: Wiley Press.

Rousanville, B., Jones, C., Novelly, R., & Kleber, H. (1982). Neuropsychological functioning in opioid addicts. *Journal of Nervous and Mental Disease, 170,* 209–216.

Rulf, R., Marshall, L., Klauber, M., Blunt, B., Grant, I., Foulkes, M., Eisenberg, H., Jane, J., & Marmarou, A. (1990). Alcohol abuse and neurological outcome of the severely head injured. *Journal of Head Trauma Rehabilitation, 5,* 21–31.

Satz, P., Fletcher, J., & Sutker, L. (1976). Neuropsychologic, intellectual, and personality correlates of chronic marijuana use in native Costa Ricans. *Annals of the New York Academy of Sciences, 282,* 266–306.

Schneider, J., & Chasnoff I. (1992). Motor assessment of cocaine and polydrug exposed infants at age 4 months. *Neurotoxicology and Teratology, 14,* 97–101.

Segal, R., & Sisson, B. (1985). Medical complications associated with alcohol use and the assessment of risk of physical damage. In T. Bratter & G. Forrest (Eds.), *Alcoholism and substance abuse.* New York: The Free Press.

Smith D., & Seymour, R. (1994). LSD: History and toxicity. *Psychiatric Annals, 24,* 145–147.

Smith, E., Ehrlich, P., & Seymour, R. (1991). Heavy marijuana use and recent memory impairment. *Psychiatric Annals, 21,* 80–90.

Spiers, M., Schomer, M., Blume, M., & Mesulam, M. (1985). Temporolimbic epilepsy and behavior. In M. Mesulam (Ed.), *Principles of behavioral neurology.* Philadelphia: F. A. Davis.

Streissguth, A., Barr, H., & Sampson, P. (1990). Moderate prenatal exposure: Effects on child IQ and learning problems at age 7½ years. *Alcoholism: Clinical and Experimental Research, 14,* 648–649.

Tarter, R., Edwards, K., & Van Thiel, D. (1988). Neuropsychological dysfunction due to liver disease. In E. Tarter, D. Van Thiel, & K. Edwards (Eds.), *Medical neuropsychology: The impact of disease on behavior.* New York: Plenum Press.

Tashkin, D., Wu, T., & Djahed, B. (1988). Acute and chronic effects of marijuana smoking compared with tobacco smoking on blood carboxyhemoglobin levels. *Journal of Psychoactive Drugs, 20,* 27–31.

Taylor, D., & Ho, B. (1978). Neurochemical effects of cocaine following acute and chronic injection. *Journal of Neuroscience Research, 3,* 95–100.

U.S. Department of Health and Human Services. (1991). *Prevention resource guide: College youth* (Publication No. ADM 91–1803). Washington, DC: U.S. Department of Health and Human Services.

Washton, A., & Gold, M. (1984). Chronic cocaine abuse: Evidence for adverse effects on health and functioning. *Psychiatric Annals, 14,* 733–743.

Washton, A., & Tatarsky, M. (1984). Adverse effects of cocaine abuse (Research Monograph No. 49, pp. 247–254). Washington, DC: National Institute of Drug Abuse.

Wise, R. (1984). Neural mechanisms of the reinforcing action of cocaine. *Cocaine: Pharmacology effects and treatment of abuse* (NIDA Research Monograph No. 50, pp. 15–33). Washington, DC: Department of Health and Human Services.

Wyse, D. (1973). Deliberate inhalation of volatile hydrocarbons: A review. *Canadian Medical Association Journal, 108,* 71–74.

Yesavage, J., Leirer, V., Denari, M., & Hollister, L. (1985). Carry-over effects of marijuana intoxication on aircraft pilot performance: A preliminary report. *American Journal of Psychiatry, 142,* 1325–1329.

3

The Disease Model of Addiction

Dennis L. Thombs

The view that alcoholism and other addictions are disease states is pervasive in the United States today. Though many people are ambivalent about the concept, upward of 90 percent of Americans agree that alcoholism is an illness (Caetano, 1987). The disease (or medical) model is the foundation for professional practice in most alcoholism and substance-abuse treatment centers and the personal recovery philosophy for a majority of counselors in the field (Sobell & Sobell, 1987). Furthermore, the model is strongly endorsed by the membership of Alcoholics Anonymous (AA), other related twelve-step programs, and by the medical community. These groups are largely responsible for the shift in public attitude from scorn and punishment to the expectation that the alcoholic or addict will be offered treatment. Without the advent of the disease model, there would likely be very little treatment of alcoholism or other dependencies today and recovery would be a relatively rare occurrence.

HISTORIC OVERVIEW OF THE MODEL

References to alcoholism as a disease can be traced to the time of Hippocrates (Sournia, 1990). However, it was not until the late eighteenth century that physicians began systematic study of the problem of inebriety, as it was known then. In 1784, Dr. Benjamin Rush, a signer of the Declaration of Independence and a surgeon general of the Army, authored a famous article entitled "An Inquiry into the Effects of Ardent Spirits on the Human Body and Mind, with an Account of the Means of Preventing and the Rem-

edies of Curing Them." Though the article was largely a compilation of widely
held attitudes at the time, Rush used the word "disease" to describe alcoholism. A more scholarly treatise was penned in 1804 by a Scottish physician
named Thomas Trotter, who insisted that drunkenness was a disease, but one
without a clear etiology (Kinney & Leaton, 1987). The first use of the term
"alcoholism" appeared in the influential work of Magnus Huss. First published in Sweden in 1849, Huss's *Alcoholismus Chronicus* identified various
alcohol-related disorders. According to Babor (1993), this work was widely
read by physicians in both Europe and the United States.

In nineteenth-century America, the disease model of alcoholism was not
widely accepted by the general public. Alcoholics were viewed as either weak-
willed or evil. In either case, they were thought to be in need of reform, not
treatment. The moralistic condemnation of the alcoholic grew as the Temperance Movement gradually shifted from advocating moderation in drinking to
advocating abstinence (Ray & Ksir, 1996). The resulting Prohibitionist Movement gained steam in the second half of the nineteenth century and eventually lead to the passage of the Volstead Act, which ushered in national
prohibition in 1920. In the years prior to the prohibition era, alcoholism treatment languished because the alcoholic was not recognized as a sick person.
Kinney and Leaton (1987) note that hospitals for intemperate persons in Connecticut, Massachusetts, and New York were closed before 1920 because of a
lack of public support. Only after national prohibition was perceived as a
failure and repealed, in 1933, did the disease model reemerge as an alternative to the moral view of alcoholism.

No discussion of the disease model would make sense without a review of
the origins of AA. Although the two are not identical, they share many core
concepts. In addition, AA is used as a major, if not the main, component of
disease-model treatment programs.

It is no accident that AA started in the 1930s. Alcoholics were receiving
very little help, and that which they did receive was often inadequate. Physicians understood little about the disorder and they typically viewed the problem with the same level of prejudice as the layperson. This indifference for
the plight of alcoholics, the outright disgust for them as individuals, and the
lack of effective treatment created a social environment in which a self-help
fellowship (i.e., alcoholic helping alcoholic) was the only practical solution
to stopping drinking. Largely abandoned by other institutions (family, medicine, organized religion), alcoholics devised a set of recovery principles for
themselves that evolved into AA.

The "Big Book" of AA (sometimes described as its "bible") indicates that
the first AA meeting occurred in Akron, Ohio, during June of 1935 (Alcoholics Anonymous, 1976). It was actually not a meeting, but rather a chance
encounter involving a New York stockbroker, who had been sober for about
six months, and an Akron physician who at the time was struggling with his

own drinking. The stockbroker was in Akron on a business trip. Unfortunately for him, his business venture failed and he feared that he would return to drinking. Operating on the theory that the only way he could refrain from drinking was to convince another alcoholic not to drink, the stockbroker struck up a conversation with the physician. The two men, known in AA literature as Bill W. and Doctor Bob, were the cofounders of AA. Together, they helped one another stay sober. Both of them began recruiting new members, often by visiting alcoholic patients in hospitals. The movement mushroomed in size over the next decade. By 1976, AA reported a worldwide membership of more than one million people with almost 28 thousand groups meeting in more than ninety countries (Alcoholics Anonymous, 1976).

AA literature has always referred to alcoholism as a malady or an affliction. Yet the same literature also makes many references to the alcoholic's moral shortcomings. For example, the AA work entitled *Twelve Steps and Twelve Traditions*, states, "We reluctantly come to grips with those serious character flaws that made problem drinkers of us in the first place, flaws that must be dealt with to prevent a retreat into alcoholism once again" (Alcoholics Anonymous, 1976, p. 73). Critics of AA have pointed out the inconsistency of referring to alcoholics as victims of disease and at the same time maintaining that personality defects and character flaws of the person cause alcoholism (Peele, 1989; Kaminer, 1992). Indeed, the AA philosophy is not internally consistent. It simply reflects the attitudes of Americans toward alcoholism as they existed in the 1930s and, to a great extent, in the 1990s as well. However, one can argue that it is unreasonable to expect a fellowship of laypeople to develop a philosophy that would pass muster with academics and intellectuals.

With the emergence of AA on the American scene, the disease concept gained momentum in many quarters during the 1950s. Some religious leaders were swayed by the AA literature, which blended calls for spiritual conversion with claims that loss of control over one's drinking had physiological origins. In 1956, the American Medical Association supported the classification of alcoholism as a disease (Milam & Ketcham, 1983). The scientific community, led by E. M. Jellinek, renewed the legitimacy of alcoholism research by developing a research center on alcoholism at Yale University, which in 1940 had started the *Quarterly Journal of Studies on Alcohol*. Jellinek's *The Disease Concept of Alcoholism*, which added to the credibility of the disease concept, was published in 1960.

The disease model came of age in the 1960s and 1970s. The Minnesota Model, so called in recognition of a well-known treatment agency in that state, was adopted across the country. This treatment model, which included a period of detoxification ("detox") followed by a twenty-eight-day rehabilitation program and then aftercare, emphasizes abstinence, patient education, and AA fellowship. Employee alcohol programs (forerunners to employee assistance programs) became more widely adopted by industry, leading to an increase in the number of workplace referrals to disease-model treatment programs.

CURRENT APPLICATION IN REHABILITATION SETTINGS

In the 1980s, the disease model matured with the great expansion of the private alcoholism rehabilitation industry. These new "rehabs," often part of national health-care provider chains, rely almost exclusively on the disease model to guide the provision of services to alcohol and drug dependent clients. Though in recent years changes in insurance reimbursement policies, called managed care, have spurred greater variation in service delivery, campus professionals should understand that at least 80 to 90 percent of treatment programs today have a disease-model orientation. A number of common features in contemporary disease-model programs can be identified. College professionals should be aware of these characteristics when making decisions about student referrals to treatment centers and in providing for or shaping the student's aftercare experience.

In both inpatient and outpatient programs, an intake assessment is usually conducted during the first contact with a patient. The purpose of the assessment is to determine the nature and extent of the patient's alcohol and/or drug problem. A careful history is taken, the patient's current level of functioning is assessed, the patient's family and other significant persons are consulted, and recommendations for treatment are made. Professional counselors are usually responsible for conducting the intake assessment. Depending on the nature of patients' problems, their means of payment for program cost, and the availability of openings, the client may be admitted directly into the on-site program or referred elsewhere for treatment.

Following admission to a rehabilitation program, one of the first tasks for a patient and counselor is to design a treatment plan based on the patient's needs. The treatment plan serves to organize and focus program activities for the patient while in treatment. Ideally, the patient and counselor design it together by identifying short-term goals and the therapeutic activities that will allow them to accomplish them. In typical disease-model programs, short-term goals may include the following: orientation to the policies and rules of the treatment facility, reviewing results from laboratory tests that reveal the extent of damage alcohol and/or drugs have done to their bodies, and reading, understanding, and accepting the first of AA's twelve steps ("We admitted we were powerless over alcohol—that our lives had become unmanageable"). Depending on the patient's progress on goals such as these, the treatment plan will be revised to motivate positive change. Many counselors closely monitor the patient's acceptance of AA recovery principles and reinforce the patient for "working the steps."

Sometimes those unfamiliar with disease-model rehabilitation programs assume that patients have frequent contact with attending physicians. This is typically not the case, especially after the patient is medically stable and released from a detox unit. Most patient involvement is with addictions counselors. Though preparation standards are changing in many states, a majority of counselors in the alcoholism and addictions treatment field rely on their own recovery as the basis for their clinical practice. Many recovering counselors have baccalaureate or even master's degrees, but their formal education is usually not alcoholism or addiction specific. There are both advantages and disadvantages to using one's own recovery experience to guide clinical practice, and though it is beyond the scope of this discussion to present them, it should be recognized that this is one major reason the disease model dominates the treatment field today.

Another component of disease-model programs is patient education. Many programs devote a great deal of time to disseminating information about the course or progression of alcoholism and other drug dependencies, including the biomedical consequences. Also emphasized are the actions necessary for recovery, such as learning about the twelve steps and twelve traditions of AA, sponsorship in AA, health promotion strategies, accepting the necessity of abstinence, and the like. The purpose of didactic instruction is to encourage patients to realize that their personal experience with addiction and recovery is similar to that of other addicts. This confirms for patients that alcoholism and other addictions follow a predictable disease course and identifies the steps alcoholics before them have found necessary for recovery.

AA meetings are integrated into most treatment programs today. Typically, meetings are led not by staff, but by recovering alcoholics or addicts from the community. The purpose of having meetings in treatment is obviously to facilitate learning about AA, but it is also to help patients find a "sponsor." A sponsor is a veteran AA member, usually with at least several years of stable recovery, who provides personal guidance to a person new to the program. It is up to each new member to identify and reach out to a sponsor. Many patients do not actually identify a sponsor while in rehabilitation. However, in counseling patients may be asked about their progress in obtaining sponsorship and about those qualities they would like to find in a sponsor.

In treatment, it is often said that alcoholism is a "family disease." Thus, most contemporary disease-model programs attempt to involve the patient's family in their treatment. Some activities may be didactic lectures about the course of the disease, effects on the family, recovery principles, and so on. Counseling sessions may be directed toward opening channels of communication, confronting family secrets stemming from past deceptions (e.g., an extramarital affair), encouraging the patient to begin a process of making amends to those they have harmed, planning healing activities for the family, and the like. Currently, there is some disagreement in the field about the extent to which patients should be encouraged to deal with sensitive family issues. Some argue that this work is necessary for relapse prevention. Others argue that patients should focus on themselves and those actions necessary for building a stable recovery, rather than on emotion-charged conflicts within their families that could make them vulnerable to relapse. The more conservative camp contends that family counseling should be initiated only after the identified patient has established a year of stable recovery.

A final feature of current disease-model programs is discharge planning. Elements of the discharge plan may address academic, job training, or employment concerns; the possibility of placement in a halfway house or other residential facility; the need for aftercare treatment, integration into twelve-step programs, and family counseling; and so on. Some treatment programs recommend use of disulfram for alcohol-abusing patients. Disulfram is a prescribed drug that interferes with the metabolism of alcohol. Persons taking disulfram become very sick (severe headache, chest pains, flushing, and other symptoms) if they consume even a small amount of alcohol. Taking the drug discourages an impulsive return to drinking among patients new to recovery. There are dangers to prescribing disulfram, including self-inflicted poisoning, side effects when used properly, and others. Some practitioners do not believe it is an effective therapy, noting that patients who are intent on drinking can simply stop taking the drug and a short time later return to drinking.

THEORY AND RESEARCH FINDINGS

Substance Dependence and Substance Abuse

In everyday vernacular, terms such as substance abuse, addiction, and alcoholism are often used interchangeably and without much precision. In many cases, people apply these labels in a slanderous way to those they find offensive. In addictions treatment, these terms are used more objectively and function as diagnoses. Ideally, a diagnosis should remove the condition from the moral realm and motivate clients to seek treatment.

It remains difficult at times to define alcoholism or addiction. Part of the problem in the past has been the multitude of definitions in use (Jaffe, 1993). In the United States today, the classification criteria most commonly relied upon come from the *Diagnostic and Statistical Manual of Mental Disorders*, published by the American Psychiatric Association (1994). In this compendium of mental disorders are criteria for a two-dimensional scheme defining substance dependence and substance abuse. Though some classes of drugs have unique features, the criteria apply to alcohol and most other psychoactive substances.

The DSM-IV criteria for substance dependence specifies that the disorder is present when three or more of the following symptoms or behaviors occur in the same twelve-month period:

1. Tolerance (increased doses of alcohol or another drug are required to produce effects previously achieved at lower dose)
2. Withdrawal sickness (most symptoms are the opposite of those experienced during intoxication with the same substance; for example, alcohol withdrawal may

include severe anxiety and cocaine withdrawal is characterized by depression and lethargy)

3. Frequent use of a substance in larger amounts over a longer period of time than intended (loss of control)

4. A persistent desire or unsuccessful efforts to reduce or control use of alcohol or another drug

5. A great deal of time spent in efforts to obtain a substance or to recover from its effects (e.g., a hangover)

6. Because of substance use, important activities related to social, occupational, or recreational interests are given up or reduced (e.g., neglecting studies or failing to report to work)

7. Continued use of a substance despite knowledge that a physical or psychological problem is caused or exacerbated by the self-administration of the drug (e.g., continued heavy drinking despite recognition that previous assaultive or aggressive behavior was caused by alcohol use).

In applying these criteria to traditional-age college students, it is important to note that though tolerance and withdrawal are listed first among the above criteria, neither symptom is "necessary nor sufficient for a diagnosis of substance dependence" (American Psychiatric Association, 1994, p. 178). The framers of DSM IV recognize that in some dependency patterns withdrawal may be entirely absent or play only a very minor role. Many college student drinkers (ages eighteen to twenty-two) certainly show tolerance to large amounts of alcohol, but withdrawal symptoms are rare. Nevertheless, many heavy-drinking students could meet criteria for alcohol dependence (i.e., alcoholism) if only two of the remaining five features are present. Indeed, it would not be unusual for an eighteen- to twenty-two-year-old drinker to exhibit tolerance to alcohol, frequent consumption of alcohol in larger quantities than intended, and neglect of academic work because of drinking. Such a student would be diagnosed with alcohol dependence.

Using a national sample representative of the U.S. population, Grant and colleagues (1991) found that 23.5 percent of eighteen- to twenty-nine-year-old males met DSM-IV criteria for alcohol dependence, the highest in four adult age groups. Among eighteen- to twenty-nine-year-old females, the prevalence rate was 10.1 percent. Thus, it is reasonable to conclude that a significant proportion of college students are not only engaged in alcohol abuse, but actually can be classified as alcoholic. It is imperative that student affairs professionals recognize that alcoholism is relatively prevalent among students, particularly among men, and that referrals for intensive off-campus treatment need to be made on a frequent basis.

The DSM IV recognizes that not all substance-related problems can be characterized as dependencies or addictions. Thus, criteria are listed for substance abuse, a maladaptive pattern of alcohol or drug use featuring "clinically significant impairment, or distress" (American Psychiatric Association, 1994, p. 182). Substance abuse is indicated by recurrent misuse, which includes one or more of the following: (1) results in failure to fulfill major role obligations at work, school, or home, (2) occurs in situations where it is physically hazardous (e.g., alcohol-impaired driving), (3) causes legal problems, and (4) continues despite the social or interpersonal problems it causes. In addition, for the diagnosis of substance abuse to be made these symptoms must never have met criteria for substance dependence. In essence, this is a residual category for those patterns not severe enough to be diagnosed as dependencies.

Some campus professionals may believe that many of the pathology criteria of the DSM IV represent conventional college student behavior. In the eighteen- to twenty-four-year-old college population, a number of additional factors are useful in distinguishing between "normal" college drinking and DSM IV criteria for abuse and dependence. The following motivations, behaviors, and consequences can be considered indicators of a problem that requires a referral for professional evaluation:

1. Aggression or fighting while intoxicated—students sometimes refer to this as "beer muscles"
2. A weekly pattern of drinking involving frequent, gross intoxication
3. An increasing frequency of blackouts (i.e., alcohol-induced amnesia)
4. Attending class or performing other academic work (e.g., writing papers) under the influence of alcohol or another drug
5. Frequent participation in drinking games or rituals
6. Drinking or drug use for the purposes of forgetting about problems (e.g., academic difficulties, relationship concerns)
7. Selling plasma, textbooks, or other belongings to obtain money for alcohol or drugs
8. Indiscriminate and usually unprotected sexual activity while intoxicated
9. Frequent minor injuries—which occur under the influence of alcohol (lacerations, sprains, bruises, burns, etc.)
10. A family history of alcohol or drug dependency

Etiology of Alcoholism and Other Drug Dependencies

The disease model has long been associated with the view that alcohol and drug dependencies have physiological origins stemming from genetic (inborn) vulnerabilities (Fingarette, 1988). Some in the treatment community have bordered on being dogmatic in their insistence that alcoholism, specifically, does not have psychosocial origins (Milam & Ketcham, 1983; Talbott, 1989). Thus, the disease model is usually separated from behavioral-science theories emphasizing the importance of personality, cognitive, and environmental variables, as well as learning processes. This feud, pitting physicians and other treatment personnel against academics and behavioral-science researchers, has not been productive (Gordis, 1991). An unfortunate aspect of the schism is that many "frontline" addiction treatment providers have not learned to use the disease model as a theory, but rather treat it as absolute law. Too frequently, the model is not held tentatively, as theories should be, but instead is inexorably latched onto.

Disease-model proponents have often overstated the significance of genetic factors in the development of addiction (Peele, 1985). It is not unusual in treatment programs and twelve-step meetings for recovering persons to be taught that "alcoholism is a genetic disease" or "alcoholism runs in families which makes it genetic." These simplistic notions, of course, do not adequately explain the role of genetics in alcoholism. Clearly, the inherited factor is a "susceptibility" (or vulnerability, predisposition, etc.) to alcoholism, rather than the alcoholism itself. One's genetic makeup simply increases or decreases the likelihood that alcoholism will appear in an individual (Lester, 1988). By contrast, examples of genetic diseases include cystic fibrosis, sickle-cell anemia, Down's syndrome, and Tay-Sack's (Van De Graaff & Fox, 1986).

Another common misconception related to addiction etiology involves illicit drugs. It is taught in some treatment and twelve-step programs (e.g., Narcotics Anonymous) that addiction to drugs such as cocaine, heroin, marijuana, PCP, and so on also has genetic origins. Though this may be possible, at least with some illicit drugs, at this time these assertions have no empirical basis. Virtually no scientific investigations on this issue have been conducted (Alexander, 1988; Crabbe, McSwigan, & Belknap, 1985; Nunes & Klein, 1987).

Recent research on the etiology of alcoholism makes a strong case for genetic–environment interaction, and, interestingly, the magnitude of each source of influence may be roughly equal (Kendler, Heath, Neale, Kessler, & Eaves, 1992; McGue, Pickens, & Svikis, 1992). Even the biomedically oriented National Institute on Alcohol Abuse and Alcoholism (1993) recently concluded that "The distribution of alcoholism throughout a given population indicates that genetic factors alone cannot account for the pathogenesis of this disease" (p. 61). The respective contributions of heredity and environment may differ along a variety of dimensions, including type of alcoholism (Cloninger, Bohman, & Sigvardsson, 1981), gender (Pickens, Svikis, McGue, Lykken, Hesten, & Clayton, 1991; Kendler et al., 1992), and age at onset of alcohol problems (McGue et al., 1992). For example, in several studies of adoptees, Cloninger and colleagues have identified two forms of alcoholism (Type I and Type II) that vary with respect to genetic susceptibility (Bohman, Sigvardsson, & Cloninger, 1981; Bohman, Cloninger, von Knorring, & Sigvardsson, 1984; Cloninger, 1983; Cloninger et al., 1981). Type I alcoholism is the more prevalent type and is influenced by both genetic and environmental factors. Type II alcoholism is a more severe form of the disorder and is significantly influenced by genetic factors rather than by the environment. Type II occurred only in men, with drinking problems often beginning in adolescence, and included a pattern of aggressive behavior and arrests. Twin studies have also found that genetics may influence male and female alcoholism in different ways depending upon the age at onset of alcohol problems. For example, McGue and colleagues (1992) found that genetic factors played a stronger role in male alcoholism where drinking problems began before the age of twenty. In males with an age of onset after age twenty, environment exerted the stronger influence on the development of alcoholism. In females, McGue and colleagues (1992) found alcoholism to be determined entirely by environmental factors, regardless of the age of onset. However, another twin study, by Kendler and colleagues (1992), found that genetics accounted for 50 to 60 percent of the variance in female alcoholism. Thus, at this stage of scientific inquiry it can be concluded that both genetics and environment play a role in the development of alcoholism. The respective contribution of each source of influence probably varies by age of onset, and possibly by gender. It is also likely that future research will further delineate types of alcoholism based on varying genetic and environmental influences (National Institute on Alcohol Abuse and Alcoholism, 1993).

What does this recent research on the etiology of alcoholism do to the validity of the disease model? As critics have contended, the classic model does not provide a good fit for the empirical data developed in the course of the adoption and twin studies of recent decades (Fingarette, 1988; Peele, 1985). Furthermore, a voluminous body of literature indicates that psychological, social, and developmental factors play a role in the development of alcoholism (and probably other drug dependencies) (National Institute on Alcohol Abuse & Alcoholism, 1993). At the same time, it should be recognized that the disease model was never an empirically driven theory. Its revival after the era of national prohibition occurred largely because of the neglect shown alcoholics by the scientific community. Recovering alcoholics took it upon themselves to revive the disease concept, largely through AA. Thus, it is probably not fair to expect the classic model to hold up under scientific scrutiny. It was developed with a more practical goal in mind—to get the alcoholic the help that he or she needed. Because there is no dispute that the disease model has helped hundreds of thousands of people recover from dependencies, it may be more helpful to take from it those elements that many in recovery have found useful and embrace treatment innovations offered by the behavioral sciences.

Basic Features of the Classic Disease Model

There are a number of basic features to the classic disease model that are typically taught to patients in treatment programs today. It will be helpful for campus professionals to understand them so that they can offer effective services to recovering students discharged from treatment.

Primary Disease In many treatment programs, patients are taught that they have a "primary disease," meaning that it is not the result of another condition. Alcoholism, in particular, is typically described as a primary disease process with many symptoms, including marital problems, stress, depression, other psychiatric disorders, and so forth. In essence, addictions treatment programs elevate alcohol dependency, and drug dependencies as well, to a position above other psychological or psychiatric disorders. The latter disorders are often seen by treatment staff as secondary to alcoholism and other drug addictions. Many counselors believe that if the drinking and drug use are stopped, other psychological or behavioral problems will disappear. Thus, patients are encouraged to believe that their dependency is a severe problem and is more fundamental than other psychological, behavioral, or relationship problems. The purpose of this instruction is to focus patients on their drinking or drug problem and not allow them to become sidetracked by numerous other life problems. Many treatment programs will encourage patients new to recovery to avoid working on mental health or marital problems until they can demonstrate a stable sobriety.

Disease-model treatment typically applies the primary disease concept too broadly. Without question, a portion of patients in treatment can be accurately classified as primary alcoholics or addicts. However, research shows that a slight majority of alcohol and drug dependent clients also suffer from psychiatric comorbidity, where the alcohol or drug dependency can be considered the secondary rather than the primary disorder in terms of order of onset (National Institute on Alcohol Abuse and Alcoholism, 1993). This suggests that disease-model programs need to narrow the application of the primary disease concept and develop alternative treatment strategies for those patients whose addictions are secondary to another psychiatric disorder.

Loss of Control The concept of "loss of control" refers to the alcoholic's or addict's inability to stop or limit their use of a substance once a small amount of the drug (or alcohol) has been ingested. The concept is a central feature of the disease model. In fact, the first step of AA's Twelve Steps requires that recovering alcoholics acknowledge their inability to control their drinking: "We admitted that we were powerless over alcohol—that our lives had become unmanageable" (Alcoholics Anonymous, 1976). The "Big Book" of AA also teaches, "We are equally positive that once he takes any alcohol whatever into his system, something happens, both in the bodily and mental sense, which makes it virtually impossible for him to stop. The experience of any alcoholic will abundantly confirm this" (Alcoholics Anonymous, 1976, pp. 22–23).

Jellinek's (1960) work added to the concept's credibility by proposing that one type of alcoholism, labeled gamma, was based on loss of control. Jellinek believed that once gamma alcoholics consumed a small amount of alcohol, an unknown psychological mechanism compelled them to continue drinking until drunkenness. It is not surprising that Jellinek's observations were consistent with AA teachings, as he relied heavily on the self-reports of AA members for identifying alcoholism subtypes (Jung, 1994).

Loss of control is a feature that most people with substance dependencies can identify with because it explains the frustrating and baffling experience of wanting to cut down but failing to do so. The concept is helpful to many persons in recovery who repeatedly try and fail to control their use because it informs them that this inability is a disease symptom, not a failure of will, that abstinence is the only means of recovery, and that by surrendering to the power of the disease they can give up the futile struggle to control their drinking. For many in AA and other twelve-step programs, recognizing their own loss of control and "working" the first step are spiritually uplifting and liberating experiences. The result can be increased motivation to work the AA program of recovery.

Despite the utility of the loss-of-control concept in clinical practice, researchers from the behavioral sciences have frowned on the notion for some time. The classic formulation of loss of control is not supported by objective data (Fingarette, 1988). The criticisms of the concept are numerous and the literature rebuking it relatively large. The interested reader should first examine Fingarette's (1988) *Heavy Drinking: The Myth of Alcoholism as a Disease* for an introductory review of this literature. However, a few criticisms bear mentioning here. First, the concept fails to account for why relapse occurs frequently among alcoholics. If loss of control is triggered by and occurs only after a small amount of alcohol is consumed, then why should alcoholics have any difficulty in refraining from the first drink? Second, research has demonstrated that alcoholics can drink in a controlled manner when contingencies (rewards and punishment) are carefully arranged to promote a sensible, paced drinking (Sobell & Sobell, 1976). Third, placebo research has demonstrated that even among alcoholics the amount of alcohol consumed is more closely related to their beliefs about what they are drinking (alcohol versus tonic placebo) than it is to the actual alcohol content of their drinks (Marlatt, Demming, & Reid, 1973). Fourth, teaching recovering alcoholics that they literally have a mechanism within them that prevents them from stopping after two or three drinks can have the unintended effect of turning a patient's slip into a full-blown relapse (Marlatt & Gordon, 1985). Thus, the loss of control concept remains one of the dividing points between the treatment and scientific communities.

Progression The disease model maintains that alcoholism and other addictions are progressive in nature (Talbott, 1989). That is, continued use of a substance will cause ever-worsening problems. The course of a progressive disease is relatively predictable, unless the addiction process is interrupted by treatment. The gradual deterioration of the alcoholic or addict has been described in numerous ways, though all have common features. Typically, the initial stages of a dependency are characterized by increasing tolerance, where larger and larger quantities of the drug are used to alter mood (Milam & Ketcham, 1983). In these early stages, alcoholics or addicts are completely unaware of their growing dependency on a substance. They may actually be proud of their tolerance (or ability to "handle it") at this point, though loss of control may already be established. Usually, there is little or no social impairment. Thus, others do not recognize the drinking or drug use as a problem and biomedical complications have not yet become obvious. However, the person is increasingly becoming preoccupied with use of the substance, such that when they are not using it they are thinking about doing so.

At some point, an invisible line is crossed where alcohol or drugs are not used only to enhance mood, but just to feel normal (Johnson, 1980). Now there are consequences to continued substance use and a middle stage of dependency is entered in which the alcoholic or addict begins to feel intense remorse, guilt, and anxiety about the problem. The natural tendency is to continue the drinking or drugging to block out these feelings and to rely on defense mechanisms (denial, rationalization, etc.) to cope with the harm being done to self, family, friends, or coworkers. In the middle stages of dependency, one's circle of friends changes because old friends do not want to drink or use drugs with the same high intensity. Use of the substance may become secretive. In alcoholism, specifically, blackouts may become frequent occurrences and the alcoholic develops strategies to avoid them by engaging in maintenance drinking, that is, maintaining a near constant intoxication that is at levels well below that which would cause a blackout. This type of drinking tends to conceal the problem, at least to those outside the family. Withdrawal symptoms are now a reality for the dependent person and other substances may be relied upon to medicate this condition (e.g., tranquilizers). Major life responsibilities in such roles as parent, worker, or student are often neglected and, in AA jargon, life becomes unmanageable.

The later stages of dependency involve "hitting bottom," that is, the person experiences severe consequences from his or her misuse of alcohol or drugs and because of this finally perceives a need to stop. The consequences will vary from person to person, but may include damage to an organ system (e.g., chronic gastritis or liver damage in alcoholism, recurrent chest pains and heart rate irregularities in cocaine dependence), termination of employment or academic dismissal from school, separation from spouse and children, involvement with the criminal justice system (arrest for drug possession or distribution, DWI charges, etc.), or acute psychiatric emergency (threats or attempts at suicide). The current use of the concept of hitting bottom recognizes that every alcoholic and addict will have a different bottom. Some will be lower than others, but in all cases it is assumed to be that point at which the alcoholic or addict perceives him or herself to be defeated and is willing to ask for help. In the classic disease model, this is the optimal point at which to enter treatment. However, contemporary disease-model practitioners insist that the bottom can be raised through effective intervention. For a college student, hitting bottom might mean eviction from the residence hall or academic probation or dismissal, which can be turned into an opportunity to intervene to get the student to address his or her substance abuse problem.

As with other features of the disease model, empirical support for the notion that substance dependence is invariably progressive is at best mixed.

Adams, Garry, Rhyne, Hunt, and Goodwin (1990) and Fillmore, Hartka, Johnstone, Leino, Motoyoshi, and Temple (1991) all found that drinking patterns of middle-age adults tend to be maintained into old age; that is, those who drink heavily in middle age tend to do so at more advanced ages as well. However, the amount of alcohol consumed, by itself, is not a good measure of abuse or dependence. Grant and colleagues (1991) assessed alcohol abuse and alcohol dependence in a nationwide sample using DSM III-R criteria and found that the prevalence of these two disorders decreased steadily with age. Whether this decrease can be accounted for by positive treatment outcomes or remission without treatment (i.e., spontaneous remission) is not known. It is likely that both factors play a role in the lower rates of alcohol abuse and alcohol dependence in older populations. Obviously, many thousands of Americans have been effectively treated in disease-model treatment programs. However, spontaneous remission should not be considered a rare occurrence. By some estimates, 20 percent or more of individuals with alcoholism become permanently abstinent without ever receiving any type of treatment (American Psychiatric Association, 1994). Thus, while the "progressive course" concept applies to many alcoholics and addicts, particularly those who present themselves for treatment, it may not necessarily apply to the broad spectrum of persons with alcohol and drug dependencies.

Chronicity The greatest single source of tension between the alcoholism treatment and research communities involves competing views on the issue of chronicity. The disease model maintains that alcoholism as well as other drug addictions are chronic disorders that can only be treated with total abstinence from alcohol and other illicit drugs (Marion & Coleman, 1991). Abstinence is not thought to cure an addiction, but rather to arrest its development. Thus, dependencies are likened to other chronic diseases (cardiovascular disorders, diabetes, epilepsy, etc.) where there is an identified treatment but no cure. For this reason, members of twelve-step programs refer to themselves as recovering as opposed to recovered. The former term denotes the chronic, ongoing nature of the disease requiring abstinence and long-term AA (or other twelve-step) membership for keeping it in remission.

Among disease-model proponents, treatment strategies relying on controlled drinking protocols evoke repugnance and even suspicion (Pendery, Maltzman, & West, 1982). Giving alcoholics hope that they may be able to return to safe, sensible drinking is seen as not only misguided, but even unethical professional practice (Milam & Ketcham, 1983; Marion & Coleman, 1991). The disease model asserts that alcoholics can only sustain controlled drinking (perhaps two or three drinks a day) for limited periods of time (a few weeks to a few months) before returning to abusive drinking practices. Milam and Ketcham (1983) argue that this is the case because alcoholics metabolize alcohol differently than do nonalcoholics. Marion and Coleman (1991) argue that substance use, on even an occasional basis, impairs one's ability to process new information that is necessary to build a stable recovery. Continued use interferes with the acquisition and integration of learning experiences that are part of the recovery process and allow denial and self-delusion to persist. In essence, substance use represents old behavior that makes the individual new to recovery prone to relapse.

Without doubt, abstinence is clearly the safest and most healthful strategy an alcoholic can adopt to address a drinking problem. As with other disease-model concepts though, chronicity and the universal requirement of abstinence are probably extended too far. Miller (1982) and others have noted that competently administered controlled drinking protocols are effective with about 15 percent of problem drinkers. Furthermore, there are some advantages to controlled drinking over abstinence-oriented treatment (Heather & Robertson, 1983). For example, in some alcoholics, abstinence simply does not lead to an overall improvement in life functioning and, in fact, may be linked to severe recurrent relapses. Two additional points about controlled drinking bear mentioning. First, it is most appropriate for young patients who have not had biomedical complications or serious involvement with the criminal justice system (e.g., many college students) and second, it is not indicated for recovering alcoholics who are successful at abstinence. It is a strategy that could be considered on an individual basis at the onset of treatment.

Treatment and Counseling Strategies

Though disease-model treatment programs vary, there are a number of strategies that alcoholism and addiction counselors rely on to facilitate the recovery process. Each will be briefly described.

Dealing with Denial and Confrontation Denial, a basic defense mechanism, can be defined as an inability to perceive an unacceptable reality. It is best thought of as a problem of perception, rather than as outright deception. Denial protects the ego from threat. In the context of alcoholism and addiction, the threat is recognition of one's own alcohol or drug problem and all the guilt and shame associated with the label. Massella (1991) has stated that denial is actually the "primary symptom of chemical dependence" (p. 79). After all, without the presence of denial, alcoholism and other addictions would not be progressive; that is, the substance user would recognize early on the harm they cause (to themselves, friends, and family) and stop their drinking or drug use.

Most disease-oriented practioners believe it is important to use confrontative procedures (e.g., family interventions, employee or student assistance program efforts, group confrontation) to break through the denial. The failure to stamp out all vestiges of denial makes relapse a possibility. As George (1990) has noted, it "protects the option to continue to use, which for the addicted individual is the essence of life" (p. 36).

A variety of techniques are employed to help patients accept the reality of their disease. In cases where medical symptomatology is present, patients are often presented with the results of laboratory tests. In a private meeting with treatment staff, the damage to organs is reviewed and the potential medical consequences of continued drinking or drug use is discussed. Many times patients are then encouraged to share their lab values with other patients in group therapy or during other meetings in the treatment program.

In group counseling, patients are encouraged to confront other patients about any defense mechanisms that they may display. Counselors may assign homework exercises, requesting that patients describe their use of defense mechanisms prior to entering treatment and those they use in the present. To accomplish this, they often have to ask for feedback from others about their current behavior. During activities designed to involve family members in the treatment process, the patient may be requested to remain silent while each member of their family recounts past negative experiences involving the patient's alcohol or drug use and any harm they may have suffered as a result.

Self-Diagnosis and Self-Care During the course of treatment, patients are frequently encouraged to engage in self-diagnosis; that is, patients must recognize the symptoms of addiction in themselves and apply methods of self-care (e.g., change unhealthy eating habits). Patients who are engaged in self-diagnosis have broken through much of their denial and demonstrate active involvement in their own treatment. As with other chronic diseases (e.g., heart disease, diabetes, epilepsy), effective self-care is considered crucial for positive long-term outcomes. Patients who are passive in receiving treatment and those who do not take responsibility for their recovery have poor prognoses.

Use of Twelve-Step Recovery Programs Virtually all disease-model programs incorporate AA, Narcotics Anonymous (NA), or other twelve-step recovery programs into treatment. NA and other twelve-step recovery programs (e.g., Cocaine Anonymous) grew out of AA. Though they may focus on a different drug, their recovery principles are virtually identical to those espoused by AA. Patients new to recovery are usually encouraged to focus on only the first three steps during their first year or so of sobriety. The first three steps read as follows:

We admitted we were powerless over alcohol—that our lives had become unmanageable.

Came to believe that a power greater than ourselves could restore us to sanity.

Made a decision to turn our will and our lives over to the care of God *as we understood Him.* (Alcoholics Anonymous, 1953, p. 5)

These three steps encourage patients to (1) surrender to a problem that they cannot control, (2) recognize the "craziness" of their past behavior, and (3) reach out to a force greater than themselves for spiritual conversion.

The AA (or other twelve-step program) meetings in treatment are typically organized or led by recovering individuals from the local community who have built a solid sobriety. Treatment program staff do not usually attend these meetings, even though many are in recovery themselves. However, staff professionals will engage patients in discussions about their progress at "working the steps." One purpose of this is to confront any resistance patients may have about involving themselves in AA or NA. Sometimes patients will initially believe that AA requires members to hold religious beliefs. The organization does not require members to have religious faith; in fact, many long-time members are agnostic or atheistic.

Regimentation of Program Most addiction treatment facilities today in the United States, especially inpatient and residential programs, are highly regimented with respect to patient conduct and use of time. While in treatment, the patient's day is highly structured. Patients are usually expected to awaken early, complete a variety of housekeeping tasks, check-in with staff, and so on. Each day the patient will attend educational classes, meet with a counselor, participate in group therapy, join with others for AA meetings, and eat meals with other patients. There is very little free time. Usually, patient access to television, radio, telephone, newspapers, magazines, and the like is purposely restricted so that patients will focus on themselves and their recovery. Patients who cannot comply with the program structure are given what is sometimes called a "therapeutic discharge" (i.e., they are kicked out of the program).

Relapse Prevention The classic disease model had very little to say about how to prevent a relapse other than to instruct the patient not to do it, go to an AA meeting, and call your sponsor. Today, progressive disease-model programs attempt to teach patients relapse prevention skills that they can employ outside of the treatment setting. There are a number of relapse prevention strategies described in the literature (Daley & Raskin, 1991), and most share a set of common features. For example, a component is usually included to educate patients about the nature of relapse, the factors that make one prone to relapse, and strategies for dealing with cravings. Second, patients create a personal inventory of anticipated triggers, which are the emotions, events, or situations that could cause them to relapse. Third, they identify and, while still in treatment, rehearse behaviors that will reduce their risk of relapse. Finally, they practice these new behaviors in everyday life and report their successes and failures in an aftercare phase of treatment.

Measures of Treatment Effectiveness

In disease-model programs, treatment effectiveness is determined by a variety of patient outcomes. However, the most paramount of these is abstinence from alcohol and other psychoactive drugs (excluding caffeine and nicotine). In AA teaching, there is a distinction made between sobriety and being "dry" (Kinney & Leaton, 1987). A dry alcoholic is simply an alcoholic who is not drinking at the moment, whereas the sober alcoholic, in addition to not drinking, has made fundamental changes in his or her philosophy, behavior, and lifestyle. Sobriety does not come easily. It requires extensive twelve-step work.

Beyond abstinence and sobriety, a number of other behavioral indicators demonstrate that treatment was effective. A partial list includes the following:

1. Regular and frequent attendance at twelve-step meetings (usually at least three meetings weekly)

2. Obtaining a sponsor (i.e., a mentor with several years of stable sobriety) and talking with this person on a regular basis

3. Reading educational materials on various recovery issues

4. Changing one's circle of friends, and possibly socializing with other recovering individuals

5. Removing alcohol, drugs, and any related paraphernalia from one's residence

6. Successful completion of an aftercare program (followup therapeutic activities that continue after treatment is finished)

Does treatment based on the disease model work? The answer to this very complicated question is a qualified yes. Surprisingly, there have been few randomized clinical trials testing the effectiveness of disease-model treatment programs per se (National Institute on Alcohol Abuse and Alcoholism, 1993). A number of nonrandomized clinical trials have been conducted, but the results from the investigations have to be interpreted cautiously because of possible bias associated with patient selection of treatment modality. Another problem with the existing research is that posttreatment followup assessments ve often tracked patients for only one to two years, making long-term ef- tiveness difficult to determine. Furthermore, it has become widely accepted that patient outcomes are determined by a variety of nontreatment factors, such as characteristics of the patient (e.g., mental health status, income level) and posttreatment environmental factors (e.g., family stability) (Moos, Finney, & Cronkhite, 1990). For these reasons and many others, a simple answer to the question of treatment effectiveness is not possible. However, studies do show that people who enter treatment have better outcomes than those who avoid it (Ray & Ksir, 1993). In an extensive review of treatment outcome research, the National Academy of Sciences's Institute of Medicine (1990) concluded there is reason to believe that, "treating people with alcohol problems is an endeavor that can produce very positive results" (p. 148). Interestingly, this same report notes that outpatient treatment appears to be as effective as inpatient treatment.

APPLICATIONS OF THE DISEASE MODEL

Disease Model and Assessment

Substance-abuse assessments will be at least partially formed from the values and attitudes held by the campus professional conducting the evaluation. Claims that substance-abuse assessment is completely objective are naïve. The personal biases of the evaluator almost always creep into the evaluation, especially where sensitive or ambiguous situations involving substance abuse are disclosed by a student.

Within the context of the disease model, three issues need to be considered by campus professionals in making clinical observations and interpretations and decisions about appropriate treatment. The first issue pertains to the orientation of the campus professional conducting the assessment. To what extent does the professional hold negative attitudes toward substance abusers? Professionals who view alcohol or drug abuse as immoral conduct are likely to be judgmental, which can undermine their effectiveness with a student. On the other extreme lies another question professionals should ask themselves: Is college student alcohol or drug abuse a relatively harmless rite of passage? This view tends to downplay the clinical significance of substance abuse and quite possibly results in failure to make appropriate positive diagnoses. This tendency may be linked to the professional's own substance abuse as an undergraduate.

A second issue concerns the professional's view of the appropriateness of using DSM-IV substance use criteria in the assessment of college students. One argument is that the DSM criteria were developed from clinical observations of older, more chronic populations and thus do not apply to the vast majority of college students. This view tends to lead the professional away from the disease model and likely discourages referrals to treatment programs. The counterargument, that there is no compelling reason not to apply DSM criteria to college students, is likely to result in frequent referrals to off-campus treatment. Those with a disease-model orientation would tend to view the rejection of DSM criteria as a form of "professional enabling"; that is, allowing students' harmful dependencies to progress because of a reluctance to actively intervene.

A third issue campus professionals should consider in the assessment of student substance use is the presence of any bias they may hold about the disease model itself. Academics, in particular, have been hypercritical of the disease model, and from a scientific perspective much of the criticism is deserved. However, the objective observer will also take into account the history of alcoholic mistreatment and note that the model is the basis of stable recovery for many thousands of individuals. Thus, in the assessment and referral of substance abusing college students, professionals should consider only the fit between the student and disease-model treatment, and make an attempt to set aside any personal prejudices or philosophic problems that they might have with the disease concept. It should also be realized that local treatment options may be limited to disease-model programs.

Referrals of Students to Twelve-Step Programs and Treatment

Students with substance abuse problems should understand that both twelve-step programs and disease-model treatment programs are abstinence oriented. This does not mean that members of AA will turn an intoxicated student away from a meeting. On the contrary, they will welcome newcomers who are struggling to become sober. The only requirement to attend an AA meeting is the *desire* to stop drinking. Nevertheless, campus professionals can facilitate the recovery process by emphasizing that in AA, other twelve-step programs, and formal treatment, the goal is complete abstinence from alcohol and other drugs.

Campus professionals should also be aware that many recovering individuals never go to formal treatment, but instead get sober through affiliation with AA or other similar groups. This is a particularly viable option for those that recognize their dependency and do not yet have physical dependency or other medical complications, major psychiatric disturbance, or serious involvement with the criminal justice system. The advantages of relying on a twelve-step recovery include that (1) meetings, particularly AA meetings, are held in virtually every community and on many college campuses today; (2) there is no fee; and (3) participation in twelve-step programs will not disrupt academic work. In many large metropolitan communities, AA support services publish a directory of meeting times and places. AA can also be found in the telephone book.

In preparing a student for a twelve-step meeting, the student should be advised on several points. First, meetings vary tremendously in regard to enthusiasm, warmth, member characteristics, and even structure. Some meetings focus on discussion of a specific step, others are led by speakers; some are open to the public, while others are closed to recovering alcoholics or addicts only. Thus, if a student does not like a particular meeting, they should be encouraged to attend other meetings until they find a meeting where they feel comfortable. Students will sometimes form an unfavorable opinion of AA as an organization based on one meeting. Premature conclusions such as these should be discouraged. Second, newcomers do not have to speak in meetings if they do not wish to do so. They can simply say that they are not yet ready to talk or that they are there just to listen. Third, the meetings are truly confidential. Information disclosed in meetings will not be connected to them at a later date. Fourth, twelve-step programs are not cults. They do not use coercion and members do not monitor the behavior of other members.

Referrals to treatment programs are often necessary for students who are uncertain about their dependency status, for those in obvious denial, where there is the possibility of psychiatric disturbance or medical problems, or when the student's behavior places other students at risk of harm (e.g., an alcoholic student who becomes violent when intoxicated). Depending on whether treatment is provided on an inpatient or outpatient basis, the student's academic progress may be temporarily interrupted. Even outpatient treatment will often preclude full involvement in academic work, and some students may opt for services near their home or some distance from campus.

There are two traps the campus professional should avoid in the referral process. When a student needs to be evaluated by a substance abuse specialist, it is counterproductive to engage the student in debate or argument about the disease concept and it is unnecessary to arrive at a diagnosis. The campus professional should help the student see the need for indepth assessment by a specialist.

Intellectual debate can sometimes distort accurate appraisal of one's own drinking behavior and thereby decrease the likelihood that a student will acknowledge the need for further assessment. In addition, the campus professional is not obligated to make a diagnosis nor required to use stigmatizing terms such as alcoholic or addict. In a caring and empathetic way, the student should be encouraged to view further assessment as a health protection measure.

Difficulties Faced by Recovering Students

Campus professionals must become aware that the college environment is not conducive to recovery based on the disease model or the twelve steps of AA. Many recovering students complain about the amount of partying they see around them. Sometimes they find it difficult to understand why colleges and universities do not do more to address substance abuse problems on their campuses.

As a result of being alcohol and drug free, recovering students face a number of difficulties on campus. They may experience social isolation and a loss of prior friendships with drinkers. Other students often demonstrate a lack of sensitivity to their recovery status and may not accept their abstinence. This is particularly the case when drinking students are intoxicated. Many recovering students find it uncomfortable to attend social events where alcohol is being used, especially those that involve heavy drinking. Among those in the early stages of recovery (i.e., the first year or so), feelings of threat may arise when around alcohol. This sometimes makes it difficult to find suitable living quarters. In addition, it can be irritating for recovering students to hear faculty make joking references to drunkenness, see alcohol paraphernalia in academic buildings, and repeatedly be informed of upcoming parties as announced by prominently displayed campus flyers and advertisements.

Traditionally, college and university administrators encourage students to organize themselves for action to foster change on some social issue (e.g., cultural diversity, gay rights, women's issues, etc.). They probably do not understand that because of the desire for anonymity and AA traditions that discourage political action on alcohol control, recovering students will not likely become the champions for change in drinking customs on campus. The traditions and principles of AA encourage introspection and change within the individual. The philosophy encourages those in recovery to withdraw from the drinking world, not to confront it. This is why AA members tend to socialize with one another. The absence of a visible movement against campus alcohol abuse does not mean that there is no student support for such an initiative. Support exists, not only from recovering students, but also from those who choose to abstain for other reasons and those who drink only lightly and avoid any illicit drug use. However, it is unlikely that these groups will provide the leadership necessary for change on the substance abuse problem. In contrast to other social problems that affect student life, the burden of fostering change on this issue falls on campus faculty and staff.

SUMMARY AND CONCLUSIONS

The disease model has made treatment of alcoholism and other addictions possible in the United States. Without the emergence of the model and the development of twelve-step programs, very little assistance would be offered to those suffering from drug dependencies. The model is widely used in addictions treatment because of its relative simplicity and straightforward insistence on abstinence. Though features of the disease model have been challenged by science, many alcoholic and addicted individuals have rebuilt their lives using it as a guide. Thus, the history of mistreatment, strong advocacy by the treatment community, and testimonials from recovering individuals are the social forces that have forged the disease model as it exists in current form. Within the next decade, changes in the U.S. health-care system may alter the provision of treatment services, which, in turn, might lead to revisions in the model. Science may also become a force in reshaping the model. The challenge facing treatment specialists will be to incorporate new knowledge into conventional treatment to make it more efficient and better matched to a broad spectrum of diverse clients. The challenge facing campus professionals, particularly student affairs personnel, will be to transform the campus environment in ways that will thwart the development of the disease of addiction.

REFERENCES

Adams, W. L., Garry, P. J., Rhyne, R., Hunt, W. C., & Goodwin, J. I. (1990). Alcohol intake in the healthy elderly: Changes with age in a cross-sectional and longitudinal study. *Journal of American Geriatrics Society, 38*(3), 211–216.

Alcoholics Anonymous. (1976). *Alcoholics Anonymous: The story of how many thousands of men and women have recovered from alcoholism* (3rd ed.). New York: Alcoholics Anonymous World Services.

Alcoholics Anonymous. (1953). *Twelve steps and twelve traditions*. New York: Alcoholics Anonymous World Services.

Alexander, B. K. (1988). The disease and adaptive models of addiction: A framework evaluation. In S. Peele (Ed.), *Visions of addiction: Major contemporary perspectives on addiction and alcoholism*. Lexington, MA: D. C. Heath.

American Psychiatric Association. (1994). *Diagnostic and statistical manual of mental disorders* (4th ed.). Washington, DC: Author.

Babor, T. F. (1993). Megatrends and dead ends. *Alcohol, Health and Research World, 17*(3), 177–186.

Bohman, M., Cloninger, C. R., von Knorring, A. L., & Sigvardsson, S. (1984). An adoption study of somatoform: III. Cross-fostering analysis and genetic relation to alcoholism and criminality. *Archives of General Psychiatry, 41,* 872–879.

Bohman, M., Sigvardsson, S., & Cloninger, C. R. (1981). Maternal inheritance of alcohol abuse: Cross-fostering analysis of adopted women. *Archives of General Psychiatry, 38,* 965–969.

Caetano, R. (1987). Public opinions about alcoholism and its treatment. *Journal of Studies on Alcohol, 48,* 153–160.

Cloninger, C. R. (1983). Genetic and environmental factors in the development of alcoholism. *Journal of Psychiatric Treatment and Evaluation, 5*(6), 487–496.

Cloninger, C. R., Bohman, M., & Sigvardsson, S. (1981). Inheritance of alcohol abuse: Cross-fostering analysis of adopted men. *Archives of General Psychiatry, 38,* 861–868.

Crabbe, J. C., McSwigan, J. D., & Belknap, J. K. (1985). The role of genetics in substance abuse. In M. Galizio & S. A. Maisto (Eds.), *Determinants of substance abuse.* New York: Plenum.

Daley, D. C., & Raskin, M. S. (1991). Relapse prevention and treatment effectiveness studies. In D. C. Daley and M. S. Raskin (Eds.), *Treating the chemically dependent and their families.* Newbury Park, CA: Sage.

Fillmore, K. M., Hartka, E., Johnstone, B. M., Leino, E. V., Motoyoshi, M., & Temple, M. T. (1991). A meta-analysis of life course variation in drinking: The collaborative alcohol-related longitudinal project. *British Journal of Addiction, 86,* 1221–1268.

Fingarette, H. (1988). *Heavy drinking: The myth of alcoholism as disease.* Berkeley and Los Angeles: University of California Press.

George, R. L. (1990). *Counseling the chemically dependent: Theory and practice.* Englewood Cliffs, NJ: Prentice-Hall.

Gordis, E. (1991). Linking research with practice. *Alcohol, Health, and Research World, 15,* 173–174.

Grant, B. F., Harford, T. C., Chow, P., Pickering, R., Dawson, D., Stinson, F. I., & Noble, J. (1991). Prevalence of DSM III-R alcohol abuse and dependence— United States, 1988. *Alcohol, Health, and Research World, 15*(1), 91–96.

Heather, N., & Robertson, I. (1983). *Controlled drinking.* London: Methuen.

Institute of Medicine. (1990). *Broadening the base of treatment for alcohol problems.* Washington, DC: National Academy Press.

Jaffe, J. H. (1993). The concept of dependence: Historical reflections. *Alcohol, Health and Research World, 17*(3), 188–189.

Jellinek, E. M. (1960). *The disease concept of alcoholism.* Schenectady, NY: New College and University Press.

Johnson, V. E. (1980). *I'll quit tomorrow* (rev. ed.). San Francisco: Harper & Row.

Jung, J. (1994). *Under the influence: Alcohol and human behavior.* Pacific Grove, CA: Brooks/Cole.

Kaminer, W. (1992). *I'm dysfunctional, you're dysfunctional: The recovery movement and other self-help fashions.* Reading, MA: Addison-Wesley.

Kendler, K., Heath, A. C., Neale, N. C., Kessler, R. C., & Eaves, L. J. (1992). A population-based twin study of alcoholism in women. *Journal of the American Medical Association, 268,* 1877–1882.

Kinney, J., & Leaton, G. (1987). *Loosening the grip: A handbook of alcohol information.* St. Louis: Times Mirror/Mosby.

Lester, D. (1988). Genetic theory: An assessment of the heritability of alcoholism. In C. D. Chaudron & D. A. Wilkinson (Eds.), *Theories on alcoholism.* Toronto: Addiction Research Foundation.

Marion, T. R., & Coleman, K. (1991). Recovery issues and treatment resources. In D. C. Daley & M. S. Raskin (Eds.), *Treating the chemically dependent and their families.* Newbury Park, CA: Sage.

Marlatt, G. A., Demming, B., & Reid, J. B. (1973). Loss of control drinking in alcoholics: An experimental analogue. *Journal of Abnormal Psychology, 81,* 233–241.

Marlatt, G. A., & Gordon, J. R. (Eds.). (1985). *Relapse prevention*. New York: Guilford Press.

Massella, J. D. (1991). Intervention: Breaking the addiction cycle. In D. C. Daley & M. S. Raskin (Eds.), *Treating the chemically dependent and their families*. Newbury Park, CA: Sage.

McGue, M., Pickens, R. W., & Svikis, D. S. (1992). Sex and age effects on the inheritance of alcohol problems: A twin study. *Journal of Abnormal Psychology, 101*(1), 3–17.

Milam, J. R., & Ketcham, K. (1983). *Under the influence: A guide to the myths and realities of alcoholism*. New York: Bantam.

Miller, W. R. (1982). Treating problem drinkers: What works. *The Behavior Therapist, 5*, 15–19.

Moos, R. H., Finney, J. W., & Cronkhite, R. C. (1990). *Alcoholism treatment: Context, process, and outcome*. New York: Oxford University Press.

National Institute on Alcohol Abuse and Alcoholism. (1993). *Alcohol and health: Eighth special report to the U.S. Congress* (NIH Publication No. 94–3699). Alexandria, VA: EEI.

Nunes, E. V., & Klein, D. F. (1987). Research issues in cocaine abuse: Future directions. In H. I. Spity & J. S. Rosecan (Eds.), *Cocaine abuse: New directions in treatment and research*. New York: Brunner/Mazel.

Peele, S. (1985). *The meaning of addiction: Compulsive experience and its interpretation*. Lexington, MA: D. C. Heath.

Peele, S. (1989). *Diseasing of America: Addiction treatment out of control*. Lexington, MA: Lexington Books.

Pendery, M. L., Maltzman, I. M., & West, L. J. (1982). Controlled drinking by alcoholics?: New findings and reevaluation of a major affirmative study. *Science, 217*, 169–174.

Pickens, R. W., Svikis, D. S., McGue, M., Lykken, D. T., Hesten, L. L., & Clayton, P. J. (1991). Heterogeneity in the inheritance of alcoholism. *Archives of General Psychiatry, 48*(1), 19–28.

Ray, O., & Ksir, C. (1996). *Drugs, society and human behavior* (7th ed.). St. Louis: Mosby-Year Book.

Sobell, M. B., & Sobell, L. C. (1976). Second year treatment outcome of alcoholics tested by individualized behavior therapy: Results. *Behaviours Research and Therapy, 14*, 195–215.

Sobell, M. B., & Sobell, L. C. (1987). Conceptual issues regarding goals in the treatment of alcohol problems. In M. B. Sobell & L. C. Sobell (Eds.), *Moderation as a goal or outcome of treatment for alcohol problems: A dialogue*. New York: Haworth Press.

Sournia, J. C. (1990). *A history of alcoholism*. Oxford: Basil Blackwell.

Talbott, G. D. (1989). Alcoholism should be treated as a disease. In B. Leone (Ed.), *Chemical dependency: Opposing viewpoints*. San Diego: Greenhaven.

Van De Graaff, K. M., & Fox, S. I. (1986). *Concepts of human anatomy and physiology*. Dubuque, IA: W. C. Brown.

4

Alternative Theories of Substance Abuse: Implications for Understanding Substance Abuse and Dependence in College Students

John E. Calamari and W. Miles Cox

Substance abuse and dependence is now one of the most frequently occurring adjustment disorders in adolescents, young adults, and the general population. In fact, substance use disorders are the most prevalent form of psychiatric disorder in the United States (Meyers et al., 1984). Although all age groups are affected by this pervasive difficulty, adolescents and young adults are particularly heavily affected. A substantial proportion of the adolescent population uses drugs or alcohol to the extent that their health, interpersonal relationships, or school performance is adversely affected (Johnston, O'Malley, & Bachman, 1985, cited in Bray & Krinsley, 1990).

The impact on society of this epidemic of alcohol and other drug abuse and dependence is striking. The economic consequences of substance use disorders, reflected by decreases in productivity, associated unemployment, and increases in criminal justice system expenses—to name just a few effects—have been estimated to be more than $100 billion annually in the United States (Johnson & McCown, 1993). Some people working in the field of alcohol and drug rehabilitation argue, though, that specification of the more concrete economic costs of the substance use disorders distracts from appreciation of their most tragic consequences—the resulting personal suffering of millions of individuals and their families. These more personal consequences are dramatically seen in the young adult who develops one of these disorders. In such cases, a talented, intellectually gifted, and socially concerned young person might become alarmingly transformed into a different kind of individual. The development of a substance use disorder is the antecedent to some young adults' academic failure, is a precipitant of other psychiatric conditions that often co-occur with substance use problems (e.g., depressive and anxiety disorders), and might lead to social isolation and despair. Some young adults' substance abuse can even be fatal. Fatalities can occur, for example, through substance-related accidents or as a result of overdoses of the drugs themselves. The potentially life-threatening nature of substance abuse is dramatically illustrated by the tragic death of Len Bias, a young adult with a promising future career in professional athletics.

The scope and significance of substance abuse and dependence, particularly when occurring at the important developmental stage of young adulthood, dictate that societal resources—including those directed at active scientific research—be aimed at understanding and ameliorating these problems.[1] In fact, the research of social and biological scientists who have studied addictive behaviors during the past three decades has provided the catalyst for the development of the alternative models and theories of substance use and abuse that we will describe.

Our major aim in this chapter is to review alternatives to the classic disease model of alcohol and other drug abuse problems. Throughout the chapter we compare and contrast the disease model (e.g., Jellinek, 1952) with alternative views of the complex phenomena of alcohol and other drug abuse and dependence. We use the term "disease model" to refer to a compilation of theories and associated interventions that originated from Jellinek's ideas and which today are exemplified by the Alcoholics Anonymous program (Alcoholics Anonymous, 1939, 1955, 1976), an intervention model that is often referred to as the twelve-step treatment program. We attempt to highlight the differences between the classic disease model and alternative theories through a case vignette. Although the case that we describe is fictitious, it represents a composite of our own experiences with college students with substance abuse and dependence problems. Before introducing this case, we examine some of the precipitants for the development of alternative views of substance abuse and dependence.

CATALYSTS FOR THE DEVELOPMENT
OF ALTERNATIVE MODELS

The magnitude of psychoactive substance use problems in contemporary society, and the use of psychoactive substances throughout recorded history (cf. Cox & Calamari, in press) would imply that these phenomena have been the focus of scientific scrutiny for a long time. In point of fact, it has only been relatively recently that these problems have been scientifically evaluated. Historically, substance use problems have been characterized as moral or legal issues (cf. Cox, 1987a; Johnson & McCown, 1993) which were regarded as outside the domain of mental health professionals and best left to religious and political authorities to deal with. Other factors have also helped to slow the involvement of medical and social scientists. There appears to have been a widely held belief in clinical psychology and psychiatry that traditional psychotherapeutic interventions were unlikely to be effective with substance-dependent people (Miller & Rollnick, 1991). Substance abusers' recalcitrance to standard psychotherapies was thought to result from their entrenched defensive reactions (e.g., denial and rationalization), and distinctive personality, especially antisocial features (Miller & Rollnick, 1991). However, extensive research has failed to identify a clearly defined addictive personality (Nathan, 1993). Particular personality characteristics do appear to act as one of the mediators in people's susceptibility to develop addictive disorders (Cox & Klinger, 1988, 1990), but a number of different personality typologies have been identified among alcoholics and other substance abusers (see Cox, 1987a, 1988; Johnson & McCown, 1993). Nevertheless, the widely held belief that substance abusers are generally unresponsive to treatment because of their unique personality characteristics has done little to promote research and treatment innovations. Further, excessive alcohol or other drug abuse has historically been conceptualized by some theorists as a surface symptom of more fundamental psychological difficulties (cf. Nathan, 1993, p. 467). Hence, clinicians would target the processes assumed to underlie drug and alcohol overuse (e.g., unconscious intrapsychic conflict), approaching the problem in a manner very similar to their treatment of a broad range of adjustment difficulties. Although alternative theorists highly value determination of underlying motivation to abuse substances (e.g., drinking to reduce high levels of social anxiety), the unique characteristics of substance use problems are understood to require a disorder-specific intervention. Failure to develop and apply a treatment for substance abuse problems which directly addresses the unique behavioral, cognitive, and physiological dimensions of these disorders has led to treatment failure in the past and has contributed to the belief that substance use disorders are unresponsive to psychological interventions.

The magnitude of substance abuse and dependence problems has necessitated that working models and treatment strategies be developed. However, because clinical needs predated most of the empirical work in this area, the traditional disease model and associated interventions have come to dominate the field, even though the model is not based on scientific research. Sobell and Sobell (1993) recently concluded that treatment interventions for alcohol use problems have developed in the relative absence of scientific knowledge. They further suggested that new results from addictive-behaviors research are frequently ignored by many practitioners if these findings are incompatible with their conceptualization of substance use problems. Thus, there is a rigid adherence to traditional theories and interventions among some groups that work in the addictive-behaviors field. Such dogmatism is quite different from other areas of medicine, psychiatry, and clinical psychology, where research findings often serve to precipitate relatively rapid and significant changes in clinical practice.

The result of this state of affairs is that the Minnesota Model, a twenty-eight-day inpatient treatment program based largely on the disease model of substance abuse, is the most widely used intervention in the United States today (Cook, 1988a, 1988b; cited by Sobell & Sobell, 1993). Can such extensive use of this expensive and intrusive treatment be justified given what we know about substance use disorders today? This chapter will briefly outline some of the major tenents of the disease model and discuss the support or refutation that scientific studies have provided. Before doing so, however, we present a case example of problematic alcohol use involving a college freshman. We then integrate information contained in this case example into our discussion of the disease model, the scientific findings related to it, and the development of alternative models and theories of substance abuse and dependence.

Substance Abuse of a Young Adult

Gerald Franklin enrolled as a freshman at a state university during the fall term. He was nineteen years old at the time and this was the first time that he had lived away from his middle-class family. Although Gerald had generally regarded his parents' restrictions on his behavior as reasonable, he anticipated with great pleasure the new freedom that his independent living would bring.

The relatively unrestricted living that Gerald's dormitory provided led to some significant changes in his behavior. With no one to question his whereabouts, he often stayed out very late during his first few months at college. This new routine, which he and his peers called "partying," was carried out primarily with three of his new friends from the dormitory, including his roommate Mark. The partying activities centered around going to popular local nightclubs to dance, attempting to meet women, and drinking large quantities of beer. Although Gerald, Mark, and another one of their friends were younger than the legal drinking age, they purchased false driver's licenses from an upperclassman for $50 each. Gerald was initially reluctant to spend this amount of money from his tight budget, but he was assured by his peers that this was a good (if not essential) investment for a person starting college.

Gerald's late nights and frequent heavy drinking (which sometimes involved consuming as many as fifteen 8-oz glasses of beer) strongly interfered with morning classes. Because there were no immediate contingencies for missing large morning lectures, by the sixth week of the semester Gerald had developed a pattern of missing most of his morning classes each week. Moreover, missing classes and his late nights and social activities had a negative impact on his study time, leaving Gerald significantly behind in many of his classes by the midterm. Although Gerald had graduated in the upper 20 percent of his high school class with relatively little effort, midterm exams at the university did not go well for him. He failed two of his five exams and received a grade of D on a third. These poor grades were shocking to Gerald and precipitated immediate changes in his typically gregarious and energetic personality, including the development of a mild depression. Gerald's friends, including Mark (who had fared only slightly better than Gerald on the midterms) were empathetic and supportive, but could offer only one concrete recommendation to Gerald for coping with the situation and his negative affect, namely, to go out and "get wasted."

When the phone rang at 9:30 A.M. the next morning, Mark groggily answered on the sixth ring. When the caller identified himself as John Franklin (Gerald's father), this had a sobering effect on Mark. When John asked if he could speak with Gerald, Mark immediately tried to awaken him, but Gerald responded by grumbling unintelligibly and putting his pillow over his head. Mark then tried tactfully to explain that Gerald was "under the weather" this morning and could not come to the phone. This information worried John Franklin, who requested that Gerald call him later that day at his office. John Franklin's call had been precipitated by the notice of failing classes that had been sent to Gerald's home address the previous day and that he and his wife had opened.

Gerald did not return his father's call until that evening. He felt he needed the day to clear his head and to muster the fortitude to explain the condition he was in when his father had called. During the phone conversation, Gerald's father and mother both expressed great concern about Gerald's condition that morning and his failing grades. Lacking a creative explanation for his unavailability earlier that morning, Gerald confessed that he had been out the night before and had "a few beers."

John and Mary Franklin decided to make the three-hour drive to the university the following weekend to determine what was going on with their son. Needless to say, Gerald did not look forward to his parents' visit. He became more anxious following their call, and although he had attended all his classes during the remainder of the week, his inability to concentrate during classes served only to intensify his distress. He felt hopelessly lost and behind. These feelings were a major catalyst for Gerald's going out yet again to drink with his friends that Friday night. When Gerald and his parents met the following Saturday afternoon, Gerald was sober, but he did not look well to his parents. They were most concerned about his visible anxiety and his seemingly hopeless attitude about his ability to improve his academic performance. Gerald was initially very reluctant to share any of the details of his new, problematic lifestyle, but his family's custom of frank discussion of problems and attempts to uncritically identify solutions helped him to be direct and truthful. The prominent role of Gerald's beer drinking in his problematic situation became clear, and this information was particularly distressing to his parents. The Franklins had prior experience with the devastating effects of alcoholism. Approximately ten years earlier, Mary Franklin's younger brother had been diagnosed as alcoholic. Following job loss and the near ruin of his marriage he had agreed to enter an inpatient treatment program. Since his successful completion of the program, Mary's brother has remained totally abstinent. Mary could not help but worry that Gerald had inherited the same disease she had been told her brother had—alcoholism.

Extensive discussions between Gerald and his parents filled the remainder of the weekend. They agreed that Gerald would make an appointment at the university counseling center the following Monday to seek help for his excessive drinking and his academic difficulties.

How can we best understand Gerald's problems? Had he, in fact, inherited the disease alcoholism, for which the rational response would be (from the perspective of the traditional disease model) total abstinence from the use of alcohol? How likely would it be for Gerald to succeed if his goal became never to drink alcohol again, and what would it mean if he sometimes deviated from this goal and went out to drink with his friends? In that event, what would the appropriate intervention be? We now address these and related issues as we discuss the limitations of the classic disease model of alcoholism and explore the alternative views of substance use problems.

Limitations of the Disease Model

Explaining abnormal behavior and psychiatric syndromes as analogous to physical diseases has been a popular approach, but one that has been recognized as having serious limitations (cf. Adams & Cassidy, 1993). In traditional conceptualizations of diseases, underlying physiological causes (for example, bacteria or viruses) are assumed to have caused the condition, though for many diseases the responsible physiological agent has yet to be identified. In fact, specific biological etiologies have not been discovered for most types of psychiatric disorders. In some cases where biological mechanisms have been found to play an important role in the development of a disorder, they are not considered sufficient to fully explain the etiology and maintenance of the condition. Various psychological mechanisms have also been found to play important causative roles in many forms of abnormal behavior. In the case of substance use problems in particular, biological mechanisms are today viewed as important in the development of the disorders (e.g., see the section on biological factors such as the role genetics plays in alcoholism), but substance use disorders are now widely believed to have multiple determinants (cf. Cox & Klinger, 1988, 1990; Johnson & McCown, 1993). If substance use problems are going to be seen as analogous to a disease processes, the comparison would best be made with medical conditions such as adult onset diabetes or cardiovascular disease, where lifestyle and stress are understood to play an etiologic role (cf. Gatchel, Baun, & Krantz, 1989).

Let us now return to Gerald's case and the questions that his excessive drinking raised. His behavior would most likely be viewed by proponents of the disease model of alcoholism as symptomatic of a condition that would inevitably become worse with time. Support for the contention that Gerald has the disease alcoholism would be garnered from his positive family history for alcohol problems, since the disease model views alcoholism as a largely genetically driven, progressive disease (e.g., Jellinek, 1952, 1960). Proponents of the classic model maintain that whenever individuals with the disease use any alcohol, they lose control over the amount of alcohol that they consume and their excessive consumption eventually produces physical health problems. These multiple negative outcomes eventually lead to a generally ruinous effect on the individual's life. This belief emerged from a series of uncontrolled studies conducted by Jellinek (1952), in which a sample of male alcoholics were followed over time and appeared to inevitably deteriorate to a "skid-row" type of existence. But, as Sobell and Sobell (1993) have pointed out, the suggestion that all substance use problems are inevitably progressive lacks empirical support. A series of studies (e.g., Cahalan, 1970; Fillmore, 1988; Roizen, Cahalan, & Shanks, 1978) have shown that problematic drinkers do not necessarily progress to severe alcohol dependence and the presumed calamitous life situations associated with excessive alcohol use. The lack of progressive deterioration seen in many problem drinkers has been a major force behind the continued distinction in psychiatric taxonomy (e.g., DSM IV [American Psychiatric Association, 1994]) between substance abuse, a less severe condition, and substance dependence, a more severe condition (Nathan, 1991).

The diagnostic distinction between alcohol abuse and alcohol dependence has implications for Gerald's treatment, as well as for the conceptualization and treatment of substance use disorders in general. In the classic disease model, individuals are dichotomized; they either have the disease or they do not. Other theorists have suggested that alcohol problems can better be understood as points on a continuum of alcohol use. The continuum ranges from abstinence to nonproblematic use to different types and degrees of problematic use (e.g., Cox & Klinger, 1988, 1990; McCrady, 1993; Sobell & Sobell, 1993). Thus, these alternative theorists contend that alcohol use problems may be exhibited in a variety of forms and a broad range of levels of severity. Further, research suggests that problem drinkers constitute a much larger group than severely dependent drinkers (Institute of Medicine, 1990), and recent research findings support the position that the former may be responsive to a broad range of interventions (for reviews of this issue, see Cox 1987b; Miller & Rollnick, 1991; Sobell & Sobell, 1993).

If Gerald's situation is viewed as a manifestation of alcohol abuse—a point on the alcohol use continuum where drinking has begun to cause serious life disruption but has not progressed to the level of near complete disability associated with alcohol dependence—numerous minimally intrusive, short-term, and potentially quite effective interventions could be applied. Among the treatment options available to clinicians would be short-duration motivational interviewing, which uses a structured counseling approach to help the substance abuser mobilize personal resources needed to change his or her behavior (Miller & Rollnick, 1991). Another short-duration intervention was devised by Sobell and Sobell (1993). In their Guided Self-Change Treatment (GSCT), two or three sessions designed to modify problematic cognitions and behaviors are used to analyze problematic drinking patterns, identify more effective coping procedures, and increase client motivation. A more extensive procedure for altering motivational patterns, Systematic Motivational Counseling (SMC; Cox & Klinger, 1988, 1990; Cox, Klinger, & Blount, 1996), which involves a detailed analysis of the individual's motivational structure, has been used both with substance abusers and severely dependent persons. We discuss Sobell and Sobell's (1993) Guided Self-Change intervention and Cox et al.'s (1995) Systematic Motivational Counseling at greater length later in this chapter. All of these procedures could be delivered in a university counseling center to alter abusive drinking behavior typified in our description of Gerald. Each of these treatment approaches has achieved some degree of empirical support for its efficacy, with further scientific studies ongoing.

Harm Reduction

Such alternative views and treatment approaches to substance use disorders make it necessary to consider a broader range of intervention goals. In the classic disease model, complete abstinence is considered the only viable goal for the alcoholic (cf. Alcoholics Anonymous, 1939, 1955, 1976). Other clinicians consider controlled drinking as a reasonable objective for some problem drinkers, seeing this goal as more compatible with problem drinkers' own preferences and one that is more likely for them to actually realize (e.g., Miller & Rollnick, 1991; Sobell & Sobell, 1993). Within the framework of such alternative treatments, any movement of the substance abuser from more to less problematic substance use is understood as important and is encouraged. This position has been depicted as "harm reduction," where any action taken to promote movement from greater to less harmful alcohol or other drug use is actively encouraged and supported (Marlatt, Larimer, Baer, & Quigley, 1993). As Marlatt and colleagues (1993) have described, the harm-reduction model differs from the disease model in its understanding of substance abuse problems as varying along a continuum and in the acceptance of controlled drinking as a possible treatment goal for the substance abuser. In the harm-reduction model, interventions are customized to be congruent with the level of problematic substance use observed. Primary prevention programs would be directed at individuals not presently involved in substance abuse, brief interventions would be structured for mild or moderate substance abusers, and specialized treatment, including intensive inpatient treatment, would be considered for persons with the most severe substance use problems. Further, the harm-reduction approach is not limited to individual clinical or self-management training procedures. Changes designed to reduce harm in the physical or social environment (e.g., more careful verification of student identifications at university community bars) and changes in public policy (e.g., discontinuation of liquor-company sponsorship of university events) are also considered important elements in a comprehensive approach to substance use problems. The harm-reduction model may have great relevance to the university community, where intervention resources are limited and student tolerance for interventions is finite, but a substantial problem still exists.

Applying the harm-reduction model to Gerald's situation could result in supporting efforts to limit his "partying" and associated beer drinking to Friday and Saturday nights (assuming Gerald's unwillingness to comply with the law as he is younger than the legal drinking age, and assuming that there are no specific contraindications for continued—albeit reduced—drinking, such as specific medical problems). Other intervention options for Gerald might include changing environments (e.g., a new roommate with a better track record of academic performance or movement out of a freshman dorm to a setting more supportive of academic pursuits). Attempts would be made during the intervention to precipitate Gerald's use of his existing motivational resources to accomplish a specific behavioral change that he himself chose. If functional analysis of his behavior identified specific circumstances that maintained his alcohol use (e.g., coping-skill deficits, anxiety or other mood-related problems) specific skills might be taught or coping deficits rectified as components of the treatment.

Possibly the greatest advantage of the alternative treatments for ameliorating the substance use problems of young adults attempting to progress through demanding college curricula is the substantial flexibility that these treatments offer. A number of studies (e.g., Edwards et al., 1977; Orford, Oppenheimer, & Edwards, 1976) have demonstrated that even brief counseling sessions for the purpose of giving advice about changing problematic drinking can have utility in precipitating behavioral changes in some problem drinkers or other drug abusers. Although short-duration, outpatient treatment will not be sufficient for every college student with a substance use problem, motivational enhancement interventions should be relevant for the majority of these young adults.

The burgeoning empirical approach to substance use disorders has prompted a major research effort to identify factors leading to the best match between substance abuse problems and specific treatments in an effort to maximize positive outcomes (Miller, 1992). This investigation, "Project Match," is being conducted at multiple sites throughout the United States and is the most extensive evaluation of psychosocial treatments for alcohol abuse and dependence ever to be undertaken. The goal of the project is to determine which of three treatments—a disease-model intervention (cf. Cook, 1988a); an approach designed to change cognitions and behaviors that have an impact on drinking (cf. Monti, Abrams, Kadden, & Cooney, 1989); and a motivational enhancement therapy (cf. Miller & Rollnick, 1991)—works best with which kinds of individuals (Miller, 1992). It is hoped that the results of this study will provide guidance for clinicians attempting to identify the most effective intervention for particular persons with alcohol use problems.

Gerald Franklin developed a drinking problem during his first semester at his university. His adjustment difficulties obviously went well beyond the home-to-school transition that all students must make. Excessive drinking was certainly a significant component of Gerald's problems and is something that needs to be addressed. But as we have suggested, conceptualizing Gerald's problem as alcoholism, a progressive disease process, and insisting on intrusive and expensive inpatient treatment, would not be congruent with the scientific knowledge that we have about alcohol and other drug use problems. We now explore in greater depth the research findings related to the alternative models that we have presented, and describe some of the theories which have emerged from this research. First, though, we briefly present the contemporary definitions of substance use problems. These problems are understood by nonadherents of the disease model as highly complex and caused by the interaction of a multitude of factors.

SUBSTANCE USE PROBLEMS DEFINED

The classic disease model emphasizes the role of biological factors in the etiology of substance use disorders. Tolerance and withdrawal symptoms are emphasized in such definitions. Tolerance is generally understood as a physiological process whereby greater amounts of psychoactive drugs are required to produce the same effect that was previously produced by a smaller amount. Withdrawal reactions consist of adverse physiological and psychological symptoms that develop when the use of a drug is suddenly reduced or discontinued altogether. Some theorists argue, though, that an exclusive emphasis on these processes does not do justice to the recognized cognitive and behavioral changes associated with substance use problems. Included among these changes are a growing preoccupation with obtaining the drug, associated vocational dysfunction, and social and behavioral changes that often disrupt the family and leave the individual progressively more socially isolated (cf. Johnson & McCown, 1993).

The current American Psychiatric Association definition of substance abuse is:

A. A maladaptive pattern of substance use which leads to a clinically significant impairment or distress as manifested by one or more of the following occurring within the same twelve-month period:

 1. Recurrent substance use resulting in a failure to fulfill major role obligations at work, school, or home (e.g., repeated absences or poor work performance related to substance use; substance-related absences, suspicions, or expulsions from school; neglect of children or household)

 2. Recurrent substance use in situations in which it is physically hazardous (e.g., driving an automobile or operating a machine when impaired by substance use)

 3. Recurrent substance-related legal problems (e.g., arrests for substance-related disorderly conduct)

4. Continued substance use despite having persistent or recurrent social or inter-personal problems caused or exacerbated by the effects of the substance (e.g., arguments with spouse about consequences of intoxication, physical fights)

B. Has never met the criteria for Substance Dependence for this class of substance. (American Psychiatric Association, 1994)

The American Psychiatric Association definition of substance dependence is

A. A maladaptive pattern of substance use, leading to clinically significant impairment or distress, as manifested by three (or more) of the following occurring at any time in the same twelve-month period:

1. Tolerance, as defined by either of the following: (a) need for markedly increased amounts of the substance to achieve intoxication or desired effect; (b) markedly diminished effect with continued use of the same amount of the substance

2. Withdrawal, as manifested by either of the following: (a) the characteristic withdrawal syndrome for the substance; (b) the same (or a closely related) substance is taken to relieve or avoid withdrawal symptoms

3. The substance is often taken in larger amounts or over a longer period than was intended

4. A persistent desire or unsuccessful efforts to cut down or control substance use

5. A great deal of time is spent on activities necessary to obtain the substance (e.g., visiting multiple doctors or driving long distances), use of the substance (e.g., chain smoking), or recovering from its effects

6. Important social, occupational, or recreational activities are given up or reduced because of substance use

7. Substance use is continued despite knowledge of having a persistent or recurrent physical or psychological problem that was likely to have been caused or exacerbated by the substance (e.g., current cocaine use despite recognition of cocaine-induced depression, or continued drinking despite recognition that an ulcer was made worse by alcohol consumption). (American Psychiatric Association, 1994)

The clinician is asked to specify if the substance dependence is with or without Physiological Dependence (evidence of tolerance or withdrawal as defined in criterion 1 or 2).

Substance abuse is defined as alcohol or other drug use to the extent that the person is frequently intoxicated, fails to meet important life obligations, and engages in dangerous behaviors while intoxicated, such as driving an automobile. Symptoms of tolerance and withdrawal are *not* defining characteristics of substance abuse. Substance dependence involves additional—and usually more severe—symptoms. Marked tolerance or substantial withdrawal reactions are frequently associated with substance dependence.

Review of the two sets of diagnostic criteria suggests that Gerald's problem would best be diagnosed as substance abuse. As we have previously suggested, clinicians adhering to the alternative theories that we have described would advocate multiple intervention options for approaching Gerald's drinking problem. His treatment could be structured to be minimally intrusive so as to allow him to continue his studies at the university. We now explore the empirical support for this position.

THE EMPIRICAL FOUNDATIONS
OF ALTERNATIVE THEORIES

Biological Factors

We have pointed out that in the classic disease model substance use problems are viewed as a progressive disease process, but that this position is not generally congruent with empirical findings. Nonetheless, a body of data does exist supporting hypotheses that biological factors do, in fact, play a role in the development of substance use problems. Nathan (1993) has recently reviewed the role that genetic mechanisms may play in the development of alcohol use disorders. One of the larger and more important studies was conducted with a sample of Danish alcoholics (Goodwin, Schulsinger, & Molter, 1974). These researchers found that the sons of alcoholics were four times as likely to be alcoholic as the sons of a matched group of nonalcoholics, regardless of whether these individuals had been reared by their biological parents. Other genetic studies have suggested that there are two genetically driven alcoholic subtypes that differ in the manner in which the disorder is inherited (e.g., Bohman, Sigvardsson, & Cloninger, 1981; Cloninger, Bohman, & Sigvardsson, 1981). Type I alcoholism is characterized by later development of the disorder, a high risk of alcohol-related medical problems, and low rates of antisocial behavior and social and occupational problems. The children of Type I alcoholics were found to be twice as likely to develop alcohol dependence as the children of nonalcoholics. Type II alcoholics are characterized by significant social problems, fewer medical problems, and an earlier onset of the disorder than in Type I alcoholics. The risk of alcohol dependence in the sons of these individuals was found to be nine times that of the nonalcoholics. In addition, Bohman and colleagues (1981) found that the daughters of alcoholic mothers, although adopted by nonrelatives at an early age, were three times more likely to be alcohol abusers. Despite this evidence, Searles (1988), in a review of this and other genetic research on alcoholism, suggested that these studies are methodologically flawed and that the conclusions drawn by their authors should be tempered.

Another biological factor that may be related to the development of alcohol problems involves individual differences in how people metabolize alcohol. As Goodwin (1979) pointed out, to develop alcoholism a person must be able to consume large quantities of alcohol. Observed ethnic differences in the rates at which alcohol is metabolized and the associated differences in rates of consumption appear to support this hypothesis. For example, as a consequence of deficient amounts of the enzyme necessary to metabolize alcohol, aldehyde dehydrogenase, Asians have a low physiological tolerance for alcohol and concomitant low rates of alcoholism. When the sons of individuals with extensive alcohol abuse histories are compared to males without a family history of alcoholism, a number of important physiological differences in response to alcohol ingestion are seen. Levels of two hormones, cortisol and prolactin, reliably change when people drink alcohol, but these changes are significantly smaller in the sons of alcoholics (Schuckit & Gold, 1988). Further, the sons alcoholics were found in this study to feel less intoxicated following consumption of a set amount of alcohol and demonstrated less motor-behavior disturbance in comparison to a control group without a positive family history.

Individual differences in concentrations of specific brain neurotransmitters (chemicals that control the activation of neurons in the central nervous system) have also been suggested as a biological mechanism that may help to account for individual variability in alcohol and other drug consumption. Kranzler and Anton (1994) have recently reviewed the role various neurotransmitters play in the consumption of alcohol. To date, the neurotransmitter serotonin and a class of neurotransmitters known as endorphins (endogenous opiate-like substances) have been the most extensively implicated. Further, Kranzler and Anton suggested that the effects serotonin and endorphin deregulation have on drinking may be mediated by a third neurotransmitter system involving dopamine. This system is thought to play a fundamental role in the experience of pleasure. Elucidation of the neurochemical basis of substance dependence may eventually lead to broadly effective pharmacological treatment of alcoholism and other drug problems (Kranzler & Anton, 1994).

Thus, a number of biological processes are implicated in the development or maintenance of substance use problems. These findings suggest that some individuals will be more or less likely to develop these disorders, regardless of life experiences. Although the evidence supporting an important role for biological mechanisms is compelling, these findings do not necessarily support the contention that these disorders are best understood as a progressive disease process. Identification of biological etiologic mechanisms does not suggest that individuals can be neatly dichotomized as having or not having a disease, and that those with the problem will inevitably deteriorate if they attempt moderate substance use. As has been suggested regarding abnormal behavior generally, a broad range of social learning experiences and other environmental factors will interact with vulnerability to produce substance use problems only in some people (cf. Zubin & Spring, 1977). Appreciation of this complex interaction between etiologic mechanisms sets the stage for a much broader and flexible approach to treatment intervention.

Psychosocial Mechanisms

Learning mechanisms that are seen as broadly influencing behavior have been hypothesized to play an important role in the development and maintenance of substance use problems. Attempts have been made to understand drug use as behavior maintained by environmental consequences (cf. Johnson & McCown, 1993). Psychoactive substance use is understood as sometimes developing or continuing as a result of drug-produced reductions in negative affective states. Thus, pathological substance use may be motivated by tension or distress reduction, or the modulation of anxiety and depression (cf. Nathan, 1993). Further, Vuchinich and Tucker (1988) posit that alcohol consumption will emerge as a highly preferred activity under environmental conditions where there are minimal constraints on access to alcohol and sparse alternative reinforcers. They contend that the availability of alternative reinforcers and the cost associated with gaining access to them has a major influence on drinking in the natural environment.

Recently, emphasis has been placed on the role that cognitive factors may play in the development of alcohol and other drug use disorders, and in the propensity of substance abusers to repeat patterns of problematic drinking or drug use following periods of improved control (e.g., Goldman, Brown, & Christiansen, 1987; Marlatt, 1985). The role of an individual's expectations regarding the effects of alcohol and other drug use is emphasized in these models, and expectancy effects are seen as often exerting a more powerful influence on behavior than the pharmacological properties of a drug (cf. Annis & Davis, 1988). Studies have shown that subjects' anticipation of substance-induced effects (e.g., enhanced positive affect, reduced negative affect, increased social interaction or interpersonal intimacy, sexual arousal, or reduced levels of tension) are strong determinants of actual experiences (Donovan, 1988). Further, expectancies are seen to play a critical role in mediating needed behavioral changes in substance abusers. The motivational construct self-efficacy (Bandura, 1977, 1978) has been used to explain the importance of cognitive factors to the ability of an individual to correct a substance use problem. Efficacy expectation has been defined as the judgment that one has the ability to execute a certain behavior pattern (Annis & Davis, 1988). Any treatment procedure is understood to be effective only to the extent that it increases expectations of personal efficacy, and the strength of an individual's efficacy expectations determines the nature of coping behavior employed and how long such behavior will be maintained when obstacles arise (Annis & Davis, 1988). The general aim of treatment, therefore, is to increase the client's self-efficacy, with emphasis placed on high-risk situations for problematic drinking or drug use. Although cognitive mechanisms mediate behavioral changes according to this model, the most powerful method for changing self-efficacy (and hence drinking or other drug use) is to induce changes in people's actual performance (Annis & Davis, 1988). A preferred treatment strategy is to have the client engage in homework assignments tailored to his or her high-risk situations for relapse. Mastery experiences in these high-risk situations have a powerful impact on the client's appraisal of his or her coping abilities, resulting in an increase in efficacy expectations and a change in drinking behavior (Annis & Davis, 1988).

The Etiology of Gerald's Drinking Problem

It is possible that Gerald inherited a biological predisposition that affects his use of alcohol. How could such a biological mechanism be best understood? We suggest that Gerald's positive family history for alcoholism is most accurately viewed as increasing his vulnerability to develop a drinking problem, but should not be taken as evidence that he inherited a disease that dictates that any use of alcohol on his part will inevitably lead to progressive loss of control and alcoholism. As we began to discuss, some theorists assert that development of an adjustment disorder does not result from the direct inheritance of a particular abnormality. Rather, development of the problem is influenced biologically through inheritance of a predisposition to develop a particular disorder. When this vulnerability interacts with certain environmental conditions, an adjustment problem might develop. Without this interaction between biologically driven vulnerability and environmental circumstances, typically referred to as stressors, the problem does not manifest itself. We suggest that Gerald's positive family history for alcohol use problems could best be understood as a vulnerability factor now interacting with his new life situation rather than as evidence that he had inherited a disease.

What role might psychosocial factors play in the development of Gerald's drinking problem? Beer drinking certainly is encouraged and reinforced in the university social milieu. Alternative reinforcing activities that are incompatible with alcohol consumption (e.g., involvement in intramural athletics) will need to be identified as a component of effective interventions. If specific coping-skill deficits are found to be related to Gerald's drinking, alternative adaptive responses should be identified and taught to him. For example, if Gerald's drinking proves to be related to social anxiety that he experiences at nightclubs and in other settings when he attempts to interact with other people, social skills training and related interventions designed to diminish his social anxiety should become an integral component of his treatment.

In addition, Gerald's post-midterm self-efficacy was quite low. An effective treatment for his problem drinking would need to enhance his feelings of competency and self-worth. An intervention designed to improve Gerald's self-efficacy would likely focus on setting specific, small, achievable goals; for example not going out during the week until he had studied for two hours, and then not drinking more than perhaps four glasses of beer. His small but concrete behavioral changes would be made salient to him and would be the foundation for accomplishing the more pervasive self-control that he needs.

EVOLVING ALTERNATIVE MODELS: PRECIPITANTS TO INTERVENTION

Substance Use as Environmentally Determined

As we have already begun to review, an important force in applied psychology during the past three decades has involved the systematic study of human learning and the application of resultant principles to many different problems. Abnormal behavior is understood as learned in the same manner that all other behavior is acquired. Nathan Azrin has applied the model to a broad array of behavioral disturbances. To deal with alcohol problems in particular, he developed what he has called the community reinforcement approach (Hunt & Azrin, 1973).

The community reinforcement approach involves restructuring problem drinkers' social environment. Family members become actively involved in reinforcing prosocial behaviors, and strive to refrain from any activity which might inadvertently reinforce excessive alcohol use (e.g., making dinner for a drunken spouse who does not return home until one in the morning; Sisson & Azrin, 1993). Taking Antabuse and engaging in adaptive behaviors incompatible with excessive drinking are examples of the behavioral changes that are encouraged. Other behaviors which family members would reinforce include obtaining and maintaining a job, becoming involved in enjoyable social relationships, and assertive communications with other people. Azrin and his associates developed specific procedures to encourage the development and maintenance of these skills, and a series of treatment outcome studies have reported quite favorable results (Hunt & Azrin, 1973; Azrin, 1976; Azrin, Sisson, Meyers, & Godley, 1982; see also the review by Meyers & Smith, 1995).

As we also discussed, a complete understanding of substance use problems can come only from examining environmental contingencies within the context of a person's broader life situation, rather than focusing exclusively on the rewards and costs of drinking or other drug use. Vuchinich and Tucker (1988) summarized the findings of many studies with animal and human subjects, concluding that an increased preference for alcohol develops when access to alternative reinforcers is reduced or delayed. Further, these authors concluded that some individuals drink more alcohol when the cost of gaining access to alternative reinforcers is increased, provided that the cost of drinking remains constant. These findings imply that substance abusers' general lifestyles and the broader environmental contexts in which they drink or use other drugs must be examined to assess the availability of alternative reinforcers. Individuals whose environment have adequate alternative reinforcers and who have the skills necessary to extract these rewards from their environment will be less likely to misuse alcohol or other drugs than will people who do not. Such considerations imply that the broader university community may need to be assessed to assure that adequate alternative reinforcers are easily accessible. Environments that provide many alternative, enjoyable activities that are unrelated to drug use may serve to reduce the magnitude of university students' difficulties with psychoactive substances.

Self-Regulation

Social learning mechanisms appear to play an important role in the development and maintenance of substance use problems. There is growing evidence that cognitive processes also powerfully affect individuals' propensity to excessively use psychoactive substances. Further, a number of cognitive processes have now been identified that may be able to account for how human beings accomplish behavioral changes, and specifically how people are able to ameliorate their problems with substance use. The fundamental question that researchers are attempting to answer is what motivates people to change. Here, motivation is seen not as an enduring personality characteristic; rather, it is a state of readiness or eagerness to change (Miller & Rollnick, 1991). Thus, motivation can vary across time as a function of a variety of influences. Much of the impetus for research in this area has been based on the observation that many people with addictions are able to overcome their problems without the assistance of a therapist or a formal treatment program (Miller & Rollnick, 1991). It is believed that a similar processes is involved regardless of whether the person changes on his or her own or with professional assistance (Miller & Rollnick, 1991).

Stages of Change

A useful model for accounting for the motivation to change an addictive behavior was developed by Prochaska and DiClemente (1982; summarized by Miller & Rollnick, 1991). These authors proposed that when individuals change an addictive behavior they progress through a series of predictable stages: precontemplation, contemplation, determination, action, maintenance, and often relapse. In the precontemplation stage, the individual has not yet recognized that he or she has a problem that needs changing. When people in this stage are told by others that they have a problem, their reaction is typically negative and defensive. However, as people develop an awareness of their problem, they enter the contemplation stage. In this stage, they experience ambivalence, repeatedly considering and then rejecting the decision to change. Nevertheless, if the balance can be shifted in the direction of making a change, the person moves into the determination stage. The individual now acknowledges that there is a problem that requires change, but has not yet identified a strategy for accomplishing this change. Miller and Rollnick suggested that this stage represents a window of opportunity for therapists to help the individual progress to the next stage, action. During the action stage, the individual takes specific steps to alter the acknowledged problem. However, the resulting changes must then be maintained. The model proposes that the processes that initiate behavioral changes and those that maintain the changes can often be quite different. If a relapse occurs, that is, the problem behavior begins to occur again with regularity, the individual must once again pass through at least some of the successive stages. In fact, most changes in addictive behaviors appear not to be accomplished by a single progression through the sequential stages. Rather, there are more typically repeated relapses before the desirable changes become stable.

Determining where the individual is in the change process, then, becomes critically important to how interventions should be structured in order to best precipitate changes (Miller & Rollnick, 1991). For example, attempts to move problem drinkers who are still in the contemplation stage directly into the action stage is likely to be met with resistance and failure. Such people could better be helped by assisting them to identify additional reasons to change their current behavior, additional costs for not doing so, and by helping them to increase their self-efficacy (the belief that they can, in fact, accomplish the behavior that they desire).

Individuals with substance use problems are often aware that their behavior is detrimental, and they sense that changes are needed. Helping them to progress from the contemplation stage to the determination and action stages by assisting them in mobilizing needed motivational resources can be the critical therapeutic task.

TREATMENT INTERVENTIONS BASED
ON ALTERNATIVE THEORIES

We now describe in greater detail two interventions based on alternative theories. An increasing number of such interventions are now available, and the interested reader may want to review Hester and Miller (1995), Miller and Rollnick (1991), or McCrady (1993) as additional examples of treatment approaches based on alternative theories.

The first approach reviewed, Guided Self-Change Treatment, is described in detail in Sobell and Sobell's (1993) treatment manual. The approach is designed for persons meeting diagnostic criteria for substance abuse, is very short term (lasting two sessions), and could be delivered by appropriately trained university counseling center personnel. The collaborative and educational tone of the approach, as well as its short duration, make it an attractive and cost-effective intervention for a university setting, and may foster greater acceptance by students.

We then describe Cox and colleagues' (1996) Systematic Motivational Counseling. This more extensive intervention has been applied with more severe substance abusers, including chronic alcoholics in inpatient settings, though the treatment approach can be applied across the full range of substance abuse problems. Both GSCT and SMC approaches have been and continue to be empirically evaluated and modified.

Guided Self-Change

Sobell and Sobell's (1993) treatment integrates cognitive–behavioral assessment and treatment techniques with structured homework assignments, including systematic self-monitoring and readings about alcohol-related problems. The typical procedure includes just two ninety-minute sessions, though clinicians who use the technique are encouraged to be flexible and provide additional work with clients as judged appropriate. They provided a detailed treatment manual designed for use with early-stage problem drinkers in particular, though the manual can also be used with problem drinkers at various levels of severity.

Sobell and Sobell's intervention begins by familiarizing the client with this cognitive–behavioral approach. Clients are told that they will be expected to use their own resources to resolve their alcohol problems, and that they will be asked to systematically monitor their own alcohol use, read and review handouts that will be provided to them, complete other homework assignments, and attend the two ninety-minute sessions. From the outset, the clients' role in taking major responsibility for their own changes is made explicit and the other conditions of the intervention are explained to them. Specifically, clients are expected to be sober when they arrive for each session; they are given a breath test to verify their alcohol-free status. The importance of completing the readings and other homework assignments and bringing the latter to the next session is stressed.

In general, goal setting is an important component of current alternative interventions for alcohol problems, and this process is typified by Sobell and Sobell's approach. Specifically, clients are asked to choose their own drinking goals and are provided with structured recording forms to guide them through the process. They are encouraged to formulate drinking goals that can be measured with behavioral specificity. One purpose of goal self-selection is to increase clients' commitment to change. Nevertheless, the therapist tactfully points out any information from the assessment that might be incongruent with clients' selected goals (e.g., medical contraindications for moderate drinking instead of total abstinence). Still the ultimate choice of goals rests with the clients. Systematic self-monitoring is used to determine if the aimed-for goals are met and to identify possible obstacles to meeting those goals.

Following completion of the assessment, clients are asked to review Reading 1 and complete Homework Assignment 1, both of which Sobell and Sobell include in their manual for other clinicians to photocopy and use. Reading 1 further introduces clients to the treatment, describes a behavioral analysis of drinking, and emphasizes that overcoming alcohol problems is a long-term goal whose successful attainment depends on clients' systematic and sustained efforts. In Homework Assignment 1, Part 1, clients are asked to undertake a functional analysis of their drinking, and a recording form is provided to guide this activity. Homework Assignment 1, Part 2, asks clients to provide information (again, on a recording form that is provided) about their most frequent "limited-drinking" situations during the past year. Limited drinking is defined as consuming no more than four standard drinks, and that the alcohol consumption resulted in no negative consequences. Information obtained from this exercise is then used to assess limited-drinking goals that clients may have selected, and provides further information about the functional analysis of clients' drinking.

Reading 2 in Sobell and Sobell's program further clarifies functional analytic methods for assessing problem drinking. Drinking triggers are discussed and the specific consequences of consuming alcohol are evaluated. In addition, clients are introduced to a simple technique for resolving drinking problems, and actions that clients can take to avoid relapses are described. In Homework Assignment 2, Part 1, clients are asked to apply the problem-solving skills they have learned to their own specific problem-drinking situations. This activity is expanded in Homework Assignment 2, Part 2, with clients now identifying specific aspects of their lifestyle that may contribute to their drinking problems. Various life situations are evaluated, including social relationships, leisure and recreational activities (e.g., social gathering which occurs exclusively at bars), and the general availability of alcohol. Structured recording forms are once again provided to guide clients through these homework exercises. Completed forms become the focus of the next treatment session.

Sobell and Sobell describe a number of case examples with which their procedure has been effectively applied. Application of their technique to our student Gerald's case would involve orienting him to a cognitive–behavioral interpretation of his alcohol abuse. A functional analysis of his drinking would then be undertaken, whereby the resulting behavioral recordings would be used to identify the particular circumstances that surround Gerald's drinking. An initial step in his treatment would involve collaboratively working with him to establish his particular drinking goals. Most likely, Gerald would be unwilling to commit himself to a goal of total abstinence, even though he is an underage drinker and his drinking has become very problematic. Instead, he would more likely be willing to aim to limit his drinking, for example, to weekends or two occasions per week. He might also be willing to place a limit on the amount that he would drink on each occasion (e.g., three standard drinks of beer).

The functional analysis of Gerald's drinking might reveal that he drinks only with certain people, such as his roommate Mark and other friends from his dormitory. It might also show that Gerald has failed to established friendships at the university other than with his "drinking buddies." Accordingly, Gerald and his therapist might agree that he would attempt to make other friends. The functional analysis would likely also reveal that Gerald drinks to reduce his social anxiety, particularly while attempting to interact with women. Undoubtedly, Gerald and his therapist would identify strategies for Gerald to overcome his discomfort in social situations that would be more adaptive than his attempting to do so by overindulging in alcohol.

Systematic Motivational Counseling

Cox and Klinger's (1988, 1990) motivational model of alcohol use is an integrative approach that takes into account the biological, psychological, environmental, and sociocultural variables that contribute to alcohol use and abuse. The model suggests how these various kinds of etiological variables interact with one another to lead to a final motivational pathway to alcohol use. According to the model, excessive drinking is governed by the same variables that affect people's motivational patterns generally. Individuals are motivated to acquire positive incentives that they expect will bring them pleasure, and to eliminate or avoid negative incentives that cause discomfort. The motivational model explains how drinking alcohol acquires high incentive value for particular individuals, and how it does so within the context of the other incentives in people's lives.

There is a close interplay between people's motivational structure, life satisfaction, and motivation to drink or not to drink alcohol or use other drugs. For example, to the extent that people have adaptive motivational patterns that increase their likelihood of successful and satisfying goal pursuits, their motivation to obtain emotional satisfaction by drinking alcohol will be reduced. If people have maladaptive motivational patterns that decrease their likelihood of successful and satisfying goal pursuits, their motivation to try to obtain emotional satisfaction by drinking alcohol will be enhanced. Identifying these patterns requires a detailed assessment of the problem drinker's motivational structure and how the motivation to drink alcohol is embedded in that complex structure.

Such an assessment is done in the context of Systematic Motivational Counseling (Cox et al., 1996), which begins with administration of the Motivational Structure Questionnaire (MSQ; Klinger, Cox, & Blount, 1996). Clients are asked open-ended questions that help them name and describe their current concerns in major life areas (Klinger, 1975, 1977), and the goals that they have formed associated with those concerns. In motivational theory, there are two defining characteristics of a goal: (1) It is some object or event that a person expects will bring about a desirable affective change (either an increase in positive affect or a diminution of negative affect), and (2) it is something that the person is committed to achieve. On the MSQ, respondents name their goals and concerns in sixteen major life areas, including such areas as family, friends, and significant others; finances; and occupation. Then, from menus of choices and rating scales provided in the MSQ Test Booklet, each respondent characterizes the goal striving corresponding to each concern along various dimensions. These include (1) the desired action, (2) the role that is being played, (3) the degree of commitment, (4) the expected effect on successful or unsuccessful goal attainment, (5) the expected chances of success of goal attainment, (6) temporal dimensions (e.g., when each goal is expected to be reached), and (7) the effects that continued alcohol use will have on goal attainments.

From the ratings of each respondent's goal strivings, quantitative indices are calculated from which a profile is drawn to depict that respondent's motivational structure. The profile shows the degree to which the respondent's overall motivational patterns are adaptive or maladaptive. For example, it illustrates the extent to which the person has few or many goals, is positively or negatively motivated, plays an active or spectator role in goal strivings, puts forth much or little effort to achieve goals, displays effort that is fruitful or fruitless, expects little or great joy upon goal attainments, is ambivalent or lacks ambivalence regarding goal pursuits, expects little or great sorrow upon failure to attain goals, is optimistic or pessimistic about goal attainments, feels that goals are easily accessible or distant, and the degree to which continued alcohol use will interfere with or facilitate goal attainments.

The SMC technique includes two kinds of components, the core counseling components and the motivational restructuring components. In addition to administering the MSQ and providing careful feedback on the results, the core components include such things as introducing the client to the rationale for SMC and how the counseling will proceed; preliminary exercises, such as the analysis of goal interrelationships; and the planning of specific, concrete objectives to be accomplished during the course of counseling. The restructuring components, by contrast, are individually chosen for each person, depending on that person's particular motivational needs. These components include constructing ladders that depict the hierarchical steps leading to the ultimate attainment of goals, setting between-session goals, helping the person shift from a negatively motivated to a positively motivated lifestyle, improving the person's ability to reach appropriate and realistic goals (e.g., by acquiring the skills necessary to do so), bolstering the person's self-esteem and inherent feelings of self-worth, resolving conflicts between goals and ambivalence within particular goals, relinquishing goals that are unlikely to succeed and/or be emotionally satisfying even if successful, and identifying incentives for the person's pursuit and enjoyment that previously were unknown to him or her.

Using this context as a starting point, let us briefly examine how we might enhance our client Gerald's life satisfaction while simultaneously diminishing his motivation to drink alcohol. From what we know about Gerald, it seems likely to expect that on the MSQ he would name goals related to developing a significant relationship with a woman. We might also discover that Gerald entertains a faulty belief that he will have the opportunity to interact with women only by behaving very gregariously, and further that he is able to accomplish the latter only when he is intoxicated. Thus, within the SMC framework we would need to help Gerald disengage himself from his goal of achieving gregariousness through the consumption of alcohol in order to find the romantic relationship that he is seeking. At the same time, Gerald would need help to foster the attainment of his desired goal through avenues that are more likely to succeed than those to which he is presently committed. Additional details about how to apply the counseling technique with cases like that of Gerald are provided in the SMC Treatment Manual (Cox et al., 1996).

SUMMARY AND CONCLUSIONS

We have described developments leading to a scientific understanding of alcohol and drug problems. The burgeoning empirical work in this area has been the foundation for alternative explanations, models, and developing theories of substance use and abuse. These alternative formulations are continuously evolving as ongoing scientific work is integrated into these models. Our case illustration highlighted the significantly different understandings of and responses to substance use problems by the traditional disease model and developing alternative theories. One clear advantage of the empirically driven alternative models is that they offer substantially greater flexibility in understanding and treating substance use problems. Initial evaluations of the effectiveness of treatment interventions that have emerged from these new models is encouraging. Additional study of substance use disorders must now continue, so that further refinements in professionals' manner of dealing with these pervasive problems can be realized. It is hoped that the end result will be more effective treatment interventions for the many young adults like Gerald who experience substance use problems.

NOTE

1. Throughout the chapter we use the term *substance abuse* to refer to a less severe kind of problematic substance use than substance dependence. The substance abuser's life is adversely affected, but not to the debilitating extent seen in substance dependence. Substance dependence is associated with drug tolerance and withdrawal symptoms, as well as pronounced behavioral changes. We present a comprehensive definition of these concepts in a later section of the chapter.

REFERENCES

Adams, H. E., & Cassidy, J. F. (1993). The classification of abnormal behavior: An overview. In P. B. Sutker & H. E. Adams (Eds.), *Comprehensive handbook of psychopathology* (2nd ed.) (pp. 3–26). New York: Plenum Press.

Alcoholics Anonymous. (1976). *Alcoholics Anonymous:The story of how many thousands of men and women have recovered from alcoholism* (3rd ed.). New York: Alcoholics Anonymous World Services.

Alcoholics Anonymous. (1955). *Alcoholics Anonymous:The story of how many thousands of men and women have recovered from alcoholism* (2nd ed.). New York: Alcoholics Anonymous World Services.

Alcoholics Anonymous. (1939). *Alcoholics Anonymous.* New York: Alcoholics Anonymous.

American Psychiatric Association. (1994). *Diagnostic and statistical manual of mental disorders* (4th ed.). Washington, DC: Author.

Annis, H. M., & Davis, C. S. (1988). Assessment of expectancies. In D. M. Donovan & G. A. Marlatt (Eds.), *Assessment of addictive behaviors* (pp. 84–111). New York: Guilford Press.

Azrin, N. H. (1976). Improvements in the community reinforcement approach to alcoholism. *Behaviour Research and Therapy, 14,* 339–348.

Azrin, N. H., Sisson, R. W., Meyers, R., & Godley, M. (1982). Alcoholism treatment by disulfiram and community reinforcement therapy. *Journal of Behavior Therapy and Experimental Psychiatry, 13,* 105–112.

Bandura, A. (1977). Self-efficacy: Toward a unifying theory of behavioral change. *Psychological Review, 84,* 191–215.

Bandura, A. (1978). Reflections on self-efficacy. *Advances in Behavior Research and Therapy, 1,* 237–269.

Bohman, M., Sigvardsson, S., & Cloninger, C. R. (1981). Maternal inheritance of alcohol abuse. *Archives of General Psychiatry, 38,* 965–969.

Bray, B. H., & Krinsley, K. E. (1990). Adolescent substance abuse. In E. L. Feindler & G. R. Kalfus (Eds.), *Adolescent behavior therapy handbook* (pp. 275–303). New York: Plenum Press.

Cahalan, D. (1970). *Problem drinkers: A national survey.* San Francisco: Jossey-Bass.

Cloninger, C. R., Bohman, M., & Sigvardsson, S. (1981). Inheritance of alcohol abuse. *Archives of General Psychiatry, 38,* 861–868.

Cook, C. C. H. (1988a). The Minnesota Model in the management of drug and alcohol dependency: Miracle, method, or myth? Part 1. The philosophy and the program. *British Journal of Addiction, 83,* 625–634.

Cook, C. C. H. (1988b). The Minnesota Model in the management of drug and alcohol dependency: Miracle, method, or myth? Part 2. Evidence and conclusions. *British Journal of Addiction, 83,* 735–748.

Cox, W. M. (1987a). Personality theory and research. In H. T. Blane & K. E. Leonard (Eds.), *Psychological theories of drinking and alcoholism.* New York: Guilford Press.

Cox, W. M. (Ed.). (1987b). *Treatment and prevention of alcohol problems: A resource manual.* Orlando, FL: Academic Press.

Cox, W. M. (1988). Personality theory. In C. D. Chaudron & D. A. Wilkinson (Eds.), *Theories on alcoholism.* Toronto: Addiction Research Foundation.

Cox, W. M., & Calmari, J. E. (in press). Addiction. *Encyclopedia of human biology* (2nd ed.). San Diego, CA: Academic Press.

Cox, W. M., & Klinger, E. (1988). A motivational model of alcohol use. *Journal of Abnormal Psychology, 97,* 168–180.

Cox, W. M., & Klinger, E. (1990). Incentive motivation, affective change, and alcohol use: A model. In W. M. Cox (Ed.), *Why people drink: Parameters of alcohol as a reinforcer.* New York: Gardner.

Cox, W. M., Klinger, E., & Blount, J. P. (1996). *Systematic motivational counseling: A treatment manual.* Copyrighted material available from W. Miles Cox.

Donovan, D. M. (1988). Assessment of addictive behaviors: Implications of an emerging biopsychosocial model. In D. M. Donovan & G. A. Marlatt (Eds.), *Assessment of addictive behaviors* (pp. 3–50). New York: Guilford Press.

Edwards, G., Orford, J., Egert, S., Guthrie, S., Hawker, A., Hensman, C., Mitcheson, M., Oppenheimer, E., & Taylor, C. (1977). Alcoholism: A controlled trial of "treatment" and "advice." *Journal of Studies on Alcohol, 38,* 1004–1031.

Fillmore, K. M. (1988). *Alcohol use across the life course: A critical review of 70 years of international longitudinal research.* Toronto: Addiction Research Foundation.

Gatchel, R. J., Baun, A., & Krantz, D. S. (1989). *An introduction to health psychology* (2nd ed.). New York: Random House.

Goldman, M. S., Brown, S. A., & Christiansen, B. A. (1987). Expectancy theory: Thinking about drinking. In H. T. Blane & K. E. Leonard (Eds.), *Psychological theories of drinking and alcoholism* (pp. 181–226). New York: Guilford Press.

Goodwin, D. W. (1979). Alcoholism and heredity: A review and hypothesis. *Archives of General Psychiatry, 36,* 57–61.

Goodwin, D. W., Schulsinger, F., & Molter, N. (1974). Drinking problems in adopted and nonadopted sons of alcoholics. *Archives of General Psychiatry, 31,* 164–169.

Hester, R. K., & Miller, W. R. (Eds.). (1995). *Handbook of alcoholism treatment approaches: Effective alternatives* (2nd ed.). Boston: Allyn & Bacon.

Hunt, G. M., & Azrin, N. H. (1973). A community reinforcement approach to alcoholism. *Behaviour Research and Therapy, 11,* 91–104.

Institute of Medicine. (1990). *Broadening the base of treatment for alcohol problems.* Washington, DC: National Academy Press.

Jellinek, E. M. (1952). Phases of alcohol addiction. *Quarterly Journal on Studies on Alcohol, 13,* 673–684.

Jellinek, E. M. (1960). *The disease concept of alcoholism.* New Haven, CT: Hillhouse Press.

Johnson, J. L., & McCown, W. G. (1993). Addictive behaviors and substance use: An overview. In P. B. Sutker & H. E. Adams (Eds.), *Comprehensive handbook of psychopathology* (2nd ed.) (pp. 437–450). New York: Plenum Press.

Johnston, L. D., O'Malley, P. M., & Bachman, J. G. (1985). *Use of licit and illicit drugs by America's high school students 1954–1984.* Rockville, MD: National Institute on Drug Abuse.

Klinger, E. (1975). Consequences of commitment to and disengagement from incentives. *Psychological Review, 82,* 1–25.

Klinger, E. (1977). *Meaning and void: Inner experience and the incentives in people's lives.* Minneapolis: University of Minnesota Press.

Klinger, E., Cox, W. M., & Blount, J. P. (1996). Motivational structure questionnaire for alcoholics. In *NIAAA handbook of alcoholism treatment assessment instruments.* Washington, DC: U.S. Government Printing Office.

Kranzler, H. R., & Anton, R. F. (1994). Implications of recent neuropsychopharmacologic research for understanding the etiology and development of alcoholism. *Journal of Consulting and Clinical Psychology, 62,* 1116–1126.

Marlatt, G. A. (1985). Cognitive factors in the relapse process. In G. A. Marlatt & J. R. Gordon (Eds.), *Relapse prevention: Maintenance strategies in the treatment of addictive behaviors* (pp. 128–200). New York: Guilford Press.

Marlatt, G. A., Larimer, M. E., Baer, J. S., & Quigley, L. A. (1993). Harm reduction for alcohol problems: Moving beyond the controlled drinking controversy. *Behavior Therapy, 24,* 461–504.

McCrady, B. S. (1993). Alcoholism. In D. H. Barlow (Ed.), *Clinical handbook of psychological disorders* (2nd ed.) (pp. 362–395). New York: Guilford Press.

Meyers, J. K., Weissman, M. M., Tischler, G. L., Holzer, C. E., Leaf, P. J., Orvaschel, H. A., Anthony, J. C., Boyd, J. H., Burke, J. E., Kramer, M., & Stoltzman, R. (1984). Six-month prevalence of psychiatric disorders in three communities: 1980–1982. *Archives of General Psychiatry, 41,* 959–967.

Meyers, R. J., & Smith, J. E. (1995). *Treating alcohol abuse: The community reinforcement approach*. New York: Guilford Press.

Miller, W. R. (1992). Client/treatment matching in addictive behaviors. *The Behavior Therapist, 15,* 7–8.

Miller, W. R., & Rollnick, S. (1991). *Motivational interviewing: Preparing people to change addictive behaviors*. New York: Guilford Press.

Monti, P. M., Abrams, D. B., Kadden, R. M., & Cooney, N. L. (1989). *Treating alcohol dependence*. New York: Guilford Press.

Nathan, P. E. (1991). Substance use disorders in the DSM-IV. *Journal of Abnormal Psychology, 100,* 356–361.

Nathan, P. E. (1993). Alcoholism: Psychopathology, etiology and treatment. In P. B. Sutker & H. E. Adams (Eds.), *Comprehensive handbook of Psychopathology* (2nd ed.) (pp. 451–476). New York: Plenum Press.

Orford, J., Oppenheimer, E., & Edwards, G. (1976). Abstinence or control: The outcome of excessive drinking two years after consultation. *Behaviour Research and Therapy, 14,* 409–418.

Prochaska, J. O., & DiClemente, C. C. (1982). Transtheoretical therapy: Toward a more integrative model of change. *Psychotherapy: Theory, Research, and Practice, 19,* 276–288.

Roizen, R., Cahalan, D., & Shanks, P. (1978). Spontaneous remission among untreated problem drinkers. In D. B. Kandel (Ed.), *Longitudinal research on drug use: Empirical findings and methodological issues* (pp. 197–221). Washington, DC: Hemisphere.

Schuckit, M. A., & Gold, E. O. (1988). A simultaneous evaluation of multiple ethanol challenges to sons of alcoholics and controls. *Archives of General Psychiatry, 45,* 211–216.

Searles, J. S. (1988). The role of genetics in the pathogenesis of alcohol. *Journal of Abnormal Psychology, 97,* 153–167.

Sisson, R. W., & Azrin, N. H. (1993). Community reinforcement training for families: A method to get alcoholics into treatment. In T. J. O'Farrell (Ed.), *Treating alcohol problems: Marital and family interventions* (pp. 34–53). New York: Guilford Press.

Sobell, M. B., & Sobell, L. C. (1993). *Problem drinkers: Guided self-change treatment*. New York: Guilford Press.

Vuchinich, R. E., & Tucker, J. A. (1988). Contributions from behavioral theories of choice to an analysis of alcohol abuse. *Journal of Abnormal Psychology, 97,* 181–195.

Zubin, J., & Spring, B. (1977). Vulnerability—a new view of schizophrenia. *Journal of Abnormal Psychology, 86,* 103–126.

PART II

POLICIES, PROGRAMMING, AND PREVENTION

5

Policy Development: An Essential Element in Addressing Campus Substance Abuse Issues

John H. Schuh and Elsie R. Shore

A variety of ways are available to institutions of higher education to address issues related to the possession, use, and potential abuse of alcoholic beverages. Among these are educational programs, counseling interventions, and treatment programs. None of these approaches can have their desired effect without a carefully crafted institutional policy governing alcoholic beverages. Gonzalez (1987) asserted that policy development is "an integral part of a comprehensive alcohol education and prevention program" (p. 88). Goodale (1987) added that "a policy can assist in deciding where university responsibility must end and where student responsibility must begin. The policy cannot be filed away in a dean's office. It must be enforced and visible" (p. xi).

Guidance for developing a policy that will govern the possession and use of alcoholic beverages (an alcohol policy) is available from the Council for the Advancement of Standards of Student Services/Development Programs (CAS) (1990). CAS developed a series of standards regarding alcohol and other drug policies that include the following features:

1. Policies need to be consistent with the law.
2. Policies need to promote environments free from substance abuse.
3. Policies need to define to whom regulations apply.
4. Policies need to identify prohibited behaviors.
5. Policies need to establish protocols for involving law enforcement officers from agencies on and off campus.
6. Policies need to outline procedures referring individuals to sources of assistance.

7. Policies need to define marketing guidelines for alcoholic beverages.

8. Policies need to identify guidelines for the sanctioned use of alcohol. (1990, p. 5)

These guidelines from CAS provide an excellent point of reference for an institution that is proposing to establish a policy concerning the possession and use of alcoholic beverages or review its existing policy. Nevertheless, the CAS approach assumes that appropriate background material and information are understood by policy makers who, as a consequence, have an informed point of reference from which to begin their study. That may be an erroneous assumption. Many individuals who are involved in the development of institutional policy may have very little knowledge about the factors and conditions that influence the development of policy. Policy makers may include students, who are unaware of how policies were established simply as a function of the limited amount of time they have spent on campus; faculty, who may have been appointed to a policy development group more as a function of their interest in students than their technical expertise or knowledge about the topic; and others, such as administrators or governing board members, who are involved in this activity because of their status at the institution.

This chapter has been developed to discuss what we believe are essential elements in the development of an alcohol policy. Among these elements are institutional mission and philosophy; the legal landscape, which includes principles of law as well as relevant court cases; institutional objectives in policy development; and various educational perspectives on the possession and use of alcoholic beverages. We conclude this chapter with some suggestions about the elements that might be found in an institution's alcohol policy.

MISSION AND PHILOSOPHY

The initial element of policy to be discussed in this chapter is an institution of higher education's mission and philosophy. Taken together, "mission and philosophy provide a rationale for the institution's educational programs, policies, and practices" (Kuh, Schuh, & Whitt, 1991, p. 41). When an institution's mission and philosophy are clear and coherent, students and others associated with the institution understand why things are done the way they are.

Mission

Lyons (1993) observed that "Each college or university is unique, and that uniqueness derives from a distinctive mission" (p. 3). He went on to point out that for student affairs programs to be successful a clear understanding of mission is necessary. The same is true for the development of policy. Policies must be consistent with the institution's mission and philosophy.

Regardless of the specific statement, "An institution's mission defines what a college is and aspires to be" (Kuh, 1991, p. 12). Mission statements tend to vary substantially from institution to institution. The mission statement of a small, private, church-related liberal arts institution will be very different than that of a large state university. In turn, both will be different than those of specialized institutions, such as graduate and professional schools.

Colleges and universities that are serious about their mission statement use this document to guide the development of policy and the practical affairs of the institution. For example, a private college that has a close affiliation with a church which holds as one of its tenets that members will not use alcohol is an institution that very likely will develop a policy consistent with that of the church. The policy, in this case, might be that the possession and use of alcohol is prohibited on campus and that stiff penalties are applied to those who violate the regulation. At the other end of the continuum is an institution that delivers instruction almost exclusively through correspondence and television courses so that students never go to the main headquarters of the institution. In this case, the institution might not even have an alcohol policy.

Most campuses do not fit at either end of this continuum. In fact, it is more likely they will experience the tensions of trying to balance the needs of some groups within the community who think there should be very tight regulation of the possession and use of alcoholic beverages with those who advocate a much more liberal position. The challenge policy makers face is to develop a position which balances the natural tensions of the various constituencies that comprise the campus while staying true to the mission of the institution.

Philosophy

An institution's philosophy is equally important. Institutional philosophy consists of "values, assumptions, and beliefs about human potential, teaching and learning" (Kuh, Schuh, & Witt, 1991, p. 41). Some institutions have a philosophy that all students will be treated like adults and are responsible for their actions without any form of interference from the college. Others take a more parental approach, and tell prospective students, for example, that their behavior will be tightly regulated. In the case of the former institution, a policy covering the possession and consumption of alcoholic beverages might be to let local law enforcement agencies deal with students as they do with any other citizens and let the justice system run its course. The latter institution might develop a very strict policy where student behavior is monitored very closely and infractions of the policy are dealt with directly.

To confound the situation even further, some institutions will behave differently depending on the constituency affected. For example, the college may inform students that alcohol is not permitted on campus and, accordingly, that they may not consume alcoholic beverages. Students, in turn, may point to prefootball game tailgating parties, frequented by alumni and alumnae and benefactors of the college at the football stadium, which include the liberal use of alcohol. Students might ask if hospitality events hosted at the president's house include liquor. These ambiguities and inconsistencies are significant and make the development of policy challenging.

Implications for Policy Development

Unfortunately, most colleges do not have distinctive features such as those of a church-related institution that make developing a policy governing the possession and use of alcoholic beverages relatively easy. For those institutions that are not so unique, a review of the college's mission and philosophy can be very helpful. At one set of exemplary institutions, Kuh, Schuh, and Whitt (1991) found that the mission statements of the institutions were clear and coherent. As a result, "Students, faculty and administrators have similar views of how the institution works" (p. 66). In developing a policy designed to regulate the possession and consumption of alcoholic beverages, an institution would be well advised to keep the following principles in mind:

1. The policy should emanate from the institution's mission statement.
2. The policy should be consistent with the institution's espoused and enacted philosophy.
3. The policy should be clear, easily understood, communicated in such a way that all members of the community know about it, and leave little to individual interpretation.
4. The policy should be reviewed at least as often as the institution's mission statement is revised.

THE LEGAL LANDSCAPE

The second element in developing a policy is the legal landscape. Federal laws, state laws, and local ordinances have an influence on the policy an institution might develop. Increasingly, the legal environment is having an effect on how institutions conduct business. "Law's presence on the campus and its impact on the daily affairs of postsecondary institutions have grown continuously since . . . 1978" (Kaplin & Lee, 1995, p. 1). The law cannot be ignored in developing a policy on alcoholic-beverage possession and consumption, and in many ways will shape what an institution can permit beyond a total ban of alcoholic beverages from its premises.

Federal Law

Federal law, through the distribution of highway trust funds, makes it very expensive for individual states to set the minimum age for people to possess alcoholic beverages below twenty-one (Gehring, 1991). While states have the authority to set a drinking age of less than twenty-one, federal highway funds can be withheld from those states which elect to do so with the potential price tag of millions of dollars. So, primarily as a practical matter, states have set the drinking age at twenty-one. In turn, institutions of higher education, unless they are bent on inviting a multifaceted disaster, must have a policy consistent with state law.

The Drug-Free Schools and Communities Amendments of 1989 require that institutions distribute certain information related to illicit drugs and alcohol to members of the campus community (Gehring, 1994). Among the items to be provided in this notice are standards of conduct prohibiting the possession and distribution of illegal drugs and alcohol, a description of applicable laws related to the possession and consumption of illicit drugs and alcohol, a description of counseling and treatment programs available, and a statement that sanctions will be imposed for a violation of institutional standards and a description of those sanctions (Gehring, 1994, p. 80).

State Law

A variety of state laws and local ordinances also may affect an institution's policy regarding the possession and sale of alcoholic beverages. Among these are laws regarding the licensure of entities that sell alcoholic beverages. In some jurisdictions it is very difficult and expensive to purchase a liquor license. As a consequence, it may be virtually impossible to obtain a license even if the institution desired such. Moreover, laws may be on the books that prohibit the sale of alcohol within a certain distance from a school. This is designed to protect children attending elementary and secondary schools. But since a college or university may be defined broadly as a school by state law, it very well may be unable to sell alcohol; if the institution has a lab school or preschool, such a law could well prohibit the sale of alcoholic beverages. Other states have restrictions on the possession of alcoholic beverages on state property. Were this the case, public institutions in those states may not be able to sell alcohol. Local "blue" laws may prevent the sale of alcohol on Sundays, elections days, holidays, or before a certain time each day or after a certain time each night. The point of this discussion is simply to point out that a wide range of laws will affect what an institution can do regarding the possession and sale of alcoholic beverages; institutions do not operate at their own discretion on this matter.

The Public–Private Dichotomy

Private institutions, since they are provided a bit more freedom from the influence of the state and federal legal environment than public institutions, have more flexibility in developing alcohol policies than public institutions. Correnti (1988) observed, "Although, in many ways, private institutions have more control over their legal destinies than public institutions do, unbridled license certainly does not exist" (p. 25). An obvious illustration of this, of course, is that private institutions cannot serve alcoholic beverages to minors. However, with the appropriate licenses, a private college could sell alcoholic beverages on its property in a state where the law prohibits state institutions from obtaining such a license. In that state, presumably, students (of legal age) could purchase beer in the student union of the private college where they could not at the public institution across the street.

Negligence

An important aspect of the legal landscape is that institutions must behave in certain ways or they could be held to be negligent. Barr (1988) identifies three elements in a negligence claim: (1) that the defendant (the college in this example) owed a duty of care to the claimant, (2) that the defendant (the college) breached that duty, and (3) that the breach of duty was the proximate cause of the injury. The implications of potential claims of negligence against an institution are obvious. If a policy is flawed, the institution may be vulnerable toward adverse legal judgments which could result in substantial monetary damages.

While institutions of higher education no longer are expected to watch over their students, commonly referred to as acting *in loco parentis*, they do have a duty to care. Gonzalez (1985) observed that the duty to care "requires colleges to provide due warning where there is a clear and present danger, and make sure the institution's activities, offerings, and programs meet minimum standards of care for its students" (p. 24). In practical terms this means that institutions must provide safe facilities and develop policies that provide for the safety of those associated with them. It does not mean that the college is responsible for every injury suffered on campus, nor will every person who suffers an injury on campus be compensated.

What might be a policy flaw that would lead to negligence? Part of the college's policy might include provisions about where alcoholic beverages can be consumed on the campus. If the policy did not include certain restrictions, the following incident could occur.

Suppose the policy indicates that as long as students are of legal age, they may drink anywhere they choose. As a consequence, a group of students decide to drink in an art studio where molten metals are used to make pieces of sculpture. A student suffers a horrible injury when molten metal is spilled on her by an intoxicated student, of age, who mishandles the material. In this hypothetical scenario, it is highly likely that a claim against the institution would be filed with excellent potential for success, because the college had not articulated where drinking was inappropriate and had failed to exercise a duty of care in the supervision of its studios. While this example may be extreme, it does illustrate how problems can arise because of a poorly conceived policy.

Social Host Liability

Many states have adopted social host liability laws (Barr, 1996). While the legal concept of social host liability as is manifested in the law and court decisions will vary from jurisdiction to jurisdiction (Walton, 1996), this concept generally holds that "proprietors may be liable for injuries to third persons which are the result of the negligence of another individual who became intoxicated at the proprietor's tavern" (Gehring, 1987, p. 143). "Sponsors of parties at which intoxicants are served, particularly to minors, could be found negligent under the social host doctrine" (Kaplin & Lee, 1995, p. 110). Kaplin and Lee add that a college that holds a liquor license or contracts with another party who holds one may face additional consequences if negligence claims arise out of an incident related to the possession and consumption of alcoholic beverages. With this potential exposure, a college may seriously want to consider a policy that prohibits the sale of alcoholic beverages in any case.

Perhaps as chilling is the thought of the institution having responsibility for the consequences of the misuse of alcoholic beverages provided at campus events. Barr (1996) concluded the following: "The institution may be found liable as a supervisor of student conduct, property owner, seller of alcohol, or social host" (p. 140). The institution may be liable if it serves as the host of an event where alcoholic beverages are served, with the result being a claim of negligence filed merely because it did not properly supervise the event.

Court Cases

A wide number of cases have been tried concerning the possession and consumption of alcoholic beverages by college students. While in each of the following cases the institution prevailed in a court of law, a stiff price may be paid even when the institution's position is sustained legally. In each case, individuals suffered injuries because of alcohol abuse. In addition, resources in the form of money, time, and energy were expended by the institution to win the case, and bad publicity for the institution inevitably results from these cases. Finally, the individuals whose actions were challenged by the plaintiffs suffer personal anguish in going through the legal process as defendants. In the end the institution may win, but it is not unscathed. Three cases are particularly useful in looking at policy questions.

Bradshaw v. Rawlings involved a class picnic where alcoholic beverages were served. The adviser cosigned the check that was used to purchase beer (Kaplin & Lee, 1995). After attending the picnic, a student who was riding in a car driven by a person who had become intoxicated at the picnic was badly injured in a traffic accident. A lawsuit resulted and the injured party sought monetary damages from the college. The jury found on behalf of the plaintiff and awarded over $1 million in damages. Although on appeal the judgment was overturned, little comfort can be taken from this case. Clearly, a college which would get involved in this kind of activity, including providing the beer for a picnic, did not exercise good judgment. Beyond that, no legal judgment can undo the fact that a student was permanently disabled as a result of the auto accident. Obvious policy implications arise from this case, including not having the college furnish the beer and not having an adviser sanction this kind of activity.

In *Baldwin v. Zoradi*, drinking occurred in a campus residence-hall room, after which a student was injured by a driver who became intoxicated from the drinking (Kaplin & Lee, 1995). The injured student did not prevail at trial, since the court decided that the college could not be expected to provide such close supervision that no drinking could occur. Here, too, policy implications arise. An institution, after establishing a policy, is expected to enforce it. While the institution prevailed, the claim of the plaintiff, that the college failed to enforce its policy, leads to the obvious conclusion that in establishing policy colleges have to develop policies that can be enforced as well as provide and support enforcement agents.

Finally, *Beach v. University of Utah* is a helpful case in that it illustrates another problem that can arise from drinking. An underage student, having consumed alcoholic beverages on a institutionally sponsored field trip and in full view of the adviser, fell and was injured (Kaplin & Lee, 1995). The institution prevailed at trial and won on the point that the adviser could not be expected to provide such close supervision so as to prevent the accident from occurring. As is the case with *Baldwin*, policy implications arise, especially in that the institution had a policy which prohibited drinking in this setting. The obvious legal challenge was that the institution failed to provide adequate supervision and enforcement of its policy. Any time a person violates policy in the view of the presumed event supervisor and is injured, a legal challenge is likely.

Implications for Policy Development

Even if an institution develops a policy that is completely consistent with its mission and philosophy, it is almost certain that state and federal laws and court cases will influence the emerging policy. Remember that federal law makes it very expensive for states to pass laws that make it legal for anyone under twenty-one to possess and consume alcoholic beverages; that state laws will influence how liquor may be purchased, where, and by whom; and that case law provides a rich reservoir of lessons learned from the misuse of alcoholic beverages. Finally, the principles of negligence and social host liability may assist an institution in deciding that it wants nothing to do with the possession and sale of alcoholic beverages because of the obvious risks associated with such.

EDUCATIONAL PERSPECTIVES

How Policy Contributes to Student Education

Though college and university policies regarding alcohol and other drugs are often developed in response to external mandates or legal concerns, such policies can also serve an educational function. Thus, another consideration when developing policy is its impact on the student's college experience.

Assuming, of course, that they are put into practice rather than merely put on paper, university substance use and abuse policies will lead to educational experiences and messages for students. The path from policy to student education may be direct or indirect.

The path is direct when the policy requires educational programming about substance use and abuse. Such activities include programs for the general student population; training for residence hall staff, peer leaders, and others working directly with students; educational programs for specific student groups (e.g., fraternities and sororities, foreign students, residents of campus living units); special educational interventions for students who have violated alcohol rules; counseling for students with substance abuse problems; and the like. The need for institutional commitment to its policy in the form of money and other resources is obvious; without tangible support such programs will not be established or will not endure.

Students also may be educated indirectly, living and studying on a campus that has developed and implemented regulations regarding alcohol and other drugs. Rules and guidelines on the use of alcohol at campus events, for example, establish learning situations in which students experience ways of living with alcohol (or, indeed, without it) that may be different from what they have known before. Interventions to discipline, educate, or counsel students who have violated rules or are showing signs of substance-related problems teach both those directly involved and those who witness or hear about the interventions.

Finally, policy can educate indirectly by serving as a force to counter other messages. The educational programs and policies discussed can offer alternatives to general cultural ideas about substance use. They can present models other than those of substance-abusing on-campus peers, and can debunk myths about substance use (Perkins and Berkowitz, 1986; Berkowitz, Chapter 6 of this book). The messages may be new or different from those the students themselves brought to campus as a result of earlier experiences with alcohol or other drugs.

Policy can also prohibit or limit student exposure to unhealthy, negative, or dangerous messages. The prohibition of alcohol advertisements in campus publications or the establishment of guidelines for the types of ads that will be accepted limits "education" by beer companies and liquor distributors. Such prohibitions or regulations deflect not only exhortations to use alcohol, but also messages linking drinking with sexual activity and the objectification of women, rollicking friendship and masculine hijinks, and escape from schoolwork and other responsibilities. Other restrictions on alcohol advertising on campus, such as on billboards and through sponsorships of sporting events, similarly inhibit such messages. They might also give students respite from what, without such policy mandates, could become a virtually constant bombardment of images of alcohol and drinking, a respite that might enable other images (of activities, friendship, even scholarship) to emerge.

What Students Learn

The information, attitudes, and types of behaviors learned through exposure to campus substance use and abuse policies and programs will, of course, depend on their actual content as well as on the philosophy or mission of the school. Learning is likely to occur in three general areas. Students may learn how to use alcohol in a safe and legal fashion. They may learn about the abuse of alcohol and other substances and what can be done about it. Finally, alcohol policy and programs may affect students' social-skill development.

Teaching students about safe ways to handle alcohol is complicated by the fact that the current legal drinking age is twenty-one years old (Commission on Substance Abuse at Colleges and Universities, 1994). This effectively divides the student population into two groups, with those under twenty-one subject to different rules and treated in different ways than are those of legal age. Though divided by legal status, members of the two groups are likely to be in close contact, living, working, and socializing together. Campus personnel are precluded from teaching, modeling, or expecting moderation or safe drinking practices when dealing with underage students, a stance that can be difficult to maintain in the face of frequent and often obvious drinking in this group (see Rubington, Chapter 7 of this book, for a discussion of enforcement dilemmas in residence halls).

What the presence of underage students does provide, however, is the opportunity to teach about abstaining while in a drinking environment and about including abstainers (albeit often involuntary ones) in social events. A policy which requires that parties or other campus events furnish nonalcoholic beverages in addition to beer or other alcohol creates both an expectation that underage students will obey the law and an atmosphere in which they can feel more comfortable doing so. The prohibition of alcohol-centered events, such as keg parties, can have the same effect. Events conducted in accordance with these rules can demonstrate to both underage and older students that drinking is not the only way to have fun and that abstainers are not dull or prudish people. Such events might also help students recognize that people's needs are different and that different types of people can come together in pleasant ways.

Policies that regulate the way alcohol is used at campus events can help legal-age students develop safe drinking behaviors. Some schools require food at events and trained bartenders to dispense drinks. Other policies mandate that drink service be curtailed at least one hour before the end of the event and require that designated drivers or taxicabs are available. These types of regulations show students that alcohol is a potentially dangerous drug and that there are ways to reduce the danger without giving up drinking.

As can be seen, many university policies address campus or school-related events. These occasions are more than entertainment; they can be laboratories for the development and maturation of social skills. Most students arrive at college having experience with alcohol (Eigen, 1991). However, in part because of their age, it is likely that they drank in secret with other inexperienced young people. It is also likely that they drank to get drunk. Campus events, and the rules that regulate them, can help students change their drinking patterns and develop appropriate, more "adult" behaviors.

Alcohol is often present in coed social situations. Eigen (1991) points out that many female students "will virtually never have a drink unless they are on a date or in the company of men" (p. 16), and that many college men believe that drinking and social success are related. Campus events, alcohol education programs, and programs about interpersonal relationships can help students find nonexploitive and safe ways of interacting with potential and actual romantic partners.

Student involvement in event planning teaches other kinds of social skills. While their focus will be on ensuring that everyone has a good time, university policies point out that everyone includes abstainers and those who are not able to drink (underage students, those in recovery, etc.) and that planning a good time means more than providing kegs, drinking-game paraphernalia, and some potato chips. Event planners learn that the host has some responsibility (morally and legally) for the consequences of guests' behavior and that the responsible host plans in advance for guest safety. They learn that the way an event is conceptualized and advertised (i.e., party vs. kegger) affects participants' behavior and the success of the event.

How substance abusers and violators of university policies are handled also contributes to student education and development. The most obvious educational components are programs about substance abuse for the general student population, special groups such as residence hall occupants, or those who have violated rules. Other learning takes place when students or their friends are confronted, disciplined, intervened upon, or counseled about their behavior. By these means, students can learn about substance abuse and how it is differentiated from use, a distinction that can be difficult within campus populations. They may discover that they do not have to accept intoxicated behavior when it disturbs their studies or activities or threatens their safety. They may learn that they can intervene with a friend and that intervention and treatment can prevent or curtail the damage and waste that abuse produces. And, for some, what they learn on campus will help them recognize and deal with their family histories of substance abuse.

Campus policy about alcohol and other drugs can help to create an environment filled with educational opportunities and healthy messages. Personnel, including staff, faculty, and other students, and the campus environment itself, from billboards and advertisements to social events, become conduits for the policy and its educational components.

POLICY OPTIONS

Given the need to take into account state and local laws, the institution's mission, its educational philosophy, and the goals it sets for its substance abuse policy, it is clear that no single set of statements can apply to all schools.

The Drug-Free Schools and Communities Act Amendments of 1989 do mandate, however, that universities prohibit any use of illegal substances, including the use of alcohol by underage students. The acts provide the following additional minimum requirements: the annual distribution of materials describing the health risks of substance use and abuse, available counseling programs, the college's sanctions for policy violations, and the legal sanctions at local, state, and federal levels; the establishment of sanctions, up to and including expulsion and referral for prosecution; assurance of enforcement of sanctions; and review of the program at least every other year (Commission on Substance Abuse at Colleges and Universities, 1994).

The Inter-Association Task Force on Alcohol Issues, a group created by several national organizations of college administrators, developed Model Campus Alcohol Policy Guidelines (Eddy, 1989). These go beyond the minimum, providing a number of recommendations for policy development. The group recommends that alcohol policies include the following:

1. Synopses of drinking age, regulation of sale, open container, and other pertinent laws (e.g., dram shop laws).

2. Locations where alcoholic beverages are permitted, preferably including a specific list of permitted locations.

3. Locations where alcoholic beverages may be sold, also with clear specification.

4. Guidelines regarding public and private social events within the jurisdiction of the school. Public events should be registered in advance and the following guidelines be followed: Appropriate permits should be obtained; measures should be taken to ensure that underage persons do not drink; direct access to alcoholic beverages should be limited to those designated as servers; consumption should be permitted only within a designated area; nonalcoholic beverages should be available in the same place and featured as prominently as alcoholic ones, both on site and in advertising; a reasonable portion of the budget should be designated for food; there should be no "drinking contests" permitted or promoted; the presence of alcohol should not be used to encourage attendance at events; advertisements should not mention the amount of alcohol that will be available; institutionally approved security staff should be present throughout the event.

5. A statement regarding the use of alcohol at membership recruitment functions, such as those held by fraternities, sororities, and other campus organizations.

6. A statement regarding the use of alcohol at athletic events and in athletic facilities. The statement should be specific and should apply equally to all potential attendees (students, faculty, alumni, etc.).

7. Guidelines for the marketing, promotion, or advertising of alcohol on campus.

8. Procedures for handling policy violations, including an explicit statement of sanctions to be applied. (Sherwood, 1987)

Harding (1993) provides a set of questions administrators might pose in order to evaluate their institution's alcohol policies. These include whether the policy is consistent with federal, state, and local laws; whether the policy addresses both individual and group behavior and events; whether it applies to all campus property as well as to off-campus events controlled by the university; whether it applies to the entire campus community, including administration, faculty, staff, and visitors; whether the policy is clearly stated and not contradictory in terms of the consequences of rule violation; and whether those responsible for enforcement are supported by the administration and have their authority clearly defined. Another question Harding poses is whether the policy addresses both on- and off-campus behavior. She states that the institution must be accountable for the former, and may, in the interest of good community relations, wish to have policies addressing the latter. She points out, however, that off-campus rules "may backfire if the institution is unwilling to enforce them" (p. 45).

Some Specific Policy Provisions

A look at specific regulations in place at various institutions reveals the range of particulars that might be addressed in a substance use and abuse policy as well as the range of potential responses an institution can make. Most of the provisions cited come from Eigen (1991) or *Rethinking Rites of Passage* (1994), a document produced by the Columbia University Center on Addiction and Substance Abuse. The reader is also directed to a set of reports developed by the now defunct Network of Colleges and Universities Committed to the Elimination of Drug and Alcohol Abuse (e.g., Harding, 1993).

Beer is banned at about 25 percent of American colleges; 32 percent ban hard liquor. While this certainly is one option, concerns have been expressed that banning drinking on campus serves to drive it off campus, placing students in situations that might be more dangerous than their relatively safe and supervised dorms and campus venues. Complete bans may also reduce the school's appeal to students, be unpopular with faculty or alumni/ae, and open the school to increased liability as a result of its endorsement of a policy that cannot be easily enforced (Commission on Substance Abuse at Colleges and Universities, 1994). Less contentious is the prohibition of drunkenness and disorderly behavior, a regulation that exists at almost all American colleges.

The majority of policy provisions seek to limit or define conditions under which students and others connected with the institution may use alcohol. The most traditional forms of regulation address locations where drinking can take place and times that drinking and events where alcohol is present can be held. Newer rules mandate amounts, types of beverages, and qualified servers. Universities and colleges have, for example, done the following:

1. Limited drinking events to weekends
2. Restricted Thursday night parties to groups at or above a specified GPA
3. Defined some activities as "no alcohol" events
4. Banned kegs

5. Required prior registration at events with alcohol

6. Restricted the amount of alcohol permitted at an event, based on the number of registrants

7. Limited numbers of students permitted to register and attend events

8. Required presentation of identification and hand stamping at the entrance to events

9. Mandated that nonalcoholic beverages be readily available at all functions where alcohol is available

10. Required food at events

11. Forbidden the purchase of alcohol with organizational funds

12. Forbidden members of campus organizations to dispense alcohol

13. Required trained servers to dispense alcohol

14. Instituted and funded Alcohol Awareness Weeks, BACCHUS programs, designated driver programs, and the like

15. Required members' attendance at a substance abuse education program before allowing the organization to have an event.

Policies have also addressed advertising of alcoholic beverages and events at which alcohol will be served. The target of the policy may be promotions, such as billboards, posters, and ads in student papers, done by campus organizations or by liquor and beer companies. Sponsorship of campus activities by liquor companies has also come under scrutiny. Some policies include the following:

1. Complete bans on liquor company advertisements

2. Complete bans on liquor company sponsorships of campus activities

3. Bans on hiring students as campus representatives of liquor companies

4. Forbidding or limiting liquor advertising at events or in promotions for events

5. Regulating the content of advertisements (forbidding mention of alcohol, certain types of messages, or the promotion of alcohol as the focus of activity)

6. Forbidding off-campus bars to use bulletin boards or advertise in campus papers or on campus radio stations

7. Forbidding any connection between campus logos or symbols and alcohol, such as on beer mugs, ashtrays, other drinking paraphernalia.

"If, from an alcohol risk point of view, the campus is a dangerous place, then the fraternity houses are the 'Bermuda Triangle' of the campus ocean" (Eigen, 1991, p. 8). A bright spot in this picture is that fraternities and sororities are recognizing the personal and legal dangers and are joining in the effort to reduce their risks. The National Interfraternity Conference, for example, has suggested that all fraternity parties be BYOB, with alcohol checked at the bar and distribution monitored (Commission on Substance Abuse at Colleges and Universities, 1994). The Fraternity Insurance Purchasing Group (FIPG) (1991), an organization that enables member chapters to purchase insurance, requires compliance with certain alcohol and drug regulations. Their risk-management policy includes provisions forbidding the purchase of alcohol with chapter funds; the purchase of kegs or cases; sale or provision of alcohol to minors; and cosponsorship of events with alcohol distributors, taverns, or others who sell or provide alcohol. FIPG policy also mandates dry rushes. Similarly, various universities have banned rushes, forbidden participation by freshmen/women, and/or instituted dry rushes.

As stated earlier, campus substance abuse policies must include statements of the consequences that may follow violations. Clear, noncontradictory sanctions are recommended, as is institutional support for those given enforcement responsibilities. In addition to possession of alcohol or other drugs and drunken or disorderly conduct, offenses may include possession of false ID, illegal sale of alcohol, and giving alcohol to an underaged person. Substance abuse education is a frequent sanction, especially for first-time offenders.

Although they may not be incorporated into formal policy statements, there are other issues that policy makers may want to consider. One is the availability of alternatives to drinking. In many college communities, bars and clubs are the only recreational facilities open late at night. While some feel that entertainment is not the responsibility of university personnel, others have considered providing alternatives, such as on-campus coffee houses, access to basketball courts and gyms, and special activities such as all-night film festivals.

The involvement of faculty in substance abuse prevention is another area to consider. Schools can provide training or information so that faculty members more easily recognize and respond to students having substance-related problems. Schools might also educate faculty on how their attitudes and behaviors affect student behavior (and open the school and themselves to lawsuits). In many departments, the subject of substance use and abuse can be incorporated into the curriculum. Finally, the scheduling of classes and exams can be a factor in campus drinking. At one university, where students began their "weekend" with parties on Thursday nights, the president suggested that faculty schedule exams and quizzes on Fridays, and Thursday partying decreased (Eigen, 1991). Thus, during their deliberations policy makers may also generate suggestions that can add to the university's response to substance use and abuse problems.

SUMMARY

This chapter has discussed the essential elements of an alcohol policy. These elements include a thorough understanding of the institution's mission and philosophy, an appreciation of the legal environment that helps shape an alcohol policy, information about the institutional objectives in the development of policy, selected educational perspectives on the possession and use of alcoholic beverages, and various policy options that institutions can consider in developing an alcohol policy. Our view is that a carefully crafted policy can significantly advance an institution's efforts in providing an appropriate environment related to the possession and use of alcohol, but a poorly conceived policy will take an institution down a path strewn with disasters.

REFERENCES

Barr, M. J. (1988). Institutional liability: What are the risks and obligations of student services? In M. J. Barr & Associates, *Student services and the law* (pp. 179–196). San Francisco: Jossey-Bass.

Barr, M. J. (1996). Legal foundations of student affairs practice. In S. R. Komives, D. B. Woodard, Jr., & Associates, *Student services: A handbook for the profession* (pp. 126–144). San Francisco: Jossey-Bass.

Commission on Substance Abuse at Colleges and Universities. (1994). *Rethinking rites of passage: Substance abuse on America's campuses*. New York: Columbia University, Center on Addiction and Substance Abuse.

Correnti, R. J. (1988). How public and private institutions differ under the law. In M. J. Barr & Associates, *Student services and the law* (pp. 25–43). San Francisco: Jossey-Bass.

Council for the Advancement of Student Services/Development Program. (1990). *Alcohol and other drug programs: Self assessment guide*. Athens, GA: Author.

Eddy, M. S. (1989). *College alcohol programs* (Report No. ED0-HE-88-16). Washington, DC: ERIC Clearinghouse on Higher Education (ERIC Document Reproduction Services No. ED 308 802).

Eigen, L. D. (1991). *Alcohol practices, policies, and potentials of American colleges and universities: An OSAP white paper* (Report No. DHHS-ADM-91-1842). Rockville, MD: Alcohol, Drug Abuse, and Mental Health Administration (DHHS/PHS) (ERIC Document Reproduction Service No. ED 350 928).

Fraternity Insurance Purchasing Group. (1991). *FIPG risk management manual*. NP: Author.

Gehring, D. D. (1987). Legal rights and responsibilities of campus student groups and advisers. In J. H. Schuh (Ed.), *A handbook for student group advisers* (2nd ed.) (pp. 115–149). Carbondale, IL: ACPA.

Gehring, D. D. (1991). Legal issues in the administration of student affairs. In T. K. Miller, R. B. Winston, Jr., & Associates, *Administration and leadership in student affairs* (2nd ed.) (pp. 379–413). Muncie, IN: Accelerated Development.

Gehring, D. D. (1994). Protective policy laws. In M. C. Coomes & D. D. Gehring (Eds.), *Student services in a changing federal climate: New directions for student services sourcebook no. 68* (pp. 67–82). San Francisco: Jossey-Bass.

Gonzalez, G. M. (1985). Alcohol on campus: You must ensure its responsible use—here's how. *AGB reports, 27*(4), 24–28.

Gonzalez, G. M. (1987). Alcohol policy development: A necessary component for a comprehensive education program on campus. In J. S. Sherwood (Ed.), *Alcohol policies and practices in college campuses* (pp. 87–95). Washington, DC: NASPA.

Goodale, T. (1987). Introduction. In J. S. Sherwood (Ed.), *Alcohol policies and practices in college campuses* (pp. vii–xii). Washington, DC: NASPA.

Harding, F. M. (1993). *Teamwork for healthy campuses: New York State college alcohol and other drug programs*. Albany: New York State Office of Alcoholism and Substance Abuse Services.

Kaplin, W. A., & Lee, B. A. (1995). *The law of higher education* (3rd ed.). San Francisco: Jossey-Bass.

Kuh, G. D. (1991). Characteristics of involving colleges. In G. D. Kuh & J. H. Schuh (Eds.), *The role and contribution of student affairs in involving colleges* (pp. 11–29). Washington, DC: NASPA.

Kuh, G. D., Schuh, J. H., & Whitt, E. J. (1991). *Involving colleges: Successful approaches to fostering student learning and development outside the classroom.* San Francisco: Jossey-Bass.

Lyons, J. W. (1993). The importance of institutional mission. In M. J. Barr & Associates, *The handbook of student affairs administration* (pp. 3–15). San Francisco: Jossey-Bass.

Perkins, H. W., & Berkowitz, A. D. (1986). Perceiving the community norms of alcohol use among students: Some research implications for campus alcohol education programming. *International Journal of the Addictions, 21,* 961–976.

Sherwood, J. S. (Ed.). (1987). *Alcohol policies and practices on college and university campuses* (NASPA Monograph, Vol. 7). Washington, DC: NASPA.

Walton, S. (1996). Social host liability: Risks for fraternity and student hosts. *NASPA Journal, 34,* 29–35.

6

From Reactive to Proactive Prevention: Promoting an Ecology of Health on Campus

Alan D. Berkowitz

Alcohol and other drug specialists on college and university campuses have traditionally focused their efforts on the prevention of abuse and on identification, intervention, and treatment strategies for abusers. These efforts place the abuser and his or her abuse at the heart of prevention and educational efforts. There is growing evidence, however, that an exclusive emphasis on abuse and problem behavior may unintentionally serve to perpetuate problem alcohol and other drug (AOD) use. Focusing solely on AOD use and its negative effects draws attention to extreme problem behavior and fosters a perception that the campus environment is more abusing than it really is.

In fact, on most campuses, what a majority of students believe about the AOD use of their peers is inaccurate (Baer, Stacy, & Larimer, 1991; Haines, 1996; Presley, Meilman, & Lyerla, 1995; Perkins & Berkowitz, 1986a; Prentice & Miller, 1993). This misperception can alienate and marginalize the majority of students who use responsibly or who do not use at all by leading them to feel that it is their more responsible behavior which is deviant. The emphasis on problem behavior that needs to be changed or prevented creates an environment in which pressure to conform to a false norm is exacerbated. In contrast, documenting and reinforcing already existing positive norms among students has been shown to be effective in fostering campus climates which are supportive of health-enhancing behaviors. This latter model of drug prevention, described here as "proactive prevention," is the subject of this chapter.

The proactive prevention model focuses on positive, healthy behaviors in the context of the larger campus social ecology. It is proactive because it seeks to eliminate or reduce pressures, attitudes, and beliefs which lead to increased use and abuse, rather then merely reacting to the consequences of abuse or calling attention to them. Like other models of drug prevention, it incorporates traditional primary, secondary, and tertiary intervention strategies to help abusers and prevent abuse. However, these interventions are offered within the context of a comprehensive campus program which emphasizes the larger campus climate, discourages abuse, and empowers non-using and non-abusing students and their behaviors. The following are the definitions of primary, secondary, and tertiary prevention as they are commonly used within the drug prevention field.

Primary Prevention The objective of primary prevention is to protect the individual in order to avoid problems prior to signs or symptoms of problems. It includes activities, programs, and practices that operate on a fundamentally nonpersonal basis to alter the set of opportunities, risks, and expectations surrounding individuals. Primary prevention interventions are usually directed at large groups and/or communities.

Secondary Prevention Persons who are in the early stages of problem behavior associated with alcohol and other drugs, or who are at risk for such problems are the focus of secondary prevention activities. Secondary prevention attempts to avert the ensuing negative consequences of abuse by inducing individuals, through counseling, educational programs, or treatment, to give up or change their behavior. It is often referred to as early intervention.

Tertiary Prevention Individuals who use alcohol and other drugs compulsively are the subject of tertiary prevention, which strives to ameliorate negative effects through treatment and rehabilitation. Tertiary prevention is commonly referred to as treatment, but also includes rehabilitation and relapse prevention (Office of Substance Abuse Prevention, 1989).

This chapter reviews the evolution of the proactive prevention model, presents relevant theory and research in support of the model, identifies characteristics of effective programs and the role of survey data within them, and provides examples of innovative strategies based on this model which have been effective in reducing drinking on college and university campuses.

EVOLUTION OF THE PROACTIVE PREVENTION MODEL

In the last thirty years, there has been a distinct evolution in the theories and strategies developed to reduce AOD use in educational settings (Gilchrist, 1994). Within higher education, the evolution from earlier models to a proactive prevention model has been catalyzed by the Department of Education's Fund for the Improvement of Post-Secondary Education (FIPSE) Drug Prevention Program. FIPSE has funded hundreds of college and university efforts since its inception in 1987, and has actively promoted the proactive prevention model.

The proactive prevention model incorporates strategies of earlier models of AOD prevention, providing services to prevent abuse among non-users (primary prevention), reducing the likelihood that at-risk individuals will develop problems (secondary prevention), and helping abusers into recovery (tertiary prevention). Thus, the proactive prevention model utilizes many strategies and approaches associated with other models, but incorporates these activities into a more comprehensive, campuswide program which emphasizes the strengthening of already existent healthy behaviors.

The different models of AOD prevention which have been employed on college and university campuses and their historical evolution will be briefly reviewed. Each model is based on particular theoretical assumptions about human behavior and how substance use patterns can be changed. It is best to view these models and theories as cumulative; later models incorporate and expand on earlier ones. Each theoretical advance leads in turn to new programmatic approaches to drug prevention.

Individual Change and Social Influence Models

Early AOD prevention approaches focused on the individual in isolation from a social context. These models made a number of assumptions about behavior change: that the provision of information (information-only or awareness model) or teaching of skills (skill-deficiency model) would help individuals change abusive behavior (tertiary prevention) or inculcate resistance to developing future problems among at-risk (secondary prevention) or other individuals (primary prevention). As research accumulated suggesting that peer and social influences were more important in predicting abuse than were personality, family, and social background differences, new models evolved to take into account the influence of peers, with the goal of helping at-risk individuals resist these influences (social learning and social-influence models). All these models—information and awareness, skill deficiency, and social influence—utilized interventions which focused on the potential or actual problem behavior of individuals rather than on changes in the broader social environment. To a large degree, evaluation studies and research conducted in the 1960s, 1970s, and early 1980s suggest that these approaches were ineffective in reducing abuse (Moskowitz, 1989; Rundell & Brunold, 1988).

Social Ecology or Person-in-Environment Models

The next generation of theory about AOD prevention emphasized the importance of the social environment in shaping and maintaining individual behavior. The social ecology or person-in-environment model focuses on primary prevention, viewing the entire community as the target of the intervention. Social ecological approaches employ a variety of components common to previous models, including disseminating information, teaching skills to "inoculate" individuals against use or abuse, training leaders, using media, and developing effective policies, all with the goal of helping individuals resist peer pressure to use and abuse drugs (Gilchrist, 1994). For the most part, this model focuses on negative behavior or on teaching individuals skills to resist negative influences from others, and does not call into question the accuracy of students' perceptions of their environment. Evaluation research suggests that the social ecology/person-in-environment model is more effective than previous models in preventing and reducing abuse (Gilchrist, 1994).

Misperceived-Norms Model

H. Wesley Perkins and I were among the first to point out that the well-documented influence of peers on AOD use might be due to students' *misperceptions* of peer attitudes and behaviors (Perkins & Berkowitz, 1986a). In an analysis of data collected in 1979, we demonstrated that most college students held moderate personal attitudes with respect to alcohol consumption but perceived their peers to be much more permissive or tolerant of abuse than was actually the case. The data in Table 6.1 indicate that a majority of students described their own attitude toward alcohol as one in which drinking and occasional intoxication were acceptable when this drinking did not interfere with academic or other responsibilities (personal attitude). However, the perception of most students was that their peers held a more permissive attitude, in which occasional or frequent intoxication was acceptable even when it resulted in negative consequences (perceived norm). In this model, what the aggregate of students really believe is called the "actual norm," while the incorrect belief is called the "perceived norm," or the "misperception" of the norm.

Questions evaluating the extent to which students misperceive the AOD-related behavior of their peers have since been incorporated into the CORE instrument (Presley, Meilman, & Lyerla, 1994) and other research surveys. The CORE instrument, a standardized questionnaire used to assess campus drug problems, is described in detail later in this chapter. Analysis of data collected with these instruments has led to widespread empirical confirmation of the existence of such misperceptions (Baer et al., 1991; Haines, 1996; Presley et al., 1995; Prentice & Miller, 1993).

Other research indicates that students who experience themselves as deviating from this false norm increase their drinking over time in order to conform more closely to their peers' purported behavior (Prentice & Miller, 1993). A similar convergence of behavior toward a false norm has been documented for cigarette smoking among adolescents (Chassin, Presson, Sherman, Corty, & Olshavsky, 1984; Marks, Graham, & Hansen, 1992; Sussman et al., 1988). This phenomenon (convergence of behavior toward a false norm) suggests that, when uncorrected, misperceptions may create increased pressure to drink over time and result in a worsening of substance abuse problems on campus.

Conversely, efforts to correct misperceptions can serve as a means of reducing perceived peer pressure to use alcohol and other drugs or to delay the onset of alcohol, marijuana, and cigarette use among adolescents, as has been reported by Hansen and Graham (1991). Additional support for the influence

Table 6.1
Percentage Distribution of Personal Attitudes and Perceived Campus Norms for Alcohol Use among Students (N = 1,116)

Items	Personal attitudes	Perceived norm
"Drinking is never a good thing to do."	1.4	0.1
"Drinking is all right, but a student should never get 'smashed'."	12.7	0.8
"An occasional 'drunk' is okay as long as it doesn't interfere with grades or responsibilities."	66.0	35.4
"An occasional 'drunk' is okay even if it does occasionally interfere with grades or responsibilities."	9.3	33.2
"A frequent 'drunk' is okay if that's what the individual wants to do."	9.5	29.5
(No response)	(1.0)	(1.1)

Source: Perkins & Berkowitz (1986a).
Note: Percentages do not add up to 100 because of rounding.

of peer norms is provided by data from the Monitoring the Future Project. Data from this longitudinal study were analyzed to determine that the steady decline in adolescent use of cocaine, marijuana, and cigarettes during the 1970s and 1980s could be explained by increases in the percentage of adolescents who perceived that their peers disapproved of substance use (Bachman, Johnston, & O'Malley, 1990; Bachman, Johnston, O'Malley, & Humphrey, 1988). This demonstrates that appropriate information about peers can be effectively used to change individual behavior.

Studies have demonstrated that misperceptions are held by all members of campus communities, including undergraduate and graduate students, faculty, and staff (University of Michigan, 1993), and by student leaders such as resident advisers (Berkowitz & Perkins, 1986). They are formed in response to highly visible problem behavior (such as public drunkenness), which, because of its visibility, is remembered more than responsible behavior, despite the fact that such problem behavior is exhibited by only a minority of students (Berkowitz, 1991; Perkins, 1994a).

In an important theoretical elaboration of this model, H. Wesley Perkins (1994b) suggested that misperceptions are maintained and spread by public conversations that focus disproportionately on such observable, extreme behavior. The whole campus community is thus implicated in the spread of myths and misperceptions, which creates an enabling environment for AOD abuse. This negative environment is further exacerbated by reactive AOD prevention efforts, which focus attention exclusively on the problem of abuse and its consequences and overlook the more moderate norms and healthy behaviors exhibited by most students.

This misperceived-norms model was used to develop a comprehensive approach to AOD prevention based on the correction of misperceived norms as the primary intervention strategy (Berkowitz & Perkins, 1987a). The misperceived-norms model emphasizes the use of survey data to correct misperceived norms and to tailor programs to the needs of special populations, and incorporates accurate information about campus norms into primary, secondary, and tertiary prevention activities.

The Proactive Prevention Model

A number of modifications have been made to the misperceived-norms model since its inception, and implementation of the model has been improved by new intervention strategies. In early applications of the misperceived-norms model based on Berkowitz and Perkins (1987a), the actual misperception was reported to students. However, Haines (in press) has noted that it is more important to document and report healthy behaviors and actual norms in prevention programs than to provide information about misperceptions, as presentation of the last may in fact be confusing. Application of the model has also been enhanced by improved methods for disseminating information that employ social marketing and environmental assessment strategies. This revision of the misperceived-norms model is here called the proactive prevention model of drug prevention.

The proactive prevention model is distinguished from previous approaches by its two main components: emphasizing the importance of providing accurate information about communities and normative environments, and focusing on healthy, positive attitudes and behaviors of community members. One of the goals of this approach is to empower abstainers and responsible drinkers to take a more visible role in shaping campus ecology and modeling healthy behaviors. Implementation of this model has been described in detail by Haines (1996), who used it successfully, with the modifications noted, to reduce binge drinking at Northern Illinois University.

Other recent research suggests that the negative effects of alcohol on campus are perpetuated by a small minority of heavy-drinking students who impose the negative consequences of their drinking on the non-abusing majority (Wechsler, Moeykens, Davenport, Castillo, & Hansen, 1995). In their study of almost eighteen thousand college students at 140 institutions, these researchers found that 66 percent of all respondents had experienced at least one adverse consequence from other students' drinking. Non-heavy-drinking students who attended heavy-drinking schools were 3.6 times more likely to experience problems from another person's drinking than were non-heavy-drinking students at lower-drinking-level schools. The experience of being bothered by the negative effects of someone else's drinking is somewhat analogous to the concept of passive smoking and has been termed "secondary heavy drink effects" by Wechsler and his colleagues. Campus data on the extent to which secondary heavy drink effects occur, along with information on peer disapproval, can be used within the proactive prevention model to reinforce actual norms and encourage the majority of students to become less tolerant and accepting of the negative behaviors of a minority.

Another methodology which can be used to promote the goals of the proactive prevention model is environmental risk assessment (Ryan, Colthurst, & Segars, 1994). Environmental risk assessment provides a method of analyzing the availability of alcohol (how, when, and where it is provided) to develop profiles of community risk factors which contribute to alcohol-related problems. The environmental factors which are identified often play a key role in the development and maintenance of exaggerated perceptions of use. These include the visibility and frequency of alcohol advertising and promotional materials, the visibility of alcohol use and its effects, and the prevalence of negative messages in campus media. Following identification of critical environmental risks, strategies can be developed to change their prevalence. This in turn may result in reduced misperceptions and reduced problem drinking.

While media campaigns are most effective when they report data about the local campus community, Haines (1996) has suggested that national data from the Monitoring the Future Project (Bachman et al., 1990; Bachman et al., 1988) or the Wechsler and colleagues (1995) study can be used as part of a proactive prevention strategy when local data are not available.

CHARACTERISTICS OF EFFECTIVE PROGRAMS

The proactive prevention model utilizes relevant theory and research to explain how campus environments support drug abuse and how they can be changed. To be effective, however, programs using this model must be implemented using techniques that effectively translate theory and research into action. A variety of program strategies have been associated with the effectiveness of drug prevention programs and are currently recommended by experts. These program components can be summarized under the following headings: (1) comprehensiveness—inclusion of all campus constituencies and a focus on the larger campus ecology, (2) intensity—activities which are interactive and sustained over time, (3) relevance—developmentally appropriate, peer-oriented, and tailored to the needs of different campus groups, and (4) positive—emphasizing healthy behaviors and program successes rather than abusive behavior and problems. Each component and its role within the proactive prevention model will be briefly described in greater detail and are summarized in the following list:

Comprehensiveness

Involves all campus constituencies

Permeates all aspects of the institution

Provides multiple exposure to interventions

Utilizes campus media to correct misperceived norms

Targets the community as a whole

Intensity

Activities are sustained over time

Activities require active rather than passive involvement

Activities are regular at set times and places and are dependable

Relevance

Activities are tailored to the needs of specific campus groups

Interventions focus on peer-related variables

Students are used in leadership roles

The relationship of AOD to other health behaviors is emphasized

Positive messages

Healthy behaviors are documented and reinforced

Individuals are encouraged to focus on what they can do, not on what they should not do

An emphasis on problem behaviors or problems is avoided. (*Adapted from* Berkowitz, 1990)

For the most part, these techniques and strategies focus on implementation and can be used in association with any of the theories and models that have been described.

Comprehensiveness

A comprehensive program is one that involves almost all individuals and constituencies within an institution, is incorporated into multiple aspects of their institutional experience, and includes multiple exposures to different program strategies. A comprehensive program includes faculty, staff, and students; offers activities in a variety of contexts; and utilizes campus media to document and reinforce actual healthy norms and behaviors which exist on campus. Because faculty and staff hold misperceptions similar to those of students and are often responsible for the dissemination of these misperceptions, interventions directed at faculty and staff are an important component of a comprehensive proactive prevention program.

Intensity

Intensive programs are sustained over time and require active rather than passive involvement. One-time events, such as alcohol awareness weeks or isolated programs, have limited impact which diminish over time if they are not linked to other ongoing activities. Programs that require active participation through discussion, role plays, and other experiential techniques are more effective than those which allow for passive observation, such as sitting in a classroom or lecture (Goodstadt & Caleekal-John, 1984; Oblander, 1984). Intensive programs use creative methods to capture student attention and encourage retention of information provided through more passive sources, such as campus media.

A good example of a theoretically based, intensive, peer-oriented classroom intervention based on the individual-change/social-influence model has been provided by Gonzalez (1989), who developed an experiential drug education course for college students. The course consisted of equal amounts of time spent in lectures and small group discussions led by peer facilitators. The facilitators led students in role-playing exercises on assertiveness and interpersonal communication skills, values clarification, and consumption self-monitoring exercises. Evaluation data indicated that the course was effective in reducing participants' susceptibility to drug use and abuse.

Relevance

Programs are effective when they are relevant to an individual's present-day experience. As campuses become increasingly diverse, generic one-for-all programs become less effective. To ensure relevance, programs need to accomplish the following: (1) be tailored to the specific needs of individual student groups, (2) acknowledge both the emotional ambivalence and the sense of invulnerability of young adulthood, (3) focus on positive peer-related variables (such as actual norms and peer disapproval), (4) utilize student leaders to deliver messages, and (5) acknowledge that AOD use interacts with and is a risk factor for a variety of other health and behavioral problems which must be addressed in conjunction with each other.

Until recently, the overwhelming majority of research on collegiate and noncollegiate AOD use was conducted with samples of Caucasian students. Programs designed on the basis of this research incorrectly assume that other individuals will behave and be affected in a similar fashion. In fact, a growing research literature has documented differences among groups of college students that affect the way in which they use and perceive alcohol and other drugs. These include gender differences (see Berkowitz & Perkins, 1987b; Engs & Hanson, 1989; Perkins, 1991, 1992), racial and ethnic differences (Meilman, Presley, & Lyerla, 1994; Presley, Meilman, & Lyerla, 1995), sexual orientation, participation in campus groups and subcultures such as fraternities and sororities and athletic teams, religiosity (Perkins, 1985, 1994), and familial alcoholism (Perkins, 1987; Perkins & Berkowitz, 1991). With respect to ethnicity, for example, recent data from the CORE Institute indicate that AOD use is most problematic for Caucasians and Native Americans and least problematic for Asian and African Americans, with Hispanics in-between (Presley et al., 1995). Lawson and Lawson (1989) have provided an excellent edited volume addressing group differences for a number of special populations. To whatever extent possible, prevention programs should tailor information and relevant messages to such groups and take into account their unique characteristics.

Positive Messages

As noted earlier in this chapter, negative messages that focus on problem use and its consequences tend to reinforce misperceptions, exaggerate the extent of problems, and encourage the majority of students, who hold healthy attitudes, to be silent about their beliefs and behaviors. On the other hand, media and promotional campaigns which call attention to healthy attitudes and behaviors can empower students in this silent majority to become more visible and influential. Haines (1996) suggests that effective prevention messages have the following characteristics: They are positive and promote achievable behaviors rather than those to be avoided, they are inclusive (i.e., include all elements of the target population), and they are empowering (i.e., affirm and encourage rather than scare and blame people).

THE ROLE OF AOD SURVEYS IN PROACTIVE PREVENTION

Implementation of the proactive prevention model requires that communities be provided with accurate information about behavioral norms and other factors known to influence AOD use. In the past, such data have not been available due to the fact that AOD surveys have traditionally been used primarily for needs assessment and evaluation purposes to assess changes in behavior over time. This descriptive approach overlooks the value of surveys in obtaining data that can become an integral part of the change process itself. In contrast, the proactive prevention model requires survey data on student AOD behaviors, attitudes, and perceptions—data that can be incorporated into educational programs, analyzed according to the characteristics and needs of different campus groups, and used to provide direct, ongoing feedback to students about their own behavior. This section provides guidelines for the collection of survey data within the proactive prevention model as originally proposed by Perkins and Berkowitz (1986b), and more recently by Berkowitz (1994) and Haines (1996).

Campuses that want to use survey data within the proactive prevention model can develop their own surveys or use standardized surveys which provide individual campus data. The proactive prevention model is more effective when local campus data can be collected; when this is not possible, national data and norms can be adapted for use (Haines, 1996). Data are analyzed to assess the following: the extent to which misperceived norms exist on campus, the healthy behaviors or attitudes of a majority of students, and the unique patterns of substance use among different campus constituencies. These data are then presented within primary, secondary, and tertiary prevention contexts.

Perkins and Berkowitz (1987a) compared the misperceived-norms model with more traditional approaches in terms of how survey data can be used for primary, secondary, and tertiary prevention. Within the proactive prevention model, surveys can be used to identify community-wide norms regarding alcohol use and document healthy behaviors (primary prevention), reveal norms and healthy behaviors about alcohol use patterns and attitudes of problem-prone groups to their own membership (secondary prevention), utilize alcohol survey results to create group discussion and reinforce healthy behaviors within particular social groups (secondary prevention), or utilize survey data to help clients assess themselves within the context of the larger community (tertiary prevention).

Until recently there were no standardized, easily administered, machine-scorable AOD surveys that could be used to establish national norms and provide comparable data for campuses with similar demographic features. This problem has been rectified with the development of the Centers for Disease Control's (CDC) National College Health Risk Behavior Survey (NCHRBS) and the CORE Alcohol and Drug survey.

The NCHRBS and CORE have different strengths and weaknesses. The NCHRBS measures behaviors across a variety of dimensions in addition to alcohol, including nutrition, sexuality, intentional and unintentional injury, and mental health. It is thus an excellent instrument for assessing the relationship of AOD use to other types of risk-taking behavior. The NCHRBS is an adaptation of the CDC's Youth Risk Behavior Survey (YRBS) (Kolbe, Kahn, & Collins, 1993) and will be used to help monitor progress toward "Healthy People 2000" and toward the "National Health Objectives for the Year 2000." An analysis and rationale for the questions on alcohol incorporated into the YRBS and NCHRBS have been provided by Blanken (1993). The NCHRBS is machine scorable and is usually administered in classroom settings or through campus mailings. Data from the NCHRBS can also be useful for comparison of college student populations with other, noncollege populations.

The short form of the CORE, while lacking the breadth of the NCHRBS, provides a more comprehensive overview of behaviors, perceptions, and environmental factors associated with AOD use. Another advantage of the CORE is that the answer sheet contains five blank spaces which can be used to ask questions of particular interest on individual campuses administering the survey. The CORE Alcohol and Drug Survey User's Manual that accompanies the questionnaire reviews sampling procedures, methods of survey administration, and techniques for ensuring a high response rate (Presley, Harrold, Scouten, Lyerla, & Meilman, 1994). It provides an excellent introduction to survey administration procedures which can be used with or without the CORE questionnaire itself. On most campuses, the CORE has been administered during classes or sent out through the campus mail.

Recently, a long form of the CORE has been developed which includes a second page incorporating additional questions related to myths and beliefs about AOD use, relationship to other risk behaviors (sexuality, violence, and injury), perceptions of risk and peer disapproval, perceptions of the campus environment, participation in campus activities, and negative effects of other people's drinking. The long form of the CORE takes an additional ten minutes to complete (thirty instead of twenty minutes) and has been designed to provide the kind of information necessary for implementation of the proactive prevention model.

Another potential use of surveys is to collect information that can be used to evaluate the relative effectiveness of different program activities (Berkowitz & Perkins, 1987a). This can be done by including questions assessing the extent to which survey respondents are aware of or have participated in program activities. Data analysis can then examine the relationship between program participation and changes in AOD behaviors within the campus as a whole or for specific subpopulations (Berkowitz, 1994).

The following summary points (from Berkowitz, 1994) should be considered in the development of survey instruments to assess AOD use, in evaluating the usefulness of the CORE and NCHRBS, and for assessing ways to use the optional five questions on the CORE.

1. AOD surveys should include questions which assess use patterns, motivations, negative consequences, perceptions, and other correlates for AOD use. Such questions should have an explicit theoretical rationale and/or programmatic application.

2. Demographic information should be collected which provides information on campus subpopulations and groups for whom current knowledge is lacking (i.e., ethnic and sexual minorities, nontraditional students, abstainers, high-risk populations, and individuals who have reduced their use.)

3. Whenever possible, standardized instruments should be used or questions from them should be incorporated into campus surveys. This will provide a means of comparing institutional survey data with that from other institutions with similar characteristics.

4. Surveys should be used to collect data that can be used for counseling and outreach purposes and that can provide meaningful information to the campus community about itself. Comments should be solicited from student-development specialists, administrators, programmers, and peer educators as part of the process of developing survey instruments to determine what types of information would be helpful to them.

5. Surveys can be used to help evaluate the effectiveness of AOD programs. Thus, surveys should include measures of participation in program activities to more accurately assess the relative impact of these interventions and the cumulative impact of participation in multiple interventions.

Most of these objectives can be met by using the long form of the CORE. Information on the availability of the CORE can be obtained from the CORE Institute, Center for Alcohol and Other Drug Studies, Student Health Programs, Southern Illinois University, Carbondale, IL 62901 (phone 618–453–4366). For information on the NCHRBS, contact the Centers for Disease Control and Prevention, National Center for Chronic Disease Prevention and Health Promotion, Division of Adolescent and School Health, 4770 Buford Hwy. N.E., MS-K-33, Atlanta, GA 30341–3724 (phone 404–488–5330).

CASE STUDIES: EXAMPLES OF EFFECTIVE INTERVENTIONS

In recent years the proactive prevention model has been applied effectively on college and university campuses to reduce the incidence of alcohol abuse. The concluding section of this chapter provides case studies of three campuses and one clinical case study of an alcohol abuser to illustrate how the proactive prevention model has been applied to promote the goals of primary, secondary, and tertiary prevention. The case studies also show how the model can be implemented using strategies which are comprehensive, intensive, relevant, and positive, along with techniques for effectively incorporating survey data. Haines (1996) recently provided a detailed handbook describing implementation of the proactive prevention model, which will be invaluable to anyone interested in applying this approach.

Primary Prevention (Northern Illinois University)

At Northern Illinois University (NIU) the proactive prevention model has been incorporated into a primary prevention effort aimed at supporting positive drinking norms and behaviors and reducing binge drinking. Drug-abuse prevention and treatment has been provided to students on this campus since 1972. Since 1988, annual surveys have been conducted to assess the extent of AOD use and related problems on campus. In the 1988–1989 academic year, the first year of an NIU FIPSE grant, mainstream prevention strategies were used to reduce heavy drinking. These included promotion of abstinence and moderate drinking, educating students about the negative consequences of use, and education programs for student residences and other groups. Although misperceptions were surveyed, no special effort was made to change students' misperception of the prevalence of heavy drinking (defined as six or more drinks when partying). Program outcomes at the end of this first year were disappointing: There was no change in the percentage of heavy drinkers (44%), and students continued to perceive NIU as a heavy-drinking campus (69% of students thought that most students were heavy drinkers).

During the 1989–1990 academic year, a concerted effort was made to change students' perceptions of alcohol use through a comprehensive public-information media campaign. Campus surveys had indicated that the campus newspaper was read by 75 percent of students on a daily basis and that it was the preferred source of obtaining health information for 80 percent of students. These preferences were taken into consideration in the development of the media campaign, which included the following components: (1) Advertisements were placed in the daily campus newspaper documenting actual campus norms for alcohol use, (2) flyers with information about healthy behaviors and actual campus norms were distributed around campus and in all informational programs, and (3) peer educators were used to stimulate student interest in the information campaign and to encourage students to remember the information provided. The total cost for the media campaign was only $3,000.

The third component of the program used peer educators in a unique and imaginative manner. Peer educators who were dressed in trenchcoats, fedoras, and shades—"The Money Brothers"—periodically approached tables of students in cafeterias at lunch and dinner hours. They asked the students to report the correct percentage of NIU students who were not heavy drinkers, and the percentage who did not condone drunkenness. When students responded correctly, they were awarded a dollar bill, then all students in the vicinity were awarded copies of the flyer. Students who responded incorrectly also received the flyer. This creative strategy called attention to information provided through the campus paper and provided a motivation for students to learn the information.

Following this intervention the number of students who overestimated the percentage of heavy drinkers on campus dropped by 10 percent (from 69 to 59%), and there was a corresponding decrease in the percentage of heavy drinkers (from 44 to 36%). In addition, the number of campus deaths due to alcohol was reduced from three to zero, and the percentage of students who reported alcohol-related injuries was reduced from 30 to 22 percent (Haines, 1996). These changes suggest that the campus program was effective in changing actual behavior and not just responses to surveys. National data for the same time period showed no decrease in the rate of heavy drinking, ruling out other causes for the decrease at NIU (see Figure 6.1). This program has been continued in subsequent years with similar rates of success.

Primary and Secondary Prevention (Mississippi State University)

At Mississippi State, the proactive prevention approach was utilized to launch a media campaign directed at the whole campus (primary prevention), as well as to educate the "carriers of the misperception" (faculty, administration, and campus leaders) about actual campus norms in order to reduce their role in the spread of misperceptions of campus use (secondary prevention). Because individuals who have and spread misconceptions can be considered to "have a problem" that needs to be addressed, efforts to educate them can be thought of as secondary prevention. In fact, one positive outcome of the Mississippi State program was an increased willingness on the part of faculty, staff, and students to enforce campus policies related to alcohol use.

Figure 6.1
Effects of Social Influence Media Intervention on Student Binge Drinking

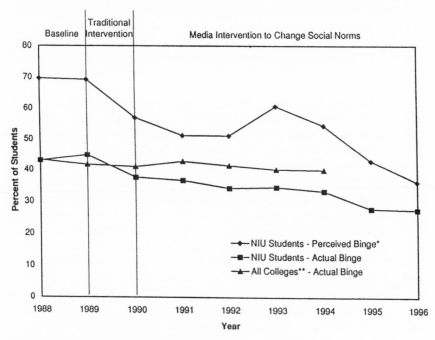

Source: Haines (1996); reprinted by permission.
*Binge defined as drinking more than five drinks when "partying."
**Data not available for 1995 or 1996.

Although campus surveys indicated that Mississippi State was traditionally a low-use campus, student and staff perceived campus use patterns to be high. This misperception led both students and staff to accept the values and actions of students who abused alcohol as being typical of the student body as a whole. Many administrators assumed, for example, that most students would object to stricter enforcement of the existing alcohol policies on campus. As part of a FIPSE drug-prevention award, CORE data were used to launch a media campaign during the 1991–1992 academic year. The campaign had five goals: (1) to counter bad publicity, (2) to create a positive campus image, (3) to direct more campus resources toward prevention, (4) to direct attention away from irresponsible student behavior toward responsible and non-using behavior, and (5) to more consistently enforce campus policies regulating alcohol use.

The media campaign had a number of components. Following the NIU program, ads were placed in the student newspaper documenting actual norms, and dollar bills were given out by students wearing "We Pass the Buck" buttons. Myth-reduction information was promulgated among students, faculty, staff, and parents of students, and was provided in classroom drug-education workshops offered to approximately 25 percent of Mississippi State's thirteen thousand students each year. Program staff gained access to the classroom by offering to present a program on days when faculty had to be absent.

In addition, a secondary prevention initiative was developed to prevent leaders who already held the misperception from conveying it to other members of the community. These leaders included faculty, administration, and student leaders, who were educated about actual norms for alcohol use on campus. Results of data collected with the CORE were summarized in a five-point ·executive summary titled "The Good News About Mississippi State," which reported information about positive behaviors and corrected misperceptions of campus norms. This information was provided to administrators through distribution of the executive summary at staff meetings. Myth-reduction information was also provided in faculty and staff newsletters and in the campus newspaper.

The campaign was so successful that after two years the "We Pass the Buck" program had to be limited to first-year students. Following these interventions, there was a statistically significant increase in the number of women who had not had a drink in the last year, a decrease in the rate of impaired driving, and a substantial increase in the number of students who did not want alcohol present at parties. This last fact was convincing for administrators, who modified alcohol-policy sanctions and enforcement procedures, recognizing that many students preferred an alcohol-free campus environment.

Secondary Prevention (The Medical College of Wisconsin)

At The Medical College of Wisconsin (MCW) the proactive prevention model was utilized to develop educational outreach programs specifically oriented to the needs of medical students. This program provides a good example of how a proactive secondary prevention effort can be tailored to the needs of a particular population.

MCW was awarded a FIPSE grant in 1989. The goals of the MCW program were to (1) support students who abstained or drank infrequently, (2) encourage students who drank moderately to maintain moderation or drink less, and (3) encourage students who drank heavily to decrease their drinking.

In the first phase of the program, data were collected from groups of students who had been targeted for educational interventions. Data included actual use patterns, attitudes toward drunkenness, perceptions of other students' use of alcohol, and perceptions of other students' attitudes toward drunkenness. Following analysis of the data, programs were presented to the target groups by medical students. A quiz-bowl format was used. The presentations focused on providing accurate information about students' alcohol use, attitudes, and behaviors, and behaviors students engaged in at parties. Campus data and supporting evidence from the literature were used to document the positive attitudes, behaviors, and choices demonstrated by a majority of students, who thought they were in a minority.

Students attending the quiz-bowl program participated in a followup survey one month later. Comparisons between students in the target group and a control group (students who did not participate in the quiz bowl) indicated that students in the target group developed more accurate perceptions of campus norms as a result of attending the program. In addition, students in the target group were found to be less vulnerable to peer pressure to drink, as measured by a "party scenario" question assessing students' level of comfort with refusing drinks when they were offered.

All three of these programs meet the criteria for effective programs outlined in Table 6.1, and used survey data according to the guidelines provided here. They were comprehensive (with respect to the target population), intensive, relevant, and utilized positive messages. Each program used data from the campus in question and developed creative strategies that were interactive and caught student attention ("The Money Brothers," "We Pass the Buck," and quiz-bowl programs).

Tertiary Prevention (An Anonymous Abuser)

Students who exhibit alcohol dependence or abuse may need a variety of clinical treatment strategies to change their behavior, including individual and group psychotherapy, inpatient treatment, and support services for special populations, such as children of alcoholics (COA). These services are provided within the proactive prevention model, but in a much broader context. At each point of contact (individual psychotherapy, group psychotherapy, judicial interventions, etc.) correct data about actual campus norms are provided in order to confront the abuser's denial and weaken enabling factors in his or her environment. The following case study illustrates how the proactive prevention model can be applied in working with substance abusers.

Mike was apprehended during his first-year orientation when he was found with alcohol in violation of campus policy. As part of his judicial hearing, accurate information about campus norms was provided, and this information was reintroduced during a mandatory educational program. When Mike decided to enter counseling voluntarily after an incident which almost got him expelled from school, his therapist was able to refer to the campus data to help address Mike's denial and claims that "everyone" was drinking like him. Data on actual use patterns and the impact of abusers on non-abusers were also incorporated into a group for students in recovery which Mike attended the next year. Similar relevant data on COA were incorporated when he participated in a COA group his junior year. Thus, although Mike's actual treatment within his campus proactive prevention program was in many ways not different from that on any other campus or clinic, the emphasis on normative, healthy behavior was used to confront his denial more effectively and provide a context for his behavior at each point in the treatment process.

SUMMARY AND CONCLUSION

Effective drug prevention programs should be based on sound theory and use effective strategies for translating theory into action. This chapter introduced the proactive prevention model of intervention, a model that attempts to reinforce and promote healthy behaviors on campus and avoids the traditional focus on problem behaviors and measures of abuse. Campus programs based on this model utilize campus data about positive norms and behavior and are integrated into primary, secondary, and tertiary prevention activities. Effective interventions are comprehensive (reach the whole campus), relevant (about the campus and its different populations), intensive (interactive and sustained over time), and promote positive messages. Recent research presented in support of the model provides evidence that the incidence of problem behavior is overestimated by students on most campuses, and that this misperception contributes to substance abuse problems. The proactive prevention model was applied in case studies of three campuses which have successfully used it to reduce problem behavior by reinforcing healthy norms.

ACKNOWLEDGMENTS

The author gratefully acknowledges the financial assistance of the Christopher D. Smithers Foundation in the writing of this chapter. I would also like to thank H. Wesley Perkins, Michael Haines, and Ron Bucknam, who collaborated in the development of the proactive prevention model, and Cathryn Goree, Michael Haines, and Barbara Lindquist, who provided material for the three case studies. Special thanks to Myra Berkowitz for her skillful editing and perceptive comments.

REFERENCES

Bachman, J. G., Johnston, L. D., & O'Malley, P. M. (1990). Explaining the recent decline in cocaine use among young adults: Further evidence that perceived risks and disapproval lead to reduced drug use. *Journal of Health and Social Behavior, 31,* 173–184.

Bachman, J. G., Johnston, L. D., O'Malley, P. M., & Humphrey, R. H. (1988). Explaining the recent decline in marijuana use: Differentiating the effects of perceived risks, disapproval, and general lifestyle factors. *Journal of Health and Social Behavior, 29,* 92–112.

Baer, J. S., Stacy, A., & Larimer, A. (1991). Biases in the perception of drinking norms among college students. *Journal of Studies on Alcohol, 52*(6), 580–586.

Berkowitz, A. D. (1990). Reducing alcohol and other drug use on campus: Effective strategies for prevention programs. *The Eta Sigma Gamman, 22*(1), 12–14.

Berkowitz, A. D. (1991). Following imaginary peers: How norm misperceptions influence student substance abuse. In G. Lindsay & G. Rulf (Eds.), *Project direction* (Module No. 2). Available from Wisconsin Clearinghouse, P.O. Box 1468, Madison, WI 53701–1468.

Berkowitz, A. D. (1994). Assessing collegiate substance abuse: Current trends, research needs and program applications. In G. Gonzalez & V. Veltri (Eds.), *Research and intervention: Preventing substance abuse in higher education* (pp. 73–100). Washington, DC: U.S. Department of Education, Office of Educational Research and Improvement.

Berkowitz, A. D., & Perkins, H. W. (1986). Resident advisers as role models: a comparison of drinking patterns of resident advisers and their peers. *Journal of College Student Personnel, 27,* 146–153.

Berkowitz, A. D., & Perkins, H. W. (1987a). Current issues in effective alcohol education programming. In Joan Sherwood (Ed.), *Alcohol policies and practices on college and university campuses* (pp. 69–85). Columbus, OH: National Association of Student Personnel Administrators Monograph Series.

Berkowitz, A. D., & Perkins, H. W. (1987b). Recent research on gender differences in collegiate alcohol use. *Journal of American College Health, 36*(2), 123–129.

Blanken, A. J. (1993). Measuring use of alcohol and other drugs among adolescents. *Public Health Reports, 108,* 25–30.

Chassin, L., Presson, C. C., Sherman, S. J., Corty, E., & Olshavsky, R. W. (1984). Predicting the onset of cigarette smoking in adolescents: A longitudinal study. *Journal of Applied Social Psychology, 14*(3), 224–243.

Engs, R. C., & Hanson, D. J. (1989). Gender differences in drinking patterns and problems among college students: A review of the literature. *Journal of Alcohol and Drug Education, 35,* 36–47.

Gilchrist, L. D. (1994). Current knowledge in prevention of alcohol and other drug abuse. In G. Gonzalez & V. Veltri (Eds.), *Research and intervention: Preventing substance abuse in higher education* (pp. 25–46). Washington, DC: U.S. Department of Education, Office of Educational Research and Improvement.

Gonzalez, G. M. (1989). An integrated theoretical model for alcohol and other drug abuse prevention on campus. *Journal of College Student Development, 30,* 492–503.

Goodstadt, M. S., & Caleekal-John, A. (1984). Alcohol education programs for university students: A review of their effectiveness. *International Journal of the Addictions, 19,* 721–741.

Haines, M. P. (1996). *A social norms approach to preventing binge drinking at colleges and universities.* Newton, MA: Higher Education Center for Alcohol and Other Drug Prevention.

Hansen, W. B., & Graham, J. W. (1991). Preventing alcohol, marijuana, and cigarette use among adolescents: Peer pressure resistance training versus establishing conservative norms. *Preventive Medicine, 20,* 414–430.

Kolbe, H. J., Kahn, L., & Collins, J. (1993). Overview of the youth risk behavior surveillance system. *Public Health Reports, 108,* 25–30.

Lawson, G. W., & Lawson, A. W. (1989). *Alcoholism and substance abuse in special populations.* Rockville, MD: Aspen Publications.

Marks, G., Graham, J. W., & Hansen, W. B. (1992). Social projection and social conformity in adolescent alcohol use: A longitudinal analysis. *Personality and Social Psychology Bulletin, 18*(1), 96–101.

Meilman, P. W., Presley, C. A., & Lyerla, R. (1994). Black college students and binge drinking. *Journal of Blacks in Higher Education, 4,* 70–71.

Moskowitz, J. M. (1989). The primary prevention of alcohol problems: A critical review. *Journal of Studies on Alcohol, 53,* 458–462.

Oblander, F. W. (1984, October). A practice oriented synthesis: Effective alcohol education strategies. *ACU-I Bulletin,* 17–23.

Office of Substance Abuse Prevention, Department of Health and Human Services. (1989). *Prevention plus II: Tools for creating and sustaining drug-free communities* (DHHS Publication No. ADM 89–1649). Washington, DC: U.S. Government Printing Office.

Perkins, H. W. (1985). Religious traditions, parents, and peers as determinants of alcohol and drug use among college students. *Review of Religious Research, 27*(1), 15–31.

Perkins, H. W. (1987). Parental religion and alcohol use problems as intergenerational predictors of problem drinking among college students. *Journal for the Scientific Study of Religion, 26*(3), 340–357.

Perkins, H. W. (1991). Confronting misperceptions of peer drug use norms among college students: An alternative approach for alcohol and other drug education programs. In L. M. Grow (Ed.), *The FIPSE drug prevention program in higher education training literature manual* (4th ed.) (pp. 453–473). Washington, DC: U.S. Dept. of Education Fund for the Improvement of Post-Secondary Education.

Perkins, H. W. (1992). Gender patterns in consequences of collegiate alcohol abuse: A ten year study of trends in an undergraduate population. *Journal of Studies on Alcohol, 53*(5), 458–462.

Perkins, H. W. (1994). The contextual effect of secular norms on religiosity as moderator of student alcohol and other drug use. *Research in the Social Scientific Study of Religion, 6,* 187–208.

Perkins, H. W., & Berkowitz, A. D. (1986a). Perceiving the community norms of alcohol use among students: Some research implications for campus alcohol education programming. *International Journal of the Addictions, 21,* 961–976.

Perkins, H. W., & Berkowitz, A. D. (1986b). Using student alcohol surveys: Notes on clinical and educational program applications. *Journal of Alcohol and Drug Education, 31*(2), 44–51.

Perkins, H. W., & Berkowitz, A. D. (1991). Collegiate COAs and alcohol abuse: Problem drinking in relation to assessments of parent and grandparent alcoholism. *Journal of Counseling and Development, 69*(3), 237–240.

Prentice, D. A., & Miller, D. T. (1993). Pluralistic ignorance and alcohol use on campus: Some consequences of misperceiving the social norm. *Journal of Personality and Social Psychology, 64*(2), 243–256.

Presley, C. A., Harrold, R., Scouten, E., Lyerla, R., & Meilman, P. W. (1994) *CORE alcohol and drug survey: User's manual* (5th ed.). Carbondale: CORE Institute, Southern Illinois University.

Presley, C. A., Meilman, P. W., & Lyerla, R. (1994). Development of the CORE alcohol and drug survey: Initial findings and future directions. *Journal of American College Health, 42,* 248–255.

Presley, C. A., Meilman, P. W., & Lyerla, R. (1995). *Alcohol and drugs on American college campuses: Use, consequences, and perceptions of the campus environment: Vol. 2: 1990–92.* Carbondale: The CORE Institute, Southern Illinois University.

Rundell, T. G., & Brunold, W. H. (1988). A meta-analysis of school-based smoking and alcohol use prevention programs. *Health Education Quarterly, 15,* 317–334.

Ryan, B. E., Colthust, T., & Segars, L. (1994). *College alcohol risk assessment guide: Environmental approaches to prevention.* San Diego: Alcohol, Tobacco and Other Drug Studies, UCSD Extension, University of California.

Sussman, S., Dent, C. W., Mestel-Rauch, J., Johnson, C. A., Hansen, W. B., & Flay, B. R. (1988). Adolescent nonsmokers, triers, and regular smokers' estimates of cigarette smoking prevalence: When do overestimations occur and by whom? *Journal of Applied Social Psychology, 18,* 537–551.

University of Michigan. (1993). *University of Michigan survey regarding alcohol and other drugs: Background and summary.* Ann Arbor: University of Michigan Initiative on Alcohol and Other Drugs.

Wechsler, H., Moeykens, B., Davenport, A., Castillo, S., & Hansen, J. (1995). The adverse impact of heavy episodic drinkers on other college students. *Journal of Studies on Alcohol, 56,* 628–634.

7

Prohibition and Freshman Residence Halls: A Study of the Enforcement of University Alcohol Policy

Earl Rubington

Thousands of freshmen experience culture shock when they arrive on college campuses in the fall. They learn that moving into university housing may cost them their drinking rights. The university says there will be no drinking in the residence halls and assigns the task of enforcing its alcohol policy to residence-hall staff. University policy, incoming freshmen, and residence-hall staff comprise the elements of an enforcement problem.

A comparison of the apparatus of enforcement during national prohibition and the enforcement policies currently on college campuses may give some idea of the complexity of the problem. In the former, professional special agents were paid to enforce the Volstead Act, which was the law for the entire population (Merz, 1970). By contrast, residence-hall staff are asked to enforce university policy, policing the very residence halls where they themselves live, work, and associate with residents. They have much more frequent and various kinds of contact with residents, have a number of other duties in addition to enforcement, are students themselves, are much closer to their charges in age, have much more in common with them, and generally share the same drinking culture, characteristics that make being an enforcement agent difficult.

The elements of this enforcement problem raise questions that have drawn little research attention. Accordingly, I set out to examine the enforcement of alcohol policy on one university campus. Over a period of three years, I studied three freshman residence halls. I collected data on alcohol violations, reporting practices of residential assistants (RAs), and sanctioning practices of residence directors (RDs) in each of the residence halls for each of the three study years (1989–1992). I argue that residence-hall staff, RAs and RDs alike, have devised a solution to the problem of enforcing an unenforceable rule. By redefining the term "responsible drinking" in a way that advances the interests of all three parties to the enforcement dilemma, they reduce the area of definitional conflict. Drawing on this interpretation, I then advance a few recommendations for college administrators who may wish to make enforcement of their alcohol policy more consistent with the facts of everyday life in freshman residence halls.

SOME APPROACHES TO COLLEGE DRINKING

Since the publication of the classic study *Drinking in College* (Straus & Bacon, 1953), college drinking studies have multiplied (Saltz & Elandt, 1986). For the most part, these studies employ questionnaires to answer the now traditional questions of who drinks what, with whom, how much, how often, where and when, why, and with what effects. Since twenty-one became the national legal drinking age, researchers have also studied what effects the raised drinking age has had on youthful alcohol consumption (Engs & Hanson, 1989). To date, however, there have been few studies of how residence-hall staff enforce age-specific prohibitions, the problems they have confronted, or the results they have achieved.

A few studies of drinking sanctions in residence halls have used a battery of research methods. Moffatt (1989) made an ethnographic study of one floor in a college residence hall and found that the residence-hall assistant changed from being a lax to a strict enforcer of college alcohol policy when the social atmosphere of his floor changed. Cohn and White (1990), comparing three kinds of disciplinary policies, found more alcohol violations in those residence halls where residents, rather than administrators, both formulated and enforced alcohol policy. When the drinking age was twenty, I interviewed residential assistants in upperclass as well as freshman residence halls (Rubington, 1990). I wanted to find out what difficulties were caused for RAs when the floors were divided into legal drinking age and underage categories. More specifically, I wanted to know how the RAs came to terms with the problems college alcohol policy made for them. When the drinking age was then raised to twenty-one, I decided to study freshman residence halls, where the conflicts in the definition of the drinking situation would be posed most sharply, for incoming residents and residence-hall staff alike.

Three theoretical perspectives guided the collection and analysis of data. Integration theorists hold that clear, consistent, and agreed-upon drinking norms and sanctions reduce rates of alcohol problems (Room, 1976; Ullman, 1958; White, 1982). For example, Americans of Chinese, Italian, or Jewish extraction, who share drinking cultures that prescribe moderate drinking and proscribe drunkenness, exhibit low rates of alcohol problems. By contrast, Americans of Irish extraction, who share a drinking culture which alternately prescribes and proscribes drinking and drunkenness, exhibit fairly high rates of alcohol problems (Bales, 1946). Thus, one broad hypothesis suggests that the greater the agreement on drinking rules and their sanctions, the more effective the enforcement of alcohol policy.

Sanctions theorists contend that swift, certain, and severe sanctions reduce violations (Silberman, 1976; Zimring & Hawkins, 1973). Their theories suggest that students are less apt to break drinking rules if the chances of getting away with it are poor and if sanctions are applied promptly. Consistent with crosscultural studies and the learning of norms that govern drinking are societal differences in the acceptance of deviant behavior in males and females. Crosscultural studies suggest that gender norms give men more license to deviate, in general, and in drinking situations in particular. (Hagan, Simpson, & Gillis, 1979; Tittle, 1980; Marshall, 1979). Gender norms suggest that men are much more likely to break college drinking rules than are women.

Role-conflict and interaction theorists both contend that the frequency of contact as well as role conflicts in groups influence both output and enforcement (Roethlisberger & Dickson, 1946; Merton, 1968). Their theories suggest that as RAs make more contact with each other, they come to share a set of enforcement norms. One educator of residence assistants has argued that the friend–RA role conflict is universal (Upcraft, 1982). Consequently, role-conflict theory would predict that the greater the role conflict, the less likely the enforcement of norms.

THE STUDY: QUESTIONS, METHOD, AND SETTING

In order to study how residents and residence-hall staff resolved conflicts over the definition of the drinking situation, I focused on three areas: the frequency of alcohol violations, RAs' reporting practices, and RDs' enforcement policies. The studies, covering the academic years of 1989–1990, 1990–1991 and 1991–1992, sought answers to the following four questions:

1. How effective was alcohol policy?
2. How did residents' compliance vary with RAs' reporting practices?
3. How did residents' compliance vary with RDs' sanctioning practices?
4. Did a stricter alcohol policy have the effect sanctions theory would predict?

South, East, and West Halls are the three City University (CU) freshman residence halls in which these studies took place (names of all persons and places are fictitious). The three halls, practically identical in architecture and layout, housed men and women students on alternate wings: South and West had eight wings (five male), and East had twelve (eight male). Each floor has its own RA, who receives a small stipend—room and board and the use of a telephone. In addition to their other duties, such as supervision, information, referral, programming, and counseling (Upcraft, 1982; Blimling & Miltenberger, 1990), RAs are required to report infractions of residence-hall rules.

CU's alcohol policy says residence-hall staff will enforce state laws forbidding possession and consumption of alcoholic beverages by persons under twenty-one (less than 5% of entering first-year students are twenty-one or older). CU's Housing Handbook defines this policy to residents of university housing. RDs make that policy clear to all residents at their first meeting at the start of the academic year. RAs are then supposed to repeat that policy when they hold their first meeting with residents of their floor.

CU's residence-hall policy requires RAs to report violations and RDs to take disciplinary action as needed. The sanctions imposed vary according to the gravity and frequency of violations. In previous years, disciplinary actions for alcohol violations escalated in the following sequence: verbal warning, warning letter, letter of censure, meeting with the RD, meeting with the judicial administrator, referral to CU's Alcohol and Drug Program.

CU officials instituted a stricter alcohol policy at the start of the 1991–1992 academic year. The new policy required that residents meet with the RD soon after their first alcohol violation. After these meetings, RDs generally imposed an educational sanction. For example, they might ask the violator to attend an alcohol education movie, make a presentation on alcohol to residents of their floor, or write a paper on drinking and driving. The second offense mandated attendance at six weekly programs run by the Alcohol and Drug Program (ADP). In the event of a third offense, the student might be required to repeat the six-week ADP sessions or, if the charges were more serious, face Student Court. Thus, in contrast to previous years, the very first infraction drew an immediate face-to-face response from residence-hall authorities.

Infraction of residence-hall rules can come to an RA's attention at any time of day. However, RAs are most likely to come upon violations of the rules when they are on duty. RAs are on duty approximately a dozen times each quarter. During the year, a single RA will be on duty on weekdays (Monday, Tuesday, and Wednesday); on weekends (Thursday, Friday, Saturday, and Sunday), two RAs do "double duty." When on duty, RAs make three rounds of the building on weekdays (at approximately 8:00 P.M., 10:00 P.M., and midnight); on weekends, they add a fourth and final round at 1:00 A.M.). On rounds, they check on health, safety, welfare, and respond to a variety of violations. After each round, they record infractions on discipline cards and make more detailed entries in the staff log.

Three categories of infractions (which sometimes occur simultaneously) are alcohol, noise, and all others. Alcohol violations include being in the presence of alcohol, underage drinking (in lobby, hallway, bathroom, stairway, elevator, room), possession, drunkenness, and the like. Noise includes loud voices, stereos, radios, or musical instruments. All others includes such infractions as hallway sports, vandalism, throwing objects out windows, insubordination, and so on. Noise is generally what attracts RAs' attention; after requesting admission to a noisy room, they frequently discover that drinking has been going on in the room.

Data for this three-year study come from several sources. Much of the data come from tabulation and analysis of all violations RAs reported and recorded on discipline cards for all three residence halls for the three academic years (1989–1992). When filled out completely, discipline cards contain the resident's name, room number, date and time of infraction, site and kind of infraction, the resident's attitude (cooperative or uncooperative), and the RA's initials. Additional data came from interviews I conducted with RDs, GAs (graduate assistants), and RAs. A lesser amount of data come from examining entries in logs kept in staff offices and observation of interaction in those same offices.

ALCOHOL VIOLATIONS IN THE RESIDENCE HALLS

In each of the three study years and each of the three residence halls studied, most alcohol violations took place in the fall quarter (Table 7.1). In all instances, both the number and percentage of alcohol violations dropped appreciably after the fall quarter.

Most alcohol violations occurred in the week before the start of fall-quarter classes. Table 7.2 presents alcohol violations by week for the fall quarter of the 1991–1992 school year. RAs reported 62, or 30 percent of the fall quarter's total violations in that week. Similarly, in the previous year, RAs reported 101,

Table 7.1
Alcohol Violations in Three Residence Halls, 1989–1992

	1989-1990			1990-1991			1991-1992		
	South	East	West	South	East	West	South	East	West
Fall violations	154	320	229	236	260	170	142	187	172
% alcohol	63	40	52	53	27	47	54	44	31
Winter violations	68	238	100	131	180	74	64	90	92
% alcohol	31	22	49	37	41	32	31	50	11
Spring violations	24	*	32	42	139	28	12	74	83
% alcohol	7	*	50	45	52	46	25	42	14

*Data unavailable.

Table 7.2
Alcohol Violations by Week of Fall Quarter, 1991–1992

Week	South	East	West	Total
First	20	22	20	62
Second	3	0	1	4
Third	2	8	6	16
Fourth	2	1	5	8
Fifth	1	6	4	11
Sixth	13	15	2	30
Seventh	2	3	0	5
Eighth	1	15	2	18
Ninth	17	3	0	20
Tenth	7	3	6	16
Eleventh	2	0	3	5
Twelfth	0	3	0	3
Thirteenth	4	0	0	4
Total	74	79	49	202

or 35 percent of the total of the fall quarter's alcohol violations in the week preceding the start of classes.

Additional temporal uniformities turn out as might be expected. Two-thirds of the recorded alcohol violations took place between 10:00 P.M. and midnight on the weekend. The weekend for many CU students starts Thursday nights, in part because so many of them have no Friday classes. And the weekend, of course, is for many students "party time."

Social uniformities also turned out as might be expected. Male first-year students, compared with female first-year students, were twice as likely to come to the attention of RAs for alcohol violations. Table 7.3, which crosstabulates both violators' and RAs' gender, shows that men are three

Table 7.3
Alcohol Violations by Gender, South Hall and West Hall, Fall Quarter 1990

South Hall RAs

Violators	Men		Women		Total
Men	16	73%	33	68%	49
Women	6	27%	15	32%	21
Total	22	100%	48	100%	70

West Hall RAs

Violators	Men		Women		Total
Men	12	80%	30	83%	42
Women	3	20%	6	17%	9
Total	15	100%	36	100%	51

times as likely to be written up as women. Men were also twice as likely to repeat alcohol violations.

As many RAs noted in the interviews, once freshmen learn that they cannot drink in the dorms, they give up the idea of drinking there and quietly find places outside the residence hall where they can drink. At CU, possible new locations include three public drinking establishments within walking distance, nearby student apartment houses, and fraternity parties. As other observers have noted, more stringent enforcement of university drinking rules has not reduced drinking. It has simply changed its location (MacDonald, 1988). Nevertheless, the marked drop in alcohol violations as reported by RAs attests to the effectiveness of CU's more stringent alcohol policy.

The drop in alcohol violations offers some tangential support for the social-integration hypothesis of alcohol problems. This hypothesis holds that when drinking customs and sanctions are well understood and agreed upon, alcohol problems are more apt to be infrequent. Attrition in rates of alcohol violations suggests that freshman residents learn that patterned evasion of drinking norms, accepted behavior everywhere else, is not tolerated in their residence halls. They find RAs enforcing drinking rules inside the residence hall which are evaded or broken with impunity on the outside. In this process of resocialization, through a process of trial and error (what some RAs call "testing"), freshmen learn that residence-hall staff will enforce college alcohol policy.

In addition, the marked reduction of alcohol violations by quarters supports those axioms of sanctions theory which say that swift and certain sanctions are more likely to deter people from misconduct. Similarly, the more stringent alcohol policy of 1991–1992 seems to have had precisely the intended effect that sanctions theory would predict. Table 7.1 shows violations for each hall for the fall, winter, and spring quarters. The number of alcohol violations for three academic years drops considerably in five of the six instances. Thus, as disciplinary actions become swifter and more certain (save in the case of Cole's tenure as RD of South Hall in 1991–1992, to be discussed), alcohol violations dropped accordingly.

Certainly, sanctions by themselves cannot fully explain these uniformities. In addition to sanctions, changes in precollege drinking patterns, organizational rhythms, and the collegiate calendar of work and play (Gusfield, 1991) need to be included for a more complete explanation. Some studies, for example, show that both quantity and frequency of drinking may be leveling off somewhat among all segments of the youthful drinking population (Johnston, O'Malley, & Bachman, 1988). The increased emphasis on health and the dangers of drinking may have somewhat reduced the internal and external pressure to drink in each of the years studied (Cahalan, 1988). And, as one theory of deviant behavior holds, involvement (time spent in conventional activities) decreases the number of opportunities to engage in rule breaking (Hirschi, 1969; Cherry, 1991). Finally, and perhaps most important, freshmen have to make a host of adjustments to a vast array of new and changing situations, which may lead to less time and effort devoted to drinking (Becker, Geer, & Hughes, 1968).

RA STYLES OF ENFORCEMENT

Resident assistants constitute the first line of defense of CU's alcohol policy. RAs learn or develop an enforcement style, experience problems, sometimes change their prohibition-agent role, and, in the process, influence student compliance with alcohol policy. The average tour of duty for an RA is probably two years, with some serving for three and others for only one year. Thus, being an RA is not quite the same thing as having an occupational career. Nevertheless, there are developmental sequences that do take place in the course of an RA's experience. The natural history of an RA's career has its own stages, crises, defining events, and changes over time, as do numerous occupations and professions. Persons in the RA's social circle, such as RDs, other RAs, and residents of the building as well as of their own floor, all have some influence on how RAs enforce drinking rules. Over the course of the RA's career, some persons exercise more influence than others.

CU requires that an RA have some prior experience as a resident in a college residence hall at CU or elsewhere. Most RAs had prior encounters with college alcohol policies when they were freshmen in one of CU's residence halls. Those who were drinkers reported a variety of experiences with their own RAs when they were freshmen. Most of them experienced considerable laxity in enforcement of drinking rules. A few recalled being written up for alcohol violations when they were freshmen, but most reported that they drank with impunity in the residence hall. One male said he got drunk once a week throughout the year without ever being written up. Others recalled their RAs inviting them into their room for a drink or joining a drinking party already in progress in a resident's room. Still others noted that when the RA came upon them drinking in their rooms, he or she simply closed the door. One informant noted that her RA used to call on the phone and warn them when the RA on duty would be making rounds. Thus, most RAs, even before they became RAs, were familiar with ubiquitous student drinking and lax enforcement of residence-hall alcohol policy.

The formal training to become an RA is generally limited to lectures. Informal training comes mostly from observing veteran RAs. Discussion after watching confrontations between RAs and residents also provides information on how to act when making rounds. The fall quarter generally pairs a first-year RA with a veteran on rounds. Ultimately, most RAs create their own particular style by blending various approaches and techniques they observed veteran RAs using when making rounds. Key aspects of a seasoned RA style include being matter-of-fact when confronting residents, deciding who will take charge when on "double-duty," using humor to defuse situations, and taking control of the situation quickly. In addition, veteran RAs' styles change according to where, when, and with whom they may be dealing. When making rounds they are more apt to be formal, particularly when confronting residents of floors other than their own. Confrontations with residents of their floor are much more apt to be informal.

Soon after the residence-hall director has oriented the whole building to the rules, RAs repeat that orientation in their first floor meeting at the start of the academic year. After mutual introductions, they may repeat what the RD has said about the rules: "No drinking in the building for anyone under twenty-one. Those who drink will be written up." The RAs then go on to indicate how they define and interpret the drinking rules, and how they intend to enforce them.

Some simply say nothing at all on the subject. Others tell their floor to read the Housing Handbook, since it spells out all the rules and regulations they need to know. Some will simply say, "Don't drink here." Others will say, "If I don't see it, smell it, or hear it, there's nothing I can do about it. If I see it, I write you up." One RA reported that he told his floor, "I know you're gonna be drinking. Be quiet. Be in control. Don't let it get out of hand." Some Housing Office personnel have told RAs to be strict in the beginning, to act like a top sergeant, and, later, determine whether to remain strict. While some followed that advice, others imply from the start that they will be lenient in enforcement, and that they would rather be seen as friends than as police. Thus, RAs often set the tone for their floor during their initial orientation.

In time, they develop what they call their styles of enforcement, usually one of three types: (1) by-the-book, (2) laid-back, or (3) in-between. Those who describe themselves as in-between say that they are not quite as punctilious as a pure by-the-book RA nor are they quite as relaxed and lenient as the pure laid-back RA. For most if not all of the fall quarter, RAs are more apt to be by-the-book, women somewhat more so than men. In the beginning, they are eager to learn as well as to establish their identity as RAs. They view the initial weeks of the quarter as the time when residents will test them to see whether they will enforce the rules. Will they be strict or lenient; will they give people breaks, the benefit of the doubt? Are they going to be "hardasses," "cool," or "marshmallows"?

Changes in RAs' relationships with their residents can cause problems for other RAs in the building. Many of these changes come under the heading of having lost control of their floor. One common case is that of a first-year RA who started out wanting to be friends with residents only to complain later that they were taking advantage of the situation. One RA described the problem RAs who start out wanting to be friends can expect to have. He said, "Common sense says it's easier to go from hard to soft than from soft to hard." While these RAs have lost control despite their presence on their own floor, others have lost control because of their absence. A new boyfriend or girlfriend, an outside job, or campus commitments (clubs, athletic teams) take some RAs off their own floors. They become less visible and have less and less contact with residents of their floor.

When some RAs lose control of their floors, it makes extra work for all the other RAs. "Wild floors" become known rapidly because more violations of all types of residence-hall rules occur on them. All the RAs on staff become quite familiar with these floors because they make more work for them when they are on duty and have to make rounds. A classic case of nonenforcement, for example, occurred on one floor of South Hall in 1989–1990. Vincent, the floor RA, wrote up only one resident of his floor during the course of the whole year. Largely because of his policy of noninvolvement, other RAs considered his floor the most unruly in the building. Sorting discipline cards by floor and room number revealed that over the course of the year Vincent's floor produced an excess of enforcement activity for all seven of the other RAs.

In each of the three years, every residence hall produced an extreme example of both an overenforcer and an underenforcer. In East Hall in 1989–1990, for example, this generated staff conflict between the by-the-book and the laid-back factions. Polarization simply increased problems all the way around for RAs, residents, and the RD. In perhaps no other year was the demarcation between the two styles so clear and so well understood by everybody in the building.

Through reading the staff log, listening to discussions at staff meetings, or experiencing it directly, RAs come to know about RAs who have been lenient in enforcing the rules, or, in some instances, have actually violated the rules. For example, a resident about to be written up for an alcohol violation may complain that "my RA lets me" or "the other RAs let me." RAs learn that other RAs sometimes look the other way when they come upon a violation of the alcohol rules. On rarer but more striking occasions, RAs have entered rooms when not on duty only to find another RA drinking with an underage resident (a major source of conflict in East Hall in 1989–1990).

Some RAs dislike writing up residents. One said, "I don't like to get people in trouble." Another said, "I feel uncomfortable writing people up for things I did just the year before." Most point out that they "aren't looking for trouble" when they make rounds, and that they do not want to be thought of as "the Gestapo." Thus, violations have to be blatant before they will take action. Persons drinking in hallways or walking in them with open containers, loud partying and sounds of drinking, or actually seeing people drinking (because they left the doors to their room open) are some examples of inescapable violations.

A partial explanation for the marked decrease in alcohol violations in both winter and spring quarters may be the fact that RAs move toward the center, the middle-of-the-road stance, finding that peace on rounds can best be kept by adopting the in-between style. By being neither overenforcers nor underenforcers, they strike a happy balance, thereby keeping to a minimum the number of enemies they make among residents as well as reducing the trouble they could have made for their fellow RAs and their RD. Without the presence of both negative role models (overenforcer and underenforcer), it is unlikely that they would have been able to arrive at the output norms and work styles they ultimately adopted.

THE ROLE OF THE RESIDENCE HALL DIRECTOR

CU's Housing Office personnel say that the RD sets the tone for the building. This statement implies that residence halls may have different social atmospheres which are influenced by how RDs define policy, direct their RAs, and enforce discipline. If so, residence-hall "tone" may help explain some sources of variation in alcohol violations and their enforcement. Tone, for example, may have a bearing on both the frequency of alcohol violations and the number of repeat violators.

As Table 7.1 shows, there have been some rather sharp reductions in the number and percentage of alcohol violations reported during the three-year study. For example, alcohol infractions dropped 19 percent in East Hall in 1990–1991, and another 28 percent in 1991–1992. South Hall registered the largest reduction, when alcohol infractions fell 35 percent in 1991–1992. Taken together, these reductions suggest that a stringent alcohol policy reduced alcohol violations.

On the other hand, one instance of an extremely high percentage of alcohol infractions and another of no reduction calls the policy into question. In the second year of the study, 1990–1991, alcohol violations rose 53 percent in South Hall. Similarly, in the last year of the study infractions in West Hall rose by 2 percent. Together with the relatively large number of total violations in East Hall, the data suggest that the ways RDs administered sanctions might have some bearing on these reported violations. In addition, recidivism in alcohol violations may bear some relationship to how RDs discipline their residents. The percentages of men who were written up for two or more alcohol violations in the fall quarter of each of the three years varies. (Since only sixteen women were repeaters in the three years, they have been excluded). Tabulations of the percentage of male repeaters show that both South Hall (32%) and East Hall (32%) had the highest percentages in 1990–1992.

From interviews and analysis of discipline cards and staff logs, it became possible to develop a typology of RDs as discipline agents. RDs could expect residents to conform or to violate the drinking rules, and they could be quick or slow in applying the designated sanctions as outlined in the Housing Office Handbook. This yields four types: CQ, expect conformity, quick to apply sanctions; CS, expect conformity, slow to apply sanctions; VQ, expect violations, quick to sanction; and VS, expect violations, slow to sanction. Over the three-year study period, there were seven RDs, two of whom directed the same hall for two consecutive years. Three of the four possible types appeared and affected alcohol violations and number of repeaters.

In 1989–1990, a man, N. Bach, who expected residents to drink, directed South Hall. South Hall RAs complained that "nothing happened" after they wrote up residents, and that they found Bach to be slow in sanctioning violators. The disciplinary procedure has the following steps: The RD writes a letter to the student violator, states the problem, and requests the two meet on a date the RD specifies. The RD then directs an RA to hand deliver the letter to the resident. From the RA's point of view, Bach was slow writing the letters and arranging both delivery and meetings, hence the delay in the administration of sanctions to repeaters. Although moderate in its percentage of alcohol violations, South Hall had a high number of repeat violations.

In that same year, D. Ell, a woman, directed West Hall. Expecting students to drink, she met with residents very soon after they were written up for violating a rule. Her RAs uniformly praised her because she consistently supported them in hearings with student violators and was prompt and consistent in meting out sanctions. As a result, that year West Hall had both fewer alcohol violations and fewer alcohol-violation repeaters than the other two halls.

Also in 1989–1990, W. Gold, a woman, directed East Hall. She expected students to drink but was not prompt in sanctioning alcohol violations. Her RAs also complained that nothing happened after they wrote residents up. During her tenure, RAs reported more staff and personality conflicts between the by-the-book RAs and the laid-backs. They also complained of both inconsistency and lack of support. During that year, West Hall had a very high number of both alcohol violations and repeaters.

In 1990–1991, M. Cole, a man, took over as South Hall's RD. Cole expected residents to drink and was notoriously slow in meeting with violators and dispensing sanctions. For example, one RA wrote in the staff log that a certain resident had already been written up five times for alcohol violations. He wondered when Cole planned to do something about the resident. One explanation for his behavior is that Cole did not regard punishment as the way to teach freshmen "responsible drinking." In his view, "If you tell them to close the door when they drink, you're only teaching them how to cheat." As noted earlier, during Cole's tenure South Hall had the most alcohol violations and alcohol repeaters.

D. Ell returned as West Hall's RD in the second year of the study. She still expected residents to drink but became a little slower in applying sanctions. One of her RAs characterized her as being more laid-back compared to how she had run West Hall the previous year. She acknowledged less frequent contact with her staff, attributing it to the acquisition of a boyfriend. Alcohol violations, first time as well as repeats, increased moderately during her second term.

W. Gold also returned as East Hall's RD in 1990–1991. In general, her second year was much like her first. On the whole, she continued to expect violations while still being desultory in administering discipline. West Hall remained high on alcohol violations and repeat violators.

In 1991–1992, M. Olds, a married woman, directed South Hall. Unlike the other RDs, she expected her residents to conform to the no-drinking rule and she was quick to apply sanctions. Fairly high alcohol violations coupled with few alcohol repeaters characterized her administration. That her RAs reported few other violations suggests that she had them focus on a more rigorous enforcement of alcohol policy.

J. Kane, a woman, ran West Hall in 1991–1992. Expecting residents to drink, she was quick to apply the new sanctions. West Hall had about as many violations as South Hall but somewhat fewer alcohol repeaters.

In 1991–1992, D. Buck, a woman, directed East Hall. She expected residents to drink. As with most other RDs, Buck held that if two residents were sitting in their room watching television and having a couple of beers, they were "drinking responsibly." She was, however, quick to apply sanctions to those residents who had been written up. She held strongly to the belief that residence-hall staff should be consistent in their enforcement of the rules. Under her, East Hall had a moderate amount of alcohol violations and only a few repeaters.

While this typology is certainly not the last word on the subject of residence-hall administration of discipline, it does bear out two important points. For one, whether RDs expect conformity or violation of the drinking rules and whether they are quick or slow to sanction, they can exert some influence on the frequency of first-time as well as repeat violations. In addition, this conceptualization does seem to support the view that all three parties to drinking rules and their enforcement devised, over time, a set of relationships which shaped both compliance and enforcement.

THE ETHIC OF "RESPONSIBLE DRINKING"

For alcohol educators, responsible drinking means that persons understand the action of alcohol, know their limits, make informed choices when it comes to drinking, and are prepared to accept the consequences of their behavior when they drink. For residence-hall staff, responsible drinking means something entirely different. Simply put, drinking is responsible when it keeps the residence-hall peace.

Residence-hall staff take it as inevitable that freshmen are going to drink and that there is no stopping them. They claim that most freshmen drink and that many of them have fake IDs. Staff see empty cans and bottles in the lavatory trash cans as well as in the recycling bins. Residents tell them about their hangovers and they overhear conversations about parties and drunken escapades. They see or hear their residents vomiting in the bathrooms late at night or early in the morning, and they come to know those rare residents who do not get out of bed until midafternoon. They know about the vandalism and verbal, physical, and sexual assaults that sometimes happen during or after drinking. And they are aware of the rare instances when they or other RAs have had to call campus police to take a student to the nearest hospital because of alcohol poisoning.

For RAs, drinking is a problem if it makes trouble for them in their various capacities, but most particularly when they are on duty and making rounds. Understandably then, residents who drink behind closed doors, with fewer people in their room and with voices and stereos lowered, are drinking responsibly. They are not, as Ell phrased it, "calling attention to themselves." And clearly they are not making trouble for the RAs.

RAs can start out proactive and then slowly, over the course of three quarters, become reactive (Reiss, 1970). At the start of the fall quarter, RAs use more aggressive tactics. For example, when they are in the lobby, they seek to intimidate residents whom they think are trying to sneak alcohol into the building. Although they are not permitted to examine gym, duffel, or hockey bags, look into the refrigerators which many students have in their rooms, or even to enter rooms without students' permission, in the beginning of the academic year they do ask residents to open bags or refrigerators when they suspect them of containing alcoholic beverages. Needless to say, they catch a number of naïve first-year students who are unaware of their right to refuse. Certainly, the drive they put on in the early weeks of the fall quarter must discourage some residents.

Over the course of the academic year, however, RDs, RAs, and residents work out an accommodation to residence-hall alcohol policy. The three parties to the no-drinking rule evolve an unwritten agreement whose terms comprise the ethic of responsible drinking. They agree that responsible drinking means drinking with discretion. Thus, any drinking that goes on behind closed doors without attracting the RAs' attention is responsible drinking.

The marked decline in alcohol violations in both the winter and spring quarters attests at least in part to the workings of the agreement. Most RAs, for example, responding to questions about changes in residents' actions by quarters, commented that residents learned "what they can and cannot get away with." If for many it meant not drinking in the building, for others it meant learning the best times for sneaking alcohol into the building, adjusting their drinking to the RAs' rounds, and becoming aware that they do not have to say what is in bags or refrigerators. For most, however, it probably means being more discreet when they drink in the residence hall. The reciprocal of residents' discretion is the gradual relaxation of proactive enforcement of the no-drinking rule. When all parties comply with the terms of the unwritten contract, the hallways reflect a negotiated peace.

REDUCING ALCOHOL PROBLEMS IN FRESHMAN RESIDENCE HALLS

What are some answers to the questions that initiated this three-year study? How do first-year college students respond to the age-specific prohibition which residence-hall life imposes on them? What role do RAs play in obtaining residents' compliance with prohibition? Are observed variations in residents' compliance related to how RDs conceive and enforce alcohol policy? And does a more stringent alcohol policy reduce alcohol violations in residence halls?

Before summarizing the results and discussing reduction of alcohol problems in freshman residence halls, both the limits and the assumptions on which these suggestions are based need to be made clear. There are upwards of three thousand colleges and universities in the United States today. Colleges vary in alcohol policies and enforcement, residence-hall philosophies, and residence-hall architecture (Blimling & Miltenberger, 1990). Thus, the findings reported here are more apt to apply to large urban universities with residence-hall philosophies centered more on residence-hall order than on student development. Similarly, they are more apt to apply if the residence halls are standardized (medium to high-rise, thirty-five to fifty students per floor, corridor arrangements, small double rooms, one resident assistant per floor), with a number of public drinking establishments and liquor stores within easy walking distance.

The study documents a number of uniformities: a high number of alcohol violations in the week before classes start, decreasing frequency with each subsequent week of the fall quarter, a lesser amount in the winter quarter, and an even smaller amount in the spring. In addition, there were relatively low numbers of repeat violators (e.g., in 1989, 15 out of 80 violators among the 388 residents of South Hall were repeaters). All these factors suggest that aggressive surveillance during RA rounds and writing up of alcohol violations, particularly in the fall quarter, enable RAs to discourage most freshmen from blatantly violating the age-specific prohibition.

Can RDs influence alcohol violations or the reporting practices of their RAs? Yes, but to a limited degree. Directors who are slow to sanction residents may engender, at least for a time, overenforcers among some of their RAs. But as often if not more so, laxity in dealing with residents who have been written up reinforces laid-back RAs and influences others to relax their vigilance.

Did the stringent alcohol policy work? Overall it appears that the new policy moved all parties, RDs, RAs, and residents alike, toward more stringent enforcement. By-the-book RDs, like Olds, certainly hastened the drive toward stringency, while lax enforcers, such as Cole, undermined it.

The comparison of these two RDs suggests that future research might focus on the shadows RDs cast over their residence halls. Olds, while assisting students who were moving into her building, saw one of them carting a case of beer up to his room. Olds instructed him and his parents to remove the case immediately. This event made a big impression on her RAs as well as on RAs in other buildings. By contrast, Cole, notorious among the other RDs as well as his own staff as being extremely laid-back, (he antagonized the other three RDs when he suggested that condoms be made available to all residents) was quite outspoken that the working agreement on "responsible drinking" in fact taught students how to cheat instead of how to be in control of their drinking. His philosophy, too, cast its shadow on his hall.

As noted, however, enforcement is at best only a partial explanation for student drinking behavior. Once classes begin, freshmen have to adapt to the calendar and rhythms of college life. Adjusting to the demands of classes and of study, the routines of residence-hall living, the management of time (including the work week and the weekend), making new friends, and learning the system of campus organizations are but a few of the changes incoming freshmen have to make (Becker, Geer, & Hughes, 1968). Among freshmen drinkers, clique formation probably exerts more influence on drinking patterns than college alcohol policy (Cherry, 1991). Nonetheless, this study demonstrates that policy and its enforcement can have an appreciable effect on the behavior of freshmen students in their residence halls.

The findings of this three-year study suggest that decreasing alcohol violations go hand in hand with the evolution and emergence of the ethic of "responsible drinking." Compliance with the ethic means that students will drink
in ways that reduce *public* alcohol problems. As long as those who drink do
not come to the attention of residence-hall staff, they are considered to be
drinking responsibly. In the process of living and working together, all three
parties to the age-specific prohibition have devised a workable compromise
to a rule that has been traditionally regarded, in most other quarters of urban
life, as unenforceable.

The findings of this study lend support to the integration hypothesis and
sanctions and role-conflict theories. By the same token, suggestions for how
to reduce alcohol problems in freshman residence halls can be derived from
those theoretical perspectives.

The Integration Hypothesis

To begin with, the study affords some support for the integration hypothesis. Over the period of the academic year, particularly during the fall quarter,
residence-hall staff defined what would be the operative drinking customs as
well as their sanctions. The staff made it clear that those customs and sanctions applied to the residence hall, the place where all parties resided. How
might this finding be applied with a view to further reducing alcohol violations? Just as RAs pointed out that many (if not most) freshman residents
failed to read the Housing Handbook, so it is also clear that both RDs and
RAs did not really spell out clearly and consistently in their initial orientations what they meant by acceptable levels of drinking and how it would be
enforced. Only when acceptable levels of drinking are generally known to all
and accepted by all can norms emerge by consensus.

If all staff would spell out this code of drinking conduct—in effect, the
operative rules governing alcohol policy—in advance, the social learning process might well take place a lot quicker. In their initial orientations, RDs
could state succinctly the rules and the sanctions. They could restate what the
Housing Handbook says about what happens after the first, the second, and
the third alcohol violation, all the time being precise and giving specific examples. Then, when RAs oriented their residents to their floor they could
spell out the code in finer detail, paying particular attention to how to evade
sanctions. All RAs would simply say something like this during the initial
orientation: "Don't drink here. If you do, I and all the other RAs will write
you up if we see you drinking. If you must drink, do so behind closed doors,
with only a few people in the room. Keep the voices and stereos down. And
don't play any drinking games."

If all RAs simply make this kind of matter-of-fact announcement unam-
biguously, then all except the most adventurous of residents will pay heed.
And to the extent that residents now have the drinking situation clearly de-

fined, there could well be more drinking in residence halls but with fewer alcohol violations. In that case, Ullman's hypothesis would be confirmed in action. All three parties come to a quicker consensus on the revised set of customs and sanctions that informally supplant CU's formal alcohol policy of age-specific prohibition.

Sanctions Theory

If sanctions are perceived as certain and are applied quickly, they are more likely to be effective, according to sanctions theorists. When CU's alcohol policy mandated meeting with the RD after the first alcohol violation, the number of reported alcohol violations went down. On the other hand, in those instances where RDs were slow to meet with alcohol offenders, repeats increased while RAs complained that "nothing happens." Thus, other things being equal, anything which speeds up disciplinary reactions increases effectiveness of policy. GAs, in the standard procedure in some of the residence halls, first reviewed all discipline cards at the end of the week and then compiled a list of violators who had to meet with the RD. Letters summoning violators to a meeting with their RD were then sent out the following week. If RDs reviewed the previous night's infractions each morning and issued summons almost immediately, this might very well speed the sanctioning process.

Role Conflict

RAs are well aware of the ubiquity of the friend–RA conflict, the problems it poses for them, and the difficulty of knowing where, when, and with whom to draw the line. The presumption is that anything that reduces role conflicts increases the effectiveness of alcohol policies. Time spent on both formal and informal training would be more useful if it presented real as opposed to hypothetical situations. Some residents are quite skillful at getting close to RAs with a view to turning the relationship to personal advantage. RAs must accept the fact that they are leaders. This means that they cannot put themselves under any obligation to their followers. Thus, for example, accepting a piece of pizza is much like drinking with another person. It puts one on the same plane and reduces status differences. RAs frequently reported how residents, when being written up, would say, "I thought we were friends." Training sessions can include any number of actual situations which RAs have faced. These situations give incoming RAs some idea of the kinds of situations which threaten their status as RAs. Social distance maintains respect and reduces chances that residents will claim special favors or treatment because of friendship.

RAs are well aware that they favor residents of their own floor, and that they are more lenient with them and less formal in enforcing the rules. Some actually feel guilty about being lax with their own residents and seek to make a change, something that is rather hard to do. One way to sustain their identity as RAs is in the situation of rule enforcement. Thus, when making rounds they can maintain consistency throughout all three quarters by holding to the view that when enforcing the rules they are just doing their job, that their actions are based on rules rather than relationships.

Thus, anything that maximizes social distance between RAs and residents shores up their authority, whereas anything which minimizes or reduces social distance between them and residents of all floors, their own as well as others, jeopardizes their authority. Whenever possible, new RAs should at least be juniors. Increasing the age gap increases social distance. Similarly, selecting RAs who do not drink is another possible way of increasing social distance.

SUMMARY AND CONCLUSIONS

Compared with enforcement of national prohibition (1920–1933), enforcement of age-specific prohibition in freshman residence halls has turned out to be infinitely more complex. Association, "patterned evasion" (Williams, 1970) of underage drinking laws, and university alcohol policy (policy says that students will obey state laws prohibiting underage drinking) are three conditions making for complexity. Close and frequent association of RAs with residents compromises their authority as enforcement agents, just as patterned evasion of underage drinking calls their enforcement actions into question. What caps it all is an official campus policy which assumes that its rule is enforceable.

Given the contradictions that perennially beset residence-hall staff, the solution they evolve yearly to the enforcement problem becomes as understandable as it is workable. When RAs state and act on the principle of seeing or hearing no evil, they establish a set of operative rules in the place of official college alcohol policy. Considering that only 20 percent of all residents violate that policy, 80 percent of whom are one-time offenders, the ethic of "responsible drinking," ultimately shared and understood by all who live and work in the residence hall, works rather well.

The present study has tried to show some of the conditions making for compliance and enforcement of official alcohol policy in one private urban university. It has closed with some suggestions for making the operative rules a little bit more effective without calling for major changes in the social structure of enforcement. Its goal has been to point the way to reducing alcohol problems in freshman residence halls within the terms of the working agreement the three parties have developed. Where official college alcohol policy enunciates the unenforceable norm, "don't drink," residence-hall people proclaim a more realistic policy when they say, "If you drink, make no trouble."

REFERENCES

Bales, R. F. (1946). Cultural differences in rates of alcoholism. *Quarterly Journal of Studies on Alcohol, 6,* 480–499.

Becker, H. S., Geer, B., & Hughes, E. C. (1968). *Making the grade.* New York: John Wiley.

Blimling, G. S., & Miltenberger, L. J. (1990). *The resident assistant.* Dubuque, IA: Kendall/Hunt.

Cahalan, D. (1988). *Understanding America's drinking problem.* San Francisco: Jossey-Bass.

Cherry, A. I. (1991). A social bond: An application of theory in the study of alcohol use among college students. *Journal of Alcohol and Drug Education, 36,* 96–113.

Cohn, E., & White, S. (1990). *Legal socialization: A study of norms and rules.* New York: Springer-Verlag.

Engs, R. C., & Hanson, D. J. (1989). University students' drinking patterns and problems: Examining the effects of raising the purchase age. *Public Health Reports, 103,* 667–673.

Gusfield, J. R. (1991). Benevolent repression: Popular culture, social structure and the control of drinking. In S. Barrows & R. Room (Eds.), *Drinking: Behavior and belief in modern history* (pp. 399–424). Berkeley and Los Angeles: University of California Press.

Hagan, J., Simpson, J. H., & Gillis, A. R. (1979). The sexual stratification of social control. *British Journal of Sociology, 30,* 25–38.

Hirschi, T. (1969). *The causes of delinquency.* Berkeley and Los Angeles: University of California Press.

Johnston, L. D., O'Malley, P. M., & Bachman, J. G. (1988). *Illicit drug use: Smoking and drinking by America's high school students, college students, and young adults.* Rockville, MD: National Institute of Drug Abuse.

MacDonald, K. (1988). The effectiveness of the New York State purchase law. Unpublished paper.

Marshall, M. (1979). *Beliefs, behavior, and alcoholic beverages.* Ann Arbor: University of Michigan Press.

Merton, R. K. (1968). *Social theory and social structure.* New York: The Free Press.

Merz, C. (1970). *The dry decade.* Seattle: University of Washington Press.

Moffatt, M. (1989). *Coming of age in New Jersey: College and American culture.* New Brunswick, NJ: Rutgers University Press.

Reiss, A. J. (1970). *The police and the public.* Chicago: University of Chicago Press.

Roethlisberger, F. J., & Dickson, W. J. (1946). *Management and the worker.* Cambridge: Harvard University Press.

Room, R. (1976). Ambivalence as a sociological explanation: The case of cultural explanations of alcohol problems. *American Sociological Review, 41,* 1047–1065.

Rubington, E. (1990). Drinking in the dorms: A study of the etiquette of RA–resident relations. *Journal of Drug Issues, 20,* 451–462.

Saltz, R., & Elandt, D. (1986). College student drinking studies, 1976–1985. *Contemporary Drug Problems, 13,* 117–159.

Silberman, M. (1976). Towards a theory of criminal deterrence. *American Sociological Review, 41,* 441–461.

Straus, R., & Bacon, S. D. (1953). *Drinking in college.* New Haven: Yale University Press.

Tittle, C. (1980). *Sanctions and deviance.* New York: Praeger.

Ullman, A. D. (1958). Sociocultural backgrounds of alcoholism. *Annals of the American Academy of Political and Social Science, 315,* 48–54.

Upcraft, L. (1982). *Residence hall assistants in college.* San Francisco: Jossey-Bass.

White, H. R. (1982). Sociological theories of alcoholism. In E. L. Gomberg, H. R. White, & J. A. Carpenter (Eds.), *Alcohol, science and society revisited* (pp. 205–232). Ann Arbor: University of Michigan Press; New Brunswick: Rutgers Center of Alcohol Studies.

Williams, R. M. (1970). *American society.* New York: Alfred A. Knopf.

Zimring, F. F. E., & Hawkins, G. J. (1973). *Deterrence: The legal threat to crime control.* Chicago: University of Chicago Press.

PART III

ASSESSMENT, INTERVENTION, AND TREATMENT

8

Assessing Alcohol Problems in Student Populations

Patrick D. Smith, Dedra B. Wells,
and Katurah Abdul-Salaam

While concerted efforts have been made to increase alcohol awareness and decrease drinking among college students, problem drinking on university campuses across the country continues at alarming rates. National survey data indicate more stable and higher rates of heavy drinking among students at colleges and universities than among same-age peers (Johnston, O'Malley, & Bachman, 1991). Recent studies have reported alcohol use rates from 88 to 95 percent among college students, with as many as 80 percent reporting alcohol use in the past thirty days (Johnson, O'Malley, & Bachman, 1991). It has been reported that 1.1 million young people in the United States alone abuse alcohol (Presley, Meilman, & Lyerla, 1994; Saltz & Elandt, 1986; Johnston, O'Malley, & Bachman, 1991; Pope, Ionescu-Pioggia, Aizley, & Varma, 1990; Smith, 1991). Most of what we know about the rates of drinking and problem drinking among students has been from survey data, since most alcohol-related problems among college students go undetected and treatment needs go unmet.

Recently, the U.S. Surgeon General estimated that college students spend $4.2 billion on alcoholic beverages annually and called for a reduction in alcohol use on college campuses (Office for Substance Abuse Prevention, 1991). The continued heavy and frequent use of alcohol among college students in the United States has also become a primary subject of concern to college administrators (Wechsler, Isaac, Grodstein, & Sellers, 1994). The Carnegie Foundation reported that presidents of U.S. colleges and universities identified substance abuse, specifically alcohol abuse, as the most pressing problem on campuses today (Carnegie Foundation for the Advancement of Teaching, 1990). While identification, assessment, and treatment of college students with alcohol problems are significant concerns for all individuals involved in working with this population, most college personnel report feeling unclear about how best to intervene on a student's behalf.

This chapter is meant to be a practical, "hands-on" guide for college personnel about some of the more important aspects of the assessment process. First, we will focus on the unique and vital role that college personnel can play in the overall assessment process. A basic training model for college personnel will be outlined and utilized throughout the chapter. This model has been developed to help college personnel understand and feel comfortable with their role in referring students for drug and alcohol assessment. Second, we will discuss how to identify students who may be in need of assessment for alcohol problems and will highlight some of the most common warning signs and risk factors for college personnel to be mindful of. We will also discuss in this section how an understanding of the various definitions of problem drinking among college students and drinking-related consequences can impact how we decide who to refer for assessment. Third, we will describe the referral process and will outline procedures that college personnel can follow when referring a student for assessment. Fourth, we will give the reader a more comprehensive understanding of what takes place in the assessment itself and give some examples of typical assessment procedures. In this assessment procedure section, we will also give a brief overview of some of the assessment tools most often used with college students. Finally, we will discuss how the results of the assessment are utilized to help the student receive the appropriate level of treatment and how college personnel can be involved in the followup phase of the assessment.

THE POTENTIAL ROLE FOR COLLEGE PERSONNEL

College personnel have been taking on an increasingly active role in identifying and referring students who may be in need of treatment for problem drinking. Many colleges and universities have made attempts to prepare their employees for this role. The ASK Training Program was developed to help college personnel understand and feel comfortable with this role (Smith, 1994).

The anacronym ASK has two meanings in this training program. First, the motto of the program is, "When in doubt, ASK!" Sometimes college personnel are not sure whether a student's drinking constitutes a problem. The objective of this training program is to help an individual know what signs to look for and to know how to intervene. When they find themselves wondering whether there is a problem or not, they are encouraged to go ahead and check it out with the student. They are only asking whether it is a problem by intervening and possibly making a referral. The final determination of whether it is a problem and what level of treatment may be needed will be reached via a comprehensive assessment.

Second, the ASK anacronym stands for three criteria to help us understand who should intervene. When we look at who is in the best position to confront an individual about his or her drinking and to follow through to see that the individual receives appropriate assessment and treatment, we ASK the following:

Who has the Ability to observe changes in baseline behavior?
Who has the Sense of responsibility to intervene?
Who has the Knowledge of how to facilitate a referral?

These three simple criteria are the hallmark components of the ASK Training Program. The training program outlines behavior changes to look for, increases college personnel's sense of responsibility to intervene on behalf of students, and teaches how to facilitate a referral for assessment and treatment. By covering these three basic components of the program, the ASK Training Program breaks down barriers that often keep college personnel from getting involved in intervention.

Once one knows what behaviors to look for, it is much easier to determine whether the individual in question may be in need of assessment. With an appreciation of their sense of responsibility to intervene and the knowledge of how to facilitate a referral, college personnel can play a vital role in helping a student with a drinking problem get the help that is needed. If they find themselves trying to determine whether to intervene with a particular student, the motto of the ASK Training Program is, "When in doubt, ASK!" It is believed that it is the role of the college personnel simply to ask, by intervening and making a referral, "Does this student's drinking constitute a significant problem?" It is the role of the assessment professional to answer that important question.

While many junior high and high school students with problematic drinking patterns are confronted by friends, neighbors, school personnel, and other caring adults in their lives, it probably comes as no surprise that it is their parents who are most likely to confront them about their drinking and follow through to seek assessment and treatment for their alcohol problem. Their parents have the opportunity to monitor their behavior on an ongoing basis and to notice if their behavior becomes different from their normal behavior. Even if their friends notice such changes in their behavior, they are often reluctant to confront them and are very unlikely to help facilitate a referral for proper assessment and treatment.

For college students living away from home, it is often the resident assistant on their floor of the residence hall or one of their instructors who is in the best position to notice important changes in their baseline behavior. Even if these college personnel have the ability to notice warning signs and feel a sense of responsibility for the college student's well-being, they often will choose not to intervene. This is particularly likely if they do not think it would do any good or they simply do not know where to turn for help. Without proper knowledge of how to facilitate a referral, concerned others can feel powerless and, hence, be more reluctant to get involved.

It is often the case, even among health-care professionals, that "one doesn't ask what one doesn't want to hear." A physician, for example, working in an acute outpatient care clinic often may not delve into questions about substance abuse among her adolescent patients if she is not fully aware of the local resources that can be offered for such problems. In the case of cigarette smoking, resident physicians have been found to more thoroughly assess their patients' smoking habits and to become actively involved in smoking-cessation counseling when they see it as their responsibility as a physician to address their patients' smoking (Smith & Portilla, 1995). This sounds simple and basic, yet is of particular importance since we would have erroneously assumed that all physicians in the 1990s share this sense of responsibility equally. Further study revealed that the two best predictors of physicians' sense of responsibility were their appreciation of the harmful effects of smoking and their belief that their patients expected them, as physicians, to intervene and to address their smoking problem (Smith & Portilla, 1995).

For us, then, to expect college personnel to be involved in the identification and referral of students with potential drinking problems, we must increase their sense of responsibility to intervene by increasing their appreciation of the harmful effects of problem drinking and by helping them to understand that students expect them, as college personnel, to intervene. While most are well aware of the harmful effects of problem drinking among students, those who have the most complete information regarding these devastating effects and who have the strongest beliefs about these effects are most likely to be involved in identifying and referring students in need of assessment. Furthermore, those who feel most comfortable in their role as college personnel to intervene on a student's behalf and believe that the student expects them to will also be more likely to do so.

IDENTIFYING STUDENTS IN NEED OF ASSESSMENT

When attempting to decide whether a student's drinking behaviors warrant a referral for assessment, we must take into account what constitutes problem drinking among college students. Many of the difficulties that we face in our attempts to accurately determine rates of drinking and problem drinking among college students and to appropriately identify those students in need of assessment and subsequent treatment for their alcohol-related problems have been created by our lack of agreement upon developmentally appropriate definitions of problem drinking in a university setting. Clearly, how we define problem drinking affects who we identify as needing assessment for their alcohol use and related consequences.

If researchers and clinicians have failed to come to agreement on what constitutes alcohol abuse or problem drinking in older adult populations, then it should come as no surprise that there has been even more confusion and disagreement about problem definitions for college student drinkers. Brennan and colleagues (1986) noted that this lack of definition is widely viewed as the greatest methodological deficiency in research on college students. The implications for identification of students in need of further assessment are apparent. Many of the traditional definitions of problem drinking have been based on older, male, inpatient populations. Hence, the definitions do not adequately address problem drinking in a college population for a number of reasons.

Similarly, while there is general consensus that the definitions of "alcohol dependence" and "alcohol abuse," as outlined by the *Diagnostic and Statistical Manual for Mental Disorders* (American Psychiatric Association, 1994), do not adequately capture problem drinking of college students (Smith, Kriesberg, & Volpicelli, 1987), they are often utilized in clinical work and research with the student population. The limitations of these criteria are similar to those of most criteria based on more traditional definitions of problem drinking and are addressed in this section. For a description of these criteria, see Chapter 4.

QUANTITY–FREQUENCY OF DRINKING

Quantity–frequency measures of drinking have often been utilized as the sole or primary source of information in understanding and evaluating problem drinking. This is problematic, since many older adolescent and young adult college students may experience greater problems associated with lower quantity and frequency of alcohol consumption when compared to older adults. These greater problems occur because of lack of experience with drinking or underdeveloped tolerance. Also, most college students may not have been abusing alcohol long enough to have experienced some of the more serious medical complications and physiological dependence. These physiological reactions are often used as criteria for classification of problem-drinking status. Thus, many college student problem drinkers could be omitted based on traditional definitions of problem drinking and missed by traditional methods of assessment (false negatives). Further, if college personnel utilized this definition as the criterion to identify which student drinkers were in need for further assessment, they would be underreferring many problem drinkers with low quantity–frequency of drinking but significant alcohol-related problems.

Conversely, patterns of frequent heavy binge drinking are also considered more normative in a college student population. Thus, many student drinkers with a high quantity–frequency of alcohol consumption may be classified as problem drinkers by more traditional means of assessment but may not experience the negative consequences of older adult drinkers with comparable quantity–frequency of drinking. Many clinicians and researchers have debated this issue and have questioned the degree to which more traditional assessment methods are developmentally appropriate for use with a college-age population.

It has become well accepted that many students with high quantity–frequency of alcohol consumption while in college return to non-abusive patterns of drinking after graduation or leaving college. (The reasons for this return to non-abusive drinking are thought to be, in part, because of the increased focus on establishing a career and beginning a family by these former students.) While many young people will experiment with alcohol and drugs and even use them regularly for a period of time, the majority will not develop serious problems or significant negative consequences in their lives (Bailey, 1989). Data suggest that most adolescents and young adults "mature out" of alcohol abuse (Kandel & Logan, 1984), so use of traditional assessment methods may yield false positives or overestimate rates of problem drinking among college students. It should be noted, however, that there are significant risks involved even with binge drinking that is considered normative and does not lead to long-term alcohol abuse (e.g., date rape, transmission of sexually transmitted diseases, drunk driving, accidents, injuries, etc.). While such a drinking style would not be appropriately labeled problem drinking in a more traditional sense, it is still a drinking outcome of critical importance for a college student population.

It is also important to note here that the role of college personnel in identifying and referring an individual who may be a problem drinker is very different from that of the assessment professional who needs to accurately identify the student's drinking as problematic or not. Again, we think of the motto of the ASK Training Program, "When in doubt, ASK!" We expect that, based on this model, there will be more students identified and referred than there are students who will complete the assessment process with a diagnosable drinking problem. That is to say, it is better to overrefer and have problem drinking ruled out than to underrefer and miss the opportunity to address a student's significant alcohol problem. The role is to simply ask, "Is this a problem or is it normative?" A comprehensive assessment will then help to answer this question. In summary, then, while quantity–frequency of drinking may not be necessary nor sufficient in determining whether a student's drinking is problematic, high quantity–frequency of drinking should be enough to lead college personnel to ask the question, "Is this a problem?" and make a referral.

IMPAIRMENT OF SOCIAL ROLES

Traditional methods of measuring problem drinking also focus on impairment of social roles. Often, the social roles included for assessment (e.g., marriage, career) are not salient for a college student population and difficulties involving more pertinent issues for college drinkers (e.g., impaired school performance, missed classes, regretted sexual experiences) are omitted (Hurlbut & Sher, 1992). Once again, reliance on more traditional assessments of problem drinking could yield false negatives and grossly underestimate the important negative consequences of drinking among college-age drinkers. College personnel are in an excellent position to pick up on those markers most salient to the college student population. Here, the idea is that if a student's drinking is impairing his or her abilities in any way, there is more than enough reason to identify and refer the student for further assessment.

In addition, since the definitions have been primarily based on data from older adult male alcoholics, assessment tools have traditionally not been gender sensitive and women have been underidentified and underreferred for assessment. Pope and colleagues (1994) addressed the complications associated with using these assessment tools to compare males' and females' relative problems with alcohol.

An individual is frequently classified as a problem drinker based on the quantity of alcohol consumed in one sitting or on reported multiple negative consequences resulting from their drinking. The first of these two criteria ignores that women's bodies, in general, have a higher percentage of fat and less water per pound than men's bodies. When alcohol is ingested, it is distributed in total body water; therefore, an equivalent amount of alcohol per pound will result in a higher blood alcohol level for women than for men (Blume, 1990). In addition, women experience more day-to-day variation in peak blood alcohol levels than men. This variation, which appears to be related to the menstrual cycle, makes it more difficult for women to predict the effects a given amount of alcohol will have on their bodies (Johnson, 1991). The average per capita alcohol consumption for women in the United States is only about half that for men, with women consuming an average of 0.44 oz of alcohol per day and men consuming 0.91 oz per day. Women in alcohol treatment programs also have lower consumption rates than men (4.5 oz per day for women and 8.2 oz per day for men) (Blume, 1990). Thus, assessing male and female drinkers using the same quantity–frequency criteria to classify problem drinkers may be overestimating the differences between male and female drinkers by not appreciating that females are at risk at lower levels of alcohol intake than males (Whitehead & Layne, 1987). When utilizing quantity–frequency of drinking as an indicator of need for further assessment, college personnel should be mindful of these important gender differences so they do not underrefer college women.

The second of these two criteria, negative consequences associated with drinking, is also problematic. Again, most of the negative consequences included in traditional assessment instruments are based on reports of male alcoholics. Hence, many of the consequences that are addressed (e.g., problems with the law, getting into fights because of your drinking) are more common for males than for females. It has been reported that males have a tendency to be more aggressive, have more behavior problems at school, and exhibit more externalizing behaviors, in general, than females, regardless of drinking status (Prior, Smart, Sanson, & Oberklaid, 1993). Conversely, females tend to report more internalizing consequences of drinking (e.g., anxiety, depression) than males and have been found more often to drink to get drunk (Pope et al., 1994; Petersen, Sarigiani, & Kennedy, 1991; Waite-O'Brien, 1992). Pope and colleagues (1994) highlighted the need for current assessment of drinking and problem drinking to include more female-oriented internalizing consequences so that differences in prevalence rates between males and females are not overestimated. It is important for college personnel to be aware of these gender differences when identifying and referring students in need for assessment. Reliance on more traditional definitions of alcohol problems focusing more on externalizing consequences would yield underreferral of college women with significant problem drinking.

Finally, researchers and clinicians alike have argued the value of characterizing problem drinking as a more multidimensional construct. That is, problem drinking does not have to be defined as alcohol dependence or binge drinking. In a college student population, true alcohol dependence is probably relatively rare, while binge drinking is quite common. Yet both outcomes are equally important constructs of study and can both result in serious negative drinking-related consequences. Assessment that can be sensitive to both drinking outcomes is optimal and the individual whose task it is to identify and refer students in need of assessment should keep in mind both levels of problem drinking so that they do not fail to refer students who may have significant alcohol-related problems.

DRINKING-RELATED CONSEQUENCES AND ASSOCIATED HIGH-RISK BEHAVIORS

College personnel should have a clear understanding of the drinking-related consequences and associated high-risk behaviors that may serve as warning signs of a significant drinking problem. A comprehensive appreciation of these associated factors can help in the identification of students in need of further assessment. These problems can range from simple injury to death. Some common drinking-related consequences are declining school performance, getting into unwanted sexual situations, minor injuries, hangovers, and major accidents.

In a recent study conducted by the U.S. Department of Education, students of ninety-six colleges and universities were surveyed. Results indicated that 36 percent of all students had driven while intoxicated on at least one occasion. In addition, 33 percent reported getting into an argument or fight because of drinking, 30 percent reported missing classes secondary to their drinking, and 23 percent indicated that they had performed poorly on a test because of their drinking behavior (Presley et al., 1994). In fact, alcohol-related problems often play a role in why some students delay or discontinue university studies altogether (Nystrom, Perasalo, & Salaspuro, 1993). College personnel have the unique opportunity to notice these behaviors early on and refer the student for comprehensive assessment.

Binge drinking is often associated with the more serious consequences of drinking. Binge drinking has been defined as consuming five or more drinks in one sitting (Sadowski, Long, & Jenkins, 1992). According to Presley, Meilman, and Lyerla (1994) binge drinking is frequently associated with residence-hall damage, sexual assault, fights, blackouts, and drunk driving. These are behaviors that are easily detected by college personnel and should indicate the need for further assessment. Wechsler and colleagues (1994) reported that in a study of 17,096 college students, over 50 percent of the subjects reported experiencing negative consequences directly related to binge drinking (44% were classified as binge drinkers, with 19% being frequent binge drinkers). In this study, 90 percent reported having had a hangover, 63 percent reported doing something they regretted, 61 percent reported having missed a class, 54 percent indicated they had forgotten where they had been or what they had done, 62 percent of the male subjects and 49 percent of the females had driven while drinking, and 53 percent of the males and 48 percent of the females had ridden with someone who was under the influence of alcohol or drugs. What is important to note is that these negative consequences of binge drinking occur regardless of whether the drinker in question can accurately be classified as a problem drinker. Even if a college student experiences only one binge-drinking episode in his or her life, the risk of negative consequences from that drinking episode remains high. It is better to refer for assessment and have the assessment professional rule out the need for treatment than to miss the opportunity to potentially prevent some of these negative alcohol-related outcomes.

Not only is binge drinking potentially harmful to the person, it also is disruptive to others who are forced by situation to be around them. For example, students who do not binge drink but live in dormitory, fraternity, or sorority houses are at risk of negative consequences simply because of exposure to heavy binge drinkers. These students reported a high rate of experiencing secondary binge effects, which include being insulted or embarrassed, experiencing an argument, being physically assaulted, having their property damaged, taking care of drunk friends or other students, being interrupted while sleeping or studying, experiencing unwanted sexual advances, or being victims of date rape or sexual assault (Wechsler et al., 1994). It is often the case that others around binge drinkers and problem drinkers have valuable information regarding the student's drinking behaviors. College personnel often have the ability to obtain information from the student's friends, roommates, and other key people to help in making the determination regarding need for further assessment.

Driving while intoxicated is a serious negative consequences of alcohol on college campuses. Alcohol-related accidents account for nearly one-half of all fatalities on the road and constitute the leading cause of death to America's youth (Wechsler et al., 1994). College students report extremely high rates of drunk driving. Hurlbut and Sher (1992) reported that 54 percent of the college students surveyed had driven when they knew they had had too much to drink. Presley, Meilman, and Lyerla (1994) found that 35 percent of their subjects had driven while intoxicated and Werner, Walker, and Greene (1994) found that 10 percent of their subjects had driven drunk six or more times.

In an age when AIDS and other sexually transmitted diseases are a major concern with youth, unplanned and unprotected sexual activity is of great concern. Unfortunately, these negative consequences often occur as a result of drinking. Wechsler and colleagues (1994) found that students who frequently engaged in binge drinking were seven to ten times more likely to engage in unprotected and/or unplanned sexual activity. Hurlbut and Sher (1992) found that 47 percent of their sample had, because of drinking, gotten into sexual situations they later regretted. Binge drinking has also been associated with occurrences of sexual assault and date rape (Wechsler & Isaac, 1992). While college personnel may not always be aware of a particular student's negative sexual consequences of drinking, it is advisable to be mindful that such problems may be indicative of an alcohol problem.

Alcohol has also been associated with many unnecessary deaths on college campuses. It is the leading cause of all accidental deaths (e.g., falls) on college campuses (Wechsler et al., 1994). Older adolescent students with substance abuse problems are 2.1 to 3.7 times more likely to report suicidal ideation or behavior than students who do not abuse alcohol or drugs (Levy & Deykin, 1989). Presley, Meilman, and Lyerla (1994) found that 5.5 percent of the 51,971 students they surveyed thought about or tried to commit suicide as a consequence of using alcohol and/or other drugs. Any suicidal ideation or attempt should be seen as a warning sign indicating the need for further assessment.

Alcohol abuse is also associated with negative consequences that are not as severe, but are still damaging to the individual drinker. Presley, Meilman, and Lyerla (1994) reported percentages of students that had experienced negative consequences because of using alcohol and/or other drugs in the past year: 62.8 percent had experienced a hangover, 21.7 percent had a hangover more than five times, 23.4 percent had performed poorly on a test or important project, 13.5 percent had trouble with police or college authorities, 7.7 percent had damaged property, 33.3 percent had been in an argument or fight, 50.1 percent had been nauseated or vomited, 35.6 percent had missed a class, 29 percent had been criticized by someone they knew, 11.7 percent thought they might have a drinking or drug problem, 28.2 percent had memory loss, 39.3 percent had done something they had regretted, 5.7 percent had tried unsuccessfully to stop using, and 16.1 percent had been hurt or injured.

Hence, when identifying and referring students for assessment of drinking problems on college campuses, one needs to include the full range of negative drinking-related consequences that are endemic to the student population. It is often the case that we do not keep in mind the more subtle adverse consequences of drinking even when these consequences can lead to very poor outcomes for students. At the very least, even the most subtle of the adverse consequences of drinking can contribute to delay or termination of university studies, which can have a serious impact on the individual's life. Early identification and referral for assessment for alcohol-related problems can significantly impact a number of college students who would have otherwise suffered from these negative consequences of drinking.

MAKING A REFERRAL

Remember that, based on the ASK Training Program, the knowledge of how to facilitate a referral is a key component. College personnel can only be effective in identifying students in need of further assessment for alcohol-related problems if they are aware of the available resources for referral. Knowledge of the basic assessment process and the individuals and/or agencies in the area who conduct these assessments will have a tremendous impact on one's ability to effectively identify those students who may need intervention.

One of the first contacts to be aware of is the counseling center at the college or university. Sometimes this is affiliated with the university health center. While some university campuses may have more than one such service, others may not have any. The first step should be to become familiar with the services provided on campus. If college personnel are unaware of such services on their campus, the admissions office can be a good place to start. Also, most colleges and universities have, at the minimum, some health-center services for students. One should contact the director of the student health center to find out what assessment and treatment services are available to students with drug and alcohol problems. Many training programs in the helping professions have their own clinics and counseling centers, so places for college personnel to keep in mind include clinical psychology programs, counseling psychology and educational psychology programs, and social work programs. The director of student services at the college or university may know of some of these resources and other special resources for alcohol awareness, assessment, and treatment initiatives on campus.

It may be that there are no alcohol assessment services on some campuses and that an individual needs to look into such services in the community at large. College personnel should take the time to familiarize themselves with all such services to increase their effectiveness in making an impact on students' drinking problems. Local services they should know about include hospital-based clinics that do assessment and treatment, the local community mental health center, and private practitioners in the area who provide these services. Most communities have active twelve-step groups and many have hotlines that may provide helpful information.

Once an individual has identified the primary services available for college students in their community, it is a good idea for them to get to know the key contact person(s) in that agency so that subsequent referrals can go as smoothly as possible. Referring a student for assessment of his or her drinking and related consequences is not an easy thing to do, and some familiarity with the referral source may increase college personnel's comfort in doing so. It is important to remember that this contact person can be a resource in many ways. If an individual questions whether a student's specific situation warrants intervention, it is a good idea to discuss the situation with such a professional. Also, these professionals and their organizations often offer training for individuals in the community who are in the role of identifying, screening, and referring individuals for further assessment. These professionals also may offer their assistance in planning an intervention with the student and can walk college personnel through, step-by-step, various options for the initial intervention. Professionals in the field of substance abuse have worked over the years to develop some basic guidelines to assist in planning an initial intervention with the drinker and a chapter of this book specifically addresses this issue, outlining college personnels' potential role in the intervention process (see Chapter 9).

OVERVIEW OF THE ASSESSMENT

The importance of early screening and identification of alcohol problems among college students has been emphasized in terms of preventing and minimizing adverse social, economic, and medical consequences for the students (Skinner, Holt, & Israel, 1981). Once again, the assessment of drinking problems among college students should focus on assessing whatever the problem is and then trying to characterize the drinking problem rather than assess whether a student drinker fits someone's predetermined definition of what they consider to be problematic. The map is not the territory, but is to be used to better understand the territory. So are the assessment tools to be used to better understand whatever drinking problems an individual is experiencing.

In general, the best approach to assessing a student's drinking and related problems is to utilize basic background information, drinking history and patterns of drinking, family history of drinking problems and other mental health concerns, and psychological testing to build a converging pattern of level of risk. The assessment professional must look at the various risk factors and develop a profile of risk based on information from each of these vital domains.

When conducting an assessment, the assessor must attempt to understand an individual's present behavior in the context of what is going on in their life at the current time. The individual conducting the assessment strives to better understand the cognitive, motivational, and emotional component that contributes to the current behavior. He or she then looks at what has gone on in the individual's life up to this point that may have contributed to the person's attitudes, beliefs, and current behavior.

This is an overly simplified description of the goals of any assessment, including the assessment of substance abuse. Applying these generalized goals to the assessment of problem drinking among college students, then, we first must understand the student's drinking and drinking-related behavior in the context of his or her environment. Since each college and university has its own set of norms around drinking and related behaviors, these behaviors have to be understood within the context of the "subculture" created by that particular college. It is also often the case that certain residence halls or fraternities and sororities have their own set of norms about drinking and related behaviors and this is important information to have when trying to fully understand the individual student's drinking. The individual's context can also have a temporal component. For example, students' drinking can often get more out of control during certain times of the year (e.g., spring break, finals week, freshmen initiation). While student drinkers are still at risk for negative consequences associated with their drinking during these times (probably at increased risk) it is important to understand their behavior in the context of what is normative for their subculture during that specific time.

There may also be cultural and ethnic influences that are important for assessment professionals to understand. What may be abnormal drinking or drug use for one individual may be normative for another based on their ethnic and cultural environments. Appreciation of these influences can help to safeguard against overestimating a student's problem based on standards and criteria that may not be culturally sensitive.

While it is important to look at a student's drinking in relation to the context of the campus climate or the student's cultural and ethnic background, other criteria may indicate that the student's drinking is problematic regardless of how normative it may be for his campus or cultural environment. The cognitive, motivational, and emotional contributions to the behavior being assessed are important. Two individuals with strikingly similar patterns of drinking may, indeed, report very different attitudes about drinking and may drink for different reasons. While it is well accepted that a drinker may not be able to accurately describe why they drink, they are usually able to be very specific about what they expect from drinking alcohol. Furthermore, specific expectancies about drinking (e.g., alcohol will reduce my tension, drinking alcohol makes me feel more assertive) have been found to significantly predict patterns of drinking among college students (Brown, 1985; Smith, 1991; Smith, Stahl, & Rivers, 1992). By understanding an individual's expectancies about alcohol, one can more fully understand the motivational component of the individual's drinking. Thus, expectancy models have been favored over attitude and belief models when trying to understand problem drinking (Stacy, Widaman, & Marlatt, 1990).

There is much to be understood by studying the variability or pattern of drinking in addition to simple quantity–frequency measures of alcohol consumption. Brown (1985) described using a measurement of three drinking styles, later described as three distinct factors of drinking: quantity–frequency factor, alcohol-related problems factor, and context of drinking factor (Smith et al., 1992). Smith (1991) described a fourth factor, a family history factor, and emphasized the need to generate drinking styles from each of the four factors. Assessment of a more multidimensional problem-drinking construct can yield a greater understanding of negative alcohol-related outcomes from binge drinking to alcohol dependence.

Taking into account the domains of information and influence that are of interest to the assessment professional, it will also be helpful to know what a typical assessment looks like from the perspective of the student being assessed. The student is likely to meet initially with an individual who will conduct an intake interview. This interview covers many of the domains outlined, including basic information that can help the assessor decide what further assessment may be needed. Basic demographic background information will be obtained in addition to family history of drinking problems and other related mental health concerns. The patient's own drinking history and pattern of drinking will be obtained as well as other related concerns, such as anxiety, depression, or sleeplessness. If, for example, the student indicates experiencing symptoms of depression, the assessment may include a more formal screen for depression.

In addition to the face-to-face interview with the assessment professional, the student is likely to complete a battery of self-administered paper-and-pencil screening tools to further evaluate the students drinking history, patterns of drinking, and drinking-related consequences. It is optimal to obtain information from a variety of different sources via a variety of different approaches. Thus, information from the face-to-face clinical interview with the student, the self-administered instruments completed by the student, and information obtained from significant others (e.g., parents, friends, teachers, school officials, etc.) are all important in providing the pieces to the overall puzzle to be completed so that there is a better understanding of the student's relative level of risk. College personnel can provide crucial information in the assessment process and are often called on to do so. Again, this may be in the form of a face-to-face or telephone interview with the assessment professional to ask about changes in behavior that the college personnel have had the opportunity to observe, or may be in the form of a paper-and-pencil checklist asking similar information. The following section is an overview of some of the standardized assessment tools utilized in evaluating alcohol and drug abuse among college students. While this is not an exhaustive list of tools available, it can serve as a guide to some of the more commonly used assessment measures.

STANDARDIZED ASSESSMENT TOOLS

The Rutgers Collegiate Substance Abuse
Screening Test (RCSAST)

The RCSAST was designed to address substance abuse problems in the young adult age group. The RCSAST is a twenty-five-item true–false questionnaire based on the structure of the Michigan Alcoholism Screening Test (MAST) but adapted for the young adult population. The questionnaire contains items related to substance abuse and its effect on school work and college life in general. It also contains questions about problem drinking. Respondents are asked, for example, if they use substances because they are shy with other people, to escape worries or troubles, or to increase self-confidence. Also included are questions pertaining to substance use and emotional consequences such as decreased ambition because of alcohol and/or drug use (Bennett et al., 1993).

Bennett and colleagues (1993) conducted a study with a college student population to determine if the RCSAST could differentiate between problem and nonproblem users. The results determined that with the optimal cutoff score of five, 94 percent of problem users were correctly identified and 84 percent of the control subjects were classified as nonproblem users. This gives the RCSAST a positive predictive value of 85.8 percent.

Six questions were endorsed by over 50 percent of the problem users: Has alcohol ever interfered with your preparation for exams?; Has your efficiency decreased since drinking and/or using other drugs?; Is your drinking and/or drug use jeopardizing your academic performance?; Have you ever felt remorse after drinking and/or using other drugs?; Have you ever had a complete or partial loss of memory as a result of drinking or using other drugs?; Is drinking or using other drugs affecting your reputation? These six questions either had low or no response from the control group.

Young Adult Alcohol Problems Screening Test (YAAPST)

The Young Adult Alcohol Problems Screening Test was designed specifically for college students. It is a relatively short questionnaire (twenty-seven items), easy to administer, and has a high reliability and validity. It was geared to college students in a variety of ways. Items measure negative consequences of alcohol, including blackouts, hangovers, and alcohol dependence. The YAAPST assesses whether the problems have occurred in the student's lifetime or recently (within the past year), as well as the frequency of occurrences in the past year to gauge severity of the problem. The YAAPST results can identify students who are experiencing multiple consequences of their drinking, can indicate the severity of each consequence for the student's life, and can specify areas to be targeted for prevention and intervention (Hurlbut & Sher, 1992).

The YAAPST can be used as a screening tool and to identify areas for intervention. The YAAPST can also be used to obtain descriptive information. For example, in research reported by Hurlbut and Sher (1992), five items were endorsed by 47 percent or more: Have you driven a car when you knew you had too much to drink to drive safely (54%)?; Have you had a headache (hangover) the morning after you had been drinking (73.1%)?; Have you showed up late for work or school because of drinking, a hangover, or an illness caused by drinking (75.6%)?; Has drinking ever gotten you into a sexual situation which you later regretted (47%)?; Have you awakened the morning after a good bit of drinking and found that you could not remember a part of the evening before (53.1%)?

Sensitivity and specificity (ability to accurately identify problem drinkers without underdiagnosing those who are and overdiagnosing those who are not) for the YAAPST depend on the cutoff scores, which should be determined based on the situation. For example, a cutoff score of four gives 92 percent sensitivity and 57 percent specificity, whereas a cutoff score of eight yields a sensitivity score of 58 percent and a specificity score of 91 percent (Hurlbut & Sher, 1992).

CAGE

The CAGE questionnaire can be given verbally or written. It is relatively short and easy to administer. CAGE is an acronym that represents questions about Cutting down (Do you ever feel the need to cut down on your drinking?); Annoyance by criticism (Are you ever annoyed by criticism of your drinking?); Guilty feelings (Do you ever feel guilty after drinking?); and Eye-opener (Do you ever feel the need to have a drink first thing in the morning?) (Ewing, 1984). This is then scored by giving one point to each positive response. Two positive responses generally constitute a positive test; however, in a college population even one positive response warrants further investigation. Past research indicates a specificity of 89 to 96 percent and a sensitivity of 75 to 85 percent (Ewing, 1984) However, the CAGE was developed for adults and to detect alcoholism and not problem drinking. It may, therefore, lose some of its sensitivity in the college population (Smith & Kreisberg, 1987).

Perceived Benefit of Drinking Scale (PBDS)

The Perceived Benefit of Drinking Scale is a brief clinical instrument useful in screening college students who may be problem drinkers. It consists of five true–false statements: Drinking helps me forget, drinking helps me be friendly, drinking helps me feel good about myself, drinking helps me relax, and drinking helps me be friends with others who drink (Petchers & Singer, 1987). The PBDS has well-established reliability and validity. It does not obtain direct information on how much or how often a subject drinks; however, it assesses a person's opinion on the benefits of drinking. Generally, three positive responses indicate the need for further investigation for potential drinking problem.

The Alcohol Expectancy Questionnaire (AEQ)

The Alcohol Expectancy Questionnaire (Brown, Goldman, Inn, & Anderson, 1980) is a structured 120-item questionnaire concerning the potentially positive effects of alcohol consumption. Items are answered in a true–false format and scored to yield six subscales. Recent research has called attention to the need to determine not only the endorsement of alcohol expectancies but also their strength (Conners & Maisto, 1988; Collins, Lapp, Emmons, & Isaac, 1990). Various alcohol expectancies have been found to be predictive of drinking patterns among college students. The six alcohol expectancies measured by the AEQ include (1) global positive changes, (2) sexual enhancement, (3) social and physical pleasure enhancement, (4) social assertion, (5) tension reduction, and (6) arousal with feelings of power. A more comprehensive understanding of an individual's expectancies about the effects of drinking can help identify those at risk of more serious problems and can help the treatment provider in assessment and treatment planning.

The Trauma Score

Past research has shown that trauma history can indicate a problem with alcohol (Antti-Poika, 1988; Keso, Kevisaari, & Salaspuro, 1988). Skinner and colleagues (1984) developed a questionnaire based on this theory. The Trauma Score represents a five-item questionnaire that asks the following: Since your sixteenth birthday, have you had any fractures or dislocations to your bones or joints, have you been injured in a road traffic accident, have you injured your head, have you been injured in an assault or fight, and have you been injured after drinking? As with the CAGE, two or more affirmative responses indicate the need for further assessment.

The Michigan Alcoholism Screening Test

The Michigan Alcoholism Screening Test was developed by Selzer (1971) and was the first validated and published instrument to screen for alcohol abuse. It is a twenty-five-item questionnaire that can be administered in a written format or as a structured interview. Over the years there have been several abbreviated versions of the MAST: the MmMAST, the B-MAST, and the SMAST (Nystrom et al., 1993). The MAST has been credited with high sensitivity, but it is sometimes lacking in specificity (Jacobson, 1989). Nystrom, Perasalo, and Salaspuro (1993) found two questions in particular that could cause false positive results: Have you ever attended a meeting of Alcoholics

Anonymous?; Has drinking ever created problems between you and your spouse? These questions need to be reworded because they do not specify whose drinking. Many family members and friends attend AA meetings with a problem drinker, and the second question could be answered yes if the spouse's drinking had caused problems. When the questions were reworded, the authors found six false-positive scores on the original based on one of the two questions, and specificity increased from 69.8 to 75.5 percent; sensitivity was 100 percent for both.

The Alcohol Use Disorders Identification Test (AUDIT)

The Alcohol Use Disorders Identification Test was developed by a group of researchers at the World Health Organization for the ten-country AMETHYST project (Babor, Korner, Wilber, & Good, 1987). It was developed to address perceived limitations in other instruments. The instrument was designed to include information on the quantity–frequency of alcohol consumed, questions to determine patterns of pathological drinking such as the frequency of binge drinking, a format to assess the presence of DSM-III criteria, a response format which allows differentiation between past or recent use, and clinical data such as physical findings or laboratory tests (Babor et al., 1987).

The AUDIT contains two sections. The first is a ten-item scale that assesses alcohol use in the past year by obtaining information on quantity and frequency, binge drinking, two CAGE questions, and five questions related to lifetime alcohol abuse (Fleming, Barry, & MacDonald, 1991). The second is a Clinical Screening Procedure which involves trauma history assessment and an examination.

Fleming, Barry, and MacDonald (1991) found that the two items that received the most positive response were the items that asked about blackouts (91% of the females, 84% of the males) and family members objecting to drinking (52% of the females, 45% of the males). For screening purposes, they determined that an optimal cutoff score of thirteen would reduce the number of false positives while still keeping a high sensitivity.

The Substance Abuse Subtle Screening Inventory (SASSI)

The Substance Abuse Subtle Screening Inventory was developed by Glen A. Miller to diminish the possibility of subjects from "faking good." Often substance abusers will respond to self-report questionnaires dishonestly by minimizing the amount or frequency of substance use. SASSI reduces this possibility by the use of the "subtle" questions. These questions do not directly question substance use but they refer to a subject's behaviors that are related to health, social interaction, emotional states, preferences, needs, interests, and values (Kerr, 1994).

SASSI is a fifty-two-item true–false questionnaire. It is a relatively easy test to administer and score. It claims to be on the fifth-grade reading level and can be hand scored in about one minute. It can be administered to males and females eighteen years or older (Vacc, 1994).

SASSI offers data for five scales: the Obvious Attribute Scale (OAT), which measures the subjects readiness to admit to substance abuse problems; the Subtle Attributes Scale (SAT), which is the measurement that is resistant to deception; the Denial scale (DEN), which can identify a subject's conscious or unconscious resistance to test-taking; the Alcohol versus Drug Scale (ALD), which determines if a subject has a preference for alcohol or drugs; and the Family versus Controls Scale (FAM), which is used to measure how similar the subject is to other family members with a substance abuse problem (Kerr, 1994).

According to Kerr (1994), who reviewed SASSI, "The SASSI is almost as good as its promotion claims it to be. It seems to have been responsibly developed, and it is clearly created with the practitioner in mind." SASSI also provides a manual that is helpful to those who wish to understand and administer it.

Minnesota Multiphasic Personality Inventory–2 (MMPI)

The MMPI is a questionnaire that provides information on personality and psychopathology, and has evolved to also provide information on substance abuse. The most notorious subscale that has developed out of the MMPI for the detection of substance abuse is the MacAndrew Alcoholism Scale (MAC). The MAC examines the possibility of addiction based on a subject's general behaviors (Weed, Butcher, McKenna, & Ben-Porath, 1992). There is a great deal of research that supports the premise that personality characteristics play a role in whether an individual will develop a substance abuse problem (Cook & Winoker, 1985; Hesselbrock, Meyer, & Keener, 1985; Khantzian & Treece, 1985).

The MMPI has been credited with the ability to determine what type of personality would be more likely to abuse alcohol (Svanum & Ehrmann, 1992). However, the MMPI has also received its share of criticism. A major limitation is that the MMPI has generally been tested with a biased sample, alcoholics in treatment (Svanum & Ehrmann, 1992). The MMPI is a fairly lengthy measurement and is time consuming to score. It can only be administered by a licensed psychologist or under a psychologist's direct supervision.

ASSESSMENT RESULTS AND FOLLOWUP

After the assessment professional or team comes to some initial conclusions about the student's level of risk and need for subsequent treatment, they share the assessment and requisite recommendations with the student and significant others. The results of the comprehensive assessment may be helpful in breaking down the student drinker's initial denial and in engaging their commitment to the treatment process. Sometimes, the student's parents may be minimizing their son's or daughter's drinking problem and the assessment results can serve the same function for them.

The assessment professionals, when outlining a plan for treatment, often rely on the same significant others who were involved in providing information during the assessment to assist in carrying out the overall treatment plan. College personnel can often be involved in helping to monitor, encourage, and support the student in his or her treatment. They are often called on by the treatment professional for periodic updates to monitor the relative progress the student is making in the treatment process.

SUMMARY AND CONCLUSIONS

College personnel can have a tremendous impact on the lives of the students they come in contact with. It is important for all college and university personnel to appreciate their potential role in identifying students in need of assessment for alcohol- and drug-associated problems. They can optimize their readiness for this role by following the guidelines of the ASK Training Program: (1) increase their ability to observe important changes in students' baseline behavior via greater awareness of key warning signs to watch for; (2) increase their sense of responsibility as college personnel to intervene on a student's behalf by increasing their appreciation of the devastating consequences of drinking and drug use for college students and by making them aware that students expect them to intervene; and (3) increase their knowledge of how to facilitate a referral by becoming aware of how the process works and whom to contact when the need arises. It is not always apparent whether a student needs an assessment for their drinking or drug use, but the rule of thumb is, "When in doubt, ASK!" It is suggested that college personnel always err on the side of overreferring for assessment. Again, they are simply asking whether the student's drinking or drug use constitutes a problem. The assessment professional will answer the question.

Assessment professionals look at many factors to answer that question. Quantity and frequency measures of drinking are utilized to map out the student's drinking or drug use pattern. They also obtain information regarding how drinking and/or drug use has impaired the student's social roles and what negative consequences and associated high-risk behaviors have accompanied the student's drinking and/or drug use. When doing the assessment, the professional is trying to be aware of gender, ethnic and cultural, and subcultural factors that may be important to fully understand the student's drinking and/or drug use. The professional conducting the assessment may interview the student's family, friends, and other individuals that may have information about the student's drinking or drug use or recent behavior changes.

Finally, the assessment professional relies on converging data from all these sources to determine whether the student has a drinking and/or drug problem and what treatment may be most appropriate. A more comprehensive understanding and appreciation of the assessment process can assist college personnel in the demanding task of identifying students who may need assessment for drug or alcohol problems. By actively being involved in this process, college personnel can have a vital impact on the drinking and drug use of their individual students and the college campus at large.

REFERENCES

American Psychiatric Association. (1994). *Diagnostic and statistical manual of mental disorders* (4th ed.). Washington, DC: Author.

Antti-Poika, I. (1988). *Alcohol intoxication and abuse in injured patients.* Unpublished manuscript.

Babor, T., Korner, P., Wilber, C., & Good, S. (1987). Screening and early intervention strategies for harmful drinkers: Initial lessons for the AMETHYST project. *Australian Drug and Alcohol Review, 6,* 325–339.

Bailey, G. (1989). Current perspectives on substance abuse in youth. *Journal of the American Academy of Child and Adolescent Psychiatry, 28,* 152–162.

Bennett, M., McCrady, B., Frankenstein, W., Laitman, L., Van Horn, D., & Keller, D. (1993). Indentifying young adult substance abusers: The Rutgers collegiate substance abuse screening test. *Journal of Studies on Alcohol, 54,* 522–527.

Blume, S. (1990). Chemical dependency in women: Important issues. *American Journal of Drug and Alcohol Abuse, 16,* 297–308.

Brennan, A. F., Walfish, S., & Aubuchon, P. (1986). Alcohol use and abuse in college students: Social/environmental correlates, methodological issues, and implications for intervention. *International Journal of Addiction, 21,* 475–493.

Brown, S. (1985). Expectancies versus background in the prediction of college drinking patterns. *Journal of Consulting and Clinical Psychology, 53,* 123–130.

Brown, S., Goldman, M., Inn, A., & Anderson, L. (1980). Expectations of reinforcement from alcohol: Their domain and relation to drinking patterns. *Journal of Consulting and Clinical Psychology, 48,* 419–426.

Carnegie Foundation for the Advancement of Teaching. (1990). *Campus life: In search of community.* Princeton, NJ: Author.

Collins, R., Lapp, W., Emmons, K., & Isaac, L. (1990). Endorsement and strength of alcohol expectancies. *Journal of Studies on Alcohol, 51,* 336–342.

Connors, G., & Maisto, S. (1988). The alcohol expectancy construct: Overview and clinical applications. *Cognitive Therapy and Research, 12,* 487–504.

Cook, B., & Winoker, G. (1985). A family study of familial positive vs. familial negative alcoholics. *Journal of Nervous and Mental Disease, 173,* 175–178.

Ewing, J. (1984). Detecting alcoholism: The CAGE questionnaire. *Journal of American Medical Association, 252,* 1905–1907.

Fleming, M., Barry, K., & MacDonald, R. (1991). The alcohol use disorders identification test (AUDIT) in a college sample. *The International Journal of the Addictions, 26,* 1173–1185.

Hesselbrock, M., Meyer, R., & Keener, J. (1985). Psychopathology in hospitalized alcoholics. *Archives of General Psychiatry, 42,* 1050–1055.

Hurlbut, S., & Sher, K. (1992). Assessing alcohol problems in college students. *Journal of American Medical Association, 41,* 49–58.

Jacobson, G. (1989). A comprehensive approach to pretreatment evaluation: I. Detection, assessment, and diagnosis of alcoholism. In R. K. Hester & W. R. Miller (Eds.), *Handbook of alcoholism treatment approaches: Effective alternatives* (pp. 517–543). Elmsford, NY: Pergamon Press.

Johnson, S. (1991). Recent research: Alcohol and women's bodies. In P. Roth (Ed.), *Alcohol and drugs are women's issues* (pp. 32–36). Metuchen, NJ: Scarecrow Press.

Johnston, L. D., O'Malley, P. M., & Bachman, J. G. (1991). *Drug use among American high school seniors, college students and young adults: 1975–1990* (Vol. 2). (DHHS Publication No. ADM 91-1835). Washington, DC: U.S. Government Printing Office.

Kandel, D., & Logan, J. (1984) Patterns of drug use from adolscence to young adulthood: I. Periods of risk for initiation, continued use, and discontinuation. *American Journal of Public Health, 74,* 660–666.

Kerr, B. (1994). Review of the substance abuse subtle screening inventory. In *Mental measurements yearbook* (Vol. 11) (pp. 249–251). Lincoln, NE: Buros Institute of Mental Measurement.

Keso, L., Kevisaari, A., & Salaspuro, M. (1988). Fractures on chest radiographs in detection of alcoholism. *Alcohol and Alcoholism, 23,* 53–56.

Khantzian, E., & Treece, C. (1985). DSM-III psychiatric diagnosis of narcotic addicts: Recent findings. *Archives of General Psychiatry, 42,* 1067–1071.

Levy, J., & Deykin, E. (1989). Sucidiality, depression, and substance abuse in adolescence. *American Journal of Psychiatry, 146,* 1462–1467.

Nystrom, M., Perasalo, J., & Salaspuro, M. (1993). Screening for heavy drinking and alcohol-related problems in young university students: The CAGE, the Mm-Mast and the trauma score questionnaires. *Journal of Studies on Alcohol, 54,* 528–533.

Office for Substance Abuse Prevention. (1991). Take a look at college drinking. *OSAP Bulletin,* May.

Petchers, M., & Singer, M. (1987). Perceived-benefit-of-drinking scale: Approach to screening for adolescent abuse. *Journal of Pediatrics, 110,* 997–1081.

Petersen, A., Sarigiani, P., & Kennedy, R. (1991). Why more girls? *Journal of Youth and Adolescence, 20,* 247–271.

Pope, H., Ionescu-Pioggia, M., Aizley, H., & Varma, D. (1990). Drug use and life style among college undergraduates in 1989: A comparison with 1969 and 1978. *American Journal of Psychiatry, 147,* 998–1001.

Pope, S., Smith, P., Wayne, J., & Kelleher, K. (1994). Gender difference in rural adolescent drinking patterns. *Journal of Adolescent Health, 15,* 359–365.

Presley, C., Meilman, P., & Lyerla, R. (1994). Development of the CORE alcohol and drug survey: Initial findings and future directions. *Journal of American College Health, 42,* 248–255.

Prior, M., Smart, D., Sanson, A., & Oberklaid, F. (1993). Sex differences in psychological adjustment from infancy to 8 years. *Journal of the American Academy of Child and Adolescent Psychiatry, 32,* 291–304.

Sadowski, C., Long, C., & Jenkins, L. (1992). Does substance abuse treatment have self-schematic effects? *The Journal of Psychology, 127,* 323–327.

Saltz, R., & Elandt, D. (1986). College student drinking studies, 1976–1985. *Contemporary Drug Problems, 13,* 117–159.

Selzer, M. (1971). The Michigan Alcoholism Screening Test: The quest for a new diagnostic instrument. *American Journal of Psychiatry, 127,* 1653–1658.

Skinner, H., Holt, S., & Israel, Y. (1981). Early identification of alcohol abuse: 1. Critical issues and psychosocial indicators for a composite index. *Canadian Medical Association Journal, 124,* 1141–1153.

Skinner, H., Holt, S., Schuller, R., Roy, J., & Israel, Y. (1984). Identification of alcohol abuse using laboratory tests and a history of trauma. *Annals of Internal Medicine, 101,* 847–851.

Smith, D., Kreisberg, J., & Volpicelli, A. (1987). Screening for problem drinking in college freshmen. *Journal of American College Health, 36,* 89–94.

Smith, P., Stahl, K., & Rivers, P. (1992). The role of personality preference variables in the prediction of college students drinking patterns. Paper presented at the Southeastern Psychological Association Convention, New Orleans, LA, March.

Smith, P. D. (1991). *The prediction of drinking factors among college students: A cross-cultural comparison.* Unpublished doctoral dissertation. University of Nebraska, Lincoln.

Smith, P. D. (1994). ASK Training Program: A model for training college personnel in substance abuse intervention. Paper presented to the University of Arkansas–Little Rock, Little Rock, AR, August.

Smith, P. D., & Portilla, M. G. (1995). Predicting pediatric residents involvement in smoking cessation counseling: The role of smoking cessation expectancies. Paper presented to the Southern Society for Pediatric Research, New Orleans, LA, February.

Stacy, A., Widaman, K., & Marlatt, G. (1990). Expectancy models of alcohol use. *Journal of Personality and Social Psychology, 58,* 918–928.

Svanum, S., & Ehrmann, L. (1992). Alcoholic subtypes and the MacAndrews alcoholism scale. *Journal of Personality Assessment, 58,* 411–422.

Vacc, N. (1994). Review of the substance abuse subtle screening inventory. *Mental Measurements Yearbook* (Vol. 11) (pp. 251–253). Lincoln, NE: Buros Mental Measurements Institute.

Waite-O'Brien, N. (1992). Alcohol and drug abuse among female adolescents. In G. Lawson & A. Lawson (Eds.), *Adolescent substance abuse—etiology, treatment, and prevention* (pp. 367–379). Gaithersburg, MD: Aspen.

Wechsler, H., & Isaac, N. E. (1992). Binge drinkers among college students. *Journal of American Medical Association, 267,* 2929–2931.

Wechsler, H., Isaac, N. E., Grodstein, F., & Sellers, D. E. (1994). Continuation and initiation of alcohol use from the first to the second year of college. *Journal of Studies on Alcohol, 55,* 41–45.

Weed, N., Butcher, J., McKenna, T., & Ben-Porath, Y. (1992). New measures for assessing alcohol and drug abuse with the MMPI-2: The APS and AAS. *Journal of Personality Assessment, 58,* 389–404.

Werner, M., Walker, L., & Greene, J. (1994). Screening for problem drinking among college freshman. *Journal of Adolescent Health, 15,* 303–310.

Whitehead, P., & Layne, N. (1987). Young female Canadian drinkers: Employment, marital status and heavy drinking. *British Journal of the Addictions, 82,* 169–174.

9

Intervening with Substance-Abusing College Students

Eugene R. D. Deisinger

Substance abuse continues to be a significant problem at colleges and universities throughout the country. Approximately 93 percent of college students report having consumed alcohol at some point in their lifetime, with 88 percent of college students reporting use of alcohol in the last year. While alcohol is far and away the drug of choice for college students, some 50 percent of college students have used illicit drugs in their lifetime, with 29 percent having used in the last year and 15 percent having used in the last month (Johnston, O'Malley, & Bachman, 1992). Not only are college students using alcohol and other drugs, but they are often using them heavily. Over 40 percent of college students consumed five or more drinks in a sitting at least one time in a two-week period (Johnston, O'Malley, & Bachman, 1992; Wechsler, Davenport, Dowdall, Moeykens, & Castillo, 1994) and as many as one-third of students report that they drink for the express purpose of getting drunk (Wechsler & Isaac, 1992). Binge drinking (i.e., consuming more than five drinks per sitting) has been referred to as the "number one substance abuse problem in American college life" (Commission on Substance Abuse at Colleges and Universities, 1994, p. i). In the past five years, emergency room admissions for alcohol overdose (in college communities) have increased 15 percent (Commission on Substance Abuse at Colleges and Universities, 1994). The National Institute on Alcohol Abuse and Alcoholism (1993) has reported that the highest rates for alcohol abuse and dependence are among persons between the ages of eighteen and twenty-nine, with an estimated 10 to 15 percent of college students experiencing significant alcohol-related problems (Eigen, 1991).

Students with substance abuse problems set off a "ripple effect" across their communities. Substance abuse contributes to or causes a multitude of consequences, including medical illnesses and physical injuries, physical and sexual assaults, unwanted pregnancies, sexually transmitted diseases, relationship difficulties, depression, suicide, legal problems, decreased academic performance, and decreased retention (Wechsler et al., 1994). These consequences impact not only the individual substance abuser, but ripple out to his or her family, friends, roommates, and classmates. The negative effects continue to ripple out across the institution, negatively affecting its prestige, reputation, and desirability (Commission on Substance Abuse at Colleges and Universities, 1994).

Despite the prevalence of alcohol and other drug problems among college students, no single model of prevention, intervention, assessment, or treatment has emerged that is commonly used across campuses (Dean, Dean, & Kleiner, 1986; Eigen, Brenowitz, & Henshaw, 1993). This is due, in part, to the differing needs that exist across campuses. However, this lack of unified vision is also reflective of a dearth of research and program-evaluation efforts. Very few programs have been sufficiently evaluated to be relied on as guides for institutions seeking to develop prevention and intervention programs. To assist institutions struggling with issues related to alcohol and other drug abuse, the American College Health Association (1987) made five recommendations. It advocated that institutions develop and conduct needs assessments, provide primary prevention programs, examine the effects of the campus environment on students' substance abuse problems, and conduct outcome evaluations of its efforts to reduce substance abuse. The association also stated that, while colleges and universities should focus on prevention and long-term changes on campus, they must also provide secondary prevention (intervention) programs addressing the present needs of students, faculty, and staff.

THE ROLE OF INTERVENTION IN DEALING WITH SUBSTANCE ABUSE

Intervention is, thus, one part of a larger process of addressing substance abuse problems on college campuses. Primary prevention efforts are designed to thwart the development of problem drinking patterns before they occur. In contrast, early intervention efforts are designed to interrupt problem drinking patterns before they become severe and to direct a person to appropriate services, such as screening, assessment, education, or treatment. These screening and assessment services are designed to evaluate the severity of problematic use and to match the individual to educational or treatment services meeting his or her specific needs. These services assist the person in reducing his or her problem drug use and in developing coping skills which enable the person to return to a higher level of functioning and greatly reduce the risk of future problems associated with alcohol or other drug abuse (Morrill, Hurst, & Oetting, 1980).

Programs based on an early intervention model are predicated on the notion that one need not wait for problems to worsen before action is taken. The old adage maintained that an alcoholic or addict needed to "hit bottom" before he or she would be motivated to change. This motivation would only occur when the person's life finally fell completely apart because of their drinking. They would need to have lost their job, their spouse, their car, and their dog in order to be willing to change. This view of motivation is not supported, especially among persons with lower levels of severity of dependency. In fact, there is ample evidence that substance dependency is much easier and more cost effective to treat when it is identified early in the process and the affected person is effectively connected to appropriate treatment services (Heather, 1989; Nathan, 1988). The process of intervention brings "the bottom" up to meet the person by helping them experience the consequences of their substance abuse before losing everything.

This chapter will focus primarily on the process of intervening with individual students believed to be experiencing problems with substance abuse. The chapter will define intervention and identify key components of the process, discuss methods and applications of intervention concepts, and identify issues to be addressed in developing intervention processes. It is intended not as a directive on how to do interventions, but as a guide for faculty, staff, and students.

THEORY AND RESEARCH

Suchman and Broughton (1988) commented on the specific challenges and complexities of addressing substance-abusing college students, saying, "The development of a university based substance abuse counseling program requires a broad view of substance use and abuse as being part of the development of a student's lifestyle in a university environment. This view requires an understanding of student development, the university environment, the effects of specific drugs, and the psychology of the individual student" (p. 145).

This is not to suggest that every person wanting to initiate an intervention should have expertise in every possible facet of the intervention process. To suggest this would likely intimidate even the most ardent advocate of student health. Rather, the comment by Suchman and Broughton is a reminder that substance abuse is a complex, multifaceted problem and one which will likely require a multidimensional response to attain the desired goal. University community members engaging in the intervention process will benefit from developing their skills in using intervention strategies, acknowledging the limits of their abilities, and involving other persons who might complement their skills. A team approach to intervention better provides for the support and resources that will improve outcome. A team approach does not require that a group of people actually conduct the intervention, but rather that a variety of resources are utilized to prepare for the intervention.

Defining Intervention

Vernon Johnson (1986), a leader in the field of substance abuse intervention and treatment, defines intervention as, "A process by which the harmful, progressive, and destructive effects of chemical dependency are interrupted and the chemically dependent person is helped to stop using mood-altering chemicals and to develop new, healthier ways of coping with his or her needs and problems" (p. 61).

In a similar way, Williams and Knox (1987) define intervention as "a process in which an individual is not allowed to avoid the natural and logical consequences of his or her alcohol related behavior" (p. 98). These two definitions have at least two elements in common. First, both statements view intervention as part of a process. Intervention strategies are part of a dynamic, methodical series of actions that advance one toward a specific goal. From this perspective, intervention is not seen as a goal or an end in itself. Rather, it is a means to an end, a tool that can be used to assist students experiencing difficulties with alcohol or other drugs.

The metaphor of intervention as a tool may be helpful in training university staff to assist impaired students. The metaphor implies that one can learn to intervene, just as one learns to use other tools. Experience and training will improve the effectiveness of the tools used. This allows for a greater sense of confidence and effectiveness on the part of the person conducting the intervention. There is also an implication of the importance of context in the tool's use—intervention does not occur in a vacuum. A rake is a wonderful tool for cleaning up leaves, but quite inadequate for digging a hole.

How an intervention is conducted is greatly affected by the context in which the intervention might occur. The close friend who seems to have trouble staying awake in class after a long night out likely requires a different approach than the colleague who often smells of alcohol at work in the morning, keeps a bottle of bourbon in the desk, misses faculty meetings regularly, and is verbally abusive when drinking. The circumstance will provide a guide to the approach to be taken (whether to use a rake or a shovel) with the person whom we are concerned about.

However, having a shovel does not mean that we only dig holes. Indeed, we may want to clear snow with it. Therefore, the context affects not only the tool selected, but the purpose for which the tool is used. I have noted that the circumstances leading up to the intervention impact on how the individual is approached. These same circumstance also guide us in deciding on the goal of the intervention. In the examples given, we may just want to offer an expression of care and concern for our sleepy friend. Simply hearing that someone has noticed a change and is concerned may allow him or her to get back on track. The abusive colleague, on the other hand, may need to better understand the inappropriateness of his or her behavior and to be referred for assessment and possible treatment services.

Using the tool metaphor in training staff has seemed to help them let go of the fear that there is only one right way to conduct an intervention and therefore a fair likelihood of failure. It also opens up discussions regarding the context and process of interventions. Traditional substance abuse programs and intervention efforts have erred in tending to rely on the use a sledgehammer when a tack hammer (or maybe even a feather duster) would have done the job just as well. A growing body of literature has demonstrated the limitations of the harsh confrontation approach in dealing with substance abuse. The directive–confrontational approach has been associated with increased client resistance and increased alcohol use at followup, as compared to more empathic–motivational interviewing approaches (Miller, Benefield, & Tonigan, 1993).

In addition to intervention being a tool that can be used to help persons having difficulties with substance abuse, it also assists interveners in taking care of themselves. Taking an active role in assisting another person often helps concerned others have more hope, feel more optimistic, and feel more powerful as a person. All are valuable parts of the helping process.

Both definitions of intervention presented earlier refer to an alteration in an individual's pattern of alcohol use. This alteration in use may come about through exposing the individual to the consequences of his or her alcohol use (i.e., to bring the bottom up to meet the substance abuser). Intervention also lets the substance-abusing person know that their drug use is affecting other people. A common statement made by people dependent on alcohol or other drugs is, "My drinking is none of your business, it doesn't affect you." The intervention process allows us to inform the drinker that their behavior does, indeed, impact on us. If Tom, Dick, and Mary are concerned about George's drinking, they can inform him that his drinking-related behavior (e.g., busting up Tom's stereo, vomiting on Dick's floor, and sexually harassing Mary) harms other people and is not acceptable. Hearing this message from others, particularly from several who care for the drinker or drug user, challenges the notion that they live in a vacuum in which no one is hurt by them or concerned about them. Through this eye opening, the individual is better able to evaluate the impact of his or her alcohol (or other drug) abuse and move toward more healthy ways of living. Intervention, then, is a powerful tool for making people more aware of their behavior and its effect on others, and for getting people connected to resources that can help them change.

Components of Intervention—A Model

In examining the process of intervention, it seems reasonable to develop an understanding of the components of the process. Doob (1993) describes the process of an intervention as "the efforts of one or more persons to affect one or more other persons when after an event the former, the latter, or both perceive a problem requiring resolution" (p. 1). Inherent in Doob's statement are several decisions regarding the intervention process: What indicates a need for intervention, who should do it, and how should it be done to have an effect?

Identification of Students at Risk The first consideration is the rationale for intervening. An intervention is initiated because a problem has been identified and determined to be in need of resolution. Determining what is a problem and whether the problem needs resolution are decisions that are highly dependent on personal (and institutional) values as well as on one's knowledge of the signs of substance abuse or dependency. Therefore, knowledge of these signs (and of self) are critical prerequisites to conducting effective interventions.

Substance abuse and dependency tend to affect many facets of a person's life. The signs that may indicate that a person is experiencing difficulty with alcohol or other drugs can be cognitive, social, physical, or emotional, including these:

Cognitive

Decreased attention, concentration, and/or motivation

Memory loss (blackouts)

Poor judgment or decision making (taking unnecessary risks)

Lowered academic performance (missed class, lower grades)

Social

Relationship difficulties (family, friends, dating partners, roommates, etc.)

Legal and/or financial problems resulting from alcohol or other drug use

Not upholding social obligations (e.g., missing work)

Physical

Frequent physical illness

Significant changes in eating or sleeping patterns

Difficulty in limiting intake of alcohol or other drugs when intending to

Loss of consciousness from drinking (passing out)

Drinking "the morning after" to alleviate physical discomfort

Predictable patterns of unhealthy alcohol or other drug use

Emotional

Dramatic mood swings and personality changes (seems like a different person)

Verbal or physical aggression (fights, arguments)

While there is no one profile of heavy-drinking college students, several characteristics have been documented. Heavy-drinking college students are often males, first-year students, members of the Greek system living in Greek houses, students with disabilities, gay or lesbian students, and students from dysfunctional families (Bloch & Ungerleider, 1988; Helwig & Holicky, 1994). Often, faculty and staff will contact our campus substance abuse program indicating that they have noticed something amiss about one of their students but are

unsure of its significance. In addition to praising these people for their atten-
tiveness to (and care for) their students, I have also encouraged them to visit
with the students about their concerns. A common theme in these consulta-
tions has been, "When in doubt—Check it out!"

Empowering Intervention Agents A second decision to be addressed in
the intervention process is in regard to the roles of the participants in the
intervention. Several authors have described the importance of training faculty and staff in early identification, intervention, and referral strategies (American College Health Association, 1987; Laitman, 1987; Moore & Forster, 1993).
Training sessions serve to enhance faculty and staff members' skills in intervening with students. More important, these sessions (when facilitated as dia-
logues) serve as a forum for the staff to discuss their attitudes, values, and
beliefs about substance abuse and to get support for the role of being an active helper for students.

I have found that the majority of faculty and staff members are strongly
committed to student welfare and are very willing to intervene with students
experiencing difficulties. The issues that most often hold them back are a
belief that they do not have the skills to "do it right," concern about how their
supervisor will view their actions (i.e., does the boss see intervention as part
of their job), and fear of liability if they confront someone who turns out not to
have a problem. By responding to these concerns, the institution can assist faculty and staff in becoming effective interveners. The most important step is to
assist them in developing their intervention skills. Supervisory staff should also
be trained in these skills (and their importance) so that supervisors recognize
early intervention as a vital part of their staff members' role in maintaining a safe
and healthy work environment. Concerns about liability can often be allevi-
ated by focusing staff on how the intervention is done, rather than on whether
it is done. An "intervention" that is conducted as a means of harassing, em-
barrassing, or punishing someone may likely leave the intervener open to
potential liability (morally if not legally). However, a person conducting an
intervention from a position of care and concern, who is sure of his or her
facts, involves others knowledgeable about the facts, and recognizes that the
health of the student is ultimately the student's responsibility would be much
less likely to experience significant liability. Where liability is a major concern, staff should consult with the university's legal counsel. The institution
can address faculty and staff concerns about liability by standing behind their
efforts to aid students and by developing policies that encourage faculty and
staff to intervene and to support the health and well-being of students.

Doob (1993) identified several attributes of the intervener that have an
impact on the intervention process. Effective interveners have confidence in
themselves and the appropriateness of their intervention. They have a high
level of adaptability, being able to modify their interventions to the demands
of a particular problem, situation, or person. Effective interveners develop
their knowledge of issues relevant to the problems they are addressing and

the people they are seeking to assist. Effective interveners are those who are both available and willing to respond to persons needing assistance. Finally, effective interveners make their care and concern known to their students, indicating they are willing to help. I have found that students often do not believe particular faculty or staff to be approachable or invested in helping them. Yet when those same faculty or staff members are finally invited to assist with the student, many are willing to help out in any way they can. Faculty and staff need to actively express their willingness to help students to overcome the fear that students often experience in approaching a person in a power position. Students' awareness of a climate of care and concern will aid in inspiring their confidence in the intervener and trust in his or her abilities and intentions.

In addition to being aware of strengths and positive attributes (and letting students know about them), it is also important for the intervener to be aware of his or her limitations and weaknesses. The most effective interveners are often those who best model healthy or appropriate behavior. Given this, it is important for interveners to display consistency between their own behavior and the standards they espouse to their students. Kottler (1992) challenges student-affairs professionals to confront their own hypocrisy in working with students, emphasizing their impact as models for students. A faculty member who is known to "get wasted" with some of her students after every Tuesday evening seminar is likely to have great difficulty being taken seriously were she to try to intervene with students she was seriously concerned about. The institution that maintains rigid prohibitions against student alcohol use of any type and then hosts faculty training forums where alcohol is served is not likely to be taken seriously on the issue of substance abuse. Kottler encourages self-examination of the impact of our modeling for students, and how this modeling is influenced by our own unresolved issues. Through identification and resolution of these issues we make ourselves more effective with students and model the very processes we seek to teach them.

Informal versus Formal Intervention Strategies

Informal interventions are those facilitated by peers and that do not involve elements of force or leverage in encouraging the student to respond to the intervention. Formal interventions are more structured and are facilitated by supervisors, administrators, or mental health professionals, often in the context of a legal, judicial, or administrative process (Kinney & Peltier, 1986; Meilman, 1992; Williams & Knox, 1987).

In a survey of 115 directors of college counseling centers, Stone and Lucas (1994) found support for the concept of *disciplinary education*, in which a student is required to participate in an educational intervention (such as an educational program) as a result of inappropriate behavior. However, counseling center directors reported a great deal of ambivalence about the appropriateness of *disciplinary counseling* as a consequence of formal intervention. Disciplinary counseling refers to mandatory, rehabilitative counseling of (or intervention with) students, and occurs at the request of staff dealing with disciplinary issues. Disciplinary counseling tends to occur as a result of a student having problems associated with alcohol or other drug use, with the goal of assessing or evaluating the student.

Stone and Lucas (1994) discuss the importance of a variety of issues (confidentiality, informed consent, dual roles, client autonomy, etc.) related to disciplinary counseling and the necessity of thinking through these issues prior to engaging in disciplinary counseling. Programs should clearly communicate, with clients and with referral sources, what is to remain confidential and what is not. Clients should be fully informed about what their choices are as well as what the consequences of these choices are. Roles should be clearly defined regarding responsibilities for counseling, and for enforcing student conduct. Where possible, one staff member should not have responsibility for both counseling and enforcement of student conduct.

Another major issue to be addressed is how the counseling service will be viewed, by the client as well as by the university community. Whether the counseling service will be seen as educational, punitive, judgmental, a cure-all, or a dumping ground for problem students will depend, in large part, on how the agency addresses the issues involved in referral and counseling of referred students. The perception of how well the agency deals with these issues will greatly determine the community's willingness to use the agency's services.

In a study on the impact of a residence-hall-based formal intervention program, Williams and Knox (1987) found that few problem-drinking students were identified by residence-hall staff, although sources other than resident assistants became more active in making referrals for assessment and treatment of alcohol problems. Through the course of the project, residence assistants showed a significant decrease in their perception of alcohol problems among their residents. Williams and Knox suggest this may reflect a decreasing willingness of residence staff to confront problem drinking among their peers. The authors suggest that an Employee Assistance Program model of direct, formal intervention (where students are referred to treatment services through judicial or formal processes) may have limited utility with college students. They suggest that informal intervention and referral strategies would likely be more helpful and better utilized. In a similar way, Kinney and Peltier (1986) noted that "formal interventions have become a mainstay of moving the individual with an alcohol problem into treatment. This model needs to be adapted to the college population, and students concerned about other students appropriately involved" (p. 232). This move from formal to informal intervention models is directed toward helping students help students. This will make a more significant impact on college student substance abuse than will relying solely on faculty, staff, and administrators to address the issue through judicial processes.

Individual versus Group Intervention

A question that often arises is whether an intervention should be done by one concerned person or by a group of concerned persons. It is important to have people present who have direct knowledge of the substance abuser's problems, but there is a danger in having too many people present. When more than seven or eight others are involved in the intervention the substance abuser often feels ganged-up on and becomes overly defensive, focusing more on protecting him or herself than on listening to feedback from the group. Particularly for a first intervention, it is usually most helpful to limit the group to two to four people. If additional interventions are needed (as the substance abuser's behavior affects more people), then it is often helpful to involve more concerned people in the intervention.

Determining that an intervention needs to occur and identifying the participants leads to a final decision to be addressed—how the intervention will occur. The next section describes a model of intervention and its applications.

METHODS OF INTERVENTION

Setting the Tone

Choose a time and place when the student is likely to be most receptive to your feedback. The middle of the hallway between classes is not a good time to address these issues. The setting should provide privacy and a sense of safety for the student, and neither the student nor the intervener should be under the influence of alcohol or other drugs at the time of the meeting. Check out your motives for initiating the intervention. Be sure you are approaching the intervention from a perspective of care and concern versus a desire to punish or humiliate. Avoid judging, labeling, or diagnosing the person's problems. One should avoid getting into an argument about whether the abusive drinker is an alcoholic. Often the drinker will attempt to divert the confrontation from the harmfulness to him or herself and others of his or her drinking behavior to reasons he or she cannot be classified as an alcoholic. The confronters should stick to the facts and point out how the drinker's behavior has been destructive and hurtful to him or herself and others.

The Intervention Process

The four steps for talking with a student about his or her alcohol use are taken from suggestions by the Office of Substance Abuse Prevention (1991a, 1991b). They can be summarized as follows:

1. **Emphasize your care and concern.**
   Tell the person why you are talking with him or her.

Remind the person of your relationship with him or her.

2. Describe the behavior(s) that you are concerned about.

Be specific about the details.

Focus on what you know to have happened.

3. Express your concern about the behavior.

Tell the person how you feel about the behavior.

Tell the person how their behavior has affected you.

4. Outline what you would like to see happen.

Identify the changes you would like to see happen.

Identify consequences that will occur if the behavior continues.

Identify resources where he or she can get assistance.

Set a timeline for following up with the person.

Discuss Your Reasons for Talking with the Student State your care and concern openly, role-modeling openness about feelings. Remind the person of your relationship with them; for example, "Sue, we have been friends for a long time, and I have noticed some things that have concerned me." Doing this reminds the person that you have an investment in him or her and also lets him or her know you want to talk about important issues. This allows the person to prepare emotionally for what you have to say.

Describe the Behavior That Is Causing You Concern Be as specific as possible and restrict your comments to behaviors you have witnessed or experienced. Emphasize differences in behavior, attitude, and personality that occur when the person drinks. It is generally helpful to plan ahead for the intervention. If you are doing it alone, plan out and write down your concerns. This will help keep you focused and better ensure that you have said what you wanted to say. If you are doing the intervention with a group of people, the group should meet beforehand and talk with each other about their concerns, decide what order people will speak in, and help people to focus on their concerns rather than speaking for other people. In talking with Sue you might say something to the effect of, "Sue, I have noticed that you have passed out after drinking four times this past month and that on three other occasions you couldn't remember what happened during the time you had been drinking. I also noticed that you fell down the stairs last night when you were coming home from the bar."

Express Your Concerns Regarding the Behavior Talk openly about the impact of the person's behavior on you. Substance abusers often think that their drug use affects no one but themselves. Talking about your anger, fear, frustration, and so on may help the substance abuser realize that their drug use is affecting others. Getting back to Sue, you might say, "Sue, I was really scared last night when you fell down the stairs. I was worried you had really hurt yourself. I'm afraid that you may hurt yourself again."

Describe the Changes That You Would Like to Have Happen and Identify Any Consequences That Will Occur if the Behavior Continues Offer a variety of solutions, choices, and resources and invite the person to do the same. To Sue you might say, "I would like you to visit with a someone at the counseling service. They can help you look at your drinking and help you decide what changes you would like to make with it. What can you do to help me be less worried about you?" Involving the person in the decision making increases the likelihood that he or she will take responsibility for his or her own well-being.

Enhancing Readiness for Change

Vernon Johnson (1986) described the goal of an intervention as breaking down an alcohol-dependent person's defenses so that the individual might see and accept the reality of his or her drinking. The acceptance of this reality would facilitate change on the part of the dependent person. This goal is based on a traditional model of alcohol dependency that assumes both the presence of denial to obfuscate the problem drinking and an inherent lack of motivation for change on the part of the alcohol-dependent person. In the face of such defensiveness and absence of motivation, it would make some sense to utilize strategies of harsh confrontation and directiveness (i.e., the sledgehammer) to impact on the impaired individual.

However, the view of motivation as being an individual, static trait is not always supported, particularly with less severely dependent persons (such as those more typically found on college campuses). With these individuals, motivation (for change in drinking behavior) may more accurately be seen as a dynamic, interactive state (Miller & Rollnick, 1991). This motivational state is influenced not only by the dependent person but by the intervener and other external factors. In fact, resistance and motivation levels change in response to external conditions and intervention strategies. Miller and Sovereign (1989) and Miller and Rollnick (1991) describe the following components of effective interventions, using the FRAMES model:

Feedback is provided regarding an individual's level of risk.

Responsibility for change is recognized as belonging to the individual, with the intervener promoting and supporting an internal locus of control for the individual.

Advice and recommendations are offered regarding specifics of what and how to change.

Menus of alternatives are provided, encouraging the individual's choice of options.

Empathy for and understanding of the individual are critical.

Self-efficacy of the individual (belief in one's own abilities) is promoted by the intervener.

Readers desiring more in-depth information on the FRAMES strategy are encouraged to read Miller and Rollnick (1991).

In a study of residential treatment, Brown and Miller (1993) found motivational techniques to be related to greater participation in treatment and lower alcohol consumption by clients at a three-month followup. In a similar way,

Conoley, Padula, Payton, and Daniels (1994) found clients increased their implementation of counselors' recommendations when the recommendations were of low difficulty, were consistent with the clients' perception of the problem (as well as the clients' values and world view), and when the counselor emphasized and utilized clients' strengths to move toward the recommended actions. These studies provide support for the view of motivation as a dynamic state that is subject to influence by the intervener or therapist.

Institutional and Environmental Factors

In addition to the individual factors that have been discussed, there are also important environmental factors that impact on the intervention process. A survey of five thousand college students found that 50 percent feel as though they are treated like a number and feel a sense of anonymity on campus (Boyer, 1988). Forty percent of students did not feel a sense of community on campus and nearly two-thirds did not feel comfortable talking with a professor about personal issues. These depictions of the lack of connection that students experience on campus provide some understanding of the need for intervention as well as some insight into why intervention can be so difficult. In the absence of a sense of connectedness (or in an attempt to create such a sense), students may turn to alcohol or other drugs for comfort and solace. The same lack of connectedness that may have contributed to problematic use also makes it all the more difficult to intervene with students, as they perceive faculty and staff as unapproachable and the institution as uncaring. In laying the groundwork for a successful intervention program, it is important to identify strategies and mechanisms to contribute to a sense of a caring climate on campus. The active demonstration of care and concern, through the process of intervening with students' problems early on, is one part of developing a caring climate. Recognizing and reinforcing the strengths and healthy behaviors of those students who do not need intervention is also a means of supporting the caring climate.

While the purpose of this chapter is to provide a resource for confronting an individual's substance abuse, it should be noted that this intervention does not occur in a vacuum. It is important to have mechanisms in place that address aspects of the university climate as well as individual students. Without modifications of some environmental influences, students who have responded effectively to interventions will find themselves back in environments that support their return to unhealthy patterns of drug use.

PRACTICAL EXAMPLES AND APPLICATIONS

Identifying High-Risk Students

The University of New Mexico offers a "Drinker's Check-up" (Miller & Sovereign, 1989) to identify students who may be at high risk for alcohol dependency. Ads are placed through the campus paper offering a free, confidential check-up that is not intended as a treatment for alcoholics but as an informational health service to drinkers. During the course of the four-hour check-up, the student participates in a one-hour informational session designed to provide an overview of the process and to enhance motivation for participation. Students choosing to continue with the check-up undergo a two-hour assessment interview, completing a variety of brief screening tools to evaluate their alcohol use (and its effects). Following the assessment interview, students are invited back for a one-hour feedback session during which they receive a personalized profile (oral and written) with results of their use presented in relation to normative data on other students. Miller and Sovereign note that the check-up appears to attract students with significant alcohol use and alcohol-related concerns. These students do not identify themselves as problem drinkers and would be unlikely to seek out formal treatment services. The check-up provides an opportunity for self-intervention and assistance in a manner similar to checkups offered to evaluate blood pressure and cholesterol. Outcome data on the Drinker's Check-up project indicate that participants show a significant reduction in alcohol consumption at a six-week followup. Strategies similar to the Drinker's Check-up have been developed at other institutions with similar results.

Baer (1993) describes the High Risk Drinker's Project at the University of Washington, in which interventions are conducted to challenge students' beliefs about alcohol, increase students' motivation to examine their drinking behaviors, and encourage self-change or utilization of professional treatment services. The intervention is an ongoing project which begins with the screening of all entering students to identify high-risk users. A stepped care (or graded intensity) approach is then applied, whereby minimal services and resources are used up front and more intensive services are reserved for those students with more significant problems related to their alcohol use. This approach provides for a more cost-effective use of limited resources than does a "shotgun" approach in which many students are targeted to receive the same intensive level of service, regardless of their need.

Computer-Assisted Intervention Strategies

In the computer age, it is not surprising to find electronic media being used to facilitate early interventions. Rathbun (1993) describes the use of an online computerized screening instrument that is available to students, faculty, and staff at the University of Michigan at Ann Arbor. This brief, anonymous self-evaluation was accessed by approximately 150 to 200 students, faculty, and staff each month during the first twelve months of its operation and was related to an increase in requests for further assessment of concerns related to alcohol use. In using computerized self-assessments, care should be taken to provide information that will allow for adequate followup by the person using the program. That is, if the self-assessment helps people come to the conclusion that they need assistance with their alcohol or other drug use, the tool should also provide information about how to get such assistance, by identifying campus and community resources.

Skinner (1993) also describes the use of computerized tools to facilitate early intervention efforts by substance abuse professionals. He notes that computerized assessment programs are low in cost, efficient, and provide rapid scoring, immediate feedback, and individualized reports. All of these factors can serve to increase the availability and accessibility of intervention and assessment services to potential clients.

Faculty as Interveners

Rapaport (1993) drew on instructors of English composition classes to have students participate in a writing assignment with the goal of clarifying their personal position about the role of alcohol in their life. Students were to discuss how their experiences with alcohol (positive and negative) and their personal values influenced their current use of alcohol. Rapaport believes that such self-reflection leads to increased awareness of vulnerability to alcohol problems and possibly to change in high-risk behavior.

Empowering Student Health Staff in Conducting Interventions

In a study of students seen at a university health service, Hickenbottom, Bissonette, and O'Shea (1987) found that 15 percent (of those who drank) said that a physician had asked them about their alcohol use. Only 25 percent (of students noting a physician's questioning of their alcohol use) said that the physician had discussed medical or social consequences of their alcohol and other drug use. In a community in which large numbers of students use alcohol heavily, it appears that a number of intervention opportunities are being missed by health-care providers.

Kinney and Meilman (1987) noted the importance of health-care professionals (physicians, nurses, psychologists, social workers, counselors, etc.) being aware of community and institutional resources for addressing substance abuse concerns of college students. They encouraged health service providers to refer students to substance abuse services in a knowledgeable manner and provided the following recommendations for enhancing patient compliance with a referral for substance abuse services.

First, the referring clinician must have active involvement in the case. A casual suggestion for a student to address their substance use will likely have a minimal impact. Health-care providers must take an active role in asking questions about a student's alcohol or other drug use, in providing direction for change, and in providing followup services to students identified as at risk. Without such active involvement, students fall between the cracks all too easily.

Second, the patient should make an appointment with a specific individual (at an assessment or treatment facility) for a specific time. If substance abuse assessment or treatment services are indicated, the student should be invited to contact the provider while still in the office. While it is often helpful for the physician to call the provider for the student (to ensure availability of services) it is important to allow the student to make the appointment for services. This allows the student to begin to take responsibility for and control of his or her health needs. Having an appointment with a specific person is often more comfortable to students than having an appointment with an anonymous entity. This increased comfort with the services being recommended will increase compliance with recommendations.

Third, the patient should be scheduled for a followup appointment with the referring clinician after his or her contact with the substance abuse professional. As noted, it is often quite easy for patients to fall between the cracks. Scheduling a followup visit after their first contact with the substance abuse provider helps ensure that the patient is connected with the service delivery system. It also provides the health-care provider with a better sense of the outcomes of his or her referrals. A two-way release of information should be obtained between the clinician and the substance abuse professional so that they can collaborate on developing a treatment plan.

Fourth, prepare the patient positively for a meeting with the substance abuse professional. Students often have many misconceptions and fears about what the experience (of meeting with a substance abuse counselor) will be like. Health-care providers should increase their knowledge of the various providers in their area, so that they can speak positively to patients about the provider to whom they are referring. Brochures or informational materials can be obtained from various providers and displayed prominently in offices and throughout the clinic.

Fifth, convey a sense of concern, respect, and hope for the patient. As when dealing with many illnesses and disabilities, it is easy for patients to become discouraged and hopeless about overcoming their concerns, particularly when they experience relapses in their condition. Faculty and staff can help sustain students' hopefulness and recovery by normalizing the experience of relapse. They can let the student know that relapses are common with substance dependence (as they are for many serious illnesses). They should encourage students not to view relapse as a failure, but as an opportunity to identify additional resources and means of sustaining their recovery. Relapse is often a teachable moment and another opportunity to help the student maintain awareness of the damaging consequences of their use.

SUMMARY AND CONCLUSIONS

A well-developed intervention strategy is an integral part of successful substance abuse programs at colleges and universities. Substance abuse problems that are identified early in their development have consistently been shown to be easier and more cost effective to treat. Intervention is a critical part of the process of assisting students in obtaining necessary treatment services. Done from a perspective of care and concern, intervention is an empowering experience for both the substance-abusing student and the intervener. University faculty, staff, and students are encouraged to develop their skills in conducting effective interventions with others at risk. (See the appendix to this chapter for selected additional resources.) As the campus community becomes more active in recognizing and responding to the needs of its members, a climate of care and compassion can develop and thrive.

APPENDIX: SUGGESTED RESOURCES
FOR DEVELOPING INTERVENTION SKILLS

The following is available through

The Johnson Institute
7151 Metro Blvd.
Minneapolis, MN 55435
Phone: 1–800–231–5165

- *Intervention: How to help someone who doesn't want help*, by Vernon Johnson

The following materials are all available through

National Clearinghouse for Alcohol & Drug Information
P.O. Box 2345
Rockville, MD 20847–2345
Phone: 1–800–729–6686

- *Faculty Member's Handbook: Strategies for Preventing Alcohol and Other Drug Problems*
- *Program Administrator's Handbook: Strategies for Preventing Alcohol and Other Drug Problems*
- *If Someone Close Has a Problem with Alcohol or Other Drugs* (pamphlet)

REFERENCES

American College Health Association. (1987). Statement on college alcohol and drug abuse. *Journal of American College Health, 36,* 64.

Baer, J. S. (1993). Etiology and secondary prevention of alcohol problems with young adults. In J. S. Baer, G. A. Marlatt, & R. J. McMahon (Eds.), *Addictive behaviors across the life span: Prevention, treatment and policy issues.* London: Sage.

Bloch, S. A., & Ungerleider, S. (1988). Targeting high-risk groups on campus for drug and alcohol prevention: An examination and assessment. *International Journal of the Addictions, 23,* 299–319.

Boyer, E. L. (1988). College, the quality of life. *Journal of American College Health, 36,* 259–263.

Brown, J. M., & Miller, W. R. (1993). Impact of motivational interviewing on participation and outcome in residential alcoholism treatment. *Psychology of Addictive Behaviors, 7,* 211–218.

Commission on Substance Abuse at Colleges and Universities. (1994). *Rethinking
rites of passage: Substance abuse on America's campuses.* New York: Columbia University, Center on Addiction and Substance Abuse.

Conoley, C. W., Padula, M. A., Payton, D. S., & Daniels, J. A. (1994). Predictors of
client implementation of counselor recommendations: Match with problems,
difficulty level, and building on client strengths. *Journal of Counseling Psychology, 41,* 3–7.

Dean, J. C., Dean, H. E., & Kleiner, D. L. (1986). Alcohol and drug college treatment
programs: A proposal. *Journal of Substance Abuse Treatment, 3,* 95–101.

Doob, L. W. (1993). *Intervention: Guides & perils.* New Haven, CT: Yale University
Press.

Eigen, L. D. (1991). *Alcohol practices, policies, and potentials of American colleges
and universities: An OSAP white paper.* Rockville, MD: U.S. Department of
Health and Human Services, Office of Substance Abuse Prevention.

Eigen, L. D., Brenowitz, L., & Henshaw, R. (1993, May). *College alcohol & other
drug prevention strategies.* Paper presented at the American College Health
Association Annual Conference, Baltimore, MD.

Heather, N. (1989). Brief intervention strategies. In R. K. Hester & W. R. Miller (Eds.),
Handbook of alcoholism treatment approaches: Effective alternatives. New
York: Pergamon.

Helwig, A. A., & Holicky, R. (1994). Substance abuse in persons with disabilities: Treatment considerations. *Journal of Counseling & Development, 72,* 227–233.

Hickenbottom, J. P., Bissonette, R. P., & O'Shea, R. M. (1987). Preventive medicine
and college alcohol abuse. *Journal of American College Health, 36,* 67–72.

Johnson, V. E. (1986). *Intervention: How to help someone who doesn't want help.*
Minneapolis: Johnson Institute Books.

Johnston, L. D., O'Malley, P. M., & Bachman, J. G. (1992). *Smoking, drinking, and
illicit drug use among American secondary school students, college students,
and young adults, 1975–1991: Vol. 2. College students and young adults.*
Rockville, MD: U.S. Department of Health and Human Services, National Institute on Drug Abuse.

Kinney, J., & Meilman, P. (1987). Alcohol use and alcohol problems: Clinical approaches for the college health service. *Journal of American College Health,
36,* 73–82.

Kinney, J., & Peltier, D. (1986). A model alcohol program for the college health service. *Journal of American College Health, 34,* 229–233.

Kottler, J. A. (1992). Confronting our own hypocrisy: Being a model for our students
and clients. *Journal of Counseling & Development, 70,* 475–476.

Laitman, L. (1987). An overview of a university student assistance program. *Journal
of American College Health, 36,* 103–108.

Meilman, P. W. (1992). Alcohol education and treatment: On the use of leverage in the
college setting. *Journal of American College Health, 41,* 79–81.

Miller, W. R., Benefield, R. G., & Tonigan, J. S. (1993). Enhancing motivation for
change in problem drinking: A controlled comparison of two therapist styles.
Journal of Consulting and Clinical Psychology, 61, 455–461.

Miller, W. R., & Rollnick, S. (1991). *Motivational interviewing: Preparing people to change addictive behavior.* New York: Guilford Press.

Miller, W. R., & Sovereign, R. G. (1989). The check up: A model for early intervention in addictive behaviors. In T. Loberg, W. R. Miller, P. E. Nathan, & G. A. Marlatt (Eds.), *Addictive behaviors: Prevention and early intervention.* Amsterdam: Swets & Zeitlinger.

Moore, D. D., & Forster, J. R. (1993). Student assistance programs: New approaches for reducing adolescent substance abuse. *Journal of Counseling & Development, 71,* 326–329.

Morrill, W. H., Hurst, J. C., & Oetting, E. R. (1980). *Dimensions of intervention for student development.* New York: John Wiley.

Nathan, P. E. (1988). Alcohol dependency prevention and early intervention. *Public Health Reports, 103,* 683–689.

National Institute on Alcohol Abuse and Alcoholism. (1993). *Eighth special report to the U.S. Congress on alcohol and health* (NIH Publication No. 94-3699). Washington, DC: National Institutes of Health.

Office of Substance Abuse Prevention. (1991a). *Faculty member's handbook: Strategies for preventing alcohol and other drug problems.* Washington, DC: U.S. Department of Health and Human Services.

Office of Substance Abuse Prevention. (1991b). *Program administrator's handbook: Strategies for preventing alcohol and other drug problems.* Washington, DC: U.S. Department of Health and Human Services.

Rapaport, R. J. (1993). Student self-reflection on alcohol consumption: A writing assignment. *Journal of College Student Development, 34,* 378–380.

Rathbun, J. (1993). Development of a computerized alcohol screening instrument for the university community. *Journal of American College Health, 42,* 33–36.

Skinner, H. A. (1993). Early identification of addictive behaviors using a computerized lifestyle assessment. In J. S. Baer, G. A. Marlatt, & R. J. McMahon (Eds.), *Addictive behaviors across the life span: Prevention, treatment and policy issues.* London: Sage.

Stone, G. L., & Lucas, J. (1994). Disciplinary counseling in higher education: A neglected challenge. *Journal of Counseling & Development, 72,* 234–238.

Suchman, D., & Broughton, E. (1988). Treatment alternatives for university students with substance use/abuse problems. In T. M. Rivinus (Ed.), *Alcoholism/chemical dependency and the college student.* New York: Haworth Press.

Wechsler, H., Davenport, A., Dowdall, G., Moeykens, B., & Castillo, S. (1994). Health and behavioral consequences of binge drinking in college: A national survey of students at 140 campuses. *Journal of American Medical Association, 272,* 1672–1677.

Wechsler, H., & Isaac, N. E. (1992). Binge drinkers at Massachusetts colleges: Prevalence, drinking style, time trends and associated problems. *Journal of American Medical Association, 267,* 2929–2931.

Williams, F. G., & Knox, R. (1987). Alcohol abuse intervention in a university setting. *Journal of American College Health, 36,* 97–102.

10

Treatment of Substance Abuse Problems

Kenneth C. Gregoire

One component of a comprehensive approach to reducing the adverse impact of substance abuse on our college campuses is to improve access to and facilitate treatment for students who exhibit problems with mood altering substances, including alcohol, the primary substance of abuse. A recent survey (Johnston, O'Malley, & Bachman, 1994) shows that 41 percent of college students engage in heavy drinking. They also found a trend toward increased use of illicit drugs among eighth graders, the college students of tomorrow. Furthermore, broad-based on-campus prevention programs do not always influence those most in need of assistance—the heavier drinkers (Bloch & Ungerleider, 1988). Thus, the likelihood is great that college personnel will continue to encounter large numbers of students who, because of drug use, are underachieving and presenting management problems in social, classroom, and dormitory settings. These same students are vulnerable to dropping, flunking, or being expelled from college because of substance abuse.

Faced with this prospect, it is likely that college personnel will have a number of questions about substance abuse treatment. Does treatment help? Will students be able to continue in school while in treatment? What behaviors and changes can we expect to see as students proceed through treatment? What types of support and assistance are needed for students who are trying to address substance abuse issues? How can college personnel help—or conversely, what are we doing that might actually be contributing to the problem?

The subject of treatment, particularly as it applies to college students, is a complicated one. To begin with, college students are often at a transition point in their lives, moving from adolescence to early adulthood. Thus, the decision as to whether they should be treated in adolescent programs or in programs designed for adults can be complicated and difficult. College students live in settings and surroundings which, at worst, may promote abuse of substances or, at least, may be uncomfortable for the recovering student. DuPont (1988), for example, suggests that there are a number of factors which "perpetuate the connection between drugs and campuses" (p. 41). These include the following: (1) being in an age group when incidence and prevalence of alcohol and other drug use peaks; (2) having discretionary money and time; (3) being in an environment that encourages experimentation with ideas and lifestyle, independent thinking, and questioning of authority and dogma; and (4) weakening or absence of social controls from family, spouse, or employers. These factors by themselves do not cause substance abuse. In fact, several have positive aspects which can promote the movement of a college student from adolescence to early adulthood. For the student at risk for substance abuse, however, they can provide a rich environment for the development of problems.

The changing landscape of the treatment field and shifts in societal views of chemical dependency further complicate treatment decisions for both college students and other chemically dependent people. Society seems to have reverted to punishment rather than treatment as a response to the chemically dependent person, and access to treatment has diminished at all levels of care (National Association of Addiction Treatment Providers, 1991). Even when a college student agrees to seek treatment, availability may be limited. Decisions about the type of treatment to be provided to college students are often more complex, and students may face stigma associated with the decision to enter therapy.

THE MINNESOTA MODEL OF TREATMENT

Any discussion of treatment for substance abusers should include consideration of what is often referred to as the Minnesota Model of treatment (Spicer, 1993; see also Thombs, Chapter 3 of this book). A majority of contemporary treatment programs, both private and public, incorporate many elements of this approach. Such programs are typically designed to treat those who show marked deterioration and dependence (Miller, 1993). Programs based on the Minnesota Model, generally speaking, accept and teach the following:

- Alcoholism and other drug addictions are diagnosable disorders or illnesses.
- Abstinence needs to be the primary treatment goal.
- Chemical dependency is treatable.
- The chemically dependent person needs to be treated with the same dignity and respect as people with other illnesses.
- The whole person must be treated (including body, mind, and spirit).
- A rehabilitation model of treatment is more effective with chemically dependent individuals than a medical model.

Spicer (1993) lists the following components as central to this rehabilitation model: (1) Treatment professionals and patients collaborate in defining the path of recovery; (2) changes in lifestyle habits become the focus of treatment; (3) treatment focuses on the long term; (4) treatment is multidisciplinary; and (5) rehabilitation relies on natural support systems. In addition, Minnesota Model programs frequently incorporate ideas and practices from the self-help program of Alcoholics Anonymous into their programs.

There is currently a lively debate centering around chemical dependency treatment. Many are questioning the effectiveness of traditional treatment programs and many are proposing alternative approaches to treatment (Calamari & Cox, Chapter 4 of this book). In the course of the debate, traditional Minnesota Model treatment programs are often portrayed as inpatient programs requiring a twenty-eight-day stay, adhering to inflexible requirements such as abstinence goals for all clients, and being unwilling to look at alternative treatment techniques whose effectiveness has been documented in the research literature. In practice, many treatment programs today use a wide variety of therapy techniques matched to individual patient needs, provide care at many different levels, and involve patients in the process of setting treatment goals (even the treatment goal of abstinence is, at times, creatively negotiated). The case examples presented (Linda and Bob) demonstrate the flexibility that is needed in treating chemically dependent individuals.

Bob, a farmer in his 40s, has shown a long history of alcohol related problems and several admissions to treatment. While able, as a result of treatment, aftercare and ongoing involvement in AA, to achieve extended periods of abstinence, he has shown a predictable pattern of relapsing into devastating binges, particularly after harvest each year. Each binge has ended with his readmission to treatment, often after family interventions, because, once started, Bob has been unable to stop his drinking without assistance. His binges always resulted in painful consequences such as DUIs, gambling episodes, and family quarrels, followed by remorse and depression. At the time of his last admission, his counselor suggested a different goal—that Bob work with his counselor, his family, and other supportive people to plan a drinking episode. The plan would include controls to protect against painful consequences, as well as prearranged help to insure that he would stop drinking. Bob and the family agreed that such a plan would be preferable to what had been happening. This plan for occasional nonproblem drinking was developed within a program in which the majority of patients adopt abstinence as their goal. Those familiar with the use of a patient's resistance to promote change can probably predict the outcome of this intervention: When the time came for his planned drinking episode, Bob decided he didn't really want to drink this time. In fact, Bob has stayed totally sober for the past seven years.

Linda, a 30-year-old college student, was admitted to an evening care intensive outpatient treatment program consisting primarily of psychoeducational lectures and group therapy. She sought treatment on her own because of difficulties controlling her drinking. She presented a long history of problems with alcohol, marijuana, and prescription drug abuse, as well as diagnoses for a variety of mental illnesses. She had received primary chemical dependency treatment and treatment by psychiatrists and mental health counselors but has never achieved sustained sobriety. Although, in group therapy, she was very articulate about her problems and what she has learned about herself. She continued to have difficulty remaining abstinent, which was her initial treatment goal, and continued to report problems at work, in school, and in her interpersonal relationships. As people in her group began focusing more on her problems with use of substances, Linda announced that she had decided to drop out of treatment because she particularly did not want to give up her use of marijuana. Rather than going along with Linda's plan to terminate treatment, her counselor suggested that she be seen in individual counseling for an eight-week trial period. The counselor used a number of cognitive behavioral techniques to help Linda examine her use of substances. These interventions included self-monitoring, completing decision matrices, and assessing automatic thoughts. Linda accepted this alternative and actively involved herself in the therapy, which, after one month, resulted in her acceptance of her inability to continue using substances without accompanying problems. She then chose to reinvolve herself in the intensive outpatient program and begin attending AA meetings.

What is apparent in these examples is that programs often incorporate elements from many models of treatment, including Minnesota Models, cognitive–behavioral approaches, and other social learning approaches. Existing programs find that they have an ever-expanding menu of treatment techniques, approaches, and options to choose from when working with chemically dependent people. To more fully understand the treatment of substance abuse problems, it is often helpful to consider a number of factors, including tasks and stages of recovery, setting or level of care, and modalities of treatment.

Tasks and Stages of Recovery

It is important to recognize that individuals who abuse substances can be at varying stages of acceptance and recognition of their problem and of willingness to make changes in their lives. One way to understand the process of change has been developed by Prochaska, DiClemente, and Norcross (1992). These authors present five stages of change. Efforts to help individuals who have substance abuse problems can be refined and targeted when helpers are able to accurately assess where an individual is in the change process.

The first stage of change is called the precontemplation stage. In this stage, individuals have problems associated with their alcohol and drug use but fail to identify the connection between their use and their problems, experience no anxiety over their use of alcohol and drugs, and exhibit no intention or desire to make changes in their problematic behaviors. When dealing with substance abusers in this stage, helpers with little knowledge of the change process or of substance abuse often find themselves involved in power struggles. The first task in working with a substance abuser in the initial stages of change is to form a positive working relationship which is based on trust and respect.

The next stage of change is the contemplation stage. At this stage, the individual begins to recognize the relationship between the use of alcohol and drugs and subsequent problems. He or she may begin thinking about the possibility of making changes and thinking about how life might be different without the use of alcohol and drugs. At this stage, individuals may be more susceptible to attempts by concerned others to intervene in their problematic use of chemicals. They still, however, experience considerable ambivalence about the prospect of altering their patterns of use. Helpers often prematurely lose patience with substance abusers mired in this stage of change.

The third stage presented by Prochaska and colleagues (1992) is the preparation stage. At this point individuals may well have made a decision to make changes in how they use alcohol and drugs and are actively looking for ways to accomplish this goal. They may not, however, possess the skills to make these changes or know where to turn for help. Those in a position to help substance abusers who are beginning to search for answers must have a good working knowledge of treatment and self-help resources available. Often, substance abusers will ask for help in veiled ways or only when in a state of crisis. When they do ask for help there exists a window of opportunity that may close if helpers are not able to hear the request or are not able to assist the abuser in connecting with helpful resources.

The individual moves to the fourth, or action stage, when he or she begins making observable attempts to change and experiments with new lifestyles. This stage is frequently marked by failures as well as successes in a highly variable pattern of change. Considerable support is needed for the person who is attempting to make active changes. It is important for those who are working with substance abusers to recognize that progress is not always one-directional and steady and that support can take many forms.

The last stage of change is the maintenance stage. In this stage, progress made in previous stages is consolidated, the individual continues to work on skills that have been helpful in dealing with alcohol and drug problems, and considerable energy is devoted to avoiding reversion to prior patterns of behavior. Significant attention has recently been paid to this change of stage; for example, the new area of relapse prevention is aimed at helping individuals in this stage of change.

This model illustrates the importance of considering the client's stage of change when constructing treatment plans. Individuals with substance abuse problems do not, however, progress in a predictable way from one stage to the next. They may pass through each stage several times or may go from a more advanced stage to a less advanced stage. Thus, the timing of the presentation of therapeutic interventions and the pairing of these interventions with the stage of change that the individual is in can be critical if the individual is to make progress towards resolving substance abuse problems.

Other workers have approached the notion of stages of change with substance abusers from different perspectives. Gonzales (1988) and Bell (1993) specifically addressed phases and stages of the addictive recovery process in adolescents. Gonzales presents four stages of change and emphasizes the importance of dealing with the impact of chemical abuse on the development of identity formation. Gonzales's stages are the following: (1) development of attachment to the addictive object without any connection to harm; (2) attachment to the addictive object with growing awareness of harm; (3) beginning detachment from the addictive object and engagement in a change program; and (4) development of a program of maintenance of change.

Bell (1993) gives particular attention to the phases that an adolescent goes through in the process of relapse into substance abuse after having reached the maintenance stage. These phases include (1) a return to denial, (2) avoidance of helpers, (3) gradual crisis building, (4) mobilization to return to substance use, (5) confusion and overreaction, (6) depression and behavioral loss of control, (7) recognition of loss of control, (8) option reduction, and, finally, (9) an acute relapse episode. In this model, early recognition of the process involved in relapse into substance abuse by either the substance abuser or by significant others in the substance abuser's life can result in appropriate interventions matched to the stage of relapse.

Thus, effective intervention and treatment must help individuals complete and negotiate a wide variety of tasks which can include identifying and accepting problems, improving motivation to change, detoxifying from substances, and beginning the process of stabilization. Stabilization may also include stages, such as identifying and managing post-acute withdrawal, crisis resolution, dealing with addictive preoccupation, and developing the skills needed to maintain therapeutic progress, whether measured by abstinence from mood-altering substances or nonproblematic use. Therapeutic techniques and interventions from a variety of models, including the Minnesota Model, the disease model of addiction, the social learning and cognitive–behavioral model, and brief therapy models can be applied to help individuals negotiate the stages and tasks of recovery.

Setting and Level of Care

Treatment of the college student can be provided in different settings and at a variety of levels of care. Levels of care differ in terms of structure provided and intensity of treatment. If the student enters inpatient treatment, college enrollment may need to be interrupted. Treatment on an outpatient basis, however, can be provided while the student continues in school; generally speaking, no changes in school requirements or expectations will be needed. Many universities provide some type of on-campus outpatient treatment for students with substance abuse difficulties (O'Connell & Beck, 1984; Kinney & Meilman, 1987; Gonzales, 1988; DuPont, 1988; Suchman & Broughton, 1988; Kivlahan, Fromme, Marlatt, Coppel, & Williams, 1990).

DuPont (1988) discusses the dilemma faced by counselors who work with college substance abusers, particularly when trying to help them set appropriate treatment goals. DuPont focuses on the issue of whether total abstinence from mood-altering substances should be the primary goal of treatment.

He states that the counselor needs to be very active in assisting the student to set appropriate goals. He makes the point that there is no compelling reason, for example, to assist a college student to learn how to drink responsibly if he or she is not able to use alcohol legally.

Kivlahan and colleagues (1990) take a different position, one which allows students to set their own goals. They describe a skills training program, based on the cognitive–behavioral principles used by Marlatt and Gordon (1985), which is designed to reduce the amount and moderate the pattern of alcohol consumption among college drinkers. Cognitive–behavioral techniques used in this program include self-monitoring of alcohol consumption, instruction about blood alcohol levels, limit setting, identification of high-risk situations, and development and practice of responses to high-risk situations. The goals of the program center more on risk reduction and harm minimization than on total abstinence for college drinkers.

The skills training approach is usually thought of as prevention or education rather than as a treatment program, primarily because participants may have shorter histories of abusive drug use and concomitant negative consequences. This is, however, a subtle and perhaps unimportant distinction, especially as it applies to the college population. Kivlahan and colleagues (1990) indicate that skills training may result in overall reduced drinking among college students. These researchers also have found, however, that although overall drinking may decline after skills training, many students continue to engage in occasional episodes of heavy drinking.

The *Patient Placement Criteria for the Treatment of Substance-Related Disorders*, published by the American Society of Addiction Medicine (ASAM, 1996), describes three levels of outpatient care. The first level, referred to as early intervention, consists of a variety of potential therapeutic activities aimed at helping individuals identify harmful consequences of substance abuse. At the next level, regularly scheduled sessions are provided for fewer than nine hours per week but are designed to directly treat substance abuse problems. Programs at the third level, usually referred to as intensive outpatient treatment or partial hospitalization treatment, operate either during daytime hours or in the evening and offer more than nine hours per week of structured chemical dependency treatment.

It is important to note that patients can be moved in either direction along an intensity-of-treatment continuum depending on their adjustment and individual needs. Competent assessments are critical to the process of deciding which level of care is appropriate for which patient. The stability of the patient is a primary factor when determining the appropriate level of care. See Cocores (1991) for more detailed descriptions of outpatient treatment programs.

The ASAM Patient Placement Criteria also describe two levels of inpatient treatment: medically monitored intensive inpatient treatment and medically managed inpatient treatment. Medically monitored inpatient treatment provides a highly supportive environment, twenty-four-hour observation, and multidisciplinary treatment. Medically managed inpatient treatment is appropriate for those patients who are both medically and psychiatrically unstable and who may need high levels of medical intervention and environmental support in order to stabilize. It is important to note that the various tasks of treatment, such as diagnosis, detoxification, stabilization, aftercare counseling, skill building, education, and referral can be provided at any level of care. See Dackis and Gold (1991), White and Mee-Lee (1988), or Spicer (1993) for more descriptions of inpatient and residential treatment.

Other levels of care are also available and utilized in substance abuse treatment. Extended care programs are also referred to as therapeutic communities. Generally speaking, patients who need extended care programs have already had significant treatment at some other level of care and need ongoing intensive therapy to maintain the progress made in previous treatment. Frequently, patients who are referred to extended care programs have serious emotional or sometimes physical problems concomitant to their chemical dependency. Halfway-house programs provide people a living environment with other recovering substance abusers in a setting which is supportive of recovery principles. Halfway houses provide varying levels of counseling and typically provide job placement services. Though the recent focus on problems in our health-care system has begun to dramatically change the face of treatment and the options available to chemically dependent people, most clinicians would still agree that in order to successfully treat alcoholism patients need access to a full continuum of treatment services, which should include assessment, intervention and referral, detoxification, inpatient treatment, extended care treatment, halfway-house programs, outpatient treatment of varying intensities, aftercare or continuing care, and family treatment.

Modalities

Just as treatment tasks can be accomplished at each level of care, modalities of treatment can be implemented and delivered at each level of care. Generally, when substance abusers enter treatment they are presented with a program comprised of multiple treatment modalities and adjunctive therapies. The most frequently used modalities are individual counseling, group therapy, marital and family counseling, psychoeducational activities, and milieu therapy.

Individual Counseling Many clinicians maintain that the most effective modality for treating chemically dependent patients is group therapy. However, individual counseling can serve many purposes and contribute in many ways to a comprehensive treatment plan. Although some clinicians view individual counseling as primarily supporting and preparing patients to function in a group counseling setting, individual counseling frequently serves functions that cannot be as effectively addressed in group counseling settings. For example, by building a therapeutic relationship the counselor can help a client develop motivation to change and a willingness to become involved in other forms of therapy. Some types of client defenses and negative patterns of behavior cannot be successfully challenged until a supportive, trusting individual therapeutic relationship has been established. In addition, clients bring a wide variety of concomitant problems to the therapy setting. Patients with certain interaction styles or psychological problems (e.g., avoidant or phobic of groups) may need to have initial treatment interventions delivered in an individual counseling setting.

Individual counselors often serve a case-management function for chemically dependent patients. Many patients need a wide variety of services and adjunctive therapies, and an individual counselor can ensure that the delivery of these services is effectively coordinated, see that the timing for delivery of certain therapies is appropriate, and serve as an advocate for the patient in ensuring access to appropriate services.

Individual counseling also serves the function of crisis intervention and resolution in many stages of the therapeutic process. Chemically dependent patients often find themselves in a state of crisis in many areas of their lives. Interpersonal relationship problems, legal difficulties, financial crises, and employment and/or school problems can also lead patients to be suicidal, homicidal, or in various stages of panic. Crisis intervention is often best done in an individual counseling setting, particularly when the counselor needs to play an active role with the external environment in order to protect the patient and other people. Successful resolution of the crisis is most likely to result when the individual in crisis knows, trusts, and respects the helper, conditions which are established in effective individual counseling.

Individual counseling can be very appropriate for patients who are in later stages of the change and recovery process, when they are ready to deal with other important issues. For example, patients who have endured sexual trauma early in their lives may not be prepared to deal with its impact on their functioning until they have reached a point of stable sobriety and recovery and are able to tolerate the anxiety that dealing with these issues can generate. Many find that returning to individual psychotherapy after a period of stable recovery greatly enhances their insight into past problems and improves the quality of their lives in recovery. In addition, many counselors continue to serve as a contact person for chemically dependent patients long after formal therapy has been terminated.

A special form of individual counseling that is frequently integrated into the treatment plans of chemically dependent patients, particularly in Minnesota Model programs, is individual pastoral counseling. Patients learning how to apply the twelve steps of AA to their recovery find that working with a chaplain is particularly beneficial. Patients who have serious therapeutic issues related to past behavior can benefit from working with a chaplain while doing the fourth and fifth steps of AA, which ask the person to make a moral inventory and admit the nature of his or her wrongs. While pastoral counseling is available in many programs, most such programs are sensitive to the objections of some individuals to receiving pastoral counseling due to religious considerations and provide alterative therapeutic opportunities.

Group Therapy Group therapy, in a variety of forms, has been the preferred modality of care in the substance abuse treatment community. Group settings can provide patients an opportunity to compare their problems with those of others. They may find comfort and solace in the recognition that they are not alone and realize that they will have support in trying to change. By comparing their use of chemicals to that of others they may break through the minimization and denial that has brought them to the treatment setting. Group therapies in chemical dependency programs often emphasize peer feedback, which can be provided with varying amounts of structure and direction. Some chemically dependent patients may accept feedback from peers more readily than from therapists, who are seen as authority figures to be rejected or rebelled against. Group therapies also provide individuals with an opportunity to see themselves as others do and to see how their past interactions with people influence their current ones.

Some group therapies are highly structured, task-centered, skill-building processes. Many cognitive–behavioral interventions, for example, are delivered in group therapy settings. Other group therapies are very process oriented, with the therapist assuming a much more nondirective role. While such therapy may be aimed at helping patients adopt a more active role in their recovery, more often it is focused on here-and-now types of issues and on assisting patients to learn how to constructively deal with feelings, particularly strong negative affects that have been medicated and avoided through their chemical dependency.

Individual characteristics are often taken into account in assigning patients to certain group settings. Some groups, for example, are designed to have a very heterogeneous group of clients in order to maximize the generalizability of patient progress and emphasize the fact that chemical dependency is a problem shared by a wide variety of people. Other groups, particularly those with a specific purpose or focus, have a more homogeneous group of patients. Groups may focus on certain issues, such as assertiveness, women's or men's issues, grief resolution, or relapse prevention. Also, groups may be restricted to certain types of clients, such as adolescents or cocaine patients, and may be designed to focus on problems unique to these populations.

Marital and Family Counseling A common finding in treatment-outcome research is that spouse and family involvement in the treatment process frequently improves the chemically dependent individual's chances for a successful outcome (Harrison, Hoffmann, & Streed, 1991; McCrady, 1991). McCrady has discussed a number of roles that the spouse can assume in treatment with the chemically dependent patient. Spouses can provide collateral information about the client's use of alcohol and other drugs and other patterns of behavior. It is not uncommon for substance abusers in treatment to give inaccurate information because they do not remember, as a result of defense mechanisms such as denial and rationalization, or because they are deliberately presenting false information in order to escape painful consequences. Thus, information from the spouse can be helpful, both in providing an accurate record and in confronting the client's ways of dealing with the world.

Another role the spouse can take is as a support to the chemically dependent person for desirable changes in behavior. Helping couples build positive feedback and rewards into their interactions can be a difficult but important part of therapy, as by the time such couples get to treatment there is often a long history of feelings of hurt and anger to be overcome. Spouses also can help in the delivery and use of an adjunctive therapy, such as the use of Disulfiram, a drug that when combined with alcohol produces flu-like symptoms, nausea, and heart palpitations, and is often used in treating alcoholics. Research shows that when spouses observe spouses taking Disulfiram, compliance with therapy is increased (Azrin, Sisson, Meyers, & Godley, 1982). In fact, involving the spouse in many aspects of therapy generally increases the client's overall compliance with treatment.

Spouses are often able to learn to identify the ways that they have unintentionally been enabling the chemically dependent person to continue to abuse alcohol or other drugs; for example, by assuming the chemically dependent person's responsibilities, inadvertently reinforcing drinking, or sabotaging treatment progress. Involving the spouse or family member in therapy assists in the development of positive healthy methods of supporting the addicted individual in efforts to maintain a sober lifestyle. A number of writers have expanded on the impact of familial chemical dependency on family members and the role of treatment in helping family members deal with their problems (Jackson, 1954; Cork, 1969; Black, 1981; Brown & Yalom, 1995). Some colleges provide separate and supportive programming for family members of alcoholics (Landers & Hollingdale, 1988).

Psychoeducational Lectures and Activities Part of the process of helping substance abusers recover from their problems is to educate them about their disorder or disease and assist with the development of a management plan. Chemical dependency programs provide such assistance in much the same way as do other health-care organizations treating illnesses such as heart disease, cancer, and diabetes in holistic ways. As can be seen by the sample of topics delivered in one outpatient treatment center, lectures tend to focus on helping the individual as a whole develop, grow, and recover:

Primary Treatment

Week One

Monday	What Is Addiction?	How It Works
Tuesday	How We Defend Ourselves	Step One
Wednesday	Relapse Prevention Group	

| Thursday | Religion vs Spirituality | Steps Two and Three |
| Friday | Personality Concepts/Addiction | Medical Aspects |

Week Two

Monday	Family Concepts/Dynamics	Steps Four and Five
Tuesday	Dual Addiction/Cross Tolerance	Steps Six and Seven
Wednesday	Relapse Prevention Group	
Thursday	Feelings of Inferiority	Steps Eight and Nine
Friday	Responsibility and Recovery	Sex and Recovery (Includes STD Education)

Week Three

Monday	Addiction and Anger	Step Ten
Tuesday	Dry Drunks	Step Eleven
Wednesday	Relapse Prevention Group	
Thursday	Shame and Guilt	Step Twelve
Friday	Symptoms of Recovery	Solution Thinking

Relapse Prevention

Week One	Relapse Model	Levels of Change
Week Two	Personal Triggers	Sober Self/Addict Self
Week Three	Social Pressure	Feelings Creation
Week Four	Understanding Anger	Anger Management
Week Five	Daily Hassles and Uplifts	Tension/Relaxation
Week Six	Stress Management	Urges and Cravings
Week Seven	Pity-Punish Cycle	OTC Dangers
Week Eight	Coping Behaviors	Prevention Skills
Week Nine	Relapse Limiting	Relapse Action Plan

Psychoeducational lectures and activities often combine the structured provision of information with what could be considered active group therapy. Here-and-now examples from clients' lives are often addressed in lectures, skill deficits are explored, and positive coping behaviors are identified and rehearsed. One goal of these activities is for clients to become active rather than passive partners in the process of treatment.

Milieu Therapy One of the basic aims of residential and inpatient treatment is to provide and facilitate the development of a therapeutic community, a core group of positive, motivated, supportive, and caring patients who can help each new patient develop insight into problems and motivation to change. The development of commitments to each other and the ability to help each other in recovery become powerful therapeutic tools in themselves. Counselors can work within milieu therapy to provide creative ways of dealing with patient problems. A counselor may, for example, ask a patient who is well progressed in therapy to serve as a buddy for a new patient who is coming into treatment angry and resistant. A patient who is relatively introverted and needs to learn how to interact more comfortably with unfamiliar people may be asked to serve as a greeter of new patients. The patient who takes himself or herself too seriously and lacks the ability to have fun without alcohol and drug use may be asked to collect jokes from other people in the therapeutic community and begin learning how to tell them at community team meetings in the evening. Treatment is structured so that therapy proceeds twenty-four hours a day and continues outside of the therapist's office or group room. This provides an optimal environment for patients to learn new behaviors in a low-risk setting.

Assigning Patients to Treatment

Decisions about the type, length, and level of treatment that would be optimally effective with a given individual can be difficult and complex. Patient placement criteria adopted by the American Society of Addiction Medicine (ASAM, 1996) can be useful in guiding these decisions. The criteria are organized into six dimensions: (1) acute alcohol and/or drug intoxication and/ or potential withdrawal, (2) biomedical conditions and complications, (3) emotional or behavioral conditions and complications, (4) treatment acceptance or resistance, (5) relapse potential, and (6) recovery environment. Problems relative to any of these categories are considered pertinent to decisions regarding the appropriate treatment of chemically dependent patients. The ASAM patient placement criteria also includes a set of criteria for adolescent patients. Younger college students might be better served using these criteria when making treatment decisions.

Clinicians have tended to make a number of assumptions when applying such criteria (Harrison, Hoffmann, & Streed, 1991). The severity of problems, frequency and quantity of substance use, ability to abstain (believing that treatment will not be effective if the individual continues to use substances), and the presence of concomitant problems in other areas of the person's life are relevant to decisions about level of care, length of treatment, and type of treatment. In reality, there are many extraclinical factors that influence decisions about treatment plans, including job or school demands, third-party payor restrictions, family responsibilities, availability of treatment, and the preference of the patient.

APPLICATIONS TO COLLEGE STUDENTS

Treatment Issues

Most college students who either voluntarily seek treatment or are coerced into seeking treatment are young and, presumably, in the early stages of addiction or problem use. As such, they have suffered less as a result of their substance use, are less accepting of the severity of their problems, have a greater tendency to blame others or external circumstances for their substance problems, seek external rather than internal solutions to their problems to a greater extent, and look more to others to protect them from the natural consequences of their behavior. They may engage in more minimization, active cover-up of problems, and manipulation of authority figures and potential helpers than later-stage alcoholics and drug addicts. They may also, at times, comply with treatment procedures rather than become truly therapeutically involved. As a result, therapeutic interventions need to include more intensive strategies for motivating the student and assisting him or her in problem identification. As mentioned, the tendency of many helpers in working with individuals at this stage of change is to engage in confrontation and argument. The result is generally that the substance abuser becomes more resistant or terminates the relationship. Motivational interviewing (Miller & Rollnick, 1991; Rollnick & Morgan, 1995), an approach that has been developed in an attempt to assist helpers in avoiding power struggles with resistant individuals or early-stage substance abusers, might be especially useful with college students.

Research on the treatment of adolescent substance abusers illuminates some of these points. Walfish, Massey, and Krone (1990) found that adolescents receiving residential treatment for substance abuse were similar to adult substance abuse patients in that they showed an elevation on the Pd (psychopathy) scale of the Minnesota Multiphase Personality Inventory. Unlike adult samples, however, adolescents did not show an elevation on the Depression scale, meaning that these adolescents were not experiencing significant internal distress and were likely more resistant to treatment and less accepting of their problems. Kaminer, Tartar, Bukstein, and Kabene (1992) found that adolescents receiving treatment for substance abuse who were likely to be noncompleters of treatment tended to have a concomitant conduct disorder, while those who completed treatment tended to have a concomitant affective disorder. This study is relevant to treatment of young substance abusers because one of the findings of the outcome studies discussed later in this chapter is that positive outcomes are related to the length of time that individuals stay involved in treatment activities. Certainly, one of the main challenges in treating college substance abusers is that of engaging them and keeping them in treatment. College students must be considered high risks to drop out of treatment prematurely if appropriate treatment interventions are not implemented at the beginning of the process. The message seems to be that if you are going to treat those with substance abuse disorders, do it right the first time.

College students present unique treatment challenges where recovery environment issues are concerned. They are, for example, frequently exposed to large numbers of peers who abuse chemicals and will not support them in efforts to remain abstinent or even to use chemicals in a moderate, nonproblematic fashion. Many college students are living apart from home and family for the first time and have not yet developed healthy substitute support systems. These factors can trigger relapse and need to be taken into account when planning treatment interventions and in efforts to prevent relapse. Brown, Vik, and Creamer (1989) found that while relapse rates of treated adolescent substance abusers were comparable to treated adult substance abusers, relapse in adolescents was more specifically and more frequently related directly to social pressure to drink. Raniseski and Sigelman (1992) found that the adolescent substance abusers who were most resistant to treatment were those who reported the greatest concerns about peer pressure. Managing recovery environment issues, thus, seems to be a critical factor in successfully treating college students with substance use disorders.

Total abstinence from all mood-altering substances is frequently a treatment goal for individuals with substance abuse disorders. This goal can seem more unreasonable and unattainable to young people than it does to older, later-stage chemically dependent individuals. Related to this is the fact that many treatment programs also strongly encourage involvement in AA and other twelve-step programs, which have small numbers of young people among their members. Many young college students have difficulty integrating into these self-help groups and identifying with group members; as a result they may not only drop out of self-help groups but also leave treatment programs which stress such involvement. The dilemma faced by treatment providers is often whether to treat this resistance as a denial of addiction and continue to encourage involvement in AA and total abstinence, or to help the individual look for potentially healthy support systems that are more immediately acceptable, and to work with the student on preferred but, perhaps, riskier treatment goals.

The young college student admitted to treatment for substance abuse disorders is also more likely to be a polysubstance abuser than are older individuals seeking treatment. This presents complicated treatment issues and difficulties in making accurate diagnoses. The symptoms of substance abuse can frequently mimic those of a wide variety of mental disorders, including affective, personality and even psychotic disorders. Usually, the substance abuse must be treated first, or at times concomitantly, before the whole diagnostic picture becomes clear. Even when disorders other than the substance use disorder are present, these disorders typically do not respond to treatment until the substance abuse has been managed.

The young college student who is exhibiting reasonably serious alcohol or drug-related problems may well show a history of such problems dating back into early adolescence. Some come from families with a history of alcoholism. As a result, these students may be markedly more immature than their peers, may be struggling with different developmental challenges and tasks, may have progressed further along the path of addiction, and may be significantly less likely to mature out of problematic use of alcohol and other drugs, as apparently happens with many college-age substance abusers. Identifying, reaching, and involving high-risk students in therapeutic activities is an important but difficult goal. Klein (1989) surveyed college students and found that as problematic use of substances rise, students report significantly less willingness to use potentially helpful resources. Also, there appears to be a poor match between the resources that are currently available on most college campuses and what students report they feel comfortable using.

Other research has indicated that even basic steps which could be taken to identify and refer students who have shown problems with substance abuse are not being taken. Hickenbottom, Bissonette, and O'Shea (1987) found that only 15 percent of students reported that they had been asked about their use of alcohol by a physician or other health professional. Over 90 percent of these students said they would change their drinking behavior if advised to do so by a physician. While we cannot expect that simple interventions like helpful advice will result in significant changes among those with substance use disorders, it seems clear that much more could be done on college campuses, even with existing resources, to intervene earlier with those students who are at risk. There is evidence which suggests that helpers such as medical and college personnel who are trained in brief intervention techniques can provide substance abusers with considerable assistance (Hester & Bien, 1995).

The expectations to achieve at high levels, which are a part of college life, present potential relapse triggers that are particularly salient for college students. Behaviors which could put the student at risk include skipping meals, eating poorly, staying up all night to study, and using caffeine or other stimulants to stay awake to study or to enhance performance. Procrastinating, cheating on exams or papers, and/or taking other shortcuts which leave the individual feeling guilty and inadequate also can trigger relapse. Other strong negative affects can also present relapse triggers for recovering college students, as their pattern in many cases has been to medicate these affects with chemicals and, as a result, they have not learned positive coping skills. Examples include fear of classroom presentations, anger and conflict with authority figures and rules that are seen as arbitrary, boredom during those periods of time when not faced with exams or project deadlines, and anxiety when feeling overwhelmed by demands. Most students who receive treatment for substance use disorders need an ongoing continuing-care plan to assist in the process of building skills necessary to deal with the demands of college life and to prevent relapse. It is critical to help the student and those who are influential in his or her life to realize and accept that primary treatment merely lays the foundation for continuing recovery and a series of recovery tasks and activities.

Stages of Recovery

College students in early stages of treatment and recovery may show a number of different adaptations. Knowing what to expect from such students and which patterns are common and to be expected can be helpful when attempting to assist the student.

Most college personnel are probably familiar with the experience of encountering students who, as a result of substance use, are actively in crisis and either directly or indirectly making a plea for help. Recognizing that their behavior is, in fact, a plea for help can be difficult, as most substance abusers do not directly ask for help, but rather call attention to their difficulties through outwardly destructive behavior (antagonism, rebellion, aggression) and/or self-destructive behavior (poor performance, dropping out, suicidal gestures or attempts, overdoses). Such individuals may be feeling overwhelmed by problems and may be having to cope with the painful external consequences of alcohol or drug-related behavior, such as court fines or mandates, lost relationships, and school disciplinary actions. Any additional demands or stressors may be experienced as intolerable and precipitate dramatic methods of escape and protection which, in turn, become management problems for college personnel. Even routine, day-to-day living tasks can be experienced as overwhelming and intolerable.

In working with a student in crisis, helpers must be prepared not only to be very supportive and understanding, but also to be very active in helping the student manage the immediate crisis and develop hope that he or she can avert disaster. Helpers must also recognize that there is a window of opportunity in working with students in crisis, as at these times they may be more receptive to suggestions and therapeutic interventions.

One common adjustment seen in early recovery results when individuals have moved dramatically toward acceptance of their addiction through a conversion-like process; some consider themselves to have experienced a spiritual awakening. Such people see everything in a new way and may become evangelistic with friends, teachers, administrators, and others in an attempt to educate others about substance abuse and even to encourage them to examine their own use of substances. In class, these students can be enthusiastic, outspoken, talkative, committed to their ideas, and resistant to a variety of views—delightful to have in some classes but disruptive in others. It is important to remember that, for this person, the changes made in recovery and the stability of sobriety are still tenuous. They also tend to take on more than they are prepared for. The first major disappointment can lead to feelings of disillusionment, disappointment, and questioning of the validity of their treatment experience and new views.

The student may also be devoting large amounts of time to recovery activities and may need assistance in balancing these activities with school responsibilities. It is not uncommon for people in early recovery to use their addiction and involvement in recovery activities as an excuse for continued irresponsibility in other areas of life, a stance seemingly supported by AA sponsors and therapists who tell them that their sobriety comes first. What is not always apparent with a person in this stage of recovery is the tremendous amount of support and help that is needed, despite appearances. In addition, there are many issues and tasks which the person is not yet stable enough to confront; the task of stabilizing and maintaining abstinence requires most of his or her attention and energy.

In the earliest stages of recovery, the individual must narrowly focus on avoiding substance use and dealing with such realities as post-acute withdrawal symptoms. This person is busy learning about addiction, attending many self-help meetings, establishing a relationship with a sponsor (if involved in AA), reading recovery literature, making amends to those who have been harmed, learning how to do twelfth-step work, and so on. They are focusing on very basic issues, such as eating properly, getting enough sleep, trying to build structure and routine into their life, establishing support structures, and abandoning old destructive friends and support systems.

As individuals begin to achieve some degree of stable sobriety and recovery, different patterns of behavior emerge and they begin to struggle with changing issues. Such individuals appear to have developed greater wisdom as a result of past experiences, are more tolerant of others, have an increasingly balanced view of drinking and drugging problems, and are not so evangelistic in their relationships with others. They are, however, most often genuinely willing and able to help others in need and frequently assume leadership roles in college settings.

With stability, the individual becomes prepared to confront tougher, more complex issues and problems which may have played a precipitating role in the chemical dependency or, if left unresolved, could lead to relapse. Such issues might include the effects of incest or other forms of sexual trauma, long-standing problems with intimate relationships, family problems, chronic affective disorders, or any number of personality characteristics which present barriers to high-level personal functioning. People in this stage of recovery may also give way to the tendency to buy each new self-help book, wave, or trend and have difficulty balancing new information with what they have learned in the past. They may also abandon what has worked for them in the past. The task in this stage is for individuals to begin to consolidate changes, to integrate information, and to continue building skills which make them more effective in all areas of their life. Many people begin in this stage of recovery to achieve levels of functioning which neither they nor anyone else ever expected they could.

Case Examples

John is a nineteen-year-old second-year college student who is involved in continuing-care counseling with a university counselor at the student health center. He received primary treatment for chemical dependency during the past summer, has been totally abstinent from mood-altering substances for seven months, and has continued to be active in AA. He continues to have difficulty in his class work, primarily as a result of missing deadlines, procrastinating, and underperforming. John is an extroverted young man who can be particularly charming when asking for special consideration and privileges.

His counselor has recently received John's permission to work with a number of his instructors in an attempt to help him identify specific problem areas interfering with his overall performance. The counselor discovered that this young man has been open with instructors about being chemically dependent but has frequently used the AA admonishment that he should put his recovery above all else as a tool in his arsenal for rationalizing irresponsible behavior and for avoiding full responsibility for his life. He told a professor recently that he had not been able to submit an assignment on time because, "I was asked to go on a twelfth-step call and was up till four in the morning and was too exhausted to finish my paper." The counselor also discovered that instructors were either dealing with John with frustration and no support or were overly cautious in dealing with him, believing that to do the wrong thing would push him toward relapse. The counselor found instructors open to suggestions on how to deal with John and suggested that they use variants of the following message when he showed signs of irresponsibility and manipulation: "You know, John, how much I recognize, respect, and understand the courage and the effort that is needed to recover from addiction. I know that you put a lot of time and effort into recovery and I am behind you all the way. I understand that you need to attend AA meetings, spend time with your sponsor, and I know that twelfth-step work is a part of the recovery process. From what I know of AA and treatment, though, I believe neither would want you to use what they are saying as a way to avoid major responsibilities. AA and therapy, as I understand them, teach responsibility and how to become more effective and accountable. Now, I don't want in any way to discourage you or get in the way of your recovery. Neither do I want to do anything which will enable you to continue to avoid responsibility and be less effective than you can be. I think it is important for me to penalize you as I would any other student for turning this paper in late, but I also am giving you a chance to turn the paper in, to demonstrate that you can do the work, and I would like to work with you to learn what went wrong in this process and what I can do to help you ensure that the next paper is in on time. I think it is very important that you go over what happened here with your sponsor or therapist and I am offering to talk both with you and your therapist about this."

The therapist also began working with John on such skills as structuring his time, building problem-solving skills, and developing study habits and skills. The therapist continued to work with instructors and family members, encouraging them to provide consistent reinforcement for responsible behavior, improved problem-solving skills, better organization of time, and accountability. It is important to remember in working with students such as John, who have a history of substance abuse through adolescence, that they lack the skills and maturity of other students their age and need a very active therapist willing to use many different interventions to help them catch up.

Jane is an eighteen-year-old college student enrolled in her freshman year. She has been asking her parents since the midpoint of the first semester to allow her to drop out of school. Jane's father is a recovering alcoholic and three of her older siblings have had substance abuse problems. All have had treatment and currently two of the three are recovering and substance free.

Jane not only reported problems with alcohol dating well back into middle adolescence, but also indicated that since coming to college she has been drinking more heavily and has been experimenting with marijuana and cocaine. At the time of her first interview, she was also very thin and appeared to be malnourished. A more thorough assessment revealed a high likelihood that Jane is also anorexic and bulimic.

After talking at length with her parents and her counselor and seeing that successful treatment was a possibility, Jane decided that she would like to remain enrolled in her classes and finish the semester. The original treatment plan included having her counselor work with Jane and her advisor at school to determine whether combining continued enrollment with treatment was possible. A brief inpatient admission to a chemical dependency program was arranged to further assess her physical status, help her stabilize with respect to the effects of her use of alcohol and drugs, and to help her manage cravings and compulsions to resume use of substances. Following this brief period of stabilization, Jane would begin an evening-care program, consisting of therapy three to five evenings per week to deal with her substance abuse patterns. After Jane showed signs of stabilization, active involvement in self-help groups, and diminished cravings, she would also receive, as a part of her evening-care program, individual counseling with a therapist specializing in eating disorders. Her parents were in full agreement with the plan and indicated that they would be very active in ensuring that Jane complied with the various treatment recommendations and followed through on her commitment to pursue treatment on a continuing basis for an extended period of time.

There are a number of issues which are relevant to Jane's treatment. First, the initial assessment indicated that Jane's physical status was such that she needed further medical evaluation and treatment in a setting where she could be observed closely. It was clear that Jane had a number of problems and questions about which problems were primary, which were secondary, and which should be addressed first, and these concerns were important to her ultimate response to treatment. For many clinicians the standard rule of thumb is that substance abuse problems generally need to be treated before an individual can have any realistic opportunity to resolve other mental or emotional problems. In Jane's case, however, it is clear that the anorexia and bulimia were potentially life threatening and needed to be quickly addressed. The decision, after thorough assessment, was that she should be started in a chemical dependency program, that the anorexia and bulimia would be monitored throughout this period until she was fully free of substances, and, at that point, she would begin treatment for both problems at the same time. It was stressed, to her parents and to Jane, that progress in terms of the eating disorder would be tied to her ability to stay free from abuse of substances.

The second issue is that the successful treatment of substance abusers frequently depends on the ability of a number of providers and salient people to work together. In this case, the chemical dependency counselor effectively served not only as a therapist but also as a case manager, helping the patient move from one service to the next and combine continued enrollment in school with treatment for her substance abuse, physical difficulties, and eating disorder. The third issue is that, while the therapist felt that Jane may actually have met criteria for residential care of longer duration, a number of factors suggested that Jane could benefit from the treatment plan as devised. These included the fact that Jane was accepting of her problems and open to treatment, and that her parents were stable, influential with the patient, supportive of her treatment efforts, and willing to do what they could to ensure her continued cooperation with the treatment plan. Treating Jane as an outpatient without the supportive recovery environment would present the possibility that she would drop out of treatment prematurely, failing to make the transition from one level and type of service to the next as her treatment progressed.

Other Issues

College personnel often find themselves in a unique position to be helpful to students who are confronting substance abuse issues. They may, however, be equally likely to become part of the problem instead of being part of the solution. McMillin and Rogers (1994), in evaluating the nature of relapse in substance-abusing patients, have identified a number of ways in which therapists can inadvertently contribute to treatment failures. These fall into the following categories of behaviors: (1) power struggles, (2) defocusing on addiction, (3) devaluing sobriety, (4) mixing treatment models, (5) discouraging AA attendance, (6) encouraging harmful dependence, (7) becoming a guru, and (8) expecting relapse. These types of behaviors can be pitfalls for anyone who is in a position of managing or attempting to help substance abusers. The following are specific examples of each type of error as it might be made in working with college students.

Power Struggles Power struggles between helpers and substance abusers over tangential issues are probably a particularly likely event with young people who are actively working out identity issues, in part by rejecting what is old and familiar. Helpers can get hooked into struggles over issues that have little to do with substance abuse, see the abuser as resistant, and increase the likelihood that the individual will drop out of therapy or school. Power struggles with early adults or late adolescents often occur over their appearance, choice of acquaintances, music and literary preferences, attempts to emulate famous role models, and leisure and recreational pursuits and interests.

Defocusing on Addiction One common way that this occurs is when helpers fail to recognize the stage of change and/or recovery that best characterizes the individual. For example, helpers may identify issues such as the effects of sexual trauma, codependency, maturational difficulties, or a host of others and encourage people to begin focusing on these before they are willing or able to do so, at the same time failing to help the individual with the primary goal of addressing the substance abuse. In working with young people, a therapist or helper may see the use of chemicals as an expression of rebellion or as experimentation and fail to focus on the chemical use as a primary problem.

Devaluing Sobriety One way that this occurs in work with young substance abusers is when helpers believe that the individual is too young to be an alcoholic or drug addict and/or that too much has been made of their substance abuse. They may, either directly or indirectly, fail to validate and reinforce efforts that the young person has made to achieve a sober lifestyle.

Mixing Models There are a plethora of models for understanding substance abuse disorders and numerous techniques employed by therapists and helpers in daily practice. Helpers must be particularly careful in working with students with substance use disorders, because in late adolescence and early adulthood they may be especially sensitive to mixed messages from trusted helpers. Their stage of recovery is also an important concern, as when commitment to change is still tentative, inappropriately timed or confusing interventions can precipitate treatment dropout. An example follows.

Jerry was a young man recovering from alcoholism with two years of sobriety. He enrolled in a university intending to earn a degree which would enable him to become an alcoholism counselor. In his training, he encountered ideas questioning the disease notion of alcoholism and the value of self-help groups and promoting behavioral methods of treatment and the possibility of controlled drinking goals for some people with drinking problems. Jerry became almost an evangelistic supporter of these views and resumed drinking, with disastrous effects, particularly on his family life. As a result of an intervention (one of his professors participated in the intervention), Jerry resumed treatment for his own alcoholism and began sorting out how his exposure to these different models of alcoholism had complicated his own recovery.

Discouraging AA Attendance Young substance abusers in the early stages of addiction and recovery often have strong initial resistance to AA attendance for many reasons, not the least of which relates to their failure to accept the severity of their problems with alcohol or other substances. Such individuals can be very sensitive to any signs by helpers that they have reservations about the value of AA or the validity of aspects of AA philosophy. Such reservations may directly or indirectly sanction or encourage an individual to discontinue AA attendance. While involvement in AA is not indicated for every individual who has had problems with alcohol, it remains one of the most effective modalities for individuals who are dependent on alcohol. Helpers can, of course, allow their biases to affect their work with substance abusers in many ways. Insisting on AA attendance with resistant students, for example, can be as ineffective as discouraging AA attendance with someone who is benefiting from it.

Encouraging Harmful Dependency A common pattern for individuals who have relationships with chemically dependent people is to actually enable them to continue their substance abuse. This can be done by assuming responsibilities for the substance abuser, rescuing them from predicaments, and in a myriad of ways depriving them of the privilege of being responsible for their own behavior, thus making it possible for them to continue problematic use of chemicals. Those who are most inclined to want to help the substance abuser and who often go the extra mile to help can be easy prey for the addicted college student who is building skills such as manipulation, exploitation, and avoidance of responsibility for actions. Increased knowledge of chemical dependency will assist the nonprofessional to develop the ability to distinguish actions that can be helpful to substance abusers from those which will enable them to continue use of addictive substances.

Becoming a Guru Those in a position to help substance abusers, particularly students still dealing with such maturational issues as identity formation and individuation, need to bear in mind that it is easy to cross over from supporting and facilitating growth and recovery to inappropriate and harmful influence and a variety of forms of boundary violations. It is also not uncommon for helpers who have a large investment in the recovery of the substance abuser to lose patience quickly when the abuser does not progress at the expected rate or when the abuser relapses or proceeds in halting ways through the initial stages of change. Some helpers also find themselves taking too much credit for the progress made by substance abusers and fail to help such individuals learn and recognize their own self-efficacy. Gurus, who are human, inevitably are found to be fallible and disappoint. Individuals who have developed a sense of self-efficacy are not devastated and prone to relapse when this happens.

Expecting a Relapse In attempting to help substance abusers understand how to prevent and/or manage relapse should it occur, helpers may inadvertently give the message that relapse is to be expected, and may actually give permission for substance abusers to have occasional periods of use, or at the least set up a self-fulfilling prophecy. This can particularly be a problem in working with young abusers who do not feel defeated by chemical abuse and whose recovery skills are minimal. Thus, working with substance-abusing college students around relapse issues and relapse prevention education must be handled sensitively and skillfully.

Effectiveness of Treatment

Widespread treatment of alcoholism and other drug addictions is a relatively recent phenomenon in the United States. Treatment models, structures, and designs were developed clinically, using trial and error methods and judged in terms of what seemed to work and what could reasonably and practically be implemented in day-to-day practice. Faced with scarce resources, treatment people focused on using those resources to provide sufficient staff and adequate facilities to promote and improve patient care. Because the task of evaluating and researching the effectiveness of treatment requires significant resources and presents methodological difficulties, the development of a body of outcome literature was slow in evolving.

A number of the early studies focused on issues related to treatment setting and level of care, and, indeed, a controversy, which at times became acrimonious and contentious, developed when researchers began doing studies comparing one type of treatment to another. A number of review articles concluded that while there was evidence that treatment of alcoholism could generally be shown to have beneficial results, there was little evidence to indicate that treatment setting (specifically, inpatient vs. outpatient treatment) or intensity of treatment services were reliably related to treatment outcomes (Miller & Hester, 1986; Office of Technology Assessment, 1983; Institute of Medicine, 1989, 1990). These conclusions came at a time when pressures to reduce health-care costs accumulated at many different levels and together appear to have resulted in reduced access at all levels of care for alcoholics and other drug addicts (National Association of Addiction Treatment Providers, 1991).

There has, predictably, been a fairly intense reaction to the conclusions drawn by the early review articles. One reaction has been to more fully elucidate the many methodological difficulties which must be overcome in conducting sound evaluation of treatment outcomes and research into the effectiveness of treatment techniques. A growing number of articles deal with methodological and design issues specifically related to treatment-outcome studies of substance use disorders (Moras, 1993; Borkovec, 1993; Howard, Krause, & Lyons, 1993; Nace, 1989; Nathan & Skinstad, 1987; Sobell & Sobell, 1989; Edwards, Oppenheimer, & Taylor, 1992).

As methodological issues and problems began to be addressed, the differential effectiveness of treatments was better demonstrated. More recent studies have found, for example, that inpatient programs are more effective for blue collar workers and for workers with both alcohol and cocaine problems (Walsh et al., 1991), and that there are fewer early treatment failures in inpatient than in outpatient treatment (Pettinati, Meyers, Jensen, Kaplan, & Evans, 1993). Analysis of insurance claims of alcoholics treated on an inpatient or residential basis indicates that length of stay in treatment is related to a substantially reduced rate of readmission to a hospital for any reason during the year following treatment (National Association of Addiction Treatment Providers, 1991).

Researchers have recognized that the question of whether one form of treatment is better than another is not the relevant question and can lead to conclusions which do not hold up under closer examination. The more useful aim is to match patient, counselor, level of care, treatment goal, type of treatment interventions, and other factors and variables which result in maximum treatment benefits (Mattsen & Allen, 1991; Orford, Oppenheimer, & Edwards, 1976; McLellan, Luborsky, Woody, O'Brien, & Druley, 1983).

Given this, a number of general conclusions are reasonable. Taken as a whole, treatment of substance abuse disorders seems to be a demonstrably effective and particularly cost-effective strategy. Cost-offset studies consistently show the cost benefits of treating substance use disorders. Holder, Lennox, and Blose (1992), in their summary of research into the health-care-cost savings associated with alcoholism treatment, concluded that untreated alcoholics (employees and dependents) use health-care benefits at about twice the rate as typical insurance plan members. Following treatment, the health-care costs of alcoholics drop below pretreatment levels within two to four years and, quite possibly, eventually converge with those of typical insurance plan members.

The economic benefit of treating alcoholism is particularly pronounced for younger alcoholics. Rutgers University researchers (Langenbucher, McCrady, Brick, & Esterly, 1993) concluded that where health-care costs are concerned, treating alcoholism and probably other drug addictions will return between $2 and $10 for every $1 spent. They also point out that not only does utilization of health-care services and benefits decline for alcoholics following treatment, but it also declines for their family members. A large-scale recent study conducted by Gerstein, Johnson, Harwood, Fountain, Suter, & Malloy (1994) reports similar treatment benefits. Researchers estimated that treating individuals for chemical dependency saved $1.5 billion in the first year following treatment. These savings were attributed mostly to reductions in crime. Hospitalizations were reduced by one-third. The estimate of the ratio of benefits to costs was seven to one. Length of stay in treatment was related to positive outcomes.

A wide variety of interventions applied to substance use disorders have been shown to be effective. Among these interventions are Minnesota Model programs (Walsh et al., 1991; Pettinati et al., 1993; Harrison et al., 1991), Aversion therapy (Smith, Frawley, & Polissar, 1991), Behavior Marital therapy (McCrady, 1991), Community-Reinforcement Approach (based primarily on operant conditioning principles) (Hunt & Azrin, 1973), social skills training (Eriksen, Björnstad, & Götestam, 1986), Cognitive therapy (Beck, Wright, Newman, & Liese, 1993), Relapse Prevention therapy (Marlatt & Gordon, 1985), Antiabuse therapy (Azrin, et al., 1982), and many others.

Researchers and clinicians concerned with substance use disorders, even those coming from widely divergent perspectives and orientations, seem to be converging in several ways. There appears to be agreement that, in order to meet the needs of what really is a quite heterogeneous group of individuals, we must provide a continuum of treatment services. We need to match patients, when possible, to interventions selected from a menu of those which have demonstrated their effectiveness. Though we are still a long way from being able to do this type of patient matching with precision, we now have some guidelines and standards of practice which can be used to understand the dimensions of problems relevant to treatment planning.

Spicer (1993) describes what he calls the recovery pathways model for treatment of the chemically dependent individual. This model recognizes that people with substance abuse disorders can never be considered "fixed." Periods of progress may be interspersed with periods of difficulties or even relapse. Treatment efforts must be directed at providing services when needed and discovering ways to assess individuals' progress and needs in an ongoing fashion. Treatment services cannot be provided along a continuum which is linear; that is, from detoxification, to residential treatment, to outpatient treatment, to aftercare, and so on. Patients can be moved in any direction along the continuum of services. A patient may, for example, begin in outpatient treatment, do well, and move on to aftercare (movement from greater intensity of treatment to lesser intensity). The same patient may, however, relapse in outpatient care and be referred to residential care (a movement from lesser intensity of care to greater intensity). Again, active ongoing assessment and case management are critical elements of this model. Active case management does not mean, however, making decisions for patients, but, rather, providing them improved information and expanded options to enable them to make better decisions about their care. In short, active case management, done properly, means treating patients with increased respect.

SUMMARY AND CONCLUSIONS

College students whose substance abuse has progressed to a level which requires treatment present both common and unique therapeutic challenges. Clinical opinion and research indicate that a continuum of treatment services is necessary in order to meet the needs of substance abusers. There are a variety of treatment modalities, techniques, and interventions which have been demonstrated, either empirically or through clinical practice, to be effective with substance abusers. The clinical task is to carefully assess the needs of each individual and to match treatment plans and interventions to the specific needs of each client or patient.

Formal treatment can be brief and relatively simple in nature, or complex, long-term, and requiring significant case management and coordination. Outcome research efforts have become more sophisticated and will in the future provide clinicians with more information and guidance in terms of accomplishing the types of patient–treatment matching that will result in optimal outcomes. For now, there is considerable evidence that treatment as it is being practiced is effective and that future research can only serve to enhance our efforts.

College students present unique treatment challenges because of their age and developmental level, the recovery environment they return to, and the fact that many are in the early stages of both the addictive and change processes as understood by Prochaska and colleagues (1992). While substance abusers can present significant management problems for college personnel, knowledge of the nature and course of the disorder and the nature of treatment and change processes can greatly improve the ability to manage these problems and enhance the substance abuser's chances of recovery.

Failing to or deciding against treating substance abusers is a costly and bankrupt strategy, both in terms of perpetuating human misery and of squandering a variety of resources. In our rush to contain health-care costs it is imperative that we do not prematurely abandon treatment interventions which have been demonstrated to be effective for some of our most severely addicted individuals in favor of interventions which have not been broadly tested, clinically or empirically, but promise to save money or other resources.

There is still much to be done. Some of the tasks seem to be perpetual. It seems, for example, that we need to be vigilant about repeating that alcoholism and addiction is a disease or disorder, that those afflicted need and deserve to be treated and treated humanely, that there is much that can be done to help motivate addicted individuals to seek treatment, that the whole person needs to be treated, that punishment is not only an inappropriate response but an ineffective one, and that treatment works. There is certainly much to be learned and much we can do to improve our treatments and treatment outcomes. There is, however, a growing body of literature currently available, both empirically and clinically based, which can be useful to colleges in guiding responses to the problem of substance abuse on campus.

REFERENCES

American Society of Addiction Medicine (ASAM). (1996). *Patient placement criteria for the treatment of substance-related disorders* (2nd ed.) (ASAM PPC-2). Chevy Chase, MD: Author.

Azrin, N. H., Sisson, R. W., Meyers, R., & Godley, M. (1982). Alcoholism treatment by disulfiram and community-reinforcement therapy. *Journal of Behavior Therapy and Experimental Psychiatry, 13,* 105–112.

Beck, A. T., Wright, F. D., Newman, C. F., & Liese, B. S. (1993). *Cognitive therapy of substance abuse.* New York: Guilford Press.

Bell, T. (1993). *Motivating adolescents for treatment.* Workshop handout presented by the Cenaps Corporation, Lincoln, NE.

Black, C. (1979). *My dad loves me, my dad has a disease.* Denver: MAC.

Black, C. (1981). *It will never happen to me.* Denver: MAC.

Bloch, S. A., & Ungerleider, S. (1988). Targeting high-risk groups on campus for drug and alcohol prevention: An examination and assessment. *The International Journal of the Addictions, 23,* 299–319.

Borkovec, T. D. (1993). Between-group therapy outcome research: Design and methodology. In L. S. Onken, J. D. Blaine, & J. J. Boren (Eds.), *Behavioral treatments for drug abuse and dependence* (NIDA Research Monograph No. 137, pp. 249–289). Rockville, MD: National Institute on Drug Abuse.

Brown, S. A., Vik, P. W., & Creamer, V. A. (1989). Characteristics of relapse following adolescent substance abuse treatment. *Addictive Behaviors, 14,* 291–300.

Brown, S., & Yalom, I. D. (Eds.). (1995). *Treating alcoholism.* San Francisco: Jossey-Bass.

Cocores, J. (1991). Outpatient treatment of drug and alcohol addiction. In N. S. Miller (Ed.), *Comprehensive handbook of alcohol and drug addiction.* New York: Marcel Dekker.

Cork, M. (1969). *The forgotten children.* Toronto: Addiction Research Foundation.

Dackis, C. A., & Gold, M. S. (1991). Inpatient treatment of drug and alcohol addiction. In N. S. Miller (Ed.), *Comprehensive handbook of alcohol and drug addiction.* New York: Marcel Dekker.

DuPont, R. L. (1988). The counselor's dilemma: Treating chemical dependency at college. *Journal of college student psychotherapy: Vol. 2, no. 3/4. Alcoholism/ chemical dependency and the college student* (pp. 41–61). New York: Haworth Press.

Edwards, G., Oppenheimer, E., & Taylor, C. (1992). Hearing the noise in the system: Exploration of textual analysis as a method for studying change in drinking behaviour. *British Journal of Addiction, 87,* 73–81.

Eriksen, L., Björnstad, S., & Götestam, K. G. (1986). Social skills training in groups for alcoholics: One year treatment outcome groups and individuals. *Addictive Behaviors, 11,* 309–329.

Filstead, W. J., & Parrella, D. P. (1990). *Inpatient versus outpatient treatment for alcoholism: Examining the debate.* Park Ridge, IL: Parkside Medical Services Corporation.

Gerstein, D. R., Johnson, R. A., Harwood, H. J., Fountain, D., Suter, N., & Malloy, K. (1994). *Evaluating recovery services: The California drug and alcohol treatment assessment general report.* Sacramento: California Department of Alcohol and Drug Programs.

Gonzales, E. V. (1988). Integrated treatment approach with the chemically dependent young adult. *Journal of college student psychotherapy: Vol. 2, no. 3/4. Alcoholism/chemical dependency and the college student* (pp. 147–175). New York: Haworth Press.

Gonzalez, G. M. (1988). Theory and applications of alcohol and drug education as a means of primary prevention on the college campus. *Journal of college student psychotherapy: Vol. 2, no. 3/4. Alcoholism/chemical dependency and the college student* (pp. 89–113). New York: Haworth Press.

Harrison, P. A., Hoffmann, N. G., & Streed, S. G. (1991). Drug and alcohol addiction treatment outcome. In N. S. Miller (Ed.), *Comprehensive handbook of alcohol and drug addiction.* New York: Marcel Dekker.

Hester, R. K., & Bien, T. H. (1995). Brief treatment. In A. M. Washton (Ed.), *Psychotherapy and substance abuse: A practitioner's handbook.* New York: Guilford Press.

Hickenbottom, J. P., Bissonette, R. P., & O'Shea, R. M. (1987). Preventive medicine and college alcohol abuse. *Journal of American College Health, 36,* 67–72.

Holder, H. D., Lennox, R. D., & Blose, J. O. (1992). The economic benefits of alcoholism treatment: A summary of twenty years of research. *Journal of Employee Assistance Research, 1,* 63–82.

Howard, K. I., Krause, M. S., & Lyons, J. S. (1993). When clinical trails fail: A guide to disaggregation. In L. S. Onken, J. D. Blaine, & J. J. Boren (Eds.), *Behavioral treatments for drug abuse and dependence* (NIDA Research Monograph No. 137, pp. 291–302). Rockville, MD: National Institute on Drug Abuse.

Hunt, G. M., & Azrin, N. H. (1973). A community-reinforcement approach to alcoholism. *Behavior Research and Therapy, 11,* 91–104.

Institute of Medicine. (1989). *Prevention and treatment of alcohol problems.* Washington, DC: National Academy Press.

Institute of Medicine. (1990). *Broadening the base of treatment for alcohol problems.* Washington, DC: National Academy Press.

Jackson, J. (1954). The adjustment of the family to the crisis of alcoholism. *Quarterly Journal of Studies on Alcohol, 15,* 562–586.

Johnston, L. D., O'Malley, P. M., & Bachman, J. G. (1994). *National survey results on drug use from the monitoring the future study, 1975–1993* (NIH Publication No. 94-3809). Rockville, MD: National Institute on Drug Abuse.

Kaminer, Y., Tartar, R. E., Bukstein, O. G., & Kabene, M. (1992). Comparison between treatment completers and noncompleters among dually diagnosed substance-abusing adolescents. *Journal of American Academy of Child and Adolescent Psychiatry, 31,* 1046–1049.

Kinney, J., & Meilman, P. (1987). Alcohol use and alcohol problems: Clinical approaches for the college health service. *Journal of American College Health, 36,* 73–82.

Kivlahan, D. R., Fromme, K., Marlatt, G. A., Coppel, D. B., & Williams, E. (1990). Secondary prevention with college drinkers: Evaluation of an alcohol skills training program. *Journal of Consulting and Clinical Psychology, 58,* 805–810.

Klein, H. (1989). Helping the college student problem drinker. *Journal of College Student Development, 30,* 323–331.

Landers, D., & Hollingdale, L. (1988). Working with children of alcoholics on a college campus: A rationale and strategies for success. *Journal of college student psychotherapy: Vol. 2, no. 3/4. Alcoholism/chemical dependency and the college student* (pp. 205–222). New York: Haworth Press.

Langenbucher, J. W., McCrady, B. S., Brick, J., & Esterly, R. (1993). Executive summary. In *Socioeconomic evaluations of addictions treatment* (pp. i–iv). Piscataway, NJ: Center of Alcohol Studies, Rutgers University.

Marlatt, G. A., & Gordon J. R. (Eds.). (1985). *Relapse prevention: Maintenance strategies in the treatment of addictive behaviors.* New York: Guilford Press.

Mattsen, M. E., & Allen, J. P. (1991). Research on matching alcoholic patients to treatments: Findings, issues and implications. *Journal of Addictive Diseases, 11,* 33–49.

McCrady, B. S. (1991). Behavioral marital therapy with alcoholics. In P. A. Keller & S. R. Heyman (Eds.), *Innovations in clinical practice: A source book* (Vol. 10) (pp. 117–135). Sarasota, FL: Professional Resource Exchange.

McLellan, A. T., Grissom, G. R., Brill, P., Durell, J., Metzger, D. S., & O'Brien, C. P. (1993). Private substance abuse treatments: Are some programs more effective than others? *Journal of Substance Abuse Treatment, 10,* 243–254.

McLellan, A. T., Luborsky, L., Woody, G. E., O'Brien, C. P., & Druley, K. A. (1983). Increased effectiveness of substance abuse treatment: A prospective study of patient–treatment "matching." *Journal of Nervous and Mental Diseases, 171,* 597–605.

McMillin, S., & Rogers, R. (1994). Relapse—do therapists contribute? *Professional Counselor, 8,* 44–45.

Mental health: Does therapy help? (1995, November). *Consumer Reports,* pp. 734–739.

Miller, W. R. (1993). Behavioral treatment for drug problems: Where do we go from here? In L. S. Onken, J. D. Blaine, & J. J. Boren (Eds.), *Behavioral treatments for drug abuse and dependence* (NIDA Research Monograph No. 137, pp. 303–320). Rockville, MD: National Institute on Drug Abuse.

Miller, W. R., & Hester R. K. (1986). Inpatient alcoholism treatment: Who benefits? *American Psychologist, 41,* 794–805.

Miller, W. R., & Rollnick, S. (1991). *Motivational interviewing: Preparing people to change addictive behavior.* New York: Guilford Press.

Moras, K. (1993). Substance abuse research: Outcome measurement conundrums. In L. S. Onken, J. D. Blaine, & J. J. Boren (Eds.), *Behavioral treatments for drug abuse and dependence* (NIDA Research Monograph No. 137, pp. 217–248). Rockville, MD: National Institute on Drug Abuse.

Nace, E. P. (1989). The natural history of alcoholism versus treatment effectiveness: Methodological problems. *American Journal of Drug and Alcohol Abuse, 15,* 55–60.

Nathan, P. E., & Skinstad, A. (1987). Outcomes of treatment for alcohol problems: Current methods, problems and results. *Journal of Consulting and Clinical Psychology, 55,* 332–340.

National Association of Addiction Treatment Providers. (1991). *Treatment is the answer: A white paper on the cost effectiveness of alcoholism and drug dependency treatment.* Laguna Hills, CA: Author.

O'Connell, D. F., & Beck, T. (1984). An involuntary therapeutic group for alcohol abusers. *Journal of College Student Personnel, 25,* 547–549.

Office of Technology Assessment. (1983). *The effectiveness and costs of alcoholism treatment.* (SUDOC no.Y3.T 22/2iC 82/2/ case No. 22). Washington, DC: Author.

Orford, J., Oppenheimer, E., & Edwards, G. (1976). Abstinence or control: The outcome for excessive drinkers two years after consultation. *Behavior Research and Therapy, 14,* 409–418.

Pettinati, H. M., Meyers, K., Jensen, J. M., Kaplan, F., & Evans, B. D. (1993). Inpatient vs. outpatient treatment for substance dependence revisited. *Psychiatric Quarterly, 64,* 173–182.

Prochaska, J. O., DiClemente, C. C., & Norcross, J. C. (1992). In search of how people change: Applications to the addictive behaviors. *American Psychologist, 47,* 1102–1114.

Raniseski, J. M., & Sigelman, C. K. (1992). Conformity, peer pressure, and adolescent receptivity to treatment for substance abuse: A research note. *Journal of Drug Education, 22,* 185–194.

Rollnick, S., & Morgan, M. (1995). *Motivational interviewing: Increasing readiness for change.* In A. M. Washton (Ed.), *Psychotherapy and substance abuse: A practitioner's handbook.* New York: Guilford Press.

Seligman, M. E. (1995). The effectiveness of psychotherapy: The *Consumer Reports* study. *American Psychologist, 50,* 965–974.

Smith, J. W., Frawley, P. J., & Polissar, L. (1991). Six- and twelve-month abstinence rates in inpatient alcoholics treated with aversion therapy compared with matched inpatients from a treatment registry. *Alcoholism: Clinical and Experimental Research, 15,* 862–870.

Sobell, L. C., & Sobell, M. B. (1989). Treatment outcome evaluation methodology with alcohol abusers: Strengths and key issues. *Advances in Behavior Research and Therapy, 11,* 151–160.

Spicer, J. (1993). *The Minnesota model.* Center City, MN: Hazelden Foundation.

Suchman, D., & Broughton, E. (1988). Treatment alternatives for university students with substance use/abuse problems. *Journal of college student psychotherapy: Vol. 2, no. 3/4. Alcoholism/chemical dependency and the college student* (pp. 131–146). New York: Haworth Press.

Valliant, G. E. (1983). *The natural history of alcoholism: Causes, patterns and paths to recovery.* Cambridge: Harvard University Press.

Walfish, S., Massey, R., & Krone, A. (1990). MMPI profiles of adolescent substance abusers in treatment. *Adolescence, 25,* 567–572.

Walsh, D. C., Hingson, R. W., Merrigan, D. M., Levenson, S. M., Cupples, A., Heeren, T., Coffman, G. A., Becker, C. A., Barker, T. A., Hamilton, S. K., McGuire, T. G., & Kelly, C. A. (1991). A randomized trial of treatment options for alcohol-abusing workers. *The New England Journal of Medicine, 325,* 775–782.

Washton, A. M. (Ed.). (1995). *Psychotherapy and substance abuse: A practitioner's handbook.* New York: Guilford Press.

White, W. T., & Mee-Lee, D. (1988). Substance use disorder and college students: Inpatient treatment issues—A model of practice. *Journal of college student psychotherapy: Vol. 2, no. 3/4. Alcoholism/chemical dependency and the college student* (pp. 177–203). New York: Haworth Press.

Wilson, P. H. (Ed.). (1992). *Principles and practice of relapse prevention.* New York: Guilford Press.

11

The Role of Self-Help Groups in College Students' Recovery from Substance Abuse and Related Problems

Gary Lawson and Ann Lawson

College administrators and mental health professionals working with college students can use self-help groups as a major adjunct to the counseling and therapy they offer. Self-help groups have many advantages, including cost (usually free) and availability (often available twenty-four hours a day). They have been proven to be effective in helping individuals with difficulties ranging from drug or alcohol problems to eating disorders or adjustment to growing up in a dysfunctional family. Referral to a self-help group can often be an easy answer for college counselors. However, like all approaches to psychological and emotional problems, one approach does not work for all; careful referral can make the difference between a successful outcome and a less than positive result. This chapter is designed to help the reader make appropriate referrals by gaining an understanding of the different self-help groups that deal with substance abuse problems.

Today there are numerous self-help groups available for support in overcoming many addictions and related problems. Alcoholics Anonymous is perhaps the most well-known of these groups, but there are many others that have followed this model. These include Overeaters Anonymous (OA), Cocaine Anonymous (CA), Narcotics Anonymous, Gamblers Anonymous (GA), Alanon, Alateen, Adult Children of Alcoholics (ACA), Codependents Anonymous (CODA), Sex and Love Addicts Anonymous (SLAA), Rational Recovery (RR), Self-Management and Recovery Training (SMART), Women for Sobriety (WFS), Secular Organization for Sobriety (SOS), and a host of other groups. Many of these groups followed the AA model closely, making only a few changes in the wording of the steps. Overeaters Anonymous, for example, substitutes "food" for "alcohol" in their twelve steps. Other groups, such as Women for Sobriety, have departed further by rewriting the steps to more closely reflect the needs of their members. Rational Recovery and SMART have made a more significant departure, basing their philosophies on Rational Emotive Therapy, created by Dr. Albert Ellis (1979).

These types of self-help groups have a common focal concern in their members' obsessive preoccupation with something or someone to the point that it has taken over a major part of their lives. Overeaters are obsessed with food, Alanon members with alcoholics, SLAA members with sex and love. Often these obsessions began as a way to deal with pain and anxiety or to try to stop another person's addiction, but they grew in intensity until they became problems in their own right. For many, their lives became unmanageable and these obsessive behaviors became part of a problem which may also sustain and contribute to a family addiction cycle (Lawson, Peterson, & Lawson, 1983). Since alcoholism and other addictions are problems that, in some families, transmit from generation to generation, people from the same family may be attending several different self-help groups. For example, the alcoholic father may be attending AA, the mother Alanon, the adolescent Alateen, and the older child an ACA group. Several of these groups could be useful to a college population. Students with their own drug or alcohol problem could attend AA, NA, or CA, while students who have lived with alcoholics or drug addicts might benefit from Alanon, ACA groups, or Codependents Anonymous. A good self-help referral system could enhance any comprehensive drug and alcohol program on the college campus.

Perhaps the primary reasons for the wide acceptance of these programs are that they are readily available, they are free, they are simple to use, and they are flexible enough to be used in a manner that seems appropriate to the individual in need of them. These programs are supposed to be programs of attraction; attendance is usually voluntary. In some cases, however, judges or probation officers require individuals to attend meetings. What these individuals take from the meetings and how they utilize what they have seen and heard is up to each one—which makes the program seem more voluntary.

The basic reason that people who attend twelve-step programs are able to change their behavior is that they learn to believe that they can change. Before there is a behavior change, however, there must be motivation to change, which is usually precipitated by some negative consequence of their behavior. These consequences usually come from family members, employers, health problems, or law enforcement agencies. Among college students the consequences may take the form of failing grades or disciplinary referrals.

Motivation may be the most important factor in the treatment of adolescent and college-age substance abusers, as they usually believe that they can do anything they choose to do, including giving up drugs or alcohol without help. In addition, young adults may be fleeing their alcoholic or addict families by going off to college and may believe they have escaped all of their problems. At this stage in their development they are unaware of how their family environment may have affected their lives and their futures. They may not identify themselves as alcoholics, addicts, ACAs, or codependents. The counselor or referring person on campus may need to help the student identify the problem and help him or her accept the need for help prior to making a referral to a self-help or twelve-step group.

WHY SELF-HELP IS USEFUL

The most obvious reason that self-help groups are therapeutic is that they offer support from people with similar problems. Isolation and secrecy is often a compounding factor in addictions, and it is very freeing for a person with a problem to know that he or she is not alone in battling it, and that there is a place where he or she can speak freely about the struggle to overcome the problem. The group members also have many years of experience living with the problem and trying to overcome it. What they bring is called experiential knowledge, as opposed to professional or scientific knowledge about the problem. The experiential knowledge and understanding developed in self-help groups is specialized and different from that of professionals or lay social supports (Borkman, 1990).

Borkman (1990) lists thirteen hallmarks of self-help groups:

1. Knowledge and a frame of reference are developed by a group of people who share a common problem or predicament. It is not developed by people individually.
2. This knowledge and frame of reference is developed in a process in which individuals tell their personal stories to their peers, talking about their pain, struggles, and feelings. These stories link the personal struggle to a larger context that includes more than the individual.
3. Members also share their strength and hope with each other as they explain how they have overcome their difficulties. The inspiration of hope is an important outcome of all group therapies, brought on in part by a shift in the self-identity of the group participant from a victim or "damaged goods" to one who survives or even prevails.
4. Members take personal responsibility for their change, but use the group for support. Belonging to a group of peers with the same struggle creates self-empowerment.
5. In sharing stories with their peers, members identify the commonalties and uniquenesses of their experiences, and can learn from the ways veterans of the group have solved common problems.
6. The content of the stories that create the learning and awareness in the group members is often in the realm of the emotions as opposed to the cognitive or intellectual spheres. This emotional knowledge is not just about the pain of the problem but also concerns how the member got the motivation to address the problem honestly, to take responsibility for it, and to change it.
7. Of great interest to the group members are existential, philosophical, or transcendental meanings of their experiences. This can range from secular philosophical

issues to the twelve-step emphasis on spiritual concerns, which can be expressed in religious terms and often involves a higher power.

8. The experiential knowledge of the members is not just the raw experience of the problem, but is an awareness that is a result of a reflexive internalized process that creates learning from this experience.

9. Experiential knowledge is transmitted through action, not just words. Members must be role models for newcomers to the groups, which is more useful than providing advice.

10. A "culture" is likely to develop over time as the group evolves a consciousness based on their common experiences. Group members develop a common language and inside jokes that are foreign to outsiders.

11. As part of the resolution of the problem, members change their identity and refashion their name, identity, and characteristics that are different from the stigmatizing stereotypes of the society.

12. In varying degrees, members extend their concern to others who are not members of their group. They may lobby for political changes or advocate to overcome stereotypes, injustice, discrimination, intolerance, and stigma. The scope and degree of their activity varies considerably.

13. Those outside of the groups cannot necessarily understand or appreciate the experiential knowledge of the group members or their use of the "language of the heart." They may undervalue this experiential awareness when they compare it to rational, objective knowledge.

Though the experiential knowledge of the self-help groups is therapeutic and different from professional help, the two are not mutually exclusive. One can enhance the other if each recognizes the strengths and resources of the other. Self-help groups that are antagonistic to professionals are eliminating a different but very useful tool to their recovery. Professionals who are antagonistic to self-help groups are limiting their chance for successful treatment. Clearly, professionals have more training in research and scientific method, but self-help groups can give a distinctive kind of help, including the following:

• Emotional support from the special bonds that form among members.
• Emotional reassurance that the members are not alone.
• Role modeling by veterans, whose examples give hope.
• Assessment of how professional knowledge can be applied to one's life.
• Advocacy for the perspectives, interests, and concerns of the group (Borkman, 1990).

THE TWELVE-STEP PHILOSOPHY

The most widely known self-help group for the treatment of addictions is Alcoholics Anonymous. AA is a good example of a self-help group that meets the criteria discussed. In the late 1930s, the founders of AA devised a set of principles, known as the twelve steps, to help alcoholics achieve sobriety

(Alcoholics Anonymous, 1976). The twelve steps of AA are the basis for nearly all the other twelve-step programs. They are as follows:

1. We admitted we were powerless over alcohol—that our lives had become un-manageable.
2. Came to believe that a Power greater than ourselves could restore us to sanity.
3. Made a decision to turn our will and our lives over to the care of God *as we understood Him.*
4. Made a searching and fearless moral inventory of ourselves.
5. Admitted to God, to ourselves, and to another human being the exact nature of our wrongs.
6. Were entirely ready to have God remove all these defects of character.
7. Humbly asked Him to remove our shortcomings.
8. Made a list of all persons we had harmed, and became willing to make amends to them all.
9. Made direct amends to such people wherever possible, except when to do so would injure them or others.
10. Continued to take personal inventory and when we were wrong, promptly admit-ted it.
11. Sought through prayer and meditation to improve our conscious contact with God *as we understood Him,* praying only for knowledge of His will for us and the power to carry that out.
12. Having had a spiritual awakening as the result of these steps, we tried to carry this message to alcoholics and to practice these principles in all our affairs.

As stated earlier, Alcoholics Anonymous has been the model for twelve-step groups that have followed. The application of AA's twelve steps to other disorders has not, however, been uniformly useful. Rewording the steps—designed to help AA members stay sober—to apply, perhaps, to people with relationship problems or even to children of alcoholics may result in ele-ments that do not quite address members' needs. For example, it is not neces-sarily useful to adults whose parents are alcoholic to make amends to others.

In the beginning, AA's basic tenets were that only an alcoholic could help another alcoholic and that psychiatric or other treatment of alcoholics was usually unsuccessful (Cain, 1964). By banding together in a spirit of mutual help and understanding and by turning their lives over to God as they under-stood Him, alcoholics could manage to lead relatively normal lives. Above all, alcoholics were expected to face the fact that they must never again take even one drink; it was an explicit AA belief that once an alcoholic, always an alcoholic (Cain, 1964). For the first five years of its existence, AA had no more than a few hundred members, almost all of whom were middle-age, middle-class white men. In 1941, after the famous reporter Jack Alexander wrote an article about AA for the *Saturday Evening Post,* membership leaped to more than eight thousand (Cain, 1964). Today, the number of AA members is reported to be close to two million (Kurtz, 1990). It must be noted, however, that estimates of membership could be overstated; one person may participate in several groups and be counted several times. Nevertheless, AA and other twelve-step programs have had a major impact on our society. The movement, which Reverend Arnold Lugar referred to as a "Twentieth Century revelation of the Holy Spirit to counteract the emotional problems which our present pace of living is producing in plague-like proportions" (Emotions Anonymous, 1978, p.14), has apparently filled some need that more traditional institutions (e.g., church and family) had not been meeting.

Although AA has been credited with beginning the disease concept of alcoholism, AA's founders attempted to avoid the controversy by using the word "malady" when referring to alcoholism. Most members of AA do, however, believe that alcoholism is a disease. The most popular and most often repeated definition of alcoholism is that it is "a physical allergy, coupled with a mental compulsion" (Cain, 1964, p. 69). Most members of AA believe that alcoholism is not a "mental disorder"; they prefer to believe that "there is nothing wrong with alcoholics except alcohol."

There seems to be some disagreement about the relationship of the disease concept to compulsive drug use. Members of Narcotics Anonymous seldom view themselves as vulnerable to alcoholism, or actively alcoholic, and have been known to claim that they can drink without abusing. In contrast, today most AA members have abused other drugs as well and believe that they must abstain from all substance use. Those who identify with one group often view members of the other as somehow different, despite the fact that both groups use a twelve-step approach to recovery. Most treatment professionals also see addiction to one substance as the same as addiction to another.

THERAPEUTIC ASPECTS OF A TWELVE-STEP MODEL

Some of the therapeutic value of a twelve-step program is obvious; some of it is not quite so evident. Much of the therapeutic value of a twelve-step model comes from the steps themselves. For example, the first step—of admitting powerlessness—is the same as recognizing and admitting the problem. Most emotional, psychological, or behavioral problems improve when the person with these problems acknowledges them. This is simple on the surface, but the therapeutic dynamics of the first step are very complex and go far beyond just admitting to the problem. The real therapeutic value has to do with etiological issues of addiction, particularly the issue of control. Alcoholics drink to demonstrate their control of drinking, even when they know that they have lost control. Paradoxically, it is only by giving up control, admitting powerlessness, and turning the problem over to a "Higher Power" that the addicted person is able to regain control of his or her life. This is one of many paradoxes in a twelve-step program to promote therapeutic change.

Steps 1, 2, and 3 are designed to help the individual admit the problem, ask for help, and turn the problem over to a Higher Power. This is surrender, a letting go of trying to control that which cannot be controlled. It is not, as some may think, an abdication of responsibility for oneself. AA believes that members who follow the twelve steps will have a spiritual awakening that will lead to serenity (Kurtz, 1990). This letting go is not bad advice for any such problem.

Steps 4 through 10 are designed to deal with the guilt that alcoholics or addicts often feel for the problems they have caused others. In some cases, alcoholics drink to relieve guilt feelings, only to feel more guilty after they sober up and drink again because of the guilt. The cycle never ends, and there is always an excuse to drink or to use drugs. Steps 4 through 10 also help the alcoholic or addict deal with anger by acknowledging his or her part in it and asking for forgiveness from the other party. These steps are intended to improve the quality of the member's sobriety, which is not just abstinence from alcohol and/or other compulsions, but a fundamental change in thinking and acting (Kurtz, 1990).

Step 11 encourages the person to stay with the program and to continue the self-evaluation, while Step 12 asks the individual to carry the message to other alcoholics and to practice the twelve steps in all activities. Step 12 is one of the most therapeutic of all the steps. Not only does it provide another chance to reduce guilt for past behavior, it enables the alcoholic to build self-esteem by helping another person.

Another major therapeutic aspect of a twelve-step program is the group interaction. The things that make any group helpful to an individual—empathy, support, encouragement—happen very often in twelve-step groups. Groups may be harmful as well as helpful, however. With more than thirty-six thousand different AA groups in the United States alone, there are bound to be some groups that are not always helpful for all who attend (Lawson, Ellis, & Rivers, 1984). Groups are like families: Some are good for all, some are good for a few, and some are bad for everyone.

A new participant in a twelve-step program usually selects a sponsor from the group, someone who has a solid sobriety and can act as an individual guide. The sponsor helps the new member on an individual basis as needed. The idea is that the new member will benefit from the experience of the member who has been sober longer. Members can keep their sponsors as long as they wish; some keep them for life. Again, although the sponsor can be a source of strength, some caution is necessary. Not everyone has the ability to be therapeutic for another human being. In fact, there are individuals with the best of intentions who often give harmful advice to others or are just emotionally unavailable in a time of need.

One final therapeutic benefit of AA and most other twelve-step programs is their availability. If there is a telephone close at hand, there is someone to call twenty-four hours a day. If an alcoholic feels like drinking or an addict like using, there is usually a meeting being held nearby. This ready availability is the reason that so many treatment programs recommend AA or other twelve-step programs as a major part of their aftercare plans.

TWELVE-STEP MEETINGS

Much of the activity of AA goes on in regularly scheduled meetings, often held in church basements or other public buildings. A list of meeting sites is available from the AA Central Office in each city. There are two basic formats to AA meetings, with minor variations. A speaker's meeting involves one person telling his or her story, usually describing what he or she was like while drinking and how he or she has changed (AA, 1957). Members benefit from hearing the pain of one person's alcoholism, how the person hit bottom, and how he or she applied the twelve steps to his or her life. The second type of meeting is a step study or topic meeting. One person is the chair of the meeting and talks about how the topic relates to his or her life. Then other group members share their personal experiences with the topic or step.

At step and speaker's meetings, usually only members or potential members speak; there are open meetings where visitors are welcome. These open meetings are good opportunities for counselors who refer to these groups to directly observe the group. Visitors do not have to speak at the meetings or identify themselves as having problems.

Groups can vary in their types of members and meeting structures and topics. It would be helpful for counselors working with a college population to have a list of groups that have members in this age range and talk about topics that are relevant to these students. Starting or sponsoring groups on the college campus is one way to ensure the availability of appropriate resources. Even a small group of students may be more beneficial than a large group of older adults. Some innovative possibilities might include combining AA and ACA, thus creating a setting for students who came from alcoholic families and are currently experiencing problems with alcohol. The school counseling center or student assistance program could provide space and support for these group meetings.

Between meetings, AA members are expected to talk with their sponsors and other members and to read the AA literature. The best-known source of information is AA's "Big Book," which discusses alcoholism and the AA program. (It is called the Big Book because it was first printed, in 1939, on very thick paper in order to convince people during the Depression Era that it was worth its selling price of $2.50 [Kurtz, 1979].) Other twelve-step programs have developed Big Books that also focus on the stories of their recovering members.

Other hallmarks of AA come from their Twelve Traditions, which are guides concerning the AA philosophy. The Twelve Traditions are as follows:

1. Our common welfare should come first; personal recovery depends AA upon unity.
2. For our group purpose there is but one ultimate authority—a loving God. He may express Himself in our group conscience. Our leaders are but trusted servants; they do not govern.
3. The only requirement for AA membership is a desire to stop drinking.
4. Each group should be autonomous except in matters affecting other groups or AA as a whole.
5. Each group has but one primary purpose—to carry its message to the alcoholic who still suffers.
6. An AA group ought never endorse, finance or lend the AA name to any related facility or outside enterprise, lest problems of money, property and prestige divert us from our primary purpose.
7. Every group ought to be fully self-supporting, declining outside contributions.
8. Alcoholics Anonymous should remain forever nonprofessional, but our service centers may employ special workers.
9. AA, as such, ought never be organized; but we may create service boards or committees directly responsible to those they serve.
10. Alcoholics Anonymous has no opinion on outside issues; hence the AA name ought never be drawn into public controversy.
11. Our public relations policy is based on attraction rather than promotion; we need always maintain personal anonymity at the level of press, radio and films.
12. Anonymity is the spiritual foundation of all our Traditions, ever reminding us to place principles before personalities.

The Traditions keep groups focused on their main purpose, that of supporting people who wish to achieve sobriety. They discourage affiliation with any other organization or professionals and help groups avoid involvement in controversial issues. Groups should be autonomous and self-supporting. That is, they should not accept money or support from other sources. Anonymity is asked of AA members, who do not use their last names in meetings. This anonymity serves the purpose of protecting "the fellowship from negative publicity that may later befall the member and reminds him or her that, within the fellowship, principles come before personalities" (Kurtz, 1990, p. 104). Anonymity is viewed as more an issue of humility than of the protection of the member's confidentiality. A member of NA wrote, "The drive for personal gain in the areas of sex, property and social position, which brought so much pain in the past, falls by the wayside if we adhere to the principle of anonymity" (Narcotics Anonymous, 1987, p. 69).

CRITICISMS OF TWELVE-STEP PROGRAMS

Kurtz (1990) noted four major criticisms of AA and the other twelve-step programs: (1) Attachment to AA or another twelve-step group is an acting out of intrapsychic pathology (in other words, people exchange one addiction for another); (2) the groups are antiscience and antiprofessional; (3) the groups have never been proved effective; and (4) AA, specifically, is culturally inappropriate for other than middle-class white men. There are perhaps different degrees of truth in all these criticisms. Alcoholics Anonymous, in particular, has been taken to task in the literature many times over the years (Kalb & Popper, 1976; Tournier, 1979); it has even been compared to a cult, as long as thirty years ago (Cain, 1964). The problem with criticizing this type of organization is that many people owe their very lives to it, and they perceive any critical remarks against the program as a personal attack or as a threat to their sobriety.

Compulsive AA attendance without working the program (that is, not actively using the twelve steps and the assistance of a sponsor to make psychological and behavioral changes) is similar to an addiction. People who attend meetings and do not make changes in thinking and behaving may be hiding from life or from their families, just as they did with alcohol, other substances, or compulsions. Some members believe that reducing the number of meetings attended or "growing out of the program" and not needing the regular support of the meetings is a sign of impending relapse, and thus may pressure others to keep the same heavy schedule of meetings that was needed in early sobriety but may not be needed in later stages of recovery. Recovery, however, is a process, and progress toward health in all areas is the goal, not hiding from these problems.

The criticism of AA as antiprofessional has its roots in historical failures of psychoanalysis used to treat alcoholism. Many alcoholics died in treatment, looking for the underlying causes of their addiction while they continued to drink. Psychologists and mental health counselors have been less than eager to treat this population, leaving the bulk of treatment to paraprofessional counselors, many of whom are themselves recovering alcoholics or substance abusers. As more states require training in substance abuse in order for agencies to be licensed, and as colleges and universities add courses in this area, more professionals are becoming interested in treating substance abuse. Faced with dwindling treatment dollars and increasing competition from professionals, mistrust of professionals remains an issue for some in AA.

Clearly, AA has been effective for many people in overcoming their addictions. For these people there is no need for actual outcome or comparison studies of different treatment approaches. The idea that "what worked for me will work for you" does not necessarily encourage scientific inquiry into important questions, such as when AA works, why it works, whom it works for, and why it does not always work. A favorite cliche in the AA community is, "Utilize; don't analyze." That may be useful advice for a new member of AA, but not for treatment personnel who are trying to provide the best treatment regimen for an individual. For the latter, it is scientific and useful to analyze.

Most of the research that is available on the effectiveness of twelve-step programs has been conducted with AA or NA members. The few studies that have been done have, however, had many methodological problems. There has been a lack of agreement on the meaning of affiliation with such groups, as well as a lack of valid measures to assess the characteristics under investigation (McCrady & Irvine, 1989). Research on AA has primarily consisted of commentaries and summaries of available correlational data (Glaser & Ogborne, 1982; Kurtz, 1982; Emrick, 1987). Both correlational and controlled studies have suggested a relationship between AA attendance and more severe symptoms if the AA member relapses (Brandsma, Maultsby, & Welsh, 1980; Ogborne & Bornet, 1982; Walker, Sanchez-Craig, & Bornet, 1982).

Because of the lack of research on AA, it is difficult to know who is most likely to benefit from the program. The research "is not currently developed enough to provide us with a composite profile of the most likely AA affiliates" (Emrick, Tonigan, Montgomery, & Little, 1993, p. 53). As people who have freely chosen to attend meetings and to remain involved in the program, AA members are also not representative of all alcoholics (Galanter, Castaneda, & Franco, 1991). Their experience with AA cannot, therefore, be generalized to alcoholics who have chosen not to attend or not to continue attending. AA attendance also does not guarantee sobriety. At least half of new members of AA stop attending within three months, and 90 percent drop out by the end of a year (Miller & McCrady, 1993). Of those who continue in AA, only 70 percent of those who were sober for a year stay sober for a second year, and 90 percent of those who make it through the second year do not make the third (Doweiko, 1996).

Perhaps because of the lack of conclusive research on AA, some members have become very dogmatic about AA being the only real way to achieve sobriety. One of the major critics of AA is a newer group, Rational Recovery, which offers an alternative approach to alcoholism based on the principles of Rational Emotive Behavioral Therapy as developed by Dr. Albert Ellis (1979). One of the major complaints that the members of RR have about AA is its perceived status as the "only" alternative for the treatment of alcoholism. They see AA as a religious sect that has unlawfully become the "only" referral source for many city, state, and federal law enforcement and mental health care agencies. There may be many court cases before the matter is resolved.

The criticism that AA reflects a bias toward middle-class white men and is less effective for women, lower socioeconomic individuals, and members of ethnic groups has led to the development of alternative groups, such as Women for Sobriety for women and specialized AA groups for members of ethnic minorities, gays and lesbians, and so on. Minorities and women can receive help in twelve-step groups, but some people may object to parts of the program. Hudson (1985–1986) studied AA groups in Harlem and concluded that they were successful because the spiritual values of AA were compatible with the traditional culture of blacks. However, ethnic groups such as Native Americans, whose religion varies from Judeo-Christian beliefs, may have more difficulty with the AA philosophy and its emphasis on spirituality. This problem has also occurred for Jewish alcoholics and atheists (Kurtz, 1990).

ADULT CHILDREN OF ALCOHOLICS GROUPS

Additional problems have occurred when the AA twelve steps have been applied to problems that are not substance addictions, such as Adult Children of Alcoholics support groups. The problems that children of alcoholics suffer from are more in the area of relationship and are more closely related to psychological problems than true addictions like substance abuse. ACAs are more victims than perpetrators. They were children who were dependent on their alcoholic parents for survival. Children in these families often blame themselves for their parents' problems, because to do so gives them a sense of control over the uncontrollable. If they are flawed, then they can fix themselves, thus fixing the family. They may even be told by the alcoholic parents that their behaviors or lack of behaviors caused the former to drink.

Many of the behaviors of children of alcoholics began as adaptive responses to a chaotic environment. These behaviors became problematic for them as adults when they no longer serve this survival function. For instance, not trusting or not expressing feelings kept these children from disappointment and abuse in their alcoholic families. Trusting and expressing feelings, however, are good skills for adults who wish to have intimate relationships.

For many ACAs it does not seem appropriate to perpetuate this self-blame by admitting defects of character or making amends to people they have harmed (Steps 8 and 9). The goal for these ACAs is to stop blaming themselves for something they did not cause and cannot cure. Another danger of ACA groups is the process that occurs when members shift blame from themselves to their parents. This shift can lead to meetings full of parent-bashing without the therapeutic benefit of taking responsibility for self. If this becomes a group norm, the group can become stuck in this stage of recovery, believing that they can only belong if they see themselves as damaged by their parents. These stuck groups need to move their members toward taking personal responsibility for their current lives and future growth.

Currently, the epidemic wave of enthusiasm for ACA groups has dwindled to a small pool of struggling groups. This is probably reflective of the stages of the movement. The early stages of the movement excited millions of adults who, for the first time in their lives, connected their current problems with growing up in an alcoholic or dysfunctional family. Identification, however, is not sufficient for recovery. While the goal of AA is to support lifelong abstinence on a daily basis and maintain the identity of alcoholic, the goal of ACA is to help the members to identify their issues, resolve them, and grow out of the ACA label. ACA issues are vastly different from alcoholic or addict issues; the processes of recovery should also be different. While AA attendance may be needed for a lifetime, prolonged ACA group attendance may only keep people from truly recovering.

ACA groups may not be appropriate for all people who grew up in alcoholic families. Some may benefit from individual or group psychotherapy, and some may not need any treatment. There has, in addition, been a recent shift in the literature toward studying resilient ACAs—those who turned their difficult childhood experiences into personal strengths and resiliencies (Wolin & Wolin, 1993). Counselors wishing to refer an ACA to a support group should visit several groups to observe whether they would be helpful or harmful. Referral to a therapy group run by a licensed professional mental health provider may be more beneficial.

TWELVE-STEP PROGRAMS AND OTHER THERAPIES

The success of any effort to integrate twelve-step programs with other therapeutic approaches depends a great deal on the therapist involved. The therapist's philosophy regarding substance abuse or addiction is critical. Even such diverse approaches as those of AA and behavioral therapy can be integrated. Despite the substantial disagreements between these two approaches, particularly around the issue of controlled drinking versus total abstinence as a treatment goal, they have many aspects in common, such as the role of skills acquisition, affective change, cognitive change, and the use of social supports. Both approaches emphasize avoiding drinking environments, developing interests and activities incompatible with drinking, developing skills to use when alcohol is present, and having clearly defined behaviors to draw on when experiencing a desire to drink (McCrady & Irvine, 1989).

If the therapist understands twelve-step programs and can support the student's use of such a program, most individual therapy is compatible with a twelve-step program. It is important that the therapist and the student agree on the goals for therapy and on the usefulness of a twelve-step program. It is not therapeutic to have the therapist say one thing and the twelve-step sponsor or other group members say something else or say things that run counter to the therapist's suggestions. Most twelve-step members have accepted the value of therapy from a professional therapist. One way to combat the potential triangle of the therapist, client, and sponsor is to invite the sponsor (with the client's consent) to a therapy session so the therapist and sponsor can become allies in the process of recovery with the single goal of helping the client or member. This also reduces the chance of the client misinforming the sponsor of the therapist's advice and misinterpreting the sponsor's advice to the therapist.

Group therapy and twelve-step meetings are usually offered in the same treatment program, but the rules of conduct and the goals are different for each modality. Group therapy should not become a twelve-step meeting, nor should twelve-step meetings become therapy groups. The latter is particularly true, because there is no trained therapist available to intervene if the group situation should become therapeutically harmful. The therapist should be the controlling agent in group therapy; experienced members, general rules, and the principles of the organization usually control twelve-step meetings.

Family therapists would benefit from an understanding of other twelve-step groups available for family members, such as Alanon and Codependents Anonymous. Recently, there has been a growth and development of family therapy as a major treatment approach for addiction. Davis (1980) pointed out the similarities between AA and family therapy and suggested ways in which they might be mutually reinforcing. He stated that cessation of drinking should be the first goal in family treatment and, in general, family therapists have agreed (Bepko, 1985). Both approaches also agree that the alcoholic's drinking and resulting behavior have a profound effect on the other family members who need treatment and support themselves.

SOME NEW SELF-HELP GROUPS

With the acceptance of twelve-step programs by treatment professionals and the popular press, it is easy to believe that they work for just about everyone. Despite their growing popularity, however, the numbers are still not good. For example, if AA has 2 million members and there are more than 20 million people with alcohol problems in the United States, AA reaches fewer than one in ten people with an alcohol problem. There are many reasons for this limited range. Some people with alcohol problems are not ready for the kind of help that AA has to offer. They may not believe that they have a disease or that their problem is bad enough to require outside help. The concept of the higher power dissuades some from attending AA. As stated earlier, young adults and adolescents in the first phases of substance abuse may find it hard to relate to the older alcoholic or addict who has years of abuse. In these cases, students should be referred to groups made up entirely of college students or young adults, or alternatives to the twelve-step approach should be used.

Alternatives to twelve-step models include those devised by groups such as Rational Recovery and SMART, or groups for special segments of the population such as Women of Sobriety. Rational Recovery Systems, founded in 1986, is a national self-help organization whose purpose is to make recovery services widely available and free of charge to chemically dependent individuals, including those struggling with dependencies on alcohol, drugs, and food. The groups are open to those individuals and others interested in learning more about Rational Recovery for themselves or those they care for. RR is based on the principles of rational emotive therapy (RET), a widely accepted system of psychotherapy originated by Dr. Albert Ellis. It is not a step program like AA. It is a learning process in which a person defeats the primary dependency and gains mastery of other dependencies. RR provides a potent strategy, Addictive Voice Recognition Training (AVRT), for achieving lifetime abstinence from the offending substance. People who are interested in this approach can gain more information from Jack Trimpey's (1989) book, *The Small Book: A Revolutionary Alternative for Overcoming Alcohol and Drug Dependence*, which is available at most bookstores. Another useful book is *The Final Fix: AVRT* by Jack Trimpey, published by Lotus Press.

Recently, the Rational Recovery Self-Help Network Board, a nonprofit network of self-help meetings for recovery from addictive behavior, changed its name to Self Management and Recovery Training and decided to develop its own approach based on scientific research and Ellis's rational emotive therapy. SMART attempts to translate into a self-help format the findings of scientific research, especially research in cognitive–behavioral psychology. SMART's goal is to identify research findings which can help individuals overcome addictive behavior, and to continue to revise the SMART program in light of new research findings.

The SMART program currently focuses on the following:

1. Enhancing (and maintaining) motivation to change addictive behavior.
2. Responding to urges (cravings) without action on them.
3. Developing new ways to cope with other problems (which previously were coped with using addictive behavior).
4. Developing a positive, healthy lifestyle (in order to prevent relapse).

Some of the tools of SMART are as follows:

1. Making an evaluation of your substance use policy.
2. Becoming aware of destructive self-talk and how you can counter it.
3. Using REBT (rational emotive behavioral therapy) and/or cognitive therapy as a way to deal with unwanted emotions or low self-esteem.
4. Learning relaxation and meditation methods, which are useful if anxiety is a problem.
5. Learning to rehearse your responses in high-risk situations.
6. Devising a different lifestyle, one that is satisfying and less likely to cause relapse or ongoing boredom.
7. When drinking or using is no longer a necessary part of life, you may want to make a lifetime commitment to abstinence.

Books that may be helpful include *When AA Doesn't Work for You* by Albert Ellis and Emmit Velten, Barricade Books, Fort Lee, NJ, 1992; *Alcohol: How to Give It Up and Be Glad You Did* by Philip Tate, Rational Self-Help Press, Altamonte Springs, FL, 1993; and *The New Guide to Rational Living* by Albert Ellis and Robert Harper, Wilshire Book Company, Hollywood, CA, 1975.

Another alternative group is the Secular Organizations for Sobriety. It was also founded, in 1986, as a program that does not place emphasis on spirituality, for people who took offense to the heavy emphasis on spirituality of

AA. SOS places emphasis on personal responsibility and critical thinking. Members struggle to identify how to break their personal "cycle of addiction" (Doweiko, 1996).

Women for Sobriety, another alternative group, was founded in 1975. It addresses the issue that the AA program fails to see the very real differences between men and women. Women for Sobriety has developed thirteen core statements or beliefs, providing the member a new perspective on herself and building her self-esteem (Doweiko, 1996).

Women have traditionally been overlooked in the research on alcoholism and other addictions. They have been assumed to be just like men who have been studied and have been treated as if their addictions would respond to the same treatment as men. Feminists, however, have taken issue with the core belief of the twelve steps of AA: I am powerless over alcohol. Powerlessness is seen as the source of women's oppression within our patriarchal society. "The 12-steps were formulated by a white, middle-class male in the 1930's; not surprisingly, they work to break down an overinflated ego, and put reliance on an all-powerful male God. But most women suffer from the lack of a healthy, aware ego, and need to strengthen their sense of self by affirming their own inner wisdom" (Kasl, 1990, p. 30). Many women use chemicals because they experience themselves as powerless. Women who drink alcohol have also been stigmatized for centuries as "loose women," which further demoralizes them. The codependency movement has also been criticized as pathologizing women's socialized behavior. Berenson (1993), responding to these critiques, has proposed a new version of the twelve steps:

1. We saw that trying to control and manipulate our feelings and relationships only led to a sense of feeling out of control and powerless.
2. Recognized that our willingness to experience anger, hurt, fear, and shame could free us from blame, guilt, and self-pity and open us to help from a Higher Power.
3. Were completely willing to surrender our pain, letting it be transformed into peace and compassion, then into love, joy, and gratitude.
4. Made an honest, searching inventory of our personal principles and character, encountering both our strengths and limitations.
5. Explored with ourselves and, as appropriate, with our Higher Power and another person, the emotional impact, positive and negative, of our actions.
6. Were entirely ready to forgive ourselves and be forgiven and to congratulate ourselves and be congratulated.
7. Asked our Higher Power to help us make lasting changes.
8. Made a list of people who had hurt us and whom we had hurt and became willing to forgive them or make amends to them.
9. Reclaimed our power and accepted responsibility for our lives, standing up for ourselves, letting things be, or making direct amends.
10. Continued to act with self-respect, honoring our emotions and those of others.

11. Sought through meditation and prayer to create our destiny and to be empowered by the will and love of God, Goddess, All That Is in unfolding that destiny.

12. Having had a spiritual awakening from taking these steps, we seek to share this reality with others and to deepen our spiritual awareness in all aspects of life.

The twelve steps have also been modified to appeal to a more secular population. Behavioral psychologist B. F. Skinner (1987) wrote the Humanist Alternative Steps:

1. We accept the fact that all our efforts to stop drinking have failed.

2. We believe that we must turn elsewhere for help.

3. We turn to our fellow men and women, particularly those who have struggled with the same problem.

4. We have made a list of the situations in which we are most likely to drink.

5. We ask our friends to help us avoid those situations.

6. We are ready to accept the help they give us.

7. We earnestly hope that they will help.

8. We have made a list of the persons we have harmed and to whom we hope to make amends.

9. We shall do all we can to make amends, in any way that will not cause further harm.

10. We will continue to make such lists and revise them as needed.

11. We appreciate what our friends have done and are doing to help us.

12. We, in turn, are ready to help others who may come to us in the same way.

These steps avoid any mention of a "Higher Power," which may make them more acceptable to some people than the twelve steps in AA. Many alternatives should be considered, perhaps even before the traditional twelve-step model. In some cases, the alternatives do not require a young adult or adolescent to accept the label of alcoholic or addict as quickly as might be needed in AA. If less restrictive alternatives are ineffective, the twelve-step approach will always be there.

SUMMARY

This chapter attempted to enlighten college and university personnel, who are in a position to identify students with substance abuse problems, about the availability of self-help groups. It began with a discussion of why self-help, in general, works; presented the philosophy and therapeutic aspects of the twelve-step model; described twelve-step meetings; presented criticisms of twelve-step programs; explained how twelve-step programs work with other therapies; and introduced several new self-help programs. This thorough discussion of self-help, and particularly twelve-step programs, was provided so that the reader could make appropriate referrals by gaining an understanding of different self-help groups and which groups would be most appropriate for a student in need of help.

APPENDIX: HOW TO FIND SELF-HELP GROUPS

Al-Anon Family Group Headquarters
P.O. Box 862, Midtown Sta.
New York, NY 10018
(212) 302–7240   FAX (212) 869–3757

Alcoholics Anonymous World Services (AA)
475 Riverside Dr.
New York, NY 10163
(212) 870–3400   FAX (212) 870–3003

Narcotics Anonymous (NA)
P.O. Box 9999
Van Nuys, CA 91409
(818) 780–3951   FAX (818) 785–0923

Rational Recovery (RR)
(916) 621–4374
email: RR@Rational.org   http:\\www.Rational.org\recovery

Secular Organization for Sobriety
National Clearinghouse
Box 5
Buffalo, NY 14215–0005
(716) 834–2922
National office:
5521 Grosvenor Blvd.
Los Angeles, CA 90066
(310) 821–8430   FAX (310) 821–2610

SMART Recovery: Self-Management and Recovery Training
24000 Mercantile Rd #11
Beachwood, OH 44122
(216) 292–0220   http:\\home.sprynet.com\sprynet.mike888

Women for Sobriety
P.O. Box 618
Quakerstown, PA 18951
Dr. Jean Kirkpatrick, Executive Director
(215) 536–8026
(800) 333–1605   FAX (215) 536–8026
email: WFSobriety@aol.com   http:\\www.mediapulse.com\wfs\

REFERENCES

Alcoholics Anonymous. (1957). *Alcoholics Anonymous comes of age.* New York: Alcoholics Anonymous World Services.

Alcoholics Anonymous. (1976). *Alcoholics Anonymous: The story of how many thousands of men and women have recovered from alcoholism* (3rd ed.). New York: Alcoholics Anonymous World Services.

Bepko, C. (1985). *The responsibility trap.* New York: The Free Press.

Berenson, D. (1993). Powerlessness—liberating or enslaving? Responding to the feminist critique of the twelve steps. *Journal of Feminist Family Therapy, 3.*

Borkman, T. J. (1990). Experiential, professional, and lay frames of reference. In T. Powell (Ed.), *Working with self help* (pp. 3–30). Sliver Springs, MD: NASW Press.

Brandsma, J. M., Maultsby, M. C., & Welsh, R. J. (1980). *The outpatient treatment of alcoholism: A review and comparative study.* Baltimore, MD: University Park Press.

Cain, A. (1964). *The cured alcoholic.* New York: The Free Press.

Davis, D. (1980). Alcoholics Anonymous and family therapy. *Journal of Marital and Family Therapy, 6,* 65–74.

Doweiko, H. E. (1996). *Concepts of chemical dependency* (3rd ed.). Pacific Grove, CA: Brooks/Cole.

Ellis, A. (1979). Rational emotive therapy. In R. J. Corsini (Ed.), *Current psychotherapies* (pp. 87–108). Itasca, IL: Peacock Press.

Emotions Anonymous. (1978). *Emotions Anonymous.* St. Paul, MN: Emotions Anonymous International.

Emrick, C. D. (1987). Alcoholics Anonymous: Affiliation processes and effectiveness as treatment. *Alcoholism Clinical Experimental Research, 11,* 416–423.

Emrick, C. D., Tonigan, S., Montgomery, H., & Little, L. (1993). Alcoholics Anonymous: What is currently known? In B. S. McCrady & W. R. Miller (Eds.), *Research on Alcoholics Anonymous.* New Brunswick, NJ: Rutgers Center of Alcohol Studies.

Galanter, M., Castaneda, R., & Franco, H. (1991). Group therapy and self-help groups. In R. J. Frances & S. I. Miller (Eds.), *Clinical textbook of addictive disorders.* New York: Guilford Press.

Glaser, F. B., & Ogborne, A. C. (1982). Does A.A. really work? *British Journal of Addiction, 77,* 123–129.

Hudson, H. L. (1985–1986). How and why Alcoholics Anonymous works for blacks. *Alcoholism Treatment Quarterly, 2,* 11–30.

Kalb, M., & Propper, M. (1976). The future of alcohology: Craft or science? *American Journal of Psychiatry, 133,* 641–645.

Kasl, C. D. (1990). The twelve-step controversy. Ms. 30–31.

Kurtz, E. (1979). *Not-God: A history of Alcoholics Anonymous.* Center City, MN: Hazelden.

Kurtz, E. (1982). Why AA works: The intellectual significance of Alcoholics Anonymous. *Journal of Studies on Alcohol, 43,* 834–838.

Kurtz, L. F. (1990). Twelve step programs. In T. J. Powell (Ed.), *Working with self help* (pp. 93–118). Silver Springs, MD: NASW Press.

Lawson, G., Ellis, D., & Rivers, C. (1984). *Essentials of chemical dependency counseling.* Gaithersburg, MD: Aspen.

Lawson, G., Peterson, J., & Lawson, A. (1983). *Alcoholism and the family: A guide to treatment and prevention.* Gaithersburg, MD: Aspen.

McCrady, B. S., & Irvine, S. (1989). Self-help groups. In R. K. Hester & W. R. Miller (Eds.), *Handbook of alcoholism treatment approaches: Effective alternatives* (pp. 154–169). New York: Pergamon Press.

Miller, W. R., & McCrady, B. S. (1993). The importance of research on Alcoholics Anonymous. In B. S. McCrady & W. R. Miller (Eds.), *Research on Alcoholics Anonymous.* New Brunswick, NJ: Rutgers Center of Alcohol Studies.

Narcotics Anonymous. (1987). *Narcotics Anonymous* (4th ed.). Van Nuys, CA: Narcotics Anonymous World Service Office.

Ogborne, A. C., & Bornet, A. (1982). Abstinence and abusive drinking among affiliates of Alcoholics Anonymous: Are these the only alternatives? *Addictive Behavior, 7,* 199–202.

Skinner, B. F. (1987, July/August). A humanist alternative to AA's twelve steps. *Humanists,* pp. 5–6.

Tournier, R. E. (1979). Alcoholics Anonymous as treatment and as ideology. *Journal of Studies on Alcohol, 40,* 230–239.

Trimpey, J. (1989). *The small book: A revolutionary alternative for overcoming alcohol and drug dependence.* New York: Delacorte Press.

Walker, K., Sanchez-Craig, M., & Bornet, A. (1982). Teaching coping skills to chronic alcoholics in a coeducational halfway house: 2. Assessment of outcome and identifications of outcome predictors. *British Journal of Addictions, 77,* 185–196.

Wolin, S., & Wolin, S. (1993). *The resilient self: How survivors of troubled families rise above adversity.* New York: Villard Books.

Selected Bibliography

Alcoholics Anonymous. (1976). *Alcoholics Anonymous: The story of how many thousands of men and women have recovered from alcoholism* (3rd ed.) (the "Big Book"). New York: Alcoholics Anonymous World Services.

Alcoholics Anonymous. (1953). *Twelve steps and twelve traditions.* New York: Alcoholics Anonymous World Services.

American Psychiatric Association. (1994). *Diagnostic and statistical manual of mental disorders* (4th ed.). Washington, DC: Author.

Barr, M. J. (1988). Institutional liability: What are the risks and obligation of student services? In M. J. Barr & Associates, *Student services and the law* (pp. 179–196). San Francisco: Jossey-Bass.

Bennett, M., McCrady, B., Frankenstein, W., Laitman, L., Van Horn, D., & Keller, D. (1993). Identifying young adult substance abusers: The Rutgers collegiate substance abuse screening test. *Journal of Studies on Alcohol, 54,* 522–527.

Berkowitz, A. D. (1994). Assessing collegiate substance abuse: Current trends, research needs and program applications. In G. Gonzalez & V. Veltri (Eds.), *Research and intervention: Preventing substance abuse in higher education* (pp. 73–100). Washington, DC: U.S. Department of Education, Office of Educational Research and Improvement.

Berkowitz, A. D., & Perkins, H. W. (1987). Current issues in effective alcohol education programming. In Joan Sherwood (Ed.), *Alcohol policies and practices on college and university campuses* (pp. 69–85). Columbus, OH: National Association of Student Personnel Administrators Monograph Series.

Bliming, G. S., & Miltenberger, L. J. (1990). *The resident assistant.* Dubuque, IA: Kendall/Hunt.

Borkovec, T. D. (1993). Between-group therapy outcome research: Design and methodology. In L. S. Onkan, J. D. Blaine, & J. J. Boren (Eds.), *Behavioral treatment for drug abuse and dependence* (NIDA Research Monograph No. 137, pp. 249–289). Rockville, MD: National Institute of Drug Abuse.

Brown, S., & Yalom, I. D. (Eds.). (1995). *Treating alcoholism.* San Francisco: Jossey-Bass.

Charness, M. (1994). Brain lesions in alcoholics. *Alcoholism: Clinical and Experimental Research, 17,* 2–11.

Commission on Substance Abuse at Colleges and Universities. (1994). *Rethinking rites of passage: Substance abuse on America's campuses.* New York: Columbia University, Center on Addiction and Substance Abuse.

Cook, C. C. H. (1988a). The Minnesota Model in the management of drug and alcohol dependency: Miracle, method or myth? Part 1. The philosophy of the program. *British Journal of Addiction, 83,* 625–634.

Cook, C. C. H. (1988b). The Minnesota Model in the management of drug and alcohol dependency: Miracle, method, or myth? Part 2. Evidence and conclusions. *British Journal of Addictions, 83,* 735–748.

Cox, W. M., & Calmari, J. E. (in press). Addiction. *Encyclopedia of human biology* (2nd ed.). San Diego, CA: Academic Press.

Cox, W. M., & Klinger, E. (1990). Incentive motivation, affective change, and alcohol use: A model. In W. M. Cox (Ed.), *Why people drink: Parameters of alcohol as a reinforcer* (pp. 291–311). New York: Gardner.

Donovan, D. M., & Marlatt, G. A. (Eds.). (1988). *Assessment of addictive behaviors.* New York: Guilford Press.

DuPont, R. L. (1988). The counselor's dilemma: Treating chemical dependency at college. *Journal of College Student Psychotherapy 2,* 41–61.

Eigen, L. D. (1991). *Alcohol practices, policies, and potentials of American colleges and universities: An OSAP white paper.* Rockville, MD: U.S. Department of Health and Human Services, Office of Substance Abuse Prevention.

Emrick, C. D., Tonigan, S., Montgomery, H., & Little, L. (1993). Alcoholics Anonymous: What is currently known? In B. S. McCrady & W. R. Miller (Eds.), *Research on Alcoholics Anonymous.* New Brunswick, NJ: Rutgers Center of Alcohol Studies.

Fingerette, H. (1988). *Heavy drinking: The myth of alcoholism as disease.* Berkeley and Los Angeles: University of California Press.

Fitzgerald, H. E., & Zucker, R. A. (1995). Socioeconomic status and alcoholism: Structuring developmental pathways to addiction. In H. E. Fitzgerald, B. M. Lester, & B. Zuckerman (Eds.), *Children of poverty* (pp. 125–127). New York: Garland Press.

Fleming, M., Barry, K., & MacDonald, R. (1991). The alcohol use disorders identification test (AUDIT) in a college sample. *The International Journal of the Addictions, 26,* 1173–1185.

Galanter, M., Castaneda, R., & Franco, H. (1991). Group therapy and self-help groups. In R. J. Frances & S. I. Miller (Eds.), *Clinical textbook of addictive disorders.* New York: Guilford Press.

Gilchrist, L. D. (1994). Current knowledge in prevention of alcohol and other drug abuse. In G. Gonzalez and V. Veltri (Eds.), *Research and intervention: Preventing substance abuse in higher education* (pp. 25–46). Washington, DC: U.S. Department of Education, Office of Educational Research and Improvement.

Goldman, M. S., Brown, S. A., & Christiansen, B. A. (1987). Expectancy theory: Thinking about drinking. In H. T. Blane & K. E. Leonard (Eds.), *Psychological theories of drinking and alcoholism* (pp. 181–226). New York: Guilford Press.

Gonzalez, G. M. (1988). Theory and applications of alcohol and drug education as a means of primary prevention on the college campus. *Journal of College Student Psychotherapy, 2,* 89–113.

Greenfield, T. K., Guydish, J., & Temple, M. T. (1989). Reasons students give for limiting drinking: A factor analysis with implications for research and practice. *Journal of Studies on Alcohol, 50,* 108–115.

Haines, M. P. (1996). *A social norms approach to preventing drinking at colleges and universities.* Newton, MA: Higher Education Center for Alcohol and Other Drug Prevention.

Hartman, D. (1995). *Neuropsychological toxicology: Identification and assessment of human neurotoxic syndromes* (2nd ed.). New York: Plenum Press.

Hester, R. K., & Miller, W. R. (Eds.). (1995). *Handbook of alcoholism treatment approaches: Effective alternatives* (2nd ed.). Boston: Allyn & Bacon.

Hurlbut, S., & Sher, K. (1992). Assessing alcohol problems in college students. *Journal of the American Medical Association, 41,* 49–58.

Inciardi, J. A., Tims, F. M., & Fletcher, B. W. (Eds.). (1995). *Innovative approaches in the treatment of drug abuse: Program models and strategies.* Westport, CT: Greenwood Press.

Institute of Medicine. (1990). *Broadening the base of treatment for alcohol problems.* Washington, DC: National Academy Press.

Jansen, R. L., Fitzgerald, H. E., Ham, H. P., & Zucker, R. A. (1995). Difficult temperament and problem behavior in three-to-five-year-old sons of alcoholics. *Alcoholism: Clinical and Experimental Research, 19,* 501–509.

Jellinek, E. M. (1960). *The disease concept of alcoholism.* New Haven, CT: Hillhouse Press.

Johnson, V. E. (1986). *Intervention: How to help someone who doesn't want help.* Minneapolis: Johnson Institute Books.

Johnston, L. D., O'Malley, P. M., & Bachman, J. G. (1994). *National survey results on drug use from the monitoring the future study, 1975–1993* (NIH Publication No. 94-3809). Rockville, MD: National Institute on Drug Abuse.

Kane, J., & Lieberman, J. (1992). *Adverse effects of psychotropic drugs.* New York: Guilford Press.

Kerr, B. (1994). Review of the substance abuse subtle screening inventory. In *Mental Measurements Yearbook* (Vol. 11) (pp. 249–251). Lincoln, NE: Buros Institute of Mental Measurement.

Kurtz, L. F. (1990). Twelve step programs. In T. J. Powell (Ed.), *Working with self-help* (pp. 93–118). Silver Springs, MD: NASW Press.

Lezak, M. (1995). *Neuropsychological assessment* (3rd ed.). New York: Oxford University Press.

Marlatt, G. A., & Gordon, J. R. (Eds.). (1985). *Relapse prevention: Maintenance strategies in the treatment of addictive behaviors.* New York: Guilford Press.

McCord, J. (1988). Identifying developmental paradigms leading to alcoholism. *Journal of Studies on Alcohol, 49,* 357–362.

Miller, W. R., & McCrady, B. S. (1993). The importance of research on Alcoholics Anonymous. In B. S. McCrady & W. R. Miller (Eds.), *Research on Alcoholics Anonymous.* New Brunswick, NJ: Rutgers Center of Alcohol Studies.

Miller, W. R., & Rollnick, S. (1991). *Motivational interviewing: Preparing people to change addictive behaviors.* New York: Guilford Press.

Miller, W. R., & Sovereign, R. G. (1989). The check up: A model for early interven-
tion in addictive behaviors. In T. Loberg, W. R. Miller, P. E. Nathan, & G. A.
Marlatt (Eds.), *Addictive behaviors: Prevention and early intervention.*
Amsterdam: Swets & Zeitlinger.

Monti, P. M., Abrams, D. B., Kadden, R. M., & Cooney, N. L. (1989). *Treating alcohol dependence.* New York: Guilford Press.

Moos, R. H., Finney, J. W., & Cronkhite, R. C. (1990). *Alcoholism treatment: Context, process, and outcome.* New York: Oxford University Press.

Nathan, P. E. (1993). Alcoholism: Psychopathology, etiology and treatment. In P. B.
Sutker & H. E. Adams (Eds.), *Comprehensive handbook of psychopathology*
(2nd ed.) (pp. 451–476). New York: Plenum Press.

Nystrom, M., Perasalo, J., & Salaspuro, M. (1993). Screening for heavy drinking and
alcohol-related problems in young university students: The CAGE, the Mm-
Mast and the trauma score questionnaires. *Journal of Studies on Alcohol, 54,*
528–533.

Office of Substance Abuse Prevention. (1991). *Faculty member's handbook: Strategies for preventing alcohol and other drug problems.* Washington, DC: U.S.
Department of Health and Human Services.

Pickens, R. W., Svikis, D. S., McGue, M., Lykken, D. T., Hesten, L. L., & Clayton, P.
J. (1991). Heterogeneity in the inheritance of alcoholism. *Archives of General
Psychiatry, 48*(1), 19–28.

Presley, C. A., Harrold, R., Scouten, E., Lyerla, R., & Meilman, P. W. (1994). *CORE
alcohol and drug survey: User's manual* (5th ed.). Carbondale: CORE Institute, Southern Illinois University.

Prochaska, J. O., DiClemente, C. C., & Norcross, J. C. (1992). In search of how people
change: Applications to the addictive behaviors. *American Psychologist, 47,*
1102–1114.

Rivinus, T. M. (Ed.). (1988). *Alcoholism/chemical dependency and the college student.* New York: Haworth Press.

Rubington, E. (1990). Drinking in the dorms: A study of the etiquette of RA–resident
relations. *Journal of Drug Issues, 20,* 451–462.

Saltz, R., & Elandt, D. (1986). College student drinking studies, 1976–1985. *Contemporary Drug Problems, 13,* 117–159.

Schulenberg, J., O'Malley, P. M., Bachman, J. G., Wadsworth, K. N., & Johnston, L. D.
(in press). Getting drunk and growing up: Trajectories of frequent binge drinking during the transition to young adulthood. *Journal of Studies on Alcohol.*

Smith, J. E., & Meyers, R. J. (1995). The community reinforcement approach. In R.
K. Hester & W. E. Miller (Eds.), *Handbook of alcoholism treatment approaches:
Effective alternatives* (2nd ed.) (pp. 251–266). Boston: Allyn & Bacon.

Sobell, M. B., & Sobell, L. C. (1987). Conceptual issues regarding goals in the treatment of alcohol problems. In M. B. Sobell & L. C. Sobell (Eds.), *Moderation
as a goal or outcome of treatment for alcohol problems: A dialogue.* New York:
Haworth Press.

Sournia, J. C. (1990). *A history of alcoholism.* Oxford: Basil Blackwell.

Suchman, D., & Broughton, E. (1988). Treatment alternatives for university students
with substance use/abuse problems. *Journal of College Student Psychotherapy,
2,* 131–146.

Walton, S. (1996). Social host liability: Risks for fraternity and student hosts. *NASPA Journal, 34,* 29–35.

Washton, A. M. (Ed.). (1995). *Psychotherapy and substance abuse: A practitioner's handbook.* New York: Guilford Press.

Wechsler, H., Isaac, N. E., Grodstein, F., & Sellers, D. E. (1994). Continuation and initiation of alcohol use from the first to the second year of college. *Journal of Studies on Alcohol, 55,* 41–45.

Werner, M., Walker, L., & Greene, J. (1994). Screening for problem drinking among college freshman. *Journal of Adolescent Health, 15,* 303–310.

White, W. T., & Mee-Lee, D. (1988). Substance use disorder and college students: Inpatient treatment issues—A model of practice. *Journal of College Student Psychotherapy, 2,* 177–203.

Zucker, R. A. (1987). The four alcoholisms: A developmental account of the etiologic process. In P. C. Rivers (Ed.), *Nebraska symposium on motivation: Vol. 34. Alcohol and addictive behaviors* (pp. 27–83). Lincoln: University of Nebraska Press.

Zucker, R. A., Fitzgerald, H. E., & Moses, H. D. (1995). Emergence of alcohol problems and the several alcoholisms: A developmental perspective on etiologic theory and life course trajectory. In D. Cicchetti & D. J. Cohen (Eds.), *Manual of developmental psychopathology* (pp. 667–711). New York: Wiley.

Index

Addictive Voice Recognition Training (AVRT), 255

Adult Children of Alcoholics (ACA), 241–243, 252–253

Advancement of Standards of Student Services/Development Programs (CAS), 101–102

AIDS, 33

Alanon, 241–243

Alateen, 241–243

Alcohol abuse: alternative models, 73–74, 95; American systems of diagnosis, 3, 49, 70, 231, 254; assessment, 66–67, 165–184; biological factors, 75, 84–85, 128, 194; campus policy, 18, 101–102, 115–116 (*see also* Campus alcohol policy development); and campus professionals, 45, 56, 67–70, 95, 112, 166–168, 184, 203, 224, 229, 241; and child behavior problems, 13–14, 18, 135, 245; and "clocks," 4, 11; and college populations, 3, 8–11, 15–17, 28, 42–43, 55–56, 61, 67–69, 76–78, 108–111, 165–166, 168–170, 177, 189–190, 209–210, 221–235, 242; and computers, 202–203; definition, 24–25, 54–55, 82–84;

Alcohol abuse (*continued*)
developmental perspectives, 3–18; disease concept, 3, 6–8, 49, 74; economic benefits of treatment, 233; and environment, 4, 85–89, 121–122, 177, 201, 222–223; and ethnicity, 142–143, 251–252; freshman residence halls, 141–154; historical contexts, 4, 8, 18; history of study, 4–7, 49–52; intervention, 189–190, 204–205, 222 (*see also* Substance abuse, intervention); Minnesota Model, 210–221; moral attitudes towards, 5, 50; physiological and neuropsychological effects of, 26–31; prevention of, 119–136 (*see also* Proactive prevention model of substance abuse); probabilistic develop-mental framework, 9–12, 18; psychological factors, 86–87, 75, 194, 214–215; and sexual activity, 173–174, 190; and student overestimation of, 122–124 (*see also* Misplaced-norms model of substance abuse); treatment of, 63–66, 209–210, 234–235; and Type I alcoholism, 84; and Type II alcoholism, 57, 84. *See also* Substance abuse

About the Editors and Contributors

KATURAH ABDUL-SALAAM is the Supervisor of Assessment and Evaluation at the Connecticut Mental Health Center's and Yale University School of Medicine's Substance Abuse Treatment Units, where she is involved in providing direct assessment and treatment services for individuals and families with substance abuse issues. Ms. Abdul-Salaam is also a private consultant for Multicultural Perspective in Assessment, Consultation, and Training (MPACT) doing staff development and training focusing on issues salient to communities of color. She is actively involved in education and training of doctoral level psychology interns and resident physicians in areas of substance abuse.

ALAN D. BERKOWITZ, a licensed psychologist, is currently Scholar in Residence, University of Scranton, Scranton, Pennsylvania. He has served as a faculty member and counseling center psychologist at Hobart and William Smith Colleges. Dr. Berkowitz has written and lectured extensively on the topics of drug use and abuse in higher education and the development of rape prevention programs for men. He recently edited *Men and Rape: Theory, Research and Prevention Programs in Higher Education* and is a frequent contributor to professional journals and scholarly volumes. His research has primarily focused on the role of peer influences in drug use and on men's responsibility for preventing sexual assault.

JOHN E. CALAMARI is Assistant Professor and Director of Clinical Training, Department of Psychology, Finch University of Health Sciences/The Chicago

Medical School. He has worked extensively with clinical substance abuse and now maintains research interests in the interrelationship between anxiety and substance use disorders. His research interests include the role of anxiety sensitivity in the development and maintenance of substance use disorders.

W. MILES COX is Professor of Psychology at the University of Wales, Bangor, where he holds the Chair of the Psychology of Addictive Behaviours, the first chair of addicitive behaviours in Europe. He has conducted research and published in the area of alcohol and motivation for the past twenty years, and is internationally known for his work in motivational determinants of alcohol use. He is a Charter Fellow in the American Psychological Society and Charter Fellow and Fellow, respectively, in Divisions 50 and 28 (Addiction and Psychopharmacology) of the American Psychological Association. Cox is Founding Editor of *Psychology of Addictive Behaviors* and Past President of Division 50 of the APA, and has served on a number of grant review committees.

EUGENE R. D. DEISINGER is Assistant Director for Clinical Services at the Student Counseling Service at Iowa State University. He also is a Graduate Lecturer with the Department of Psychology at Iowa State, where he teaches graduate seminars in the assessment and treatment of substance abuse.

DEBORAH A. ELLIS is an Assistant Professor in the Wayne State University Department of Psychiatry and Behavioral Neurosciences and a child clinical psychologist. As a staff psychologist at Children's Hospital of Michigan, she provides clinical services to chronically ill children and their families. Her research interests are in the area of developmental psychopathology. She is currently engaged in longitudinal studies of behavioral impairment among children of alcoholics and preschool children with leukemia.

HIRAM E. FITZGERALD is Professor of Developmental Psychology, Chairperson of the Interdepartmental Graduate Specialization in Infant Studies and Chairperson of the Interdepartmental Graduate Specialization in Applied Developmental Science at Michigan State University, and is Executive Director of the World Association for Infant Mental Health. He is Fellow of the American Psychological Association, American Psychological Society, and the American Association for Applied and Preventive Psychology. Professor Fitzgerald's scholarly publications focus on systemic models of infant and family development, neuropsychology of stuttering, and the organization of behavior in children reared in alcoholic and/or antisocial families.

KENNETH C. GREGOIRE is a licensed psychologist in Colorado and Kansas. He has worked with chemically dependent individuals for over twenty years. He currently is Vice President, Clinical Programs, for the Valley Hope

Association, a nonprofit corporation dedicated to the treatment of chemical dependency. His current interests include clinical program development and the development of systems for improving the measurement of clinical outcomes.

ANN LAWSON is an Associate Professor of Marriage and Family Therapy at U.S. International University and a partner in the Center for Family and Psychological Studies. She is a licensed Marriage, Family, and Child Counselor, a Certified Addiction Specialist, and holds a Diplomate in Professional Chemical Dependency Counseling. Her publications include: *Essentials of Chemical Dependency Counseling, Alcoholism and the Family: A Guide to Treatment and Prevention, Alcoholism and Substance Abuse in Special Populations, Adolescent Substance Abuse: Etiology, Treatment and Prevention*, and she is co-editor of *Family Dynamics of Addiction Quarterly*. She is the former director and founder of the Children from Alcoholic Families Program, Lincoln, Nebraska.

GARY LAWSON is a Professor of Psychology at U.S. International University and a partner in the Center for Family and Psychological Studies. He is a licensed psychologist with over twenty years experience, has written and edited five books in the field of substance abuse, and is co-editor of *Family Dynamics of Addiction Quarterly*. His books include *Alcoholism and the Family: A Guide to Treatment and Prevention, Alcoholism and Substance Abuse in Special Populations, Adolescent Substance Abuse: Etiology, Treatment and Prevention, Clinical Psychopharmacology*, and *Essentials of Chemical Dependency Counseling*. He is a Certified Addictions Specialist, a Fellow in the American Orthopsychiatric Association, and is a Diplomate in Professional Chemical Dependency Counseling.

EVE E. REIDER is Codirector of the Behavioral Teratology Clinic and Affective & Anxiety Disorders Clinic in the Department of Psychiatry at the Kennedy Krieger Institute and Instructor in the Department of Psychiatry at Johns Hopkins University School of Medicine. Dr. Reider's interests focus on the relationships between parental psychopathology and family functioning and their impact on child symptomatolcgy in substance abusing families, with special emphasis on the subject of family violence in alcoholic families, and the evaluation and treatment of families with children who have chronic illness, developmental disabilities, and learning disorders.

P. CLAYTON RIVERS is Professor of Psychology and Coordinator of Substance Abuse Training in the clinical psychology training program at the University of Nebraska–Lincoln. He is the author of *Alcohol and Human Behavior: Theory, Research and Practice* and co-author of *Essentials of Chemical Dependency Counseling* (2nd Edition) (with Gary and Ann Lawson). He edited

Alcohol and Addictive Behavior, Nebraska Symposium on Motivation, Volume 34 and served on the editorial board and as Reviews Editor of the *Family Dynamics of Addiction Quarterly*. He has published in several scholarly journals including *Journal of Studies on Alcohol, International Journal of Addictions* and *Psychology of Addictive Behaviors*. Dr. Rivers's current research interests include alcohol and aging, the relationship between alcohol and sex expectancies, and the interface of the caregiving and legal systems.

EARL RUBINGTON is Professor of Sociology at Northeastern University. He is the author of *Alcohol Problems and Social Control* and co-author (with Martin S. Weinberg) of *Deviance: The Interactionist Perspective* and *The Study of Social Problems*. After making studies of halfway houses for chronic drunkenness offenders and detoxification centers for alcoholics, he has, in recent years, turned his attention to collegiate drinking and social control.

JOHN H. SCHUH is a Professor in the Department of Educational Leadership at Iowa State University, Ames. He has held administrative and faculty appointments at Wichita State University, Indiana University, and Arizona State University. Schuh has received the Contribution to Knowledge Award, the Presidential Service Award, the Annuit Coeptiis Award, and the Senior Scholar Award from the American College Personnel Association. He received the Contribution to Literature or Knowledge Award from the National Association of Student Personnel Administrators, and the Leadership and Service Award from the Association of College and University Housing Officers—International. He has served on the governing boards of ACPA, NASPA, and ACUHO-I. The author or editor of more than 125 publications, including eleven books or monographs, Schuh received a Fulbright Award to study higher education in Germany in 1994.

ELSIE R. SHORE is Professor of Psychology at Wichita State University, Wichita, Kansas. Dr. Shore's research interests include the areas of women and alcohol, workplace alcohol problems, and drunk driving prevention. She has received research grants from the National Institute on Alcohol Abuse and Alcoholism and other governmental and private research institutes. Her research has been published in leading scholarly journals, including *Addiction, Journal of Studies on Alcohol,* and *Journal of Alcohol and Drug Education*.

PATRICK D. SMITH is Clinical Chief of Substance Dependence and Concurrent Disorders at the Addiction Research Foundation, in Toronto, Ontario. Previously he was the Director of Psychosocial Services in the Division of Adolescent Medicine of Arkansas Children's Hospital and was Assistant Professor in the Department of Pediatrics of the University of Arkansas for Medical Sciences (UAMS). His clinical, teaching, and research interests focus on substance abuse among adolescents and young adults.

DENNIS L. THOMBS is Associate Professor of Health Education at Kent State University. He is the author of *Introduction to Addictive Behaviors*. Dr. Thombs has conducted original research in the area of college student health behavior. This work appears in the *International Journal of the Addictions, AIDS Education and Prevention, Health Education Research, Journal of American College Health, Journal of College Student Development*, and other scholarly publications. He teaches courses in substance abuse prevention and treatment.

DEDRA B. WELLS is Coordinator for Outreach and Research for the Adolescent Research Program of the Centers for Applied Research and Evaluation and Division of Adolescent Medicine of Arkansas Children's Hospital, Department of Pediatrics, of the University of Arkansas for Medical Sciences. Ms. Wells uses her background in communications to do training and outreach in all areas of adolescent health care.

MITCHEL A. WOLTERSDORF is a neuropsychologist in private practice in Wichita, Kansas, where he specializes in clinical and forensic diagnostics in children through adults. He is a Board Certified Forensic Examiner and Medical Examiner and holds Board seats on the Brain Injury Association of Kansas, Wichita Preferred Provider Association, and Medical Delivery Systems.

ROBERT A. ZUCKER is Professor of Psychology in the Departments of Psychiatry and Psychology at the University of Michigan, Director of the University of Michigan Alcohol Research Center, and Director of the Division of Substance Abuse in the Department of Psychiatry. His major professional interests have been the etiology of substance abuse, documentation of the effects of substance abuse on children and families, the development of preventive programing for substance abusing families, and the implementation of treatment strategies for the more severe and comorbid segments of the substance abuser population. Dr. Zucker has published almost 100 papers and seven edited books. His present research is supported by grants from the National Institute on Alcohol Abuse and Alcoholism and from the State of Michigan Center for Substance Abuse Services. He is a member of the editorial boards of *Psychology of Addictive Behaviors* and *Drug and Alcohol Dependence*, and has served on and chaired a variety of task forces concerned with the development of standards for certification of substance abuse professionals, and the training of professionals working in the substance abuse area. He has been a member of a variety of NIDA and NIAAA review panels, is currently a Fellow in APA divisions 12, 28, 29, and 50, and is also President-elect of the American Psychological Association's Division on Addictions (Division 50).